THE RANSOMWARE HUNTING TEAM

ALSO BY DANIEL GOLDEN

Spy Schools: How the CIA, FBI, and Foreign Intelligence
Secretly Exploit America's Universities

The Price of Admission: How America's Ruling Class Buys Its Way
into Elite Colleges—and Who Gets Left Outside the Gates

THE
RANSOMWARE
HUNTING TEAM

A Band of Misfits' Improbable Crusade

to Save the World from Cybercrime

RENEE DUDLEY and **DANIEL GOLDEN**

FARRAR, STRAUS AND GIROUX   NEW YORK

Farrar, Straus and Giroux
120 Broadway, New York 10271

Portions of this book previously appeared in the ProPublica series
The Extortion Economy.

Endpaper illustrations by Na Kim and Thomas Colligan.

Library of Congress Cataloging-in-Publication Data
Names: Dudley, Renee, 1985– author. | Golden, Daniel, 1957– author.
Title: The ransomware hunting team : a band of misfits' improbable crusade
    to save the world from cybercrime / Renee Dudley and Daniel Golden.
Description: First Edition. | New York : Farrar, Straus and Giroux, 2022. |
    Includes bibliographical references and index.
Identifiers: LCCN 2022022942 | ISBN 9780374603304 (hardcover)
Subjects: LCSH: Computer crimes—Prevention. | Computer security. |
    Malware (Computer software)
Classification: LCC HV6772 .D83 2022 | DDC 363.25/968—dc23/eng/20220715
LC record available at https://lccn.loc.gov/2022022942

Designed by Gretchen Achilles

Our books may be purchased in bulk for promotional,
educational, or business use. Please contact your local bookseller or
the Macmillan Corporate and Premium Sales Department at 1-800-221-7945,
extension 5442, or by email at MacmillanSpecialMarkets@macmillan.com.

www.fsgbooks.com
www.twitter.com/fsgbooks • www.facebook.com/fsgbooks

1   3   5   7   9   10   8   6   4   2

To my husband, Alket Mërtiri
—R.D.

To my wife, Kathy
—D.G.

. . . if once you have paid him the Dane-geld
You never get rid of the Dane.

—RUDYARD KIPLING, "Dane-geld," 1911

CONTENTS

Introduction: "Are You Indeed a Barbarian?"   3

1. The Man Who Invented Ransomware   17

2. The Superhero of Normal, Illinois   43

3. The Hunters Gather   63

4. The Funny War   85

5. The Price of Obsession   115

6. Stopping STOP   139

7. Ryuk Reigns   155

8. The FBI's Dilemma   169

9. The G-Man and the Dolphin   197

10. Shaking Down a City   215

11. The Extortion Economy   237

12. Lawrence's Truce   271

13. Pipeline to Tomorrow   293

    Notes   323

    Acknowledgments   343

    Index   347

THE RANSOMWARE HUNTING TEAM

INTRODUCTION: "ARE YOU INDEED A BARBARIAN?"

I n a central London neighborhood where affluence hides pockets of poverty, immigrant families from Pakistan, India, and Eastern Europe pin their hopes for their children on a small, publicly funded school. About 150 students ages five to ten attend the school, which was built more than a century ago in the Victorian style, with a brick facade and high arched windows. A modest playground adjoins a church. Many of the parents are on public assistance—or, as the English say, on the dole—and the free lunch and midmorning snack that the school provides are often their children's only meals. Even as the coronavirus pandemic ravaged the area in 2020, blitzing through public housing and terraced apartments where students' families slept four to a room, the school stayed open, its masked teachers rearranging chairs to preserve as much social distance as possible.

On a shoestring budget, in a building that's showing its age, the school gives the children a solid education and helps them adjust to English life and culture. Teachers track the students' progress by photographing them as they learn how to hold a pencil, draw a picture, or write their name. The snapshots are uploaded to a server, a powerful computer that processes data and provides services for other devices.

Because teachers photograph each child in their class at least twice a week, and the system has been in place for several years, the server stored hundreds of thousands of photos.

Matthew, an affable Englishman in his early forties with dirty-blond hair and a stubble beard, has guarded this irreplaceable trove of data on every child's learning since 2016. Although the school can only afford to pay him a few thousand pounds a year as a contractor, he is devoted to its people and mission.

Around 9:00 p.m. on Monday, November 23, 2020, someone from the school emailed Matthew that its website was down. He tried logging on but couldn't. At first, he thought he had forgotten the password. After several attempts, he realized that he was locked out. "Something's gone wrong here," he told his girlfriend, Xiao, who was sitting next to him at their kitchen table.

By 2:00 a.m., he was desperate enough to contact the help desk of the company that hosted the server. He obtained a new server and connected it to the school. With the fresh setup, Matthew could see the files listed in the directories, though he still couldn't open them. They had been renamed with the file extension ".encrypt." To his horror, he realized that the school had been hit by ransomware, one of the world's most pervasive and fastest-growing cybercrimes. An unholy marriage of hacking and cryptography, ransomware penetrates computers and renders files inaccessible without the right decryption key. The hackers then demand a hefty price for the string of characters that can unlock the information.

Evading Matthew's defenses, the hacker had entered the school's system through a web portal that teachers used for content management. An update was available, but Matthew—who manages information technology for a variety of clients and is so busy that he doesn't always remember to patch vulnerable software—hadn't installed it.

"I didn't follow my own advice. I was so frustrated, and so embarrassed," he said. "I felt like someone punched me in the stomach."

■   ■   ■

As the English novelist and essayist George Orwell once observed, "The history of civilization is largely the history of weapons." Today, digital weapons are reshaping the world, and ransomware poses what may be the greatest threat of all. It's more efficient and profitable than other cybercrimes like identity theft—and what makes it even more alarming is that criminals haven't fully exploited its potential for money and mayhem.

The frequency and the impact of ransomware attacks are widely understated because many victims don't make them public or inform authorities. But in recent years, hundreds of strains, with odd names like Bad Rabbit and LockerGoga, have paralyzed the computer systems of millions of companies, government offices, nonprofit organizations, and individuals. Exploiting society's near-total dependence on computers, criminal hackers demand thousands, millions, or even tens of millions of dollars to restore operations.

During the COVID-19 pandemic, a wave of cyberextortion crippled hospitals and other vital services, shuttered businesses and schools, and further isolated people from relatives, friends, and coworkers. Matthew saw a parallel between the two epidemics.

"It was kind of ironic, the computer virus at the same time as the real virus," Matthew said. "Both extremely contagious and virulent."

As he sifted through the digital wreckage, Matthew found a note. Titled "Hack for Life," it read in part:

All Your Files Has Been Locked! The structure and data within your files have been irrevocably changed, you will not be able to work with them, read them or see them. It is the same thing as losing them forever, but with our help, you can restore them.

We can decrypt all your files after paying the ransom. We have no reason to deceive you after receiving the ransom, since we are not barbarians and moreover it will harm our business. You Have 2days to Decide to Pay. after 2 Days Decryption Price will be Double. And after 1 week it will be triple . . . Therefore, we recommend that you make payment within a few hours.

■ ■ ■

This wasn't Matthew's first brush with ransomware. He had also worked for a software company that was attacked in 2018. For two days, he tried to recover the company's data without paying the hackers. Fearing that its reputation would suffer and investors would panic if the incident were to become public, the company grew tired of waiting and instructed Matthew to pay the 2-bitcoin ransom (about $10,000 at the time). He received the key to unlock the files, and the company moved on quietly.

What was a hiccup for a prosperous business was a potential catastrophe for a cash-strapped public school. "It would have made the assessments for the children impossible," Matthew said. "It would have cost the teachers months of work. They would have had to start from scratch. The government inspectors would have failed the school."

That night, he couldn't sleep. The next day, he alerted his superiors, who authorized him to negotiate with the attackers. The school appeared to have no choice but to reward criminals, incentivizing them to target more schools. In the meantime, Matthew and his bosses would keep the attack secret. They wouldn't report it to law enforcement, for fear of tarnishing the school's reputation. They offered an all-purpose explanation to teachers and parents who couldn't access photos or instructional materials: the system was down.

The ransom note hadn't named a price. "How much to decrypt my PC?" Matthew wrote to a Gmail address specified by the hackers.

"You have to pay 10000 euro," came the reply. "Today 10000. Tomorrow 15000. Another two days 20000."

Matthew knew the school couldn't afford that much money, so he tried to bargain by pretending the attack hadn't caused much damage. "I simply don't have 10,000 Euros to pay you, sorry, that's ridiculous. We are a poor school with small resources. We have most of the data backed up, just a few recent photos I lost. Most I can pay is 500. Let me know if that's okay."

The strategy seemed to work, as the hacker reduced the demand.

"The last amount I can accept from you is 3,000 euros. I will delete my email by tomorrow. It is better to decide soon."

Encouraged, Matthew tried to work them down even lower, "I've analyzed I have only lost around 10 photos, its not worth 3000 I'm afraid. My last offer is 750 Euros."

"1000 Euros Last Offer If you do not agree, we will have to end the conversation."

Matthew was relieved. The school could scrape together €1,000. He seemed to have averted disaster. The hackers had demanded payment in Bitcoin, which Matthew had invested in himself and knew how to obtain. He converted €1,000 to Bitcoin on an online exchange and transferred it to a digital wallet specified by the criminals. Although he didn't know it, the wallet address was associated with hackers in Iran.

"Ok it's sent," Matthew wrote. "Please let me know how to recover my files."

Then the criminals double-crossed him. "Sorry, 1000 Euros is not accepted You have to pay 10000 Euros You owe another 9,000 euros I will send you the decryption file after payment."

Matthew had been suckered. By pretending to compromise, the gang had extracted a down payment without supplying a key. Matthew was too flustered to abide by the time-honored negotiating rule "Don't let your adversary see you sweat." He scrawled a desperate appeal. "You said 1000 euros last offer and we agreed the deal," he wrote. "I have nothing more. Please don't do this to me ... Don't you have any conscience? You can't offer me the deal, and then change your mind after i paid. That's so wrong. Please, can you have a heart, there must be some good inside you? Or are you indeed a barbarian?"

The attacker refused to budge. "The amount you paid is very small My first offer and letter was 10,000 euros I do not have much to talk if you want to decrypt 9000 Euros left."

Matthew pleaded again. "If you are not a barbarian then please stick with your last offer that you made at 1000 Euros, which I have already sent you. Please be an honourable person. Even a hard criminal doesn't do this. I have no more money to give you."

"I can not accept. I'm sorry. This is not my problem."

Matthew's girlfriend, Xiao, called all her friends who worked in information technology. Everyone gave her the same answer: It was impossible to recover the files without paying the ransom. Matthew scoured the internet, hoping for a miracle. On a site called Bleeping-Computer, he came across a forum for victims of VashSorena, a ransomware strain that, like the one that had paralyzed the school's network, added ".encrypt" to the end of file names. Sorena is a Persian boy's name meaning "tribal leader," while Vash may refer to "Vash the Stampede," the outlaw hero of a popular Japanese comic book and animated television series.

"I had this ransomware today and paid the ransom but the criminal did not help," Matthew posted on the forum. Instructions there advised him to upload the ransom note and a sample encrypted file for analysis to another site, ID Ransomware, and to contact its founder, who went by the handle demonslay335. If anyone could crack the code, it would be demonslay335.

"Hi, my server that my school used to record their progress was hacked and encrypted," Matthew messaged demonslay335. "Please can you help? I'm totally stuck."

Michael Gillespie—demonslay335's real name—was in the central Illinois flatlands, six time zones away from London, working at home in a modest upstairs office that formed an unlikely front line in the war against ransomware. He and his wife, Morgan, who have eight cats, two dogs, and a rabbit, call it the "cat room." His work setup consisted of a laptop on a desk and a monitor perched on a shelf above; the only other furniture was a fraying couch. Except for a poster of *The Lion King*, his favorite movie, the beige walls were largely bare, and there were dark patches in the baseboard where the rabbit had chewed. The only window overlooked a road in his suburban neighborhood outside Bloomington.

Gangly, with glasses and a scraggly goatee, Michael bears a resemblance to a young Bill Gates. His reddish-brown hair, longer than ever because he wouldn't risk getting a haircut during the pandemic, stretched back into a low ponytail. He was wearing his usual T-shirt and jeans. As he read and answered a crush of messages, cats snuggled in his lap or crawled up his arms. When they got bored with him, they climbed on a cat tree or ate from their dishes on the floor.

Like the families at the London school, Michael was no stranger to adversity. Then about to turn twenty-nine, he'd overcome bullying in school, poverty, and cancer. When he was growing up, his family was so poor that they sometimes had to move in with friends or relatives. Michael couldn't afford college. At age sixteen, he started working at a computer repair chain called Nerds on Call and remained there for more than a decade while learning on his own to crack ransomware. After he married Morgan Blanch, his high school sweetheart, the couple struggled to pay bills. Their electricity and water were routinely turned off, their credit cards canceled, their car impounded. They almost lost their home.

None of these obstacles deterred Michael. Whenever he had a moment to spare, he decoded ransomware-infected files as a public service. Almost anonymously, without seeking recognition or reward, Michael had made himself into one of the top ransomware breakers in the world. At least one million victims worldwide have downloaded decryption tools he created. Without charging them a penny, he has saved them from collectively paying hundreds of millions of dollars in ransom. Of more than a thousand known types of ransomware, he has cracked more than a hundred.

People who are the best in the world at what they do frequently have entourages: agents, spokespeople, and groupies. Not Michael. Even the cats nestling in his lap barely distract him. The internet is his refuge and intellectual home, the place where he spends most of his waking hours and where he has gained a stature that would astonish his relatives and acquaintances in Illinois.

"He lives so heavily in the tech world that I think having bad actors involved just bothers him," said Dave Jacobs, who was the best man at Michael's wedding. "Electronic stuff is his world, and he doesn't want these things going on in it."

His online conversations with victims were strictly transactional. He didn't get involved in their lives, nor was he interested in their individual predicaments. Like Dr. Gregory House, the brilliant diagnostician played by Hugh Laurie on the TV show *House*, Michael is exasperated by those he saves. At times, he appears to share the sentiment of Charlie Brown's *Peanuts* pal Linus: "I love mankind. It's people I can't stand."

Resourceful and tireless, Michael is the most prolific member of the Ransomware Hunting Team, an elite, invitation-only society of about a dozen tech wizards who are devoted to cracking ransomware. Across the globe, this obscure band of geeky volunteers is often the only recourse for victims who can't afford—or refuse out of principle—to pay ransoms to cybercriminals. The team has cracked more than three hundred major ransomware strains and variants, saving an estimated four million victims from paying billions of dollars in ransom.

Most of the Ransomware Hunting Team members, like Michael, upend the usual stereotypes about achievement. They're improbable success stories, with a technical virtuosity that's largely self-taught. Some come from backgrounds of poverty or abuse that helped galvanize them to fight bullies. Because they're combating criminals who might retaliate against them, several hide behind aliases or online identities. Most have never met in person; few know the real name of the group's most reclusive member, a Hungarian with the Twitter handle @malwrhunterteam.

The hunters are devoted both to the cause and to one another. When one is in dire financial straits, a teammate is sure to step in with a donation or a job offer. They reside in at least seven countries—the United States, the United Kingdom, Germany, Spain, Italy, Hungary, and the Netherlands—but, in a very real sense, they live on the internet. They converse among themselves over a messaging platform, and with cybersecurity experts, consulting firms, tech aficionados, victims, and even attackers on BleepingComputer, where Matthew had posted his plea for help. Run by one of the team's founders, BleepingComputer is one part demilitarized zone, one part neighborhood pub, a place where the good and bad actors of the ransomware world intersect.

The team's members have regular jobs, typically in cybersecurity, but cracking ransomware is their passion. Several have a kind of tunnel vision; once they commit to solving a problem, they plug away at it nonstop for hours or days, oblivious to the world around them. At least three of them, including Michael, have attention deficit hyperactivity disorder, which is normally associated with being easily distracted but can also manifest itself as a state of deep, prolonged concentration called hyperfocus. They share an urge, almost a compulsion, to help humanity and fight cybercrime, like an Internet Justice League. They don't care about getting rich; otherwise, they might be devoting their skills to developing ransomware, not foiling it.

"I think we're all kind of misfits," said team member Fabian Wosar, a high school dropout who grew up in Germany but now lives and works outside London. Fabian is Michael's mentor and, along with him, the team's foremost codebreaker. "We all have weird quirks that isolate us from the normal world but come in handy when it comes to tracking ransomware and helping people. That's why and how we work so well together. You don't need credentials, as long as you have the passion and the drive to teach yourself the skills required."

The team filled a gaping void. The U.S. government was slow to respond to the growing ransomware threat. The Federal Bureau of Investigation couldn't get a handle on it, advising victims against paying ransoms but offering no practical alternative. The hackers often operated out of countries like Russia and Iran that don't have extradition agreements with the United States and tacitly condone cyberattacks on the Western world, possibly using them to gather intelligence or share in the profit. From insurers to cybersecurity firms, the private sector had little incentive to thwart ransomware; as it surged, they benefited.

The team can't crack every strain. When ransomware is done right, it's unbreakable. But some attackers make blunders, cut corners, or underestimate their adversaries. That's when the team pounces.

■　■　■

Ransomware is kidnapping updated for the digital age. Using ploys such as phishing—sending deceptive emails with malicious attachments—hackers infiltrate computers. Once inside, they detonate the ransomware and hold the computers hostage for cryptocurrency, much as kidnappers seize human beings and extract payment to release them. Such crimes can be traced back to as early as 75 BC, when pirates captured Julius Caesar and asked for 20 talents. According to Plutarch, Caesar was insulted by what he considered a low valuation of his worth and insisted on a ransom of 50 talents instead. Few other victims have been so eager to pay. In 1973, Calabrian criminals snatched the eldest grandchild of oil baron J. Paul Getty in Rome and demanded $17 million. Getty refused, saying, "I have fourteen grandchildren, and if I pay a penny of ransom, I'll have fourteen kidnapped grandchildren." Despite his bold assertion—and much like ransomware victims when they have no other recourse—he eventually paid anyway, once the amount was reduced to $3.2 million.

Another basic element of ransomware, cryptography, also goes back to ancient times. The Roman army used a cipher named after Caesar to encrypt military messages. Almost two millennia later, Nazi Germany scrambled its communications with a device called the Enigma Machine, giving it an advantage in World War II, until a team led by British mathematician Alan Turing succeeded in cracking the code. More recently, cryptography has become a backbone of the internet, safeguarding electronic banking, commerce, and communications. Unfortunately, legitimate cryptographic tools developed by government, industry, and academia have been co-opted by cybercriminals for their own purposes.

Ransomware's innovation was to weaponize the very act of encryption. Before the emergence of ransomware, hackers who breached computer systems still had a lot of work to do before they could cash in. They had to find buyers for stolen Social Security or credit card numbers, with all the associated delays and uncertainties. Ransomware made the hack itself profitable, by monetizing victims' reliance on their computers. It is a one-stop crime, so simple in concept and execution that any would-be extortionist can buy a ransomware package on the dark web—the world of online content that is not accessible through standard search engines.

In the cat room that Tuesday in late November 2020, Michael was so inundated with pleas from other victims that he barely had time to glance at the file Matthew sent him. A quick look convinced him that the school had been attacked by version 6 of an unbreakable ransomware strain, Ouroboros, named after an ancient Egyptian icon of a dragon eating its own tail.

"Ouroboros v6, not decryptable since October 2019 when they fixed the flaws," he wrote Matthew. In harried frustration, Michael added, "ID Ransomware would already have told you."

Disappointed, Matthew pushed back. "I did check the ID Ransomware earlier, and it says its a different one." Michael's own website identified the ransomware strain as VashSorena and categorized it as decryptable under the right circumstances. "Is it just a different name or is there indeed a chance I can decrypt?"

Reexamining the characters in the file name, and other indicators, Michael realized that he had mistaken VashSorena for Ouroboros. His error was understandable. Iranian hackers are believed to be behind both ransomware strains, which encrypt files in almost the same way.

Without wasting any time, Michael set to work. VashSorena's vulnerability lay in a shortcut that the criminals had taken. In order to track who paid the ransom and who didn't, VashSorena's ransom note assigned each victim a unique ID number. This was standard practice in ransomware. Also standard was that, in return for payment, each victim received a unique key to unlock the encrypted files. What was unusual was that the ID and the key were related to each other. It created an opening for Michael.

When he reverse engineered the ransomware, he discovered that it fed the ID number into a mathematical function called the derive key. Likely written by the hackers themselves, the derive key was not publicly available, but Michael could extract it using a programming tool known as a decompiler. Next, he could take the ID number from the ransom note supplied by the victim and pop it in that function. After doing some math, Michael generated the key to unlock the files. He then wrote a decryptor, a computer program that the victim can run to recover data.

In July 2020, Michael had cracked the first version of VashSorena. But, as he often did, he kept the news quiet. If the attackers learned about it, they would fix the flaw he exploited. Helping hackers polish their cryptography was the last thing the Hunting Team wanted to do. While Michael rescued at least forty victims who reached him through BleepingComputer, he didn't post his solution. This low-key approach appeared to work: although the attackers updated VashSorena five times, they didn't fix the weakness Michael identified.

Now he inserted Matthew's unique ID into the decryptor, which yielded seven possible keys. He tested them, and one worked. He sent it to Matthew.

"Took another look," Michael wrote. "It is VashSorena actually, and I was able to break your key."

It was late evening when Matthew got the message. "He did it!" he shouted. "I've got the decryptor."

Xiao yelled back from the bathroom, "How is that possible? Who is this guy?"

Following Michael's instructions, Matthew regained access to the old server and recovered the student photos and other files. "Well, amazing," he wrote Michael. "It is working. I can't thank you enough. How did you do it? The teachers and children at the school will be so grateful you could help them."

Matthew wasn't finished. He submitted an online complaint to Google, asking why it allowed a ransomware attacker to use Gmail. The search engine giant didn't respond. The London school recognized that, despite its meager budget, it had to improve its cybersecurity. At Matthew's urging, it bought a network-attached storage device, or NAS, for additional backup.

He also hatched a scheme to recoup the €1,000 from the Vash-Sorena gang. Pretending he still needed a key, he resumed negotiating with them. "The only way I can trust you again is you send me back [the Bitcoin]," he wrote. "Then I will send you the 3000 Euros total to retrieve my files."

The attacker refused. "I sold bitcoin. I have no money to give you."

Matthew upped the bait to €4,500 and then €6,000, and concocted an explanation for this seemingly irrational turnabout: "I realized I lost a lot more files than I thought."

But ransomware gangs don't give refunds. "I'm sorry," the hacker wrote, ending the conversation. "If you give me this offer for another 10 years I reject it."

Matthew came away realizing that it's almost impossible to outwit cybercriminals—unless you're the Ransomware Hunting Team.

1.

THE MAN WHO INVENTED
RANSOMWARE

E very day, on his route to the Nerds on Call office, Michael
Gillespie passed a gorgeous preserve for that quintessentially
regal insect—the monarch butterfly. The Bloomington, Illinois, parks department seeded the habitat in 2017 on a turf island to
reduce mowing costs and promote ecological diversity. On a summer
day, as many as three hundred migrating monarchs now alight on the
1.2-acre triangle of grasses and colorful flowers: white prairie clover,
pale purple coneflowers, smooth blue asters, and black-eyed Susans,
blazing saffron yellow. Beating their distinctive orange-and-black
wings, the monarchs flit from one flower to the next and sip nectar
from milkweed before resuming their journey.

More than a decade before the Bloomington habitat opened, and
nine hundred miles to the northeast, a man named Joe Popp created
his own sanctuary for monarchs and other butterflies. Popp and his
partner, Christine Ryan, bought a secluded early-nineteenth-century
stone farmhouse in Oneonta, New York, in the foothills of the Catskill
Mountains, and converted its indoor swimming pool into a lush garden with arched windows and a twenty-six-foot-high pitched ceiling.

Lovingly tended by Ryan, the Joseph L. Popp Jr. Butterfly Conservatory displays a colorful array of imported Costa Rican butterflies

darting through tropical flora, as well as rabbits, iguanas, snakes, and more exotic animals. A plaque in the entrance hall pays tribute to the "knowledge and kindness" of Popp: "Naturalist, Evolutionary Anthropologist, Writer and Brilliant Thinker."

A Harvard-educated (and subsequently Harvard-disavowed) primatologist, African adventurer, computer geek, devoted Darwinist, and all-around intellectual provocateur, the late Joseph L. Popp left behind a less admirable legacy as well: he is widely regarded as the inventor of ransomware.

In December 1989, Popp—who stood six foot one, weighed 165 pounds, wore a beard, and bore a marked resemblance to Muppets creator Jim Henson—mailed more than twenty thousand floppy disks from London to health researchers, computer magazine subscribers, and an assortment of institutions, including the World Health Organization, Chase Manhattan Bank, Shell Oil, and the Vatican. Exploiting the desperate clamor for knowledge and treatments as deaths from AIDS soared worldwide, Popp's disk featured material related to AIDS education. But when recipients ran the disk enough times, their computers froze and a message on their screen instructed them to send either $189 or $378 to a post office box in Panama to restore their access.

At the dawn of the computer era, twenty months before the launch of the world's first website, this revolutionary form of extortion caught everyone unprepared and caused widespread panic. As the Wright brothers' twelve-second flight at Kitty Hawk presaged modern aviation, so Popp's clever but primitive stunt was the forerunner of the sophisticated attacks that bedevil Michael Gillespie and his fellow ransomware hunters.

"I went into the office and people were running around," recalled Edward Wilding, who, as editor of the fledgling publication *Virus Bulletin*, acted as a liaison between police, computer experts, and victims. "Within hours, people had run the disk and frozen their computers."

Some who knew Popp attribute his attack to greed, a desire for attention, a ruthless survival-of-the-fittest credo, or simply a lifelong compulsion to poke authority in the eye. Ryan, more charitable, calls him "an anarchist in the best sense . . . With somebody that brilliant, when their brain goes haywire, it goes haywire in a big way."

Like Gillespie, Popp was a midwesterner from a less-than-privileged background. His paternal grandfather, Joseph P. Popp, a Hungarian immigrant, was a coal miner and union organizer in West Virginia; he fought with strikebreakers and reinforced his windows with chicken wire to protect against Molotov cocktails. After he was injured in a mine explosion, the family moved to Ohio. His son's and grandson's middle name, Lewis, was a tribute to longtime United Mine Workers president John L. Lewis.

Cleveland's suburbs were booming after World War II. Born in 1950, Popp grew up in Willowick, on the shores of Lake Erie. His father attended college on the GI Bill and then worked at General Electric, rising from machine operator to plant project manager over a forty-year career. His mother, Dorothy, stayed home with her five children. She was a Cleveland native and high school graduate who spoke fluent French; her father had been born in Ohio, but her mother had emigrated from Alsace-Lorraine, on the border of France and Germany.

As the eldest child and the only boy, Popp enjoyed the adoration of his parents and sisters, endowing him with considerable self-confidence. His parents, both devout Catholics, encouraged him to excel at his studies.

"Joe was always an edgy kind of guy," said Ronald Schilb, a college roommate and lifelong friend. "[But when] he was around his family, he was a good little Catholic boy. He never wanted to anger his family."

Popp supplemented his allowance by delivering Cleveland's *Plain Dealer* and collecting and selling praying mantises. He joined the Boy Scouts, where he learned to camp, row, fish, and cook outdoors over an open fire—skills that would later come in handy when he moved to rural East Africa. He would count Boy Scout canoe trips in Canada among the happiest moments of his life.

At Eastlake High School, he was shy and diligent; one classmate, a football star, expected Popp "would end up being a CPA." A rare escapade reflected a budding reluctance to conform. He and a couple of friends had been spending a summer night in a backyard tent when they decided around three in the morning to hike across town to buy sodas from a gas station vending machine. When a police officer investigating a break-in stopped to question them, Popp's friends cooperated, but Popp was suddenly nowhere to be found. He had fled into a nearby swamp, where he hid up a tree for several hours.

At Ohio State, where he enrolled in 1968, both his brilliance and his bravado became more pronounced. Popp grew his hair long, tooled around in his stylish blue two-seat Triumph Spitfire roadster, and dropped out of the Reserve Officers' Training Corps. He and Schilb invented their own diversions. They filled aluminum tent poles with marbles to make blowguns, with which they shattered Coke bottles and knocked wasp nests and squirrels off trees. On one occasion, they trapped rats on the bank of the Olentangy River, strung the corpses together, and hung them over the dining hall entrance, a wry commentary on cafeteria food. Wading into the river, which runs through the Ohio State campus, Popp captured a gigantic bullfrog. He stashed it in their shower, which the housekeeper promptly refused to clean. On vacation, they drove to the Great Smoky Mountains in Tennessee, where they backpacked through the forest and ate wild blackberries.

As sophomores, Popp and Schilb took a course on evolution. For Popp, natural selection made intuitive sense. He embraced Darwinism with religious fervor, and *On the Origin of Species* became his bible. He would later call it "the most important book of the last two centuries," adding, "You may have the impression that you understand life in general (and even biology) without having read it, but you would be mistaken."

A zoology major, he wrote his senior thesis on primates, graduating with honors and membership in Phi Beta Kappa. With a baby crow he'd found at an Ohio State field station as a pet, and a prestigious fellowship from the National Science Foundation, he headed to graduate school in anthropology at Harvard.

■ ■ ■

When Popp arrived in Cambridge, Massachusetts, a new movement was sweeping through Harvard's biology and anthropology faculty. Dubbed "sociobiology," it applied tools associated with Darwinian analysis to animal and, more controversially, human behavior. Every week, about fifteen disciples would gather near the Harvard campus in the spacious home of Professor Irven DeVore, a baboon specialist. Often they debated, drank, and gambled into the early morning. "Basically, all of the seminal papers were written in DeVore's living room at three a.m.," one attendee said.

Popp was a regular at these sessions. He was DeVore's protégé, expected to be Harvard's next baboon expert and lead the study of primates into the heyday of sociobiology. He and DeVore coauthored a paper on how male animals use aggressive behavior to maximize reproductive success. For example, they observed that apes scream or beat their chests to drive rivals away from a female, even though "greater damage could be inflicted . . . through surprise attacks"; their explanation was that intimidation has the same benefits as fighting but without the risk of injury.

Of all the seminar participants, Popp was the most outspoken. He regarded the sociobiologists' version of Darwin's theories not just as an explanation for behavior but also as commandments. Males, he argued, have a duty to gain an evolutionary edge and propagate their DNA by having as many children as possible. As he later wrote, "Life is merely an artifact of evolution—maximizing reproductive success is why we are here . . . That which increases one's reproductive success is good, that which decreases one's reproductive success is bad." For example, he approved of bigamy, because it multiplies the male's reproductive opportunities. He was less concerned with how women might feel about the matter.

"Sometimes he took these evolutionary ideas to the extreme, which is a trait that developed even more later on," said James Malcolm, another seminar student. "More than anybody else in that group, he had decided that following the exact precepts of Darwin was the way to go.

He was this extroverted guy with long hair and a slight fanatical gleam in his eye. He had this drive to him, this intensity, and he thought that following Darwin was going to be the way of the truth."

Harvard was the intellectual epicenter not just of sociobiology but of the opposition, too. Stephen Jay Gould, a paleontologist whose essays on everything from the shrinking size of Hershey bars to the improbability of Joe DiMaggio's record fifty-six-game hitting streak gained him a popular following, was a leading critic of sociobiology, calling it "speculative stories" and arguing that human behavior adapts through "cultural transmission" rather than natural selection. Nevertheless, he was one of Popp's favorite professors. Popp regarded Gould's course on evolutionary biology as the best class he took at Harvard. Popp sought him out as a mentor and sometimes used the computer in Gould's office at Harvard's Museum of Comparative Zoology.

Around this time, Popp became intrigued by computer programming. Tor Ekeland, a lawyer who often defends scientists accused of hacking, says that many of his clients are ardent social Darwinists, perhaps because there's an affinity between sociobiology and programming.

"Social Darwinism is a very logical world with inputs and outputs and binary, black-and-white thinking," Ekeland notes. "That's why you see those types of people gravitate toward programming and hacking." To hackers, a survival-of-the-fittest philosophy could justify ransomware; the victims are simply technological weaklings, doomed to extinction in the digital age.

East Africa was as alluring to up-and-coming primatologists in the 1970s as Paris had been to young writers and artists in the 1920s. Embarking on his field research in 1973, Popp was soon entranced by its beauty, its wildlife, its danger, and its people's unfamiliarity with the world he had left behind. His first stop was Ethiopia. "I went to places where villagers who had never seen a white man still had heard that 'the Americans had gone to the moon,'" he wrote in an unpublished memoir of his African adventures. "On learning that I was an American, they asked me what the moon was like. When I told them that I really didn't know, because not *all* Americans had gone, they viewed me with great suspicion. I was able to smooth over a diplomatic rift by taking out my 10-power Leitz Trinovid binoculars and letting them look at the moon under magnification."

Placated, the villagers built a hut for him, where he stayed while studying hamadryas baboons that rested on nearby cliffs. "I actually saw one band of baboons attacked by a lioness as I sat within a few feet," he wrote. "The lioness cut through the band of baboons, many of which saw her coming, and grabbed an unwary female . . . The remaining baboons screamed alarm calls and dispersed, running in all directions."

Although he occasionally returned to Ethiopia, Popp spent most of the ensuing fifteen years in Kenya. In the 1970s, he lived at a mostly deserted research station on Masai Mara, a game reserve populated by lions, elephants, cheetahs, leopards, and baboons. Because it was too dangerous to follow the baboons on foot, he watched their interactions from the wheel of his rickety Daihatsu jeep. "I think Daihatsu must mean death wish," he joked. He called out his observations, which he carefully timed with a tape recorder, to a succession of note-taking assistants—mostly female students from the United States. Drawn by his magnetism, good looks, and seemingly bright future, they not only helped him collect and analyze data but sometimes became his girlfriends as well.

The Harvard Masai Mara Baboon Research Project, for which DeVore obtained funding, covered Popp's living expenses. In his spare time, he photographed people and wildlife, and he read classic novels in the evenings by lantern light. He enjoyed wordplay: "Gnu dung is a palindrome," he reminded a researcher whose camp he visited. When he needed a root canal, he swam across a river to a dentist, Dr. Payne, whom he nicknamed "Dr. Pain." Touring Kenya, Popp caught crayfish on Lake Naivasha, went skin-diving and deep-sea fishing in the Indian Ocean, and jogged up Mount Suswa, a 7,730-foot volcano, to meet friends picnicking at the top. He rented a farm outside Nairobi, where he could decompress, see friends, and go to restaurants and movies.

"I would often time my trips from Nairobi to Masai so that I left the capital an hour or so before sunset," he wrote. "I saw an almost endless variety of wildlife. The wildebeest and zebras during their annual northern migration provided an incredible sea of glowing eyes at night. The rhythmic grunting of the wildebeest could be heard over the hum of the engine."

Popp relished hobnobbing with celebrities who passed through Masai Mara. When Henry Kissinger visited the research station, Popp gave him a dental cast of a baboon's teeth. "I got a picture of him with a baboon, which I entitled, 'Two very dominant males,'" he wrote. He heard John F. Kennedy Jr., then a student at the National Outdoor Leadership School, give an "interesting and well informed" report on snakes. He corresponded with the celebrated primatologist Dian Fossey, commiserating with her about threats to her beloved mountain gorillas from farmers encroaching on their habitat and poachers capturing the babies for sale.

"Ohio Joe," as his family dubbed him after Indiana Jones, often found himself in peril. His memoir is full of narrow escapes, though it's possible that he exaggerated them in hopes of attracting a publisher. It describes how a buffalo charged his jeep, crushing the rear door and shattering the rear window. A leopard paced the roof of his house, scanning the surrounding area for prey. He wrote of one hike in Masai Mara:

I came upon a spitting cobra. We were both startled. The cobra was about nine feet long, and such a dark black color that it looked iridescent blue. Seeing me, it raised its head about three feet above the ground and spread its hood in a threat.

Then, as I watched in amazement, it opened its mouth, and I could see its fangs move forward and out—it was only about ten feet away. It shot two streams of venom from its extended fangs, the left stream going off to the side and the right stream just passing my head at eye level, barely missing my right eye.

■ ■ ■

Although he completed his doctorate, Popp gradually lost interest in an academic career. Field research felt like drudgery. "He was not drawn to publish or perish," said his nephew Timothy Furlan. "He was drawn to adventure."

Popp did have an interest in making more money—and making it faster—than academia customarily offered. "He probably wouldn't have had too much trouble getting a professorship somewhere, but he didn't feel that he would be paid enough," said John Augustine, who, like Ron Schilb, was a college roommate and lifelong friend. "I got the impression that he wanted to be really wealthy."

Popp conceived of one get-rich-quick scheme after another. A favorite was inspired by the elephant bones that he often noticed in the grass as he tracked baboons around the reserve with his assistant and girlfriend, an Ivy League undergraduate who had intended to spend a year in Kenya but met him and stayed for four. One day, Popp reminded her of the folk legend that elephants know when their end is near and go to die in a predetermined spot. No such "elephant graveyard" has been found, but Popp suggested creating one by relocating scattered bones to an area behind the research station. They could then advertise it as an authentic elephant graveyard and charge admission to tourists. Appalled, the assistant refused to participate. Only with great difficulty did she persuade him to abandon the plan.

"He came from a regular middle-class background and wanted to do something bigger, better, more lucrative," she recalled.

Other profit-making ventures supplemented his Harvard stipend. He sold T-shirts and wildlife postcards to the tourists at Keekorok Lodge, along with copies of a field guide to Masai Mara that he and an assistant coauthored. Wearing a helmet and a hunting outfit, and shouldering an elephant gun, he led paying customers on walking safaris that often culminated in a tour of a Masai village. The Kenyan government had strict gun controls, and only with energetic lobbying did Popp procure a permit for the weapon, which he used to practice shooting, aiming at a buffalo skull at twenty yards.

Popp added pageantry to a couple of these excursions by enlisting an assistant, Robert Sapolsky, to bring up the rear, carrying a spear.

Sapolsky, a self-described "New York Jewish twerp," had no idea how to use the spear. "I decided it wasn't my thing fairly soon," he recalled.

Sapolsky was another DeVore discovery. After he graduated from Harvard in 1978, DeVore sent him to Kenya to learn from Popp for a year. Popp was "a very smart, very intellectual guy," Sapolsky said. "Once I figured out how to be invisible around him, and he decided I was in no way a threatening male to challenge his kingdom, we got along reasonably well."

Sapolsky—who would go on to an eminent career as an author and professor of biology and neurology at Stanford—soon realized that Popp was a theoretician who lacked patience for field research and became frustrated when data didn't fit his models. While Popp stayed at the station, reading up on computers and the logic behind them, Sapolsky took his place monitoring the baboons.

Popp had commandeered the best house at the research station, with East African art on the walls, a fancy bed he'd bought in Nairobi, and a cook. "In his perfect world, he would get up at eleven, be served breakfast, take a shower, lead a walk, and come back and read books on game theory," Sapolsky recalled. "We'd sit around in the evening, and he was into lots of game theory games."

Popp was uncannily good at one game, in which he and Sapolsky would write down the numbers from 1 to 10 in any order on sheets of paper. At each juncture, whoever had the higher number would win the round. In other words, if Sapolsky started with 1, 2, 3, 4, 5, 6, 7, 8, 9, and Popp chose 2, 3, 4, 5, 6, 7, 8, 9, 10, Popp would prevail each time, until he lost the last round when he had to play the number 1. Popp seemed to read Sapolsky's mind and know exactly what number he would put down next.

"He would kick your ass every time," Sapolsky said. "I recall another period where for two or three weeks, the evening's game would be him saying, 'How many of us educated Americans would it take to overthrow the Kenyan government? What if we had one Kenyan working with us?' He would go through all these different scenarios. In retrospect, no doubt a few years later, he was thinking, 'What could it take to bring a whole computer network to a standstill?'"

■ ■ ■

Popp may have been fantasizing about toppling the Kenyan government because he worried that it would give him a hard time. His various enterprises violated its prohibition against foreign researchers doing business in the country, and his house was supposed to be reserved for a government employee.

To avoid blowback, Popp cultivated the local authorities, dedicating his Masai Mara field guide to the reserve's game warden. But when Sapolsky returned to Kenya in the summer of 1980, there was a new research warden, who told Popp to move out of the house and stop his commercial activities.

Popp disregarded him. One day, the warden showed up and ordered him to leave immediately. "I heard shouting," Sapolsky recalled. "They came pouring out of this house, wrestling over a shovel. Joe took a swing at him with a shovel. The guy ran away in a panic. Joe realized he had crossed a line. He packed up his car with his gun and his suitcases and he went into hiding, after leaving a note for me, saying I needed to go to the U.S. embassy and tell them to contact Kissinger and say his life was in danger and he needed help."

According to Sapolsky, Kenyan officials were already leery of foreign researchers. They were baffled why anyone from a prestigious university would "live like some troglodyte in a game park in a leaky tent amid wildebeest shit and intestinal parasites and count how many leaves zebras eat per hour," Sapolsky said. They wondered if the visitors were poaching, smuggling animals back to the United States, or otherwise profiteering.

When Popp appeared to confirm these suspicions, the Kenyan government suspended the work of every field biologist in the country, making him a pariah among his colleagues. Desperate to resolve the situation and return to research, Sapolsky became the go-between for Popp's negotiations with the Kenyan government. Popp would leave notes on Sapolsky's windshield in the middle of the night, instructing him to speak to this or that official. Sapolsky would do so and then stick the response on his windshield for Popp.

Ultimately, Popp paid a fine and surrendered his research permit. Word reached Harvard. Likely seeking to maintain the goodwill of Kenyan authorities, Harvard apologized to the University of Nairobi in 1981 for "the difficulties and inconvenience caused by this former student."

Still, DeVore publicly defended his protégé. "Any time the Kenyan government interfered with research studies, Joe was blamed," he later told *The Plain Dealer*. DeVore died in 2014 at the age of seventy-nine.

Popp seethed over the Kenyan government's treatment of him. Its officials "hardly ever miss an opportunity to miss an opportunity to be kind or fair in their dealings with expatriate researchers," he wrote.

Despite his disgrace, Popp stayed in Kenya. Since he couldn't resume his old life there, he built a new one. He dated a dancer in the Nairobi Ballet and edited publications for the African Medical and Research Foundation (Amref), known for its Flying Doctors air ambulance services to the most remote parts of East Africa.

"Joe was head of health learning materials and known as a 'computer geek,'" recalled an Amref colleague, Nicky Blundell Brown. "He was always helpful and courteous but very much a loner."

Popp also worked as a World Health Organization consultant and sought a job with the WHO related to AIDS education. The disease, which originated in primates in Africa, was ravaging the continent, with more than 20 percent of adults infected in some countries.

"He was very interested in AIDS research," said Timothy Furlan. "He felt the research being done wasn't promising."

On a visit home to Willowick in 1988, Popp bought an expensive desktop computer and attended his twentieth high school reunion. Fulfilling every high school nerd's dream, he cut a triumphant figure. He described himself as a "scientist and publisher" and an "author, publisher in medicine, biology, computers, marathon runner," and dropped the name of the world's best-known chimpanzee expert.

"Once people heard who it was, they wanted to talk to him about his accomplishments," said the class president, Mike McCarthy. "I think he even said he met Jane Goodall one time."

Popp didn't mention the implosion of his academic career—or his latest plan to get rich.

That same year, he left Africa and moved to London. At the time, the United Kingdom had no laws specifically barring computer intrusion.

One Monday in December 1989, Eddy Willems's boss handed him a 5¼-inch disk that had arrived in the mail. They worked for a company in Antwerp, Belgium, that sold health and life insurance, and the boss explained that the "AIDS Information Introductory Diskette Version 2.0," as it was labeled, might prove useful to customers. Willems, a support engineer on the help desk, agreed to check it out.

Willems ran the program on his work computer. It asked him a series of questions about his habits and his medical history, and calculated his chances of contracting AIDS. Willems's chances of being infected were assessed at 5 percent or less. "I did well," he recalled. But for respondents identified as high-risk, the program employed the kind of blunt language often avoided by medical doctors: "Your behavior patterns are extremely dangerous and they will very likely kill you."

The information struck Willems as stale and predictable. Unimpressed, he advised his boss to pass. Then, a day or two later, when he booted up his computer, he couldn't open his files. A message flashed on the screen, informing him that it was "time to pay" for leasing the software. It instructed him to send a bank draft, cashier's check, or international money order for the amount of either $189 for a year's use of the program or $378 for the lifetime of his hard drive, payable to PC Cyborg Corp., at a post office box in Panama. Upon receipt, PC Cyborg would generate a disk to unlock his computer.

Willems was flabbergasted. "I was thinking, 'Oh my God, what did I do? We are not going to pay that.'" He worried that his computer had a bug, or that he had made some mistake.

He noticed that a blue sheet had been packaged with the disk. On the front were installation instructions, which he hadn't needed. But the back spelled out in small print what it called a "license agreement," warning of dire consequences should he fail to pay. "Your conscience may haunt you for the rest of your life; you will owe compensation and possible damages to PC Cyborg Corporation; and your microcomputer will stop functioning normally," it said.

Willems wasn't intimidated. Then twenty-seven, he had tinkered with computers since adolescence and had studied computer science in college. Rebooting with a disk that installed a copy of the Microsoft Disk Operating System (MS-DOS), he saw that his directories and file names had been encrypted with a simple code in which one number or letter corresponded to another. By breaking the code and reversing the steps, he was able to retrieve his original files.

It wasn't until he went home and turned on the evening news that he learned the scheme had gulled other people, companies, and organizations across Europe and Africa. It would become known as the AIDS Trojan, because it used AIDS education as a Trojan horse to infiltrate computers. The disk had been sent to thousands of subscribers of a London-based magazine, *PC Business World,* including Willems's company, as well as to everyone who had attended a 1988 WHO conference on AIDS. While many recipients either didn't try the disk or didn't run it enough times to encrypt their files, as many as one thousand computers were paralyzed.

Although disks were a ubiquitous method of storing data on a personal computer, few people regarded them as a security threat. Willems went on TV himself to share his solution. Victims in Belgium, Holland, and beyond thanked him with gifts of fine wine and Belgian chocolate.

After the furor died down, Willems put the disk in his desk and forgot about it. A couple of years later, he rediscovered it and decided to keep it as a souvenir. Little did he know that it would someday carry historic significance. It now hangs in his living room. When a German museum recently offered him more than $1,000 for it, he refused.

Nowhere did the attack cause greater consternation than in England, where it appeared to have originated. Compulink Information eXchange (CIX), a kind of forerunner to BleepingComputer as a forum for technical discussion, was inundated with 376 messages about the AIDS Trojan within ten days.

The freelance programmer Jim Bates was the first to crack the code in England, around the same time as Willems in Belgium. "I had the bare bones of it sorted quickly," Bates recalled. The program tried to trick users into thinking that everything was working normally while actually blocking many commands. Because it didn't alter files, just their names, "restoration can be quite simply achieved," Bates wrote in the January 1990 *Virus Bulletin*.

Like Willems, Bates didn't seek to profit from his solution, setting an altruistic precedent for Michael Gillespie and the Ransomware Hunting Team. *Virus Bulletin* made Bates's programs for removing the Trojan horse and retrieving encrypted files available for free. Only victims who wiped their hard drives clean so they could reinstall their operating systems suffered lasting damage. One university in Milan panicked and "lost ten years of astronomical observations," Bates said, making it the first true victim of ransomware. An AIDS research center in Bologna also was unable to recover a decade's worth of data.

In *Virus Bulletin*, Bates rendered his technical judgment. "While the conception is ingenious and extremely devious, the actual programming is quite untidy," he wrote, indicating that the attacker "was not particularly well schooled."

Bringing that brilliant amateur to justice was an early test for the fledgling Computer Crime Unit (CCU) of Scotland Yard's Fraud Squad. That year, Noel Bonczoszek had become the first Scotland Yard officer to use a computer to investigate a fraud. The case hinged on thousands of paper invoices, which Bonczoszek normally would have had to sort by hand. Instead, he wrote a program that flagged documents with discrepancies and identified the managers who had signed off on them. Bonczoszek then received a Home Office grant for hardware and programming to support investigations. "Once we got the computer, we taught ourselves," another Fraud Squad officer, Chris Pierce, re-called. "Noel was far more advanced than me."

Later that year, the CCU was established, and Bonczoszek and Pierce were assigned to it. The four-man team faced resistance at every turn. "There was no suitable legislation in the UK and attempts to use existing laws had failed," Pierce said. Law enforcement ignored cyber fraud "as a 'non-crime,' commerce ignored it because it was too embarrassing, and the public were totally ignorant about it, as the media did not understand it. The difference that the CCU made was that we took it seriously and we regarded these 'nerds' as criminals and not some genius."

Pierce and Bonczoszek were close friends and complemented each other well. Often called "Bonzo," Bonczoszek was brilliant and creative, a sculptor who also collected antique cameras. "He had the ideas but could easily be distracted and wander off the point," Pierce said. He also had more computer savvy than Pierce, a skilled investigator and interviewer who enjoyed public speaking and promoting the CCU.

"I am not very proficient in IT, but in 1989 we both were streets ahead of nearly all cops," Pierce said. "I remember asking a constable to send me a copy of a diskette and he sent me a photocopy of both sides. We worked in the era when police would seize the screen and leave the CPU." When the officers needed technical help, they relied on private-sector experts like Bates, the freelance programmer. "We had a wealth of interested parties to assist us," Bonczoszek said. "It was a band-of-brothers type of thing."

The AIDS Trojan posed a new challenge for the unit, which had mainly focused on hacks into academic and military networks. Pierce gloomily bet Bonzo £10 that they would never find the culprit.

They launched their investigation after being alerted by Bates as well as victims like Robert Edward Muid. Then thirty-five, Muid subscribed to *PC Business World* and knew about the threat of viruses. He had warned his colleagues at the English university where he worked not to put anything unfamiliar in their computers. But the disk that arrived in the mail seemed legitimate, and the topic of AIDS education was pertinent to his research specialty of immunopharmacology. So he inserted the disk in his university computer, which froze. Although he didn't lose his research files, because he had backed them up on another disk, he was still furious—with the hacker and with himself.

"I kicked myself for falling afoul of this," recalled Muid, who later became head of computing for the university's biosciences division. "I just thought the audacity of somebody attempting to take control of your computer, and demanding money, was something I wouldn't stand for. It was out-and-out blackmail. I contacted the police."

Popp had developed the AIDS survey at a workshop he'd led in Kenya. He then devised the encryption code separately, and altered the educational program so that it wouldn't open unless the ransomware had been installed. Aiming to stay within the law, he framed the shakedown as a voluntary licensing agreement. He also took the precaution of locating PC Cyborg in Panama, a tax haven with strict bank secrecy laws.

On a visit home to Ohio in 1989, Popp did give his friend Ronald Schilb a preview of his creation.

Schilb worried about running the disk on his new Apple computer. "I remember thinking that I did not want to mess up my new computer because I didn't have the money to buy another or have it fail on me," he said. But he felt that recipients would only have themselves to blame if their computers froze, since Popp's "license agreement" warned that "program mechanisms" would "adversely affect" the computer if the user didn't pay. "It wasn't malicious, it was money-making," he said. Popp "was explicit about removing it if you didn't want to pay for it. I'm sure that some thought they could get by without paying. Many using company computers . . . might have taken the warnings lightly."

The CCU took a less charitable view of the case. But Pierce doubted that Panama would cooperate with requests for information about PC Cyborg Corp., especially since the country's dictator, Manuel Noriega, was under indictment in the United States for racketeering, drug smuggling, and money laundering. Then a vagary of world politics tipped the balance in the investigators' favor. Nine days after the AIDS disks were distributed, the U.S. military invaded Panama, ousting Noriega. When Pierce phoned the business registration office in Panama, a U.S. marine answered. Explaining that he was in charge because the local staff "took to the hills," the marine obligingly looked up the names of PC Cyborg's partners and directors. By interviewing them, police learned that an "Elizabeth Ketema" had set up the company, purportedly by phone from Addis Ababa, Ethiopia.

Someone with a similar alias had been active in London. *PC Business World*'s publisher told police that an "E. Ketema," who purported to represent a Nigerian software company, bought the mailing list for $2,000. Ketema's handwriting and appearance—he was described as white, bearded, tall, and thin—matched Popp's.

Whoever mailed the disks had licked the stamps instead of using a postage meter, which would have required a record of the buyer's name. The saliva from the stamps was analyzed for antigens; though the procedure was less conclusive than DNA testing, at the time a rarity in criminal investigations, the results would match a sample later taken from Popp. Also, Popp's fingerprints were found in five envelopes and on the disks they contained.

The envelopes were postmarked in the London neighborhood of Kensington, one district over from Knightsbridge, where Popp had been staying. Bonczoszek broke down the door to Popp's apartment but found no sign of him.

The clincher was an encrypted disk found at the WHO's headquarters in Geneva. At Scotland Yard's request, Bates decoded it. It turned out to be a diary of the AIDS Trojan's development and test runs dating back to April 1988. The password was drjosephlewisandrewpoppjr—Popp's name plus "Andrew," presumably inserted for extra security.

The CCU also asked a government AIDS expert, Gwyneth Lewis, whether the disk's medical advice was worth paying for. Her answer was an emphatic no. The AIDS information, she found, was "alarmist" and "in certain parts inaccurate." For example, it exaggerated the odds of an unborn child contracting HIV from the mother. "The author has a rather incomplete knowledge of HIV, has presented the facts badly, and is not up to date," wrote Lewis, who was the principal medical officer of the AIDS unit of the UK's Department of Health. "This programme could cause more anxiety to the very people who need help and reassurance."

Left unanswered by investigators were two intriguing and possibly related questions: Where did Popp get the money? And did he act alone? By Edward Wilding's estimate, preparing and distributing the AIDS Trojan would have cost as much as $45,000 for disks, mailing lists, stamps, and envelopes. Popp lived like a mogul. He regularly traveled internationally, he told his family that he had bank accounts in Hong Kong and Switzerland, and he was renting a posh flat in one of London's ritziest neighborhoods. When his sister Barbara visited in October 1989, he took her to fancy restaurants and a West End production of *Les Misérables*, and they toured castles in Scotland, all on his dime.

Yet he had no obvious source of wealth. Possibly he had saved earnings from his Masai Mara field guide, safaris, and postcards. Still, his Amref salary was modest. Colleagues there mistakenly assumed that his family was supporting him. "It was understood he had his own money," Blundell Brown said.

One possibility is a deeper-pocketed investor or accomplice. "The thought occurred to me, there was someone else involved," Bates speculated. "Can you imagine licking and sticking twenty thousand stamps? It's not a job for one man."

Sapolsky heard talk that Popp "was connected with some powerful businesspeople" in Nairobi, and he believes that they staked him.

But any backer who advanced Popp money in exchange for a share of an expected windfall would have been disappointed. So far as is known, no victim paid PC Cyborg Corp. Ironically, its only revenue came from the police. During their investigation, just to see what would happen, Pierce and Bonczoszek had sent the fee without identifying themselves. There was no response. Despite its promises, PC Cyborg didn't supply a decryption tool.

■   ■   ■

About ten days after mailing the disks, Popp was preparing to speak about his AIDS survey at a WHO conference he was running in Nairobi. Another attendee showed him a newspaper article describing the novel extortion scheme that had disabled computers worldwide. Although the article didn't name him, he realized that it was referring to his disk. Stunned, realizing that his reputation would be ruined and that he might face prosecution, Popp suffered—or feigned—a breakdown. Acknowledging to the conference that he had sent the disks, he accused the colleague who had shared the article of being an Interpol agent and complained that his hotel room was bugged.

Popp headed for Nairobi's airport, where he was detained by Kenyan police, who had been notified by Interpol to look out for him. They discovered PC Cyborg seals in his luggage and seized it. He was then hospitalized. "The Kenyans informed us he was visited in hospital by American consular officials and soon afterwards disappeared," Pierce said. It seems likely that the U.S. embassy in Kenya intervened to protect a distraught American by arranging his release and his flight.

At Amsterdam's Schiphol airport, a kindly employee gave him a cup of coffee. Suspecting he had been drugged, he wrote "Dr. Popp has been poisoned" in Magic Marker on a duffel bag and waved it around for all to see.

His antics drew the attention of Dutch authorities, who notified Scotland Yard that its suspect had turned up. Still, Popp was allowed to return to the United States on Christmas Day 1989 with one of his sisters, who came to Amsterdam to take him home. Soon afterward, he and his parents went to see John Kilroy, a lawyer who had represented Popp's sister in an unrelated case. After Popp told Kilroy that he was being followed and that Interpol, Scotland Yard, and the FBI were after him, his parents asked to speak privately with the lawyer. They confided that their son was mentally ill and that they believed nobody was pursuing him.

Actually, the CCU had obtained a warrant for Popp's arrest in London on blackmail charges. The paperwork wended its way through a bureaucratic tangle—the British Home and Foreign Offices; the embassy in Washington, D.C.; the consulate in Ohio; and the U.S. Department of Justice—to the FBI. Riding the school bus in early February 1990, Popp's ten-year-old nephew heard a news bulletin on the driver's radio: "Local Harvard Whiz Kid Arrested." It was Popp.

At Scotland Yard, Pierce mounted a £10 note on cardboard and inscribed it, "On the Occasion of the Arrest of Dr. Joseph Lewis Popp Feb. 1990."

"He was only too glad to pay," Bonczoszek said.

The FBI seized Popp's computer, which contained the programming for the AIDS Trojan. The bureau sent it to England, where the CCU had the hard drive analyzed. The educational portion "was very neatly written," Pierce recalled. "It was a textbook, laid-out program. The Trojan horse part was very different and a real mess."

At the British government's request, U.S. prosecutors sought permission in the federal court in Cleveland to extradite Popp. When Popp told the court that he couldn't understand the proceedings, because he was under heavy psychiatric medication, the judge appointed two specialists to examine him. One of them concluded that Popp had become paranoid and suicidal from the shock of the news accounts, but that his condition was improving.

On the basis of the psychiatrists' reports, the prosecution and defense agreed that Popp was mentally competent to participate in the extradition hearing. Looking suitably scruffy, he attested to his delusions, including that the coffee at the airport was poisoned and that Noriega was trying to kill him. "I would say I had developed a paranoid personality outlook," he told the judge.

Popp and his lawyers portrayed the disk as a legitimate tool to educate the public and prevent the spread of AIDS. "I had the idea that, given what he viewed as a massive humanitarian crisis, he believed that his method was acceptable," Kilroy said.

Bates flew to Cleveland to demonstrate how the scheme worked. A computer was trolleyed into the courtroom, and Bates inserted the disk as well as a separate program that reduced the number of reboots needed to freeze the system. The monetary demand flashed on the screen, and when Bates tried to interrupt the encryption, a siren wailed. "They thought I was Sherlock Holmes or a close relation,"

Bates recalled. "'The judge said, 'Let the record show, the machine is making a noise like a fire engine.'"

For someone to be extradited from the United States to the UK, the alleged offenses must be serious crimes in both countries. Popp's extradition battle lasted for most of 1990. He was held without bail for months on the ground that the United Kingdom "was entitled to the delivery of the accused." In August, he was allowed to reside in a crisis shelter for two weeks as long as he called the court's pretrial services department daily. On December 20, the judge granted extradition, ruling that there was reason to believe that Popp's conduct would constitute a felony under U.S. law. She also found that the warnings packaged with the AIDS Trojan were in such small type that most users would not have read them before running the disk.

Bonczoszek and Pierce were dispatched to escort Popp to England. At the U.S. marshal's office in Cleveland, Pierce strip-searched the prisoner to check for weapons and found he was wearing a money bag around his waist with $10,000 in small bills. "My bail money," Popp said. In the UK, Pierce explained, defendants don't put up money for bail; they promise to pay. The cash was painstakingly counted at the start and end of the trip to make sure none was missing.

Popp read a paperback during the flight. "I did not get the impression there was anything wrong with Popp. He certainly did not display any mental illness to me," Pierce said. "He was very quiet and polite."

Once in England, Popp's behavior became increasingly bizarre. "His recent antics have included wearing a cardboard box, putting hair rollers in his beard to protect himself from 'radiation' and 'microorganisms' and wearing condoms on his nose," *Virus Bulletin* reported. A psychiatrist reported to London's Southwark Crown Court that Popp was "severely mentally ill" and "deteriorating."

Pierce wasn't buying it. A psychiatric hospital where Popp was placed notified police that he "had been overheard on the telephone boasting to someone he had hoodwinked the system" to avoid facing trial, Pierce said. "He was a scam artist."

While Popp may have had a temporary breakdown in Kenya from

the shock of being branded an international outlaw, he sounded calm and confident in a 1991 letter to his friend John Augustine.

"I'm staying with friends named Sandy and Glynis," he wrote. "I have to sign in daily at the local police station. The date for the trial has not yet been set. My advocate and I are confident of winning the case when it is eventually taken to trial. Generally, I am rather bored. I can't read or write well because of double vision. I have had some interesting walks around the moors. Well, I thought I'd better write so that you don't think I have fallen off the edge of the world."

Moreover, the ransomware scheme was no unhinged aberration. It was consistent with Popp's lifelong delight in mischief-making and his survival-of-the-fittest philosophy. "A bit Darwinian, that's absolutely where he was," observed James Malcolm, his fellow student in DeVore's seminar at Harvard. "He was applying selfishness and aggression. He was applying what he was studying."

As a dedicated Darwinist, and an expert on social interaction among primates, Popp would have thought deeply about how to adapt his behavior to his precarious situation. Faking insanity both served his self-interest and tickled his sense of humor—a strategy to escape punishment and mock authority at the same time.

The Southwark judge Geoffrey Rivlin, though, believed Popp—or simply wanted him off the court calendar and out of the country. In November 1991, Rivlin ruled that Popp was unfit to stand trial. While acknowledging that justice for ransomware victims remained elusive, Rivlin ordered this "very sick man" to go back to the United States as fast as he could. It was like small-town police "putting someone on the bus to the next county," Kilroy said.

Nevertheless, the case had far-reaching consequences in England. The publicity spurred Parliament to pass the Computer Misuse Act of 1990, which criminalized hacking. Under the law, impairing the operation of a computer without authorization, or hindering access to any program or data in it, is punishable by up to five years in prison. The act covers any attack, no matter where it originated, against a computer in the UK.

Authorities in Italy, where the AIDS Trojan wreaked havoc, weren't satisfied with Rivlin's cop-out. In 1993, a court in Rome sentenced Popp to two and a half years in prison for attempted extortion. Popp didn't attend the proceedings; he was safe in Texas. There would be no second extradition.

Popp never experimented with computer crime again. Once he returned to the United States, he put the AIDS Trojan behind him. He wasn't interested in discussing it privately or publicly. When a *Plain Dealer* reporter, Christopher Evans, tracked him to a gated apartment complex in Lake Jackson, about an hour south of Houston, Popp politely declined an interview.

"It's a strange case, I've got to admit that," he told Evans. "I'm not going to lose too much sleep over what is past. I feel that the future is very bright."

As usual, Popp had no evident source of financial support, but he didn't lack for company. His sister Barbara and her family lived nearby, and he sometimes had coffee with local fundamentalist Christians, whom he took pleasure in dumbfounding. Their T-shirts asked WWJD—an abbreviation for "What would Jesus do?"—so he had his own shirt printed and wore it around town. It was inscribed WWDD—"What would Darwin do?"

He tried to answer that question in an outrageous book. After being internationally humiliated, someone less arrogant might have shied away from controversy. Popp courted it. Self-published in 2000, *Popular Evolution: Life-Lessons from Anthropology* doubled down on the extreme views that he had advocated in Irven DeVore's living room a quarter century before.

Some of his advice seemed logical enough. For example, to encourage relatives to propagate the family DNA, he recommended leaving money not to them, but to their unborn children. Other lessons sounded like Swiftian satire. Teenagers should smoke, drink, and drop out of school in eighth grade, he wrote, because those behaviors correlate with having more sex and more babies. He proposed legislation against breastfeeding because of its contraceptive effect: a mother who gives formula to her baby "could produce additional offspring." In one disturbing passage, he appeared to condone rape, at least if it resulted in pregnancy. "Although one commonly hears the claim today that rape is a crime of violence, not a crime of sex, the sexual component of rape is real," he wrote. "Rape victims are not random members of the population, rather they tend to be females of reproductive age. Rapists are not random members of the population, rather they tend to be males of reproductive age."

In a letter to Augustine while working on the book, he observed that, because people raised by single mothers have higher fertility rates, "it may be that the best a father can do for his children . . . in America is to abandon them."

The irony was that he had disregarded his own philosophy: he had no children. When Augustine dared to ask why, Popp replied, "The answer is cultural load. I carry a terrible burden of relatively high educational status and First World prosperity."

Popp's views were out of step with his field. As sociobiology matured, it increasingly focused on the evolutionary advantages of cooperation and altruism. Nor had his escapade into cybercrime gone unnoticed by his onetime peers. Yet he sought endorsements from bestselling authors and former Harvard mentors, seemingly unaware that they might be reluctant to associate themselves with him. Instead, his friend Schilb, a high school biology teacher, blurbed it, saying it would "appeal to the same readership as does Stephen Jay Gould."

Behind the bravado lay hints of unease. Popp had recurrent nightmares of being attacked by lions or humans. "I'm being battered by any one of a variety of people, and I try to throw a punch at them but I can't land it with any force," he wrote to Augustine.

A rekindled relationship with Christine Ryan helped relax him. They had met in Kenya when she was an undergraduate and he was observing baboons, and again in Harvard Square in the late 1970s when he briefly returned to the United States to finish his doctorate.

After they reconnected in 1998, he said to her, "I know you're always on the internet. Please don't believe everything you read." They never talked about the AIDS Trojan.

They moved to Oneonta in 2002, and he became a friend and mentor to her teenage daughter. In 2004, he published a book-length index, *Popp's Concordance to Darwin's On the Origin of Species*, the title implying a certain equivalence between himself and his hero.

While he applied unsuccessfully for teaching jobs at nearby universities, Ryan had an idea: they should open a butterfly exhibit. It would be "for both fun and profit," Popp explained to Augustine, predicting it would attract a "good percentage" of tourists and school groups visiting the National Baseball Hall of Fame and Museum in Cooperstown, about twenty miles away. "Visitors react with a sense of joy when they are placed in a jungle room with hundreds of free-flying butterflies," he wrote.

First, though, he had to come up with the funds. Buying and rehabbing a historic farmhouse left Popp and Ryan low on cash. His bank rejected his credit application. He sought a $40,000 loan from Augustine, who turned him down. He was still raising money and preparing for the conservatory's grand opening when, on the rainy Tuesday morning of June 27, 2006, his 1993 Honda Civic, with more than 130,000 miles on it, skidded under the rear of a tractor-trailer, shearing the roof off the car. The fifty-five-year-old Popp was killed instantly.

Ryan finished the conservatory with her daughter's help and has maintained it in Popp's memory ever since. She's especially careful to preserve a stone waterfall that feeds into the goldfish pond. "He put those rocks in," she said. "It was one of the last things he did before he died."

Popp died before his invention became one of the world's most pervasive and damaging forms of cybercrime. It wasn't until several years later—after the advent of Bitcoin made it hard to trace payments—that the AIDS Trojan began, in Poppian terms, to maximize its reproductive success and engender countless progeny.

2.

THE SUPERHERO OF NORMAL, ILLINOIS

BloNo, as the Bloomington-Normal metropolitan area in central Illinois is often called, is an unusual amalgam of college and company towns. Thanks to State Farm, the area's largest employer, and Illinois State University, a distant second, the populace is largely white collar, middle class, and well educated. Both insurance and higher education are stable industries, relatively resilient during economic downturns.

The country's largest provider of home and auto insurance, State Farm covers its many policyholders for all manner of disasters—including, since 2017, ransomware attacks. There is "a steady growth in demand for this product," according to the company.

BloNo has a proud history. As an up-and-coming lawyer and politician, Abraham Lincoln often journeyed there from the state capital, Springfield, seventy miles away, to visit two key backers, David Davis and Jesse Fell. Davis, a judge, ran Lincoln's 1860 presidential campaign, helping him win the Republican nomination and the general election. Two years later, Lincoln appointed Davis to the U.S. Supreme Court. Fell, a businessman and longtime Lincoln confidant, proposed the 1858 debates with Stephen Douglas that first drew national notice to "The Railsplitter."

Fell founded the local newspaper, *The Pantagraph*. His great-grandson, Adlai Stevenson II, who worked for the family newspaper as a reporter and editor, became governor of Illinois and twice the Democratic candidate for president, losing both times to Dwight D. Eisenhower. The area was then a Republican stronghold. Democrats have since made inroads, and BloNo's red is now tinged with blue. Michael and Morgan Gillespie are part of the area's political transition, voting for both Hillary Clinton and Joe Biden.

Stevenson, Davis, and Fell are buried in Bloomington's Evergreen Cemetery. So is the infant who gave her name to one of the most beloved characters in the history of American movies. After Dorothy Gage died of pneumonia at the age of five months in 1898, her uncle, L. Frank Baum, honored his late niece by choosing the name Dorothy for the heroine of his new novel, *The Wonderful Wizard of Oz*. Near Dorothy Gage's grave stands a statue, carved from a tree stump, of her fictional namesake, gazing into the distance, with a basket over her right arm and her dog, Toto, at her feet.

Historic Route 66 bisects Bloomington's gentrifying downtown, lined by natural foods and fair trade stores and a pour-over coffee shop. Every July 4 there's a fireworks display in Miller Park, a quintessential city park with a bandstand, a zoo, mini golf, two war memorials, towering oak trees, and an artificial lake. Michael and Morgan watched the fireworks in Miller Park from the front porch of their white two-story, Craftsman-style bungalow. It occupied a corner lot on Bloomington's west side, so close to the train tracks that they could hear Amtrak's Lincoln Service roar by on its way to Chicago.

Holiday flags hung from a porch cluttered with mismatched lawn furniture. To the side of the house, enclosed by a metal fence, was a grassy patch where the Gillespies' dogs liked to sniff. Computers and equipment discarded by Nerds on Call customers were piled in the garage. Michael once hoped to repair and sell them, until ransomware consumed his spare time.

■   ■   ■

Although he has spent most of his life in central Illinois, Michael wasn't born or bred in BloNo. He's a native of Florida. His maternal grandfather, Hugh Todd, worked for the police force in Coral Gables, a Miami suburb, rising to the rank of lieutenant. Mustachioed Hugh took pride in his job. He was an extra in police-related films and television shows, enjoying a few seconds of screen time in *Police Academy 5: Assignment Miami Beach* as a police chief, and appearing in a couple of episodes of *Miami Vice*.

Hugh's daughter, Allison, earned an associate's degree in computers at Miami Dade Community College. Through a shared interest in karate, she met John Gillespie, and they began dating. As they drove to New York for a karate camp, she found out she was pregnant. Born on December 12, 1991, Michael was six weeks old at their wedding, which he attended in a onesie tuxedo. His parents—Allison was twenty-three, John twenty—were decked out in royal-blue satin karate gear, and his grandfather Hugh sang two solos.

Soon afterward, John Gillespie was laid off from a construction job in Florida. The family moved to John's mother's house in East Peoria, Illinois, and then to Peoria itself. The former headquarters of Caterpillar, which makes construction and mining equipment, Peoria is also a byword for Middle America, known for the catchphrase beloved of advertisers and campaign managers: "Will it play in Peoria?"

When Michael was four, the Gillespies resettled in Pekin, ten miles south of Peoria. With a population of 32,000, Pekin is a poor blue-collar city with a reputation as a hub for methamphetamine labs and dealers; one Pekin meth user's before-and-after photos have been featured in national anti-addiction campaigns.

John Gillespie worked on the field crew for a company called Consolidated Land Surveying, delineating sites where Verizon, Consolidated's main client, was building cell towers. Allison took college courses online in criminal justice and emergency management, and she bounced from job to job as a crossing guard, a security guard at a home improvement store, a school lunchroom server, and a cashier.

The Gillespies were devoted to their church and community. Allison delivered food to the needy, and she and John volunteered with the state's emergency services agency, communicating with tornado spotters via ham radios. They got together with other ham radio buffs at "hamfests" and outfitted their green four-door Chevy Blazer and red two-seat Chevy pickup truck with ham radios. The truck also sported half a dozen antennas on the roof and bumper as well as colored lights to alert passersby to impending disasters.

"Growing up was interesting because my house was full of voices," Michael said. "They were constantly listening not just to police scanners and fire department channels but classified radio stuff and the ham operator stuff."

Michael's parents were pro-gun zealots. After twenty-six people, including twenty children, were shot and killed in 2012 at Sandy Hook Elementary School in Newtown, Connecticut, Allison reposted a statement from the U.S. Concealed Carry Association that "more laws and more control don't equal more safety and security." John's social media postings have featured pro-gun memes and an invitation to a "grassroots rally to support gun rights" in Bloomington. Attendees were encouraged to bear arms to "serve as a fair warning for local Antifa-types who might want to crash the event."

When the Gillespies drove to Florida to visit relatives, Michael brought his Nintendo Game Boy and his stuffed cat, Kitty. Oblivious to his parents' conversation, he stared out the Blazer's window at the roofs and power lines as he imagined Kitty playing parkour, navigating an urban obstacle course. His mother was a devotee of the Justice League, especially Wonder Woman, and they sometimes detoured to Metropolis, Illinois. The city of fewer than seven thousand people on the banks of the Ohio River claims to be Superman's hometown, and it put up a bronze statue of him in 1993.

There, Michael and his parents paid their respects to the Man of Steel. The superhero stands a muscular fifteen feet high, with a single brown curl dipping over his forehead, biceps flexed, fists at his waist, red cape unfurled, and legs firmly planted atop a pedestal proclaiming TRUTH—JUSTICE—THE AMERICAN WAY.

■ ■ ■

The family struggled financially. Michael wore cast-off clothes, and his meals sometimes came from food pantries. His parents fell behind on mortgage payments on their Pekin house, and in 2003, when Michael was eleven, a bank began foreclosure proceedings. Although that action was dismissed, the Gillespies declared bankruptcy in 2008. Consolidated shut down in 2018, and John lost his job.

Michael endured hardships, but there was no lack of love. The family always had a pet, usually a cat. When he was playing outdoors or at a friend's house, his parents kept in touch with him by walkie-talkie. They encouraged his precocious interest in technology. His father taught him to repair electronics by soldering ham radios, and they played the video game *Doom* on a Gateway 2000. Michael played *Donkey Kong Country* on a used Super Nintendo that his uncle gave him. He often visited his father's mother, who was a video gamer. They gardened and cooked together, and she introduced him to online role-playing games such as *RuneScape*.

Michael loved a Lego game called *Bionicle*, in which heroes and villains face off in a mythical universe. Some pieces contained secret codes that he could enter in the official *Bionicle* website. "I was always into cryptography. I just remember being fascinated, as a kid, by the fact that you can have secrets that no one else can figure out."

He wanted more Lego sets, but his parents couldn't afford them. Instead, he and a neighborhood friend built spaceships with a large bag of mismatched Lego pieces that the playmate got at a yard sale.

Michael's elementary school recognized his talent, placing him in a gifted program. By second grade, he was doing fifth-grade math. After "picking up on the fact that I was getting into coding and stuff," he recalled, his parents enrolled him at age twelve in a programming course at Illinois Central College. A year later, he was so computer savvy that he was giving lessons to thousands of users on an online tutoring site, using graphic design software he pirated.

"I know it's bad that I just pirated an eight-hundred-dollar program, but I always thought that if I actually start making money on this, I'll actually buy it. But I didn't make money on it. So that was my logic for copping out."

Freelancing did reap an occasional windfall. A client in India once paid him $1,000 to build a website.

After middle school one afternoon, Morgan Blanch noticed a skinny boy wearing oversize clothes. He was mowing the lawn of her best friend's neighbor, an elderly woman who was berating him for not doing the job properly. "You missed a spot over here," she yelled at him.

"Oh man, that sucks for him," ten-year-old Morgan thought.

The beleaguered boy was Michael. He was helping out family friends—a mother and son the Gillespies had stayed with when they were especially strapped. Morgan never forgot her first glimpse of her future husband.

Morgan's childhood was, if anything, more turbulent than Michael's, though for different reasons. Her father, Bobby Blanch, grew up in Peoria; her mother, a diminutive brunette whose maiden name was Beth Hall, came from Pekin. They met as teenagers at Vacation Bible School. Conceived on the night of her dad's high school prom, Morgan was born in Pekin on Valentine's Day 1992, when her mother was seventeen, and her father had just turned eighteen. Her grandmother, Rita Blanch, was thirty-three at the time, and two of Morgan's great-great-grandparents were still living.

Four months later, Bobby and Beth were wed. But they were too young to handle the dual responsibilities of marriage and parenthood. "I learned very young that my needs and my wants didn't matter," Morgan said. "My parents' needs and wants were more important . . . They pretty much left us to our own devices. Nobody checked my homework. Nobody made sure I got up to go to school in the morning. If I didn't get up—if my alarm didn't go off, or I slept through it or something—I would be berated."

The dysfunction deepened as the family grew. The Blanches had a son in 1995, and a second daughter in 1997. Beth had a drinking problem, and she and Bobby argued frequently, Morgan said. Morgan became a de facto parent. By the time she was ten, she was babysitting her younger siblings as well as the family pets. Her brother, who has autism, needed extra attention.

To escape, she often stayed overnight at the home of her grandmother Rita Blanch. Rita, who worked multiple jobs, delivered the Peoria newspaper from 1:00 to 5:00 a.m., and Morgan often rode with her in the car. Yearning for a well-adjusted family life, Morgan found it on television. She rarely missed an episode of *A Baby Story*, a reality show on cable that followed loving couples through the thrills and anxieties of pregnancy to the agony of labor and the exhausted joy of having a baby.

She set her heart on being a midwife when she grew up, but soon changed her mind. "I realized I wouldn't be able to handle the negative sides, like when there's stillbirth," she said. Yet she yearned to have children. "Being a mom was what I always wanted to do. At a young age, because my mom couldn't mother me the way that I wanted her to, I started dreaming about the mother that I would be. And how I was going to make it better for somebody else, and be the thing that I couldn't have." She also developed a fondness for *The Sims*, the life simulation video game, creating a fantasy existence more fulfilling than her actual one.

In 2003, when Beth was working as a stylist at a hair salon, she filed for divorce, alleging "extreme and repeated mental cruelty." When it was finalized in 2004, she and Bobby, who was working for a flooring company, agreed that he would pay $200 a month in child support, and that the children would attend Pekin schools and be raised in the Christian faith. Bobby and Beth shared custody, and Morgan spent part of the week with each parent. That lasted for a year, until Morgan could no longer tolerate the domestic disorder at her mother's house. One night, lying in her "nasty bed," looking around at her "nasty environment," she told herself, "I don't want to do this anymore."

She marched into the living room, where her mother was still up. "I don't know how you can stand living in this," Morgan said. Never before had she challenged her mother's authority so directly. Beth snapped, grabbing and bruising Morgan's arms.

Morgan wrestled herself free and ran to her father's house. He brought her back to her mother's place. "Get everything you can carry," he said.

Inside, her mother stared her down. "Say goodbye to the rest," Beth said. "It's going to Goodwill."

Morgan never saw some of her favorite knickknacks and keepsakes again.

Beth was in a tailspin. After a domestic argument, she locked herself in the bathroom and swallowed pills. A friend knocked the door down, and Beth was rushed to the hospital. In 2006 and 2007, she pleaded guilty to drunk driving charges. Then she found the strength to transform her life. In October 2010, she wrote proudly on Facebook, "I have two years sober on Wednesday. Not a drop."

Soon after, Morgan's father retreated from society. Bobby Blanch felt self-conscious when cutting the grass or taking out the trash, as if neighbors were watching. Morgan was no longer living with him. He withdrew with his girlfriend and their daughter to an isolated house on a hilltop shadowed by pine, oak, birch, and black locust trees, at the dead end of a ten-minute drive on a dirt road marked by PRIVATE PROPERTY and KEEP OUT signs. He plowed the road himself after snowstorms and had a generator that kicked in when the power went down.

One evening outside his house, under the stars, he reflected on how he had coped as Morgan's teenage parent. "It was hard," he said. "But I was seventeen" when Beth became pregnant. "I wasn't that young. My mom was fourteen . . . I felt like, 'At least I got to seventeen.' I was an adult."

Morgan has a gorgeous contralto voice. As a fourth-grader in Pekin, she sang the patriotic country music anthem "God Bless the U.S.A." in her school's first talent show after the September 11, 2001, terrorist attacks. Her rendition brought down the house, earning praise from parents and teachers.

The next year, she chose an R&B song, "Stole," by Kelly Rowland of Destiny's Child, about talented Black teenagers who never got the chance to fulfill their potential. To Morgan's disappointment, the heartfelt protest against racial injustice fell flat. "Nobody cared for it," she said.

Anyone familiar with Pekin's history of racial discrimination might have anticipated these divergent reactions. In the 1920s, Pekin was a regional headquarters for the Ku Klux Klan, which briefly took over the daily newspaper and turned it into a mouthpiece for racism and nativism. Pekin was long notorious as a "sundown town," where Black people weren't welcome after nightfall. As signs on the south side of town put it as late as the 1970s, "Don't let the sun set on your black ass in Pekin, Illinois." The 2000 U.S. census counted only 44 Black residents in Pekin, and though that number rose to 710 in 2010, the town remained 95 percent white.

The prejudice extended to other groups. The town's founders had named it after Peking, the former name for Beijing, which was mistakenly believed to be directly on the opposite side of the globe from central Illinois. Pekin's high school athletic teams for decades were called the "Chinks." School mascots were "Chink," "Chinklette," and "Mr. Bamboo," and a local roller-skating arena was known as the "Chink Rink." At sports events, students banged a gong when a Pekin player scored.

After the school won two state basketball championships in the 1960s, the derogatory nickname became more widely known, and Chinese American groups began to protest. Pekin's government and business leaders refused to get involved, and the student body overwhelmingly voted in 1974 to keep the name Chinks. Finally, in 1980, at the insistence of a new superintendent of schools, and despite a student walkout and alumni protests that would recur for years afterward, the name was changed to Dragons. Growing up, Michael and Morgan sensed the bigotry. "Just the vibe I got from people," Michael said. "I do remember a lot of Confederate flags flying around town."

In junior high, a music teacher paired Michael with a classmate to play the ukulele and sing. Michael could strum a decent tune on the instrument, but his partner was better. So Michael, whose voice had broken in sixth grade, handled the vocals.

The teacher was surprised to hear such a deep voice from an adolescent boy. She rushed over midsong. "You have a bass voice," she said. "I need a bass in my choir." It was a fateful moment. Singing became Michael's main extracurricular activity and led him to his future wife.

Michael didn't have many friends at school. A shy, awkward computer geek who shared clothes with his mother, he was an easy target for bullying. His pants were always too short, and classmates teased that he was wearing high-waters in case of a flood.

Other kids "knew he didn't have money," Morgan said. "You know how there's always that one kid at school that everybody knows who they are because they're weird or they're the butt of people's jokes? Michael was one of those kids."

As freshmen, Michael and Morgan both participated in afterschool choir programs at Pekin Community High School. Michael was in the school's show choir, The Noteables, a song-and-dance troupe that performed at Pekin's Marigold Festival and other events. Morgan participated in an all-girls choir. When they met after practices, Morgan didn't scoff at Michael. She was overweight, which often made her feel like an outcast herself. Morgan began dating another member of The Noteables, Michael's best friend at the time. The trio hung out, with Michael as the third wheel.

When Morgan and her boyfriend split up, Michael consoled her. They walked to each other's house to play board and video games and watch movies. When they were apart, they messaged back and forth for hours on MySpace. Michael became Morgan's confidant. In front of other friends, though, she pushed him away. She was worried that they would mock her for being so close with a computer nerd. Michael had his own reservations, which he revealed to her with his characteristic bluntness.

"I could never date a fat girl," he told her one summer afternoon.

Morgan was hurt but didn't show it.

"Okay, we're just friends," she told him. "I know where you stand."

He soon regretted his insensitivity and spent the next year and a half pursuing her. But his goofiness in front of other people embarrassed her. Once, when he tried a backflip on a trampoline in her father's backyard, his knees smashed into his face, and his teeth punctured his lip. Another time, when a friend threw a lakeside party, Michael borrowed a Jet Ski and played a dangerous game of chicken on the water, racing at another rider before swerving at the last second.

Still, Morgan knew she could count on him. "We'd get annoyed because our other friends were more flighty," she said. "They weren't dependable, whereas if Michael and I made a plan, we stuck to it. And we liked that about each other."

She consulted her grandmother Rita as well as her best friend, Tricia. Both of them endorsed Michael. "Hon, best friends can make the best husbands," Rita told her. "Gosh, go to him now."

Tricia was succinct: "Give it a shot."

During Christmas break of their junior year at Pekin High, Morgan and Michael started dating.

Around the same time, sixteen-year-old Michael was looking for a job. He first applied to a flower shop. "I figured I could work with flowers, meet some girls. That's why I took French, too."

Instead, through a family friend, he landed a job that aligned with his computer skills. Like the Gillespies, Brian Ford and his family were regular worshippers at St. John's, an evangelical Lutheran church in Pekin. With an easy, close-lipped smile, a buzz cut, and a husky drawl, Brian was a genial outdoorsman who enjoyed hunting and fishing. He was also a shrewd businessman and successful entrepreneur. Throughout high school and while at Eastern Illinois University, he grew award-winning tomatoes and peppers in his own nurseries. But he didn't see a career in vegetables, so he took computer courses and got a job as a programmer at Caterpillar. In 1989, he started Facet Technologies in his basement and ran it on the side for twelve years until he quit his day job at Caterpillar. Early on, Facet fixed personal computers and handled networking for about a hundred accounts; by 2021, it was providing a wide range of tech services to five thousand businesses nationwide.

Brian believed in giving opportunities to bright high school students. He had watched Michael grow up, and the Gillespies had crowed to him about Michael's computer prowess. He knew that Michael was taking courses in networking at Pekin High. He mentioned Michael's interest to Facet's director of business solutions, Jason Hahn, whom Brian had hired at sixteen.

"There's a kid at church, smart, good with electronics, looking for a job," Brian told Jason. "Might be a good fit for us."

They brought him in for an interview. Michael seemed nervous and slightly desperate. He was worried that if he didn't get the job, he might end up laying carpet, as his and Morgan's dads had both done from time to time. But he impressed Brian and Jason, and they hired him.

In 2003, Facet had acquired Nerds on Call, a regional chain of no-frills computer repair shops. Michael started there as a part-time bench tech, doing basic work like disassembling and debugging computers. The Pekin outlet was across from the high school, and on his first day, Michael rolled up on his bicycle.

"Hey, where can I park my bike?" he asked Jason.

Soon he didn't need the bike. With his first Facet paychecks, Michael, who had gotten his driver's license a few months before, bought a rusted 1989 Chevy Blazer for $800 cash. After school, he would drive across the street to the store, or to the Nerds on Call in Peoria, twenty minutes north. "Within the same month, I got a job, got a car, got a girlfriend," he said. "Boom!" His luck continued when Pekin High raffled off a first-rate computer that he helped to build in class. With his Facet earnings, he bought more than $100 worth of tickets—and won.

As he gained more responsibility at Facet, he began to display a creative flair for problem-solving. He invented a device he called the Nuker to wipe clean old hard drives so they could be resold, and he decorated it with a tiger decal. Then he improved it, calling it Nuker 2.0 and adorning it with a lion decal.

Nerds on Call used a rudimentary ticketing system to track each job. It was written in Michael's favorite programming language, PHP, and he volunteered to refine it. In his programming class at school, he regularly finished a week's worth of assignments in a half hour and tackled ticketing the rest of the time. He upgraded the system from black and white to color, added icons, and built an app for workers in the field. Eventually, he was put in charge of its programming and integrated other Nerds on Call stores into the system. His improvements were so marketable that Facet began licensing the system to other businesses.

"For the most part, he was the main programmer for us, and he did a really good job," Brian said. "We let him roll with that on his own quite a bit."

The hardest adjustment for Michael wasn't the technical work; it was being affable. Michael did not suffer clueless coworkers or customers any more gladly than he would later put up with unwitting ransomware victims. He was accustomed to doing things his way, and he didn't welcome advice. "I don't know if he trusted people a lot," Brian said. "We had to say, 'We're here to help you.'"

Jason Hahn saw that Michael was "a little rough around the edges with his customer service." So he took him aside and offered some pointers in terms that the show choir performer could understand.

"Sometimes you've gotta act like you're in the play, and be extra nice," Jason told Michael. "When you talk to customers, they're scared of technology, and they get frustrated with it at times. We have to be the calming voice, we have to be understanding for them."

"I get it," Michael responded. "That's my bad."

Customers appreciated his vigilance. Although he had stopped going to St. John's—"Churches feel kind of cultish to me," he said—it was a Facet customer, as well as Brian's place of worship, and Michael took care of its IT needs. St. John's "depended on him for everything," the church secretary said.

He was equally enterprising at school. He and several classmates were clicking on links on Pekin High's website when they discovered a weakness that exposed sensitive information such as students' Social Security numbers. They quickly alerted their computer repair and networking teacher, Eric McCann.

"It was a vulnerability that nobody even knew about," Eric said. "They did a quick search on passwords and student accounts, and lo and behold, that file is sitting out there." Without publicizing the incident or crediting Michael and his classmates, school administrators fixed the weakness and changed everyone's passwords.

Michael's instinct for rooting out security vulnerabilities continued to deepen. He noticed that, at their lockers, other students would preset their combination locks before class so they only had to pull down on the lock when they returned. One morning, he pulled down on every lock in the hallway, leaving Post-it notes admonishing the students whose lockers he was able to open.

After school, while Michael was at Nerds on Call, Morgan worked at a McDonald's. In their senior year, they were both in the Noteables. They traveled to Nashville to perform the Ramones classic "Listen to My Heart" in a national competition on the Grand Ole Opry stage. While the group typically favored the Great American Songbook, Michael preferred listening to metal bands like Slayer and Metallica.

Morgan wanted to prepare a duet with him for a senior-year talent revue. When she teased that he was off-key—belatedly evening the score for his criticism of her weight—he got upset and quit.

In the spring of 2010, Michael graduated near the top of his class at Pekin High. Because of his class rank and strong ACT scores, he was named an Illinois State Scholar. He donned an oversize hand-me-down shirt for his yearbook photo. Brian encouraged him to go to college and work for Facet part-time, as Jason had. After all, Brian thought, Michael could sleep through most of the programming classes and still earn straight A's.

Instead, Michael accepted a full-time job at Nerds on Call, even though it paid less than $30,000 a year. His parents didn't encourage him to go to college, and he worried that, even with financial aid, it would be too expensive. "I just knew we couldn't afford it," he said. "I knew I could have applied for a lot of loans and scholarships. But even then, I knew financially it would not be feasible. I didn't want to go that much into debt." He also felt that he could learn better on his own than in a classroom. The point of college was to prepare him for a job he liked—and he already had one. During his final week of high school, he saw the names of his classmates and their college destinations posted on a bulletin board.

"Fuckers, I've already got a full-time job," he thought.

Unlike Michael, Morgan wanted to go to college. Planning to major in music, she enrolled at Millikin University in Decatur, Illinois. Decatur was seventy-five miles southeast of Pekin, but only an hour's drive south from Normal, where Facet was opening another Nerds on Call store in a strip mall on a stretch of Route 66 that had succumbed to suburban sprawl. Michael promptly transferred to the Normal store and drove from there to Decatur on weekends to see Morgan. He pirated Disney movies for her and installed Microsoft Word on the new computer she bought for school.

Morgan posted on Facebook that she was "sooooooooo excited" to register for her courses. But financial reality intruded. The textbooks drained her savings, and she had to borrow from Michael. Two months before school started, she posted that without a $5,000 loan, she would be "totally screwed. I am waaaaay too poor for college. Extremely worried about this whole money thing."

Her relatives weren't brimming with sympathy. One day she complained on Facebook, "School books are expensive when you pay out of pocket . . . how am I supposed to pay for this next year?"

"Do it the old fashon [sic] way, get a job," her maternal grandfather, Wade Hall, advised her. "Your aunt barb worked as a waitress, and it may open up new doors for you."

"Grandpa, while I'm at school, I'll already have a job, most likely in the music department," she replied. "But all of that money goes to my payments, and I won't have any time for a second job."

"Join the real world honey," Wade answered.

Once classes started, she learned the hard way that she couldn't sing her way to a music degree. "My sucky piano playing was kind of the trigger that made me rethink the whole being a music teacher thing," she wrote on Facebook. "I don't know, my brain just refuses to read music at an acceptable speed." One day, when a teacher stopped her in the middle of a piano piece and told her that she had "misread" it, she began to cry.

She also missed Michael and hated parting from him after their weekends together in Decatur. "It absolutely kills me from the inside out every time I have to say goodbye to him," she wrote. And: "Uhhh, why am I always soo unbelievably sad on Sunday nights . . . This time it's purely the fact that the one I love has to leave, and I don't know the next time I'll see him. I could never be an army wife."

She decided that, instead of a music teacher, she wanted to be a full-time mom. In October 2010, after two months at Millikin, she dropped out. She and Michael adopted a cat named Abigail Lily and found an apartment in Normal. "When I think about our life together, my fingers tingle and I know from the depths of my soul that nothing could be more right, more complete."

One day in 2011, Michael went to see Morgan's dad, chatting for two hours on various pretexts. Bobby Blanch thought Michael was building up to saying that Morgan was pregnant. Instead, Michael wanted to ask Morgan to marry him and was working up the nerve to ask for her father's blessing, which Bobby was happy to give. They got engaged in December of that year and set a wedding date for the following October.

For the bachelor party, Michael and his friends went to an isolated patch of farmland and raised nerdy hell. His best man and coworker, Dave Jacobs, brought two ten-pound pork shoulders he had roasted at home and set off homemade sparkler bombs and other fireworks. "It was like the end of *Office Space* except more so," Dave said. "One of my little devices blew an old Xbox360 that was busted about six feet in the air."

Then the guests shot up worn-out computers with guns supplied by Michael's father, who gave them a quick rundown on firearms safety. "Nobody who was too tipsy got to hold the rifles, but we put a few rounds through some old monitors," Dave said.

Under a canopy of foliage changing color, Michael and Morgan were married on a sunny afternoon in a riverside park with about a hundred guests. Beth styled her daughter's hair, and Rita Blanch officiated. Dave, who played bass guitar in a '90s cover band, deejayed the ceremony and reception. In his toast, Dave explained how he knew that Michael would be a faithful husband. Whenever a customer's computer had pornographic images left open, he said, everybody else at Nerds on Call would drool while Michael fixed the computer. Michael felt a pang of guilt about even being in the presence of smut, Dave told the guests.

Because the venue was a state park, no alcohol was allowed, but Dave stashed beer in his trunk. He and another Nerds on Call friend made repeated visits to the trunk, but they didn't tell Michael about it. "If we did he'd just be mad," Dave said.

Some hotels refused to book a room for Michael and Morgan because they weren't twenty-one yet. But the Country Inn and Suites in Peoria made an exception, and the couple honeymooned there. When the hotel supplied complimentary sparkling wine, Michael sent it back, telling staff they were underage.

The morning after the wedding, Michael woke up misty-eyed and deliriously happy. "It's our first time waking up married," he whispered to Morgan before they headed to the lobby for the breakfast buffet.

Two years later, on an afternoon in 2014, Brian Ford's younger sister called him in a panic. She had clicked on a spam attachment, and she couldn't open any files on her computer, including some cherished photos. A note from the hacker demanded hundreds of dollars to restore access. Although she didn't use the word "ransomware"— the term for this emerging type of cybercrime was not yet in common use—she was a victim of it.

Brian advised her against paying the ransom. Then he assigned the technically challenging case to Michael. It was an easy choice. Michael was so versatile that he was known as Facet's "Swiss Army Knife." He was adept at everything—programming, troubleshooting, network solutions, hardware repairs—and his communication skills had improved. He often manned the Normal store by himself, helping walk-ins and counting the cash in the register. He liked being alone because he could concentrate on his projects. For one client, he built a website that enabled car owners to renew their license plates with the state of Illinois.

The attack on Ford's sister's computer wasn't the first time Michael had heard of ransomware. A few of his clients had been hit, and he had started keeping a spreadsheet of the incidents in hopes that a solution would materialize. As he examined the computer left for him by Brian's sister, he identified the ransomware strain by its file extension as LeChiffre, which means "the cipher" in French.

When stumped by IT problems, he and his coworkers browsed the internet, and their searches for malware tips and tools often led to a site called BleepingComputer, where Michael was a registered user. He reached out via a private message on the site to Fabian Wosar, a European cybersecurity expert who often posted there and who was already gaining renown for cracking ransomware. Fabian had developed a decryption tool for LeChiffre, but in order to work, it required a sample of the malware that had encrypted Brian's sister's computer. Unfortunately, the ransomware had deleted itself without leaving any record.

"Can I crack it with brute force?" Michael asked, referring to a trial-and-error approach that depends on high-speed computers testing every possibility.

"That's not feasible," Fabian replied.

Impressed that the young American who contacted him out of the blue seemed "genuinely interested in the subject material," Fabian confirmed what Michael suspected: without a trace of the ransomware, recovery was hopeless. The encryption key was too long. "It would have taken until the heat death of the universe," Fabian told Michael.

Brian's sister never got her photos back. For Michael, the failure was a sobering lesson in how much he had to learn: "I hadn't started my journey toward reverse engineering," he said. "I was completely relying on Fabian."

But it also marked a turning point in Michael's life and was his first taste of what lay ahead.

At the office, Michael mentioned his new mentor to his friend and coworker Dave Jacobs, who had heard of Fabian as the creative mind behind the cybersecurity tools developed by Emsisoft, a global antivirus software company.

"Whoa, you actually get to talk to him directly?" Dave said. "That's pretty cool."

"Oh, yeah, I work with him on stuff," Michael replied.

"I've seen his name on software before," Dave said. "Wow, you go, man."

3.

THE HUNTERS GATHER

Michael didn't have to wait long for his next brush with ransomware. One of Facet's clients was Salem4Youth, a private boarding school and ranch for troubled teenage boys in Flanagan, Illinois, a village of wind farms and cornfields thirty-five miles northeast of BloNo.

Visitors are greeted by a sign quoting Winston Churchill: "There is something about the outside of a horse that is good for the inside of a man." Putting this adage into practice, the dozen young men living in cottages on the fifty-acre campus learn to ride and care for horses. Along with tuition revenue and donations, Salem4Youth supports itself by selling the horses.

Affiliated with a group of evangelical Mennonite churches, Salem4Youth offers online instruction, with six computer stations per classroom. Students follow a Christian homeschool-based curriculum at their own level and pace. Credits can be transferred, and nearly all the program's students graduate from high school.

Every month, a Facet technician visited the ranch to handle any IT issues. One day, when the engineer returned to the office, he dropped off the ranch's bright yellow server on Michael's desk. "They can't access their files," he said.

Michael pulled out the hard drives and scanned them. The files had been renamed, and he found a ransom note. It gave the ranch a choice:

"Wait for a miracle and get your price doubled," or pay $500 now and "restore your data the easy way . . . There is no other way to get your files, except make a payment."

Googling the file extensions online, Michael soon identified the ransomware type, called TeslaCrypt. It debuted in February 2015 and mainly targeted people in the United States and Western Europe. One unusual feature was that it encrypted folders storing computer games.

TeslaCrypt was more sophisticated than most ransomware strains at the time. It relied on an advanced form of cipher known as elliptical curve cryptography, and it used an elaborate series of interconnected secret keys to protect against decryption. There was a master key to all the networks TeslaCrypt corrupted; keys specific to each victim; "session" keys that changed each time the target computer was re-booted, as long as the malware was running on it; and keys unique to each captured file.

There were multiple versions of TeslaCrypt, each more complex than the previous one. So many victims were contacting Bleeping-Computer that the forums devoted to the strain would balloon to hundreds of pages. Lawrence Abrams, who founded and runs Bleeping-Computer, was closely tracking TeslaCrypt.

Michael didn't know Lawrence but took a chance and messaged him about the attack on Salem4Youth. Soon afterward, Lawrence re-sponded. He was setting up a task force to rescue TeslaCrypt victims, and he needed volunteers. Would Michael be interested? It was no ordinary invitation. Top cybersecurity minds from the United States and Europe were gravitating to BleepingComputer, eager to devote their skills and ingenuity to battling the growing ransomware threat. Overcoming barriers of language and geography, they were starting to work together and become familiar with one another's unique skills. Michael threw himself into the project.

Lawrence Abrams isn't a programming whiz. He rarely cracks ran-somware himself but said he knows "enough to be dangerous." His talents lie in spotting the next big cybersecurity threat, identifying the most promising people to work on it, and pulling them into his orbit.

He has transformed BleepingComputer into the cybersecurity equivalent of an eighteenth-century Parisian salon, where the best minds exchange ideas and witticisms as their admirers hang on every word. He is both host and chronicler; his authoritative posts break news about ransomware attacks and the progress made in countering them.

"We were the site everybody was coming to for ransomware problems," Lawrence said. "We attracted all the like-minded people who were passionate about it."

Lawrence, in his early fifties, is a generation older than Michael. Broad-shouldered and ruddy-faced, with graying hair, he lives in the New York City area with his wife and twin teenage sons. But he's still boyish, with a contagious joy about the fact that his life turned out to be so unexpectedly cool.

Lawrence's parents worked in the garment industry, but he was drawn to computers. He got his first computer in second grade and was soon playing video games, browsing virtual bulletin boards, and preparing accounting spreadsheets for his friends' parents. As a teenager, he romanticized computer hackers, then a new phenomenon, the way that earlier generations secretly admired Wild West outlaws like Billy the Kid or Butch Cassidy. "There's always the mystique about hackers and cybercriminals and cyberattacks," he said.

After graduating from Syracuse University with a degree in psychology, he joined a Manhattan computer consulting business, where he fixed IT problems for publishing houses, accounting firms, and Diamond District stores. Sitting at his office desk one day in 2002, Lawrence read an article about somebody who had set up a fake server, a "honeypot," to lure hackers in order to observe their tactics. Curious, Lawrence set up his own honeypot, and a short time later someone broke into his virtual machine.

Lawrence was amazed to be watching a hack in real time and couldn't resist the urge to engage with the hacker. He opened up

Notepad and wrote a message to let the hacker know he was watching. He pressed enter, and the cursor blinked on the next line. To Lawrence's wonder, the hacker wrote back, "What are you doing?"

"Well, I just set this up," Lawrence typed.

The two continued to banter. It was "a very bizarre experience," Lawrence said. "He found it amusing. I found it amusing. He wasn't doing any damage. He was very amicable." The exchange sparked Lawrence's interest in security.

Weary of corporate bureaucracy, Lawrence dreamed of becoming an entrepreneur. In 2004, still employed by the consulting firm, he toiled on a new site at night, "typing away, with the lights off" after his wife went to bed. She suggested the site's name. "Your site is really about people who are having trouble with their computers," she told him one evening. "What do you do when you have trouble with your computer? You swear at it."

BleepingComputer began as a support site for novices. Lawrence realized that competing sites weren't geared toward less tech-savvy users, referring them to manuals that were impossible for newcomers to grasp. He simplified advice about how to fix typical problems like a frozen screen, a failure to boot up, or a lost internet connection. Like Lawrence himself, BleepingComputer wasn't judgmental; its guiding principle was that there is no such thing as a stupid question.

His business model of providing tips for the uninitiated about handling glitches or hacks quickly took off. A tutorial on how to use the program "Hijack This," which is designed to spot viruses, spyware, and adware, "basically exploded the site." He brought in volunteers to advise home users on how to navigate the program and clean their computers. From then on, volunteer experts were the backbone of the site. Eventually, dozens of them would moderate forums and lead training sessions on analyzing malware.

As traffic grew, Lawrence quit his consulting job in 2008 and devoted himself full-time to BleepingComputer. The site made money from advertising and sales commissions; it's free to users. Lawrence employed three full-time reporters, plus occasional contributors, and covered ransomware and cybersecurity himself. "I hate it when anyone breaks news before us," he said. While his schedule is flexible, and he always attended his children's sports events, he never truly takes time off from the site, even on supposed vacations. "If something comes up, I'll jump on it."

Lawrence first learned of ransomware in 2012 from victims of a strain called ACCDFISA, an abbreviation for Anti Cyber Crime Department of Federal Internet Security Agency. This fictional agency was notifying people that child pornography had infected their computers, and so it was blocking access to their files unless they paid $100. Since cryptocurrency was not yet widely used, attackers instructed victims to use prepaid cards to text the payment to a specified phone number. At the time, prepaid cards were anonymous and untraceable, though they stored only small sums.

Lawrence was able to decrypt the first version of ACCDFISA. When a later version baffled him, he reached out to an acquaintance, Fabian Wosar, the creative force behind the antivirus company Emsisoft.

When an especially devious murder stumps Sherlock Holmes, the celebrated fictional detective sometimes consults his older brother, Mycroft. Heavyset and reclusive, Mycroft Holmes is "the most indispensable man in the country," less vigorous than Sherlock but even smarter. Above Mycroft's "unwieldy frame there was perched a head so masterful in its brow . . . and so subtle in its play of expression, that after the first glance one . . . remembered only the dominant mind," wrote the author Arthur Conan Doyle.

In his ingenuity, girth, and reluctance to mingle in the world, Fabian Wosar resembles Mycroft Holmes. And like Mycroft, Fabian guides a younger protégé, Michael Gillespie. Fortunately, all the clues Fabian needs are accessible on his computer, enabling him to solve mysteries that baffle everyone else without leaving his home.

Blue-eyed, balding, pallid, and unshaven, Fabian spends his days in his two-bedroom apartment near London. Brightly colored artwork depicting scenes from video games hangs on the crisp white walls, and a fuzzy brown blanket is laid out on the sofa for his cats. Figurines of characters from his favorite television show, *Doctor Who*, are neatly arranged on a bookshelf; they're gifts from his close friend and collaborator Sarah White.

He often wears T-shirts with jokey slogans; one with an Emsisoft logo read, SECURITY HACKERS: WE SOLVE PROBLEMS YOU DIDN'T KNOW YOU HAVE, USING WAYS YOU DON'T UNDERSTAND. When he speaks, he's precise and fastidious, explaining even the most complex cryptography in terms a neophyte can understand.

An insomniac, Fabian analyzes ransomware deep into the night on a giant curved monitor paired with a keyboard that glows rainbow colors. Next to the keyboard is a one-liter bottle of Pepsi Max, his caffeine fix. While working, he sometimes listens to a Spotify playlist of electronic music called MrSuicideSheep Favourites and at other times puts on a sad, romantic movie like *The Fault in Our Stars* or *Eternal Sunshine of the Spotless Mind*.

He has ADHD and the ability to hyperfocus that can be associated with it. When engrossed in a ransomware problem, he can work thirty or forty hours straight, without knowing how much time has passed. He's fidgety, constantly shifting his feet or rocking back and forth in his chair.

To relax, he occasionally partakes of edibles or magic mushrooms; he buys the mushroom spores online and grows them in a small box. Most of his meals are delivered, though he occasionally prepares foods from his native Germany, cooking sausages or baking *russischer Zupfkuchen*, a chocolate cheesecake. He doesn't have a driver's license and takes an Uber when he ventures out, mostly for doctors' appointments.

To casual acquaintances, Fabian comes across as companionable and witty. But melancholy and depression lurk close to the surface, legacies of a harrowing childhood. He was born in 1984 in Soviet-controlled East Germany when his parents were in their midforties. "Doctors actually told my mom that she should abort me because of how old she was," he said. His father was an alcoholic who drank copious amounts of beer every day. "It wasn't like that cheap and weak U.S. beer," Fabian said. "It was proper German beer." The Communist regime guaranteed jobs for everyone, and Fabian's father worked as a poultry trader. When the Berlin Wall fell and Germany was reunified, he lost his job. Fabian's mother cleaned public toilets until she got cancer and received a pension.

They lived in a working-class suburb of Rostock, a port city on the Baltic Sea notorious for anti-immigrant riots; as a child, Fabian saw neo-Nazi youth groups roaming the streets at night. Their apartment was flea-ridden, and they shared a bathroom with other tenants.

Compensating for their deprived childhoods, his parents became hoarders and filled the apartment with old bottles and newspapers. Fabian grew up without structure or rules. "I never got told that it's normal, for example, to have a shower every day." His parents were "unable to emotionally connect," and they never told him that they loved him, he said. "I got my very first hug that I can remember when I was age sixteen from my schoolmate."

His parents openly preferred his older sister and took her on family trips while leaving him home. His father physically abused him. Realizing that the beatings would end faster if he didn't react, Fabian didn't cry or fight back until he was ten or eleven, big enough to protect himself. It took a psychological toll. When he was twelve, he began having night terrors. "I pretty much screamed the entire house awake most nights," he said. After neighbors threatened to tell the landlord, his parents sent him to a psychiatrist, who helped him cope.

In school, he wore the same outfit for weeks. Like Michael Gillespie's hand-me-downs, Fabian's clothes marked him as poor, and easy prey for bullies. Applying the lesson learned at home, he didn't respond, and they got bored and stopped. They also found him useful for their schoolwork. "People knew that I had a gift to explain very complicated things in ways that make them easy to understand."

Fabian disobeyed teachers and broke rules, but schoolwork came easy to him. "I didn't even have to pay attention," he said. "If I just heard it, then I probably remembered it. I never once studied for anything." He made friends with other outcasts. They played computer games and advocated for self-serving political causes such as lowering the drinking age. They called themselves "the Freaks."

■ ■ ■

Fabian saw a computer for the first time in 1992, when he was eight and Germany was newly reunified. His father was taking computer classes in a government-run job retraining program, and Fabian visited him there. "I found them incredibly fascinating. They inherently made sense to me. I had to have one." By collecting bottles and cans, he saved enough money by the time he was eleven to buy a computer, which he hid and used in the broom closet at home. "It was a beast," fast and powerful for its time, an Intel with a fourteen-inch screen and a CD-ROM drive. He read the entire English-language manual, although the term "boot up" confused him, because *Boot* means "boat" in German. He saved up again to buy computer magazines that contained demo versions of games and programs.

Two months after he bought the computer, a floppy disk with games shared by his classmates infected it with a virus called Tequila. Fabian was entranced. "The moment I saw the computer virus for the first time, I was completely hooked," he said. His initial impulse was to create computer viruses to learn how they functioned. After reading several books that he took out from the library, he realized that he didn't have to create the viruses "any more than a trauma surgeon needed to shoot someone to learn how to remove a bullet." Instead, he collected viruses, like other kids collected postage stamps, and analyzed them. At sixteen, he developed his own anti–Trojan horse software, which he released on virtual bulletin boards. He asked users for donations, and money poured in.

Still, his depression didn't abate, and he dropped out of high school and left home. He would never see his father again. At age eighteen, with the earnings from the software he created, he moved to Vienna, where he took a job with an antivirus company. But he lost the motivation to go to the office or even get out of bed, and he quit after a few months. "I was in a really bad, bad place back then," he said.

Then he met Christian Mairoll, who founded Emsisoft in Austria in 2003. Fabian and Christian hit it off. Fabian "always was a true geek in his field and enjoyed taking software apart, including mine," Christian said. "I guess it was a bit of a challenge for both of us to get better than the other one.

"At some point we figured that we could achieve big things by teaming up and merging our knowledge. In that sense I never 'hired' him as such. I always saw him as a partner. It just happened that I focused more on the operational and business side of things and became CEO, while he got the time to go deeper and deeper into tech aspects of malware analysis and coding."

The company shifted its headquarters to New Zealand when Christian bought farmland there and began tending sheep, chickens, and fruit trees. He is proud of Fabian's accomplishments. "He's one of very few people on the planet who are able to do this kind of work," Christian said. "Or shall I call it a form of art?"

As a top executive at Emsisoft, Fabian steered the company toward the topics that interested him, including the emerging phenomenon of ransomware. In the course of his work, he became familiar with BleepingComputer and its founder. Lawrence eventually sought his help with ACCDFISA, and Fabian cracked the strain. Then the hacker released a revised version. "It was a cat-and-mouse game," Fabian said.

After his father's death, Fabian returned to Germany to take care of his mother. Gradually, he let go of his anger over his childhood. "When you keep blaming people for what they did to you, it forces you into almost a victim mentality," he said.

Fabian was one of the first security researchers to analyze a groundbreaking ransomware strain that emerged in September 2013. Known as CryptoLocker, it would usher in the modern era of ransomware—and ransomware hunting. CryptoLocker was the first major ransomware group to demand payment in digital currency. The strain penetrated computer systems through malicious attachments to fake customer support emails purportedly from FedEx and other delivery companies. Attackers demanded $300 in Bitcoin, warning that if the ransom wasn't paid in three days, they would destroy the key so that the encrypted files could never be retrieved. Its code, Fabian found, was unbreakable.

CryptoLocker was also a turning point for BleepingComputer, elevating it from a modest computer help site to a hub for ransomware fighters. "We started, out of nowhere, getting floods of people posting topics about this CryptoLocker program. No one knew where it was coming from," Lawrence said.

Lawrence learned that malware known as Zbot Trojan infiltrated Windows systems and unleashed CryptoLocker. One of the best-known "banking Trojans," Zbot was originally developed to steal passwords to financial accounts. Lawrence wrote an article about Zbot that he posted on his site before heading to a family outing at his in-laws' house. There, he excused himself to check on BleepingComputer. But when he tried to log on, he couldn't. He started freaking out.

"What's going on?" he asked himself. His web server logs were "just pounded with requests. It was like a hacker movie, where you just saw the texts rolling through. It just wouldn't stop."

He realized that, in response to his article, the CryptoLocker gang was retaliating with a distributed denial-of-service (DDoS) attack. Bots, or malware-infected computers, overloaded BleepingComputer with unwanted traffic. Unable to fix it himself, Lawrence hired an outside company. His site was down for four days. "It was horrible. I hated it. I felt violated."

Still, Lawrence couldn't help feeling flattered that the CryptoLocker gang had noticed BleepingComputer. "I knew that the developers were reading what we were writing about, what we were doing. And we had the ability to kind of change the events as things were going on. So that's where I got hooked. Since then, every single ransomware that's probably ever been out has been posted on BleepingComputer. And we ultimately will analyze it and go from there."

For Fabian, ransomware was an intriguing distraction. "I always had an interest in ransomware. I worked on it occasionally. But I needed someone to poke me," he said. That someone was his "right-hand woman," Sarah White, who had a hunch that it deserved his full attention. Her anticipation of the ransomware boom was just one example of her unerring ability, as Fabian puts it, *um die Ecke denken*— "to think around the corner."

Sarah is her real name, but White isn't. She adopted the alias to maintain her privacy and to protect herself against retaliation by ransomware gangs.

As of the autumn of 2021, Sarah was in her fourth and final year at Royal Holloway, part of the University of London, majoring in computer science and information security. She didn't take classes in her third year; instead, she earned school credit, and a salary, as a full-time software developer for Intel. She has also worked part-time for Emsisoft as a ransomware analyst since March 2016, when she was still in high school.

Born in 1998, she's petite, with shoulder-length light brown hair. While her technical skills may not match those that set Michael Gillespie and Fabian Wosar apart, she brings other qualities, including a big-picture understanding of ransomware's evolution and trends. She's invaluable in canvassing Twitter and other online sources for ransomware samples that Michael and Fabian analyze, and her contributions are credited in many of the decryption tools they release.

Sarah shares an apartment with roommates, an important step for someone accustomed to being solitary, making her feel more like a "three-dimensional person," she said. She baked her roommates a focaccia when it was "bread week" on her favorite show, *The Great British Bake Off*. She and Fabian rarely see each other in person, but they talk over WhatsApp daily. When she messages him, his devices resound not with a standard buzz but with "Yay!!"

An only child, Sarah grew up in London's southern suburbs. Her father worked in local government, monitoring health and safety in public parks; her mother cared for adults and children with learning disabilities. Neither parent had a college degree. The family's vacations to Disney World in Florida inspired an obsession with Disney movies. Like Michael, Sarah especially loved *The Lion King*.

From the time she was very young, computers were a central part of Sarah's life. A Halloween photo in 2002, when she was four, shows her smiling and wearing orange pants in front of a jack-o'-lantern and a computer with an educational game on the screen. Soon after, she raised virtual greyhounds on the website Neopets, in addition to a real-life Jack Russell terrier. At home, she became "the go-to IT person," she said. In school, she excelled in math and science. Of twenty-three students in a computer science class one year, she was the only girl.

Sarah was different in other ways as well. She describes herself as neurodivergent. Teachers noticed she was withdrawn. She also took an intense interest in niche topics, like malware. In April 2013, malware infected her grandfather's computer. Looking for answers, she came across BleepingComputer, which offered free tools she could use to scan the hard drive and fix the files. A volunteer there helped her clean the computer. "Oh, wow, this seems really cool," she thought. "Why don't I try to join that?"

Soon afterward, she enrolled in BleepingComputer's training program, which assigned reading and exercises in computer security. She came home after school and spent hours on the forums, learning to remove malware. "I was so passionate about it," she said. For her final exam, the instructor simulated injecting a type of malware called ZeroAccess into a virtual machine. ZeroAccess had penetrated millions of systems, typically when a victim opened an infected file or link. Sarah removed ZeroAccess, passed the test, and completed her training in eleven months. In 2014, after becoming one of the youngest people to graduate from the program, she joined BleepingComputer's malware response team.

While still a trainee, she participated in an online group chat about malware. Another member of the chat was someone named "FaWo," who rarely spoke. When FaWo finally weighed in, his comments piqued her interest. She decided to reach out to FaWo—who was, of course, Fabian Wosar. At first, Sarah said, "it was more me trying than him responding."

Sarah and Fabian soon realized that they shared the same interests, such as watching YouTube videos of people playing video games. Sarah could be herself with Fabian; she didn't have to fake an interest in typical teenage preoccupations like fashion or music.

One Christmas, her parents gave her an adult-sized polar bear onesie so that she could keep warm in their drafty house. She put it on, took a selfie, and sent it to Fabian. The polar bear has been their mascot ever since. Their Twitter avatars both wear polar bear onesies, drawn by the same artist as a way of thanking them for rescuing his portfolio when it was encrypted by ransomware in 2016. Fabian calls her Baby Polar Bear, and himself Big Polar Bear.

Gradually Fabian began to rely on Sarah's advice. After she told him that she hoped to make a career of eradicating malware, he arranged two internships for her at Emsisoft. As ransomware proliferated unchecked, she urged him to concentrate on it. "I see all this ransomware popping up," she told him in October 2015. "Maybe we should look into some of them and see if they're decryptable."

The next month, he discovered a flaw in the encryption algorithm of Radamant, a type of ransomware then widely sold in kits on the dark web. He created tools to unlock the first two versions of it, and Radamant's authors were evidently displeased. The next version's code contained the superfluous text "ThxForHlpFabianWosarAND-FUCKYOU!!" and "emisoft fuckedbastardsihateyou." They also named a command-and-control server "emisoftmuokod.top."

Fabian responded in a post on BleepingComputer. "I am not really sure how things work in your circles, but in my circles getting insulted by malware authors is considered the highest kind of accolade someone can get, so thank you very much for that," he wrote, adding that he had one request. "Just next time, please try to get the company name right."

On Twitter, Fabian and Sarah began following a secretive Hungarian researcher known online as MalwareHunterTeam. In his late twenties, MalwareHunterTeam has decrypted more than a dozen ransomware strains and helped break even more. He is distrustful of authority, from governments to banks, and extremely superstitious.

"Little recommendation that is very important," he tweeted in July 2021 to his legions of followers. "Don't sleep in a room where there is any kind of mirror (or at least that is not covered fully when you are sleeping)."

He separately predicted that humanity would soon face mysterious "big things" beyond anyone's imagination. "If anyone thinking about suicide nowadays, seriously just remain alive to watch," he tweeted in August of that year, "because it won't be something that happens frequently on Earth. Not even once in a few k years."

He often expressed frustration on Twitter that technology companies didn't take the threat of ransomware seriously. In August 2020, he tweeted that eight malware apps were available via Google Play: "This again shows how joke is Google 'security.'" He also made fun of what he considered another tech giant's security shortcomings: "What? You want Microsoft to concentrate on something way less important than marketing?" Four months later, he attributed the explosion in ransomware attacks to "companies fucking not caring about security, about patching, about anything basically that should be. And then thanks to authorities not caring to even act as if they do something about it."

Daniel Gallagher, who worked in cybersecurity and also began helping Michael and Fabian after coming across them on Twitter, accomplished the rare feat of gaining MalwareHunterTeam's trust and friendship. MalwareHunterTeam is "brilliant at reversing malware and understanding how it operates—finding the hidden details in the code," Daniel said. "MalwareHunterTeam is every day, nonstop, seven days a week, just constantly going at hunting malware."

A few years ago, poring over some of MalwareHunterTeam's tweets, Daniel realized that his friend was hard up financially. "Look I kinda sense that something is up," Daniel recalled messaging. "How can I help?" He offered money, but MalwareHunterTeam refused again and again. Finally, Daniel talked him into accepting some cash.

He sent $100, which was trivial to Daniel—"I spend that at Starbucks every month"—but in Hungary, it was a significant sum. Fabian also pitched in, hiring MalwareHunterTeam as a part-time software analyst at Emsisoft.

With a touch of gallows humor, MalwareHunterTeam and Daniel sometimes joked about how much richer they would be if they would only shed their scruples for a life of cybercrime. "You sit there and watch these ransomware actors clear five hundred grand on a weekend," Daniel said. "We're like, 'We could literally do that.' Those are the things you joke around about when you're tired and burnt out and getting frustrated with the amount of crime that's happening out there. It feels like you're fighting a losing battle. But we're gonna just keep fighting. You don't stop because it seems like you're not going to be able to win."

Cagily, MalwareHunterTeam said he doesn't remember how he became interested in ransomware. His greatest success in fighting it, he said, came "when Michael could decrypt ransomware thanks to I give him the samples/I cleaned it for him."

Another Eastern European researcher, who went by the handle Blood-Dolly, discovered a flaw in how TeslaCrypt, the strain that Lawrence's task force focused on, guarded its keys. Following a common approach, its developers tried to create keys by multiplying large prime numbers together. Long a source of fascination among mathematicians, prime numbers, which are divisible by only themselves and one, have many unique properties and are especially valuable in encrypting information.

But TeslaCrypt made a mistake and accidentally used numbers that weren't primes. In addition, instead of generating a protected key by multiplying two extremely large prime numbers, as is standard, some of its victim keys were the product of many smaller primes, making them less secure. BloodDolly could narrow down the field of prime numbers by using an algorithm known as a number sieve, which was effective with smaller numbers. Then, with enough computing power, he could identify TeslaCrypt's keys and unlock the encrypted files.

BloodDolly is a Slovakian named Igor Kabina, a detection engineer at an antivirus company. He took his handle from the name of a wizard he played in a Gothic game. Usually dressed in black, with deep-set eyes, a mysterious smile, and long dark hair falling below his shoulders, BloodDolly looked the part of a sorcerer. In May 2015, he posted a link to his TeslaDecoder on BleepingComputer. "I hope it will help to someone," he wrote, with a smiley-face emoji.

Realizing that the TeslaCrypt gang was adapting its ransomware in response to the steps he took against them, BloodDolly stopped posting instructions for victims about how to unlock their files. But he shared his updated tool with the task force Lawrence had assembled. Lawrence reported on his website that TeslaCrypt could be cracked but avoided describing how, for fear that the gang would identify and fix the weakness.

Through BleepingComputer, Michael connected with BloodDolly and soaked up everything that the Slovakian researcher could teach him about cracking TeslaCrypt and rescuing its victims. As they began working together, BloodDolly recalled, Michael "did struggle with brute-forcing keys," because he was using a slow programming language. BloodDolly showed him how to speed up his code.

Michael used BloodDolly's tool to obtain keys for Salem4Youth and another Facet client hit by TeslaCrypt. "I wanted to post a success story for one of my customer's systems that was hit this week," he proudly announced on BleepingComputer in August 2015. "I've just successfully decoded a few sample files at home . . . My customer is going to be thrilled we can get her photos back."

Salem4Youth restored access to its network without paying TeslaCrypt. "We appreciate everyone's help to counter evil for sure," said the program's executive director, Terry Benge.

Fabian was working to break other strains of ransomware, so he referred new TeslaCrypt victims to Michael. A victim would supply an encrypted file, which Michael would plug into BloodDolly's tool. He was soon generating customized TeslaCrypt keys around the clock using both his work and home computers, much to his wife's annoyance. Morgan would be playing *The Sims* when the avatars would slow down because Michael's program had taken over most of the computer's processing power to brute-force the TeslaCrypt keys.

Some keys could be deciphered in minutes on a laptop, while others took as long as a week on a high-powered server. The task force was helping ten to fifteen victims a day. "You had to do it for every victim," Michael said. "It's not just like a master key that decrypts everyone's files."

Extracting some of the longer keys in a reasonable amount of time required more computing capacity than Michael had at his disposal. By chance, Mission Health, a North Carolina hospital chain where Daniel Gallagher was in charge of cybersecurity, had just bought two high-powered servers. The chief information security officer allowed Daniel to use them to help the task force.

"Hey, I got $10,000 servers sitting there that are just idle right now," Daniel recalled messaging the other members. "Let's put them to use."

Michael jumped on the offer and sent a script to Daniel. "OK, run this," Michael told him. "I just need the CPU power."

"I can do that," Daniel said, and they began extracting keys together.

Michael saved so many TeslaCrypt victims that he stopped counting after a hundred. On BleepingComputer, Lawrence thanked "those volunteers who sacrificed their precious time to help victims of TeslaCrypt," singling out BloodDolly and demonslay335.

"It was huge, it was insane," Lawrence recalled. "We were cracking keys left and right. And Michael got the bug from that."

At times, Lawrence engaged directly with the TeslaCrypt hackers on behalf of victims. Once, when he let the gang know that they had deprived a mother of her photos of her son, a U.S. soldier who was killed in action, they gave her the key for free.

In May 2016, BloodDolly noticed that TeslaCrypt sites on the dark web were going offline. Sensing an opportunity, he asked the gang to release its master keys to enable victims to retrieve their files. A day and a half later, they announced that they were shutting down operations, and supplied their most recent master key. "Project closed," TeslaCrypt posted on the dark web. "We are sorry!"

■ ■ ■

Not yet members of a formal team, the hunters mainly communicated by private messages on BleepingComputer and Twitter as they battled CryptoLocker, TeslaCrypt, and other early foes. Scattered across platforms, their chats were fragmented and disorganized. They duplicated efforts and wasted time trying to figure out who was working on what, even as new ransomware strains emerged daily and exasperated victims kept knocking on BleepingComputer's virtual door.

"It got to the point where it was like, why are we doing this through private messages in the forums?" Lawrence recalled.

The hunters needed to gather. In May 2016, the same month that the TeslaCrypt attackers walked away, a malware analyst and rock drummer named Marc Rivero López, from Barcelona, Spain, had an idea that would break down the communication barriers.

Eager and affable, Marc had connected with Lawrence, Daniel, MalwareHunterTeam, and Michael, helping them analyze new threats. But the lack of coordination bothered him. "I started to see people working in their own silos," Marc said. "I was like, 'Come on, we are not working together. Let's create a community, a private one.'"

Marc realized that a necessity for any team was a communication network to which only the members had access. On May 5, he sent a Twitter message to his BleepingComputer contacts: "Hello guys, let's create a list, private, and share some stuff about ransomware. I think we can start to track new ransomware families and update the community about that, make sense?"

Daniel responded with a suggestion: "Slack for convos? Could make multiple channels." On Slack, a messaging platform, they could create chat rooms to discuss different ransomware strains.

MalwareHunterTeam was intrigued but cautious: "Hmm . . . if it's really that good, maybe we can try sometimes later."

"I think its definitely something to consider," Daniel wrote.

"Guys, Can I create the channel and invite you?" Marc asked. "Just for try?" He added a smiley-face emoji.

Marc set up the Slack, and the Ransomware Hunting Team was formed.

Besides Marc, Daniel, and MalwareHunterTeam, founding or early members included Michael, Lawrence, Fabian, Sarah, and James, a systems administrator in Italy who entered BleepingComputer's orbit in 2014 after his employer was attacked by ransomware. BloodDolly didn't join the team. He considers himself "affiliated" and still collaborates with Michael on occasion. "My involvement in Ransomware Hunting Team is indirect," he said. "I entered the bleepingcomputer to help people, and Ransomware Hunting Team has the same goal."

With users spread across numerous time zones, the team's Slack was always active. They quickly upgraded from a free version to Slack's professional service, which offered more functions. Marc initially covered the annual fee himself, but soon the teammates began sharing the cost, about $100 apiece. Michael couldn't afford it, so Marc paid for him. "He's a really good guy and he does a great job," Marc reasoned, "so why not help him if we can do it."

Marc made another vital contribution to the team's mission. He had friends at VirusTotal, an online database that collects and tests suspected malware. VirusTotal originated in Malaga, on the Spanish coast, and was acquired by Google in 2012. At Marc's request, Virus-Total gave the team a free private account. Otherwise, it would have been prohibitively expensive.

The team kept a low profile. "I don't think that anyone in the world knows that this group exists because we never spoke publicly about it," Marc said. "We are not saying any place that we have this group, which members are a part of it, and how you can enter it." It has no formal code of conduct, but members abide by certain unwritten guidelines. For example, when they crack a ransomware strain, they spread the news to victims as discreetly as possible to avoid tipping off the hackers.

"We deal with a lot of very sensitive data," Daniel said. "We are very picky on who gets let in. Do you really one hundred percent know them? Is there any indication that something about them just doesn't seem right? That they would go brag about something? Or misuse the data and bring it to whatever company they work for and try to use it for monetary gain?"

From the beginning, the teammates agreed that they would help victims for free. Later, they occasionally discussed charging for their services but each time rejected the idea. "It left a sour taste," Lawrence said.

Lawrence acted as the team's project manager. At the start, Marc was the only administrator for the team's Slack. Then he added Lawrence and Daniel. Marc also created a management channel where the three of them discussed prospective members. People don't apply to join the team; they must be nominated by a member. They also must bring a specific skill such as collecting malware samples or finding vulnerabilities. "We ask the candidate: Why do you want to be here? What can you bring of value?" Marc said. "If you're just a student wanting to learn about ransomware, this is not a group for you. Everyone in the group has a role."

Once candidates are nominated and vetted, the team votes on them. Approval must be unanimous; every member has veto power. Among the ransomware cognoscenti, an invitation to join the Ransomware Hunting Team is considered an honor. Over the years, the team has spurned half a dozen candidates and admitted about the same number.

"Team dynamic is huge," Daniel said. "There's no opportunity for anybody to be in there that's going to cause an annoyance. At that point, it doesn't matter how smart you are."

Once, Marc sent a message to the group asking for a vote on a malware researcher who had been nominated. As Marc recalled it, one team member responded, "If this guy enters the group, I will leave."

Marc defused the situation. "I want all the people happy in the group," he wrote. "So if we have a problem, this guy cannot enter. And that's it."

The group also rejected a Microsoft employee nominated by Lawrence. "In the past, Microsoft wasn't looked so fondly on by researchers," Lawrence said. "There were always security updates coming out. I personally think it was a mistake. They would have brought a lot to the table."

Despite his administrative role, Marc has never met any of his teammates. "We had planned in the beginning to do a conference in person, but we never did it." Instead, they bonded online. In 2017, Sarah, Fabian, and Michael began playing virtual party games on a simulated tabletop on Sunday nights. "I was the reason it started," Sarah said. "I wanted people to play with."

They enjoyed irreverent, fun games like Cards Against Humanity, in which players are asked a question and choose crude or politically incorrect answers from an array of cards; Broken Picturephone, akin to Pictionary except that participants make up phrases as well as drawings; and Secret Hitler, in which players divide into liberals and fascists in the Reichstag circa 1933. The objective for the fascists is to elect Hitler chancellor, and for the liberals to identify and assassinate him. Like poker, Secret Hitler requires "social deduction"—the ability to read an opponent's mind and determine if they're bluffing. It took Michael a while to catch on, but Fabian was "scarily good," Sarah said.

As the team was coming together, Michael achieved a milestone. For the first time, he reverse engineered a ransomware strain and built a decryption tool.

Named Jigsaw after the killer in the *Saw* film franchise, the ransomware spread through spam email attachments. When it infected a computer, an image of Jigsaw's puppet—with red spirals on his cheeks and a bowtie—appeared on the screen. A ransom note unscrolled, demanding $150 in Bitcoin within twenty-four hours in return for a decryption key.

"I want to play a game with you," the note said, echoing the *Saw* villain's sinister invitation. "Let me explain the rules: Your personal files are being deleted. Your photos, videos, documents, etc. But, don't worry! It will only happen if you don't comply . . . Now, let's start and enjoy our little game together!"

In an unusual feature, Jigsaw ramped up pressure on the victim by deleting files every hour that the ransom went unpaid. After three days without payment, it erased all remaining files.

But Jigsaw's cryptography was crude. Not only did it use the same key for every victim, but the key to unlock the files was hidden in the ransomware code itself, under the name "password." In April 2016, Michael, MalwareHunterTeam, and Lawrence collaborated to break Jigsaw.

Jigsaw didn't fade away. Instead, it spawned dozens of variants. Script kiddies—inexperienced hackers who use existing code rather than creating their own—tweaked Jigsaw. They translated the ransom note into languages from Vietnamese to Turkish and replaced the *Saw* puppet with everything from Hitman, a professional assassin in a video game franchise, to Pennywise, the predatory clown in a Stephen King horror novel. But the variants were flawed, and Michael cracked almost all of them.

4.

THE FUNNY WAR

In May 2016, the same month that the Ransomware Hunting Team was formally established, a group called Apocalypse began penetrating software that enables users to connect remotely to other computers. If the default language of the computers it targeted was set to Russian, Ukrainian, or Belarusian, the ransomware would stop rather than encrypt the files.

Apocalypse attracted the attention of Fabian Wosar, Michael Gillespie's mentor. Fabian quickly deciphered three variants of what he called Apocalypse's "amateurish code," and shared the keys with victims. As Apocalypse introduced six more versions, Fabian cracked them, too.

In late August, Apocalypse named a new variant Fabiansomware as a backhanded tribute to the ransomware hunter's expertise. Within the code, the gang inserted a dare: "Crack me, motherfucker!"

Fabian took it in stride. "They fell hard for me," he tweeted. "If they weren't so horrible developers, I would almost be flattered."

The new name misled some victims into thinking that Fabian was the one extorting them. "Stop your shit," one victim wrote to him over Twitter. "You encrypted my server and holding me to ransom."

"Just look up what I do before you continue to embarrass yourself," Fabian retorted. "I am a malware researcher who pissed off a ransomware gang by repeatedly decrypting their shitty ransomware and allowing their victims to decrypt their files for free."

As he had done with Apocalypse, Fabian cracked the first two versions of his namesake ransomware. In October 2016, before releasing a third version, the ransomware's frustrated developer decided to save time by running it by Fabian to see if it was bulletproof.

"Hello Fabian. I finished work on a new version, do you need a sample? I can send you."

"Sure," Fabian replied.

The developer provided a link for Fabian to access the sample. "Im 100% sure you cant crack it." Eleven minutes later: "I would like to receive the answer from you, as you like my code?"

Fabian noticed this version contained an image of his Twitter avatar—plump face, buzz cut, black-rimmed wire glasses, and goatee—with one difference: a penis pointed at him. He set aside the personal affront and started analyzing the ransomware.

"I could still [crack it] in some cases," Fabian wrote. "Not all though."

The hacker then changed his tone, praising Fabian for breaking the prior versions "like a god," and asking how he was able to solve one of them in a single day.

"Since your operations were simplistic it wouldn't take much to figure them out," Fabian explained.

"Ok, thank you for your answers," the hacker wrote. "So let's continue this funny war."

Fabian posted the modified avatar on Twitter, explaining that it would be in an upcoming version of Fabiansomware. "I wonder if this can be considered fan art," he wrote.

A week later, the Apocalypse developer resumed the conversation, making an attempt to recruit Fabian. "If you have good brain, you can engage in real business and have a lot of money, why no?"

"I have enough money to have a comfortable living," Fabian answered. "I like and enjoy my job and I don't have to worry that a SWAT team comes busting down my doors."

■　■　■

Overtures like Apocalypse's weren't uncommon. Ransomware developers reached out to compliment, insult, or banter with the hunters—and to try to manipulate them. They shared the team's fascination with ransomware and many of the same skills. They were avid readers of BleepingComputer, especially when it broke news of their exploits. As the developer of Apocalypse correctly pointed out, Fabian could have been one of the world's foremost ransomware attackers instead of one of its greatest ransomware hunters. Fabian and the hackers are "kindred spirits," Lawrence Abrams said. "It's almost like a competition between them."

Within the ranks of both hunters and hackers are self-taught, underemployed tech geeks who sometimes lack social graces, like video games, and are familiar with some of the same movies. The Hakuna-Matata ransomware strain, for instance, was named after an Oscar-nominated song from Michael Gillespie's beloved *Lion King*. Like the Ransomware Hunting Team, most of the attackers are young men. They are concentrated in Eastern Europe, although scattered globally. In countries such as Russia and North Korea, some gangs appear to enjoy a degree of government protection—and, in some cases, to be weapons in an undeclared cyberwar.

Some of the hackers pride themselves on abiding by a code of ethics. For example, they generally uphold their side of the bargain and restore computer access upon receiving a ransom. The gangs recognize that if they earn a reputation as double-crossers, future victims will be less likely to pay. They rationalize their extortion in all sorts of ways. But even when they say it isn't about the money, it probably is. Their greed is the biggest difference between them and the team.

Fabian cracked so many ransomware strains that thwarting hackers became almost routine. So he was amused when those triumphs were accompanied by the occasional outburst of theatrical praise or protest from the villain.

Beaten hackers sometimes embedded messages to their nemesis in their ransomware code. Some fawned on him: "FWosar you are the man," a developer inserted in the text of NMoreira ransomware in late 2016. "I am inspired by dudes who understand what they do.

Your bruteforcing tool was amazing, I am really impressed . . . I also didnt test the Random Number Generator, that was a stupid thing to do. Hope you can break this too, Im not being sarcastic, youre really inspiring. Hugs."

Fabian posted the compliment on social media. "At least they are polite idiots this time," he wrote. "Still idiots, though."

Others pleaded with him. "Fabian, please, don't crack me!" one attacker wrote. "It is my last attempt, If you crack this version then I will start taking heroin!"

Unmoved, Fabian broke the ransomware and built a decryptor.

More often, the hackers insulted him. Taunts like "Crack me again, Fabian! Show that you got balls!" stood out in the long lines of numbers and letters.

Like Lawrence after the DDoS attack shut down BleepingComputer, Fabian was pleased to be noticed. "They've taken the time and effort to write a message knowing that I'll probably see it and I'm clearly getting under their skin," he said. "It's a pretty good motivator to know that my work is upsetting some really nasty cyber-criminal gangs."

Sometimes, though, the insults felt like threats. One attacker advised him to "lay of [sic] the cheeseburgers you are fat!" Even though his weight wasn't a secret—he appeared portly in his avatar image and had mentioned dieting on Twitter—Fabian was unnerved. A hacker interested in his personal appearance might search for his address or family.

He also discovered that someone had set a Twitter trap for him. It was a fake Fabian Wosar account that tweeted an encoded message. When he decoded it, he found the address of a website that tracked IP addresses—the series of numbers that identify devices connected to the internet. If Fabian had visited the site from his home computer, its operators could have pinpointed his location to a city or even a neighborhood. At the time, he was still living in his hometown of Rostock, Germany.

Even more alarming were the messages that associates of the CryptON ransomware gang were sending him via online forums. CryptON attacked both home users and companies, but there was a weakness in one of its algorithms. In 2017, Fabian discovered the flaw and cracked the first three versions. In a not-so-veiled warning, CryptON's developers, who were believed to be Russian speakers, told Fabian that their friends would like to visit him in Hamburg, Germany. He had listed Hamburg as his location on LinkedIn, since it was only about two hours' drive from Rostock and better known. "They were implying that if they want to, they can get to me, so I better stay out of their business," he said.

He removed his personal details from sites like LinkedIn. But the episode was a stark reminder that his work did more than help victims recover files. Another consequence, unseen to the team's members, was the disruption of hackers' livelihoods. When Fabian cracked their ransomware, their income dried up. For some hackers, that meant they couldn't feed their families. For others, it meant waiting to buy a luxury car. And if they had ties to hostile foreign governments, the stakes were much higher, both for them and for Fabian.

He already had the Russian mob on his mind, as Rostock had a reputation for being a nexus of organized crime. The Russian chairman of Wadan Yards, a shipyard a short distance from Fabian's house, had been shot dead in an apparent contract killing in Moscow in 2011. Although there is scant evidence of overlap between traditional organized crime groups and cybercriminals, Fabian became increasingly paranoid as he noticed menacing faces staring at him in cafés and trailing him around his neighborhood grocery store.

He felt tied to Rostock. He had moved with his mother into what he described as "a really nice apartment that was in the same area she grew up in." She was dying of brain cancer, and he worried that another move would disorient her. But when she died at the end of 2017, he felt compelled to leave Germany to protect himself. He opted for the United Kingdom because of its stricter privacy laws. He knew he would miss the Baltic Sea coast, cool weather, and traditional sausages of his hometown, but he otherwise had no reason to stay.

Growing up in a beach city, Fabian loved swimming, so he thought about moving near the famous pebble beaches of Brighton, the resort on England's southern coast. He also considered Scotland, which has average monthly temperatures similar to Rostock's. But he ultimately decided that being close to Sarah White was more important than feeling connected to his past. She was about to enter college, and once she chose Royal Holloway, he moved to the London area. He resolved to live as anonymously as possible.

As Fabian prepared for his departure from Germany, Michael found himself in a strange situation—collaborating for the first time with a ransomware gang.

An Italian computer engineer, Francesco Muroni, had contacted Michael to explain that he had discovered a vulnerability in a strain called BTCWare, which targeted home users. Its method of generating keys wasn't random enough. Francesco asked Michael to build a decryptor.

"[Michael] took my proof of concept and made it more reliable," Francesco said. "I worked with him because I had a bit deeper technical knowledge. But he was incredibly good at transforming that knowledge into something people could use."

Reading the BleepingComputer forums, the BTCWare attackers learned about the decryptor. In response, they revised the ransomware. "They were trying to fix the cryptography so bad but screwing up each time," Michael said. "We'd break it, they'd release a new version, and we'd break it again." Each time, Michael had to tweak his decryption tool.

The jousting lasted six months, through nine updates. Michael and Francesco cracked the first five, but the rest broadened the pool of random numbers enough that the code couldn't be broken. At that point, most victims had no choice but to pay the ransom. But when they did, they encountered a problem: the keys supplied by BTCWare rarely recovered all their data.

The trouble was that the ransomware was riddled with software glitches that accidentally destroyed files. One, called a padding bug, erased 16 bytes at the end of a file; another overwrote encrypted files with zeros so that the information was lost forever.

To achieve his goal of rescuing victims whose backs were against the wall, Michael decided to cooperate with his archenemies. He emailed BTCWare to propose a deal. It would send him master keys to earlier versions that he was unable to break but that were no longer big moneymakers for the gang. In return, he promised to show BTCWare how to fix the glitches that were deleting victims' files in the latest version. Otherwise, he pointed out, BTCWare would lose credibility and fewer people would pay.

BTCWare agreed to provide a key for a version with the file extension ".aleta"—with one proviso. The gang's side of the bargain had to be a secret. "I can send you key only for .aleta variant but without news about BTCWARE ALETA KEY RELEASED, okay?" the hackers wrote in September 2017.

Michael didn't care about publicity for himself, but he needed to notify .aleta victims that a decryptor was now available. "With your request for no news article, are you OK with me at least publicly asking victims to contact me," he responded.

"Ok," BTCWare replied, and less than twenty-four hours later, "Progress?"

Michael asked for an original and an encrypted file. "I'll see if I can do some testing tonight in the debugger," he wrote, referring to a tool that enabled him to analyze the malware.

BTCWare complied. "Got it, will take a look when I have some time," Michael wrote. Later that day, he identified the bug and told BTCWare how to eliminate it.

"Ok," the gang answered. "Now wait while we decrypt all keys for you."

After Fabian relocated, the direct praise and taunts he'd become accustomed to receiving from hackers became less frequent. It wasn't that he was off their radar. Rather, ransomware was maturing as a business, and the hackers were becoming more professional.

Fabian had the sense that most of the hackers who'd contacted him were either solitary operators or members of a small group. By the time of his move, however, many ransomware developers were acting as part of larger gangs.

Under the ransomware-as-a-service approach, developers delegated to other hackers the task of actually spreading the ransomware. The model dates to 2014, when a strain called CTB-Locker posted a dark web advertisement selling use of the ransomware to interested "affiliates" for $10,000. In addition to the initial fee, the developer would take a roughly 30 percent cut of ransom payments. Since ransomware at that time was a volume business targeting home users, such ads attracted hackers who controlled what are known as botnets. These networks of computers that are infected and hijacked without the owners' knowledge indiscriminately spread ransomware via spam. Hackers who purchased the "off-the-shelf" kits didn't necessarily need deep technical knowledge to be successful. Dharma and Phobos, ransomware-as-a-service strains that remained popular for years, contained scanners that guided hackers to their targets.

Dark web forums became rife with advertisements for ransomware-as-a-service programs, and the model grew in popularity and sophistication. Gangs developed different ways of generating revenue, with some charging a onetime license fee and others billing for a monthly subscription. Especially once ransom demands ballooned, many developers required profit-sharing agreements that gave them a cut of each payment plus control of cryptocurrency wallets where victims sent money.

Eventually, the affiliate application process became competitive. The most ambitious gangs began to prefer affiliates with the expertise to get their ransomware inside large corporate, government, education, and healthcare targets that had much deeper pockets than home users. In job ads, prospective "employers" outlined specific qualifications, such as proficiency in Cobalt Strike, a legitimate tool, co-opted by hackers, that is used to identify system vulnerabilities. They also sought affiliates with experience in cloud backup systems; if they could encrypt businesses' backups, they would eliminate the option of restoring files without paying a ransom. The ads asked applicants to submit portfolios, with promising candidates invited for interviews.

In July 2019, an especially ambitious outfit known as REvil was expanding its operations and hiring for a "limited number of seats." Its ad, written in Russian, warned off noobs.

"Get ready for an interview and show your evidence of the quality of the installations," the ad said. "We are not a test site, and the 'learners' and 'I will try'" candidates need not apply.

REvil told candidates they would not be allowed to spread the ransomware in the Commonwealth of Independent States, which includes Russia. If hired, they would get a 60 percent cut of ransoms collected, upped to 70 percent after the first three payments. Aware that competitors, law enforcement officers, and security researchers were viewing its ads, REvil kept the details of its operation brief. "More information can be obtained during the interview," it wrote.

Groups like REvil went on hiring sprees, seeking dozens of hackers to spread their strains. Rival developers had to compete with one another for the most promising affiliate candidates, individuals in such demand that they seemed to have an advantage over their employers. Nothing could stop an affiliate from working with multiple ransomware gangs—and attacking the same victim with more than one strain.

To differentiate themselves in the fight for the best talent, some operators put large sums of Bitcoin in escrow accounts maintained by dark web forum operators. These sums, visible on the job ads, were a show of good faith—an effort to establish honor among thieves. Down the line, if a transaction went sideways, the affiliate could appeal to the forum administrator to recoup funds from that escrow account. "Unknown," a key figure behind REvil, placed $1 million in such an account.

Unknown was willing to try unconventional and brazen tactics to gain an edge over competitors, including granting a rare interview that was published on the news website of the American cybersecurity company Recorded Future. Unknown saw the interview as a novel way to generate buzz for the REvil brand.

"It seems like, why would we even need it?" Unknown told Recorded Future's Dmitry Smilyanets, himself a former hacker, referring to publicity. "On the other hand, better we give it than our competitors. Unusual ideas, new methods, and brand reputation all give good results."

While hardly anyone would call them "good," REvil did get results and rose to become one of the world's most prolific ransomware gangs. Truthfully or not, Unknown bragged about affiliates' success penetrating targets that included a ballistic missile launch system, a U.S. Navy cruiser, a nuclear power plant, and a weapons factory. Unknown suggested REvil would not unleash ransomware on these targets. "It is quite feasible to start a war," Unknown said. "But it's not worth it—the consequences are not profitable."

Unknown acknowledged the stiff competition for talented affiliates. As in the legitimate business world, some had left the thriving shop for higher pay elsewhere. "Of course, this is unpleasant, but this is competition," the hacker said. "It means that we need to make sure that people return. Give them what others don't."

Unknown was perhaps trying to reach prospective hires by boasting about the opulent lifestyle afforded by REvil's success. The hacker, who had crippled some of the world's largest companies, seemed to revel in telling an unverifiable but alluring rags-to-riches story.

"As a child, I scrounged through the trash heaps and smoked cigarette butts," the hacker said. "I walked 10 km one way to the school. I wore the same clothes for six months. In my youth, in a communal apartment, I didn't eat for two or even three days. Now I am a millionaire."

As money poured into their operations, REvil and other ransomware gangs began to mirror the practices of legitimate businesses. Just as a real-world manufacturer might hire other companies to handle logistics or web design, ransomware developers increasingly outsourced tasks beyond their purview, focusing instead on improving the quality of their ransomware. The higher-quality ransomware—which, in many cases, the Ransomware Hunting Team could not break—resulted in more and higher payouts from victims. The monumental payments enabled gangs to reinvest in their enterprises. They hired more specialists, and their success accelerated.

Criminals raced to join the booming ransomware economy. Underworld ancillary service providers sprouted up or pivoted from other criminal work to meet developers' demand for customized support. Partnering with gangs like GandCrab, "cryptor" providers ensured that ransomware could not be detected by standard anti-malware scanners. "Initial access brokerages" specialized in stealing credentials and finding vulnerabilities in target networks, and sold that access to ransomware operators and affiliates. Bitcoin "tumblers" offered discounts to gangs that used them as a preferred vendor for laundering ransom payments. Some contractors were open to working with any gang, while others entered exclusive partnerships.

"That's similar to the normal world," said John Fokker, head of cyber investigations at the California-based cybersecurity company Trellix. "When people specialize and the business is growing, they'll branch off certain services that before they had to do by themselves. You see the same thing in the underground as well."

That vast underground economy was out of sight of most victims. But a few outsourced services were what businesses like to call customer-facing. Some ransomware groups shared a call center in India, with representatives contacting employees or clients of victim organizations that hadn't paid up. Following a script provided by the hackers, the callers would describe the incident to the people on the other end of the line—who in some cases weren't even aware an attack had taken place—and then pressure them to convince the victim organization to pay.

While it's not clear whether REvil used this same Indian call center, Unknown did say in his interview with Smilyanets that direct calls provide "a very good result," adding, "We call each target as well as their partners and journalists—the pressure increases significantly."

Some gangs even outsourced their negotiations to specialized providers. Since many hackers lack a command of English, hiring a professional to communicate with victims seemed like a savvy business move. But, just like in the legitimate business world, outsourcing could backfire. With multiple groups using the same service, negotiations sometimes became jumbled. One contractor simultaneously negotiated in online chats with victims of two groups, Maze and DoppelPaymer. Relying on a script, the negotiator mistakenly failed to replace the word "Maze" with "DoppelPaymer" throughout the DoppelPaymer negotiation, causing confusion and delay.

Lizzie Cookson, a U.S.-based negotiator familiar with the victims' side of the Maze-DoppelPaymer mix-up, said the gangs' outsourcing added a "headache to this whole process."

"We've known for a long time that we're not really interacting with the developer 'face to face,' so to speak, anymore," Cookson said. "Which is too bad because things were a lot more straightforward then."

As word spread across dark web forums that ransomware was far more lucrative than other cybercrime, hackers encouraged their underworld contacts to get in on the action. They didn't need to be stuck in low-return grinds like cashing in on stolen credit card numbers. They could adapt their criminal career paths to the changing times. As the legendary martial arts film actor and director Bruce Lee famously advised, "Be water."

The cybercrime mastermind Maksim Yakubets was water. In 2009, about four years before the dawn of modern ransomware, Yakubets, then twenty-two, began his malware spree. Yakubets and his co-conspirators allegedly infected thousands of computers with malicious software they called Zeus, which captured passwords, account numbers, and other information necessary to log into online banking accounts. In a relatively labor-intensive process compared to ransomware, the Zeus co-conspirators used the ill-gotten information to electronically transfer funds from victims' bank accounts to those held by money mules. The mules moved the money to other accounts or withdrew it, smuggling the gains back to Yakubets and his group.

Through the Zeus scheme, the Ukrainian-born Russian national and his co-conspirators allegedly robbed tens of millions of dollars from municipalities, banks, companies, and nonprofit organizations across the United States. Still, Yakubets thought he could do better.

As ransomware surged, Yakubets—whose online moniker, co-incidentally, was "aqua"—became fluid. He allegedly led a group of co-conspirators who developed and deployed malware called Bugat, which was specifically crafted to defeat antivirus defenses and steal online banking credentials along with other personal information. As a joke, the group registered a server under "Evil Corp" and subsequently referred to themselves by that name, employing dozens of people to run the operation from the basements of Moscow cafés. Yakubets and his gang continuously improved the malware, later called Dridex, and added a component that would become its most important feature: a function that assisted in the installation of ransomware. With the addition, Evil Corp began attacking organizations such as the UK's National Health Service and the PGA of America with a strain called BitPaymer, demanding as much as $200,000.

BitPaymer's cryptography was unusually polished. It featured several layers of encryption and an intricate way of disguising the malware's interactions with Windows operating systems, complicating the hunters' efforts at reverse engineering. Michael Gillespie obtained a sample but couldn't make any headway. In July 2017, he and the Italian researcher Francesco Muroni analyzed the strain. Then Michael tweeted, "Confirmed Bitpaymer ransomware is not decryptable."

Swaggering around Moscow, Yakubets didn't seem to mind the publicity. Videos circulated online showing members of Evil Corp doing burnouts in luxury cars and engaging in other auto-related hijinks; Yakubets himself drove a customized Lamborghini with a license plate that translated to "Thief." The same summer that Michael tweeted about BitPaymer, Yakubets was married in a lavish celebration at a golf club near Moscow that reportedly included a performance by the well-known Russian pop singer Leonid Agutin. He spent more than $330,000 on the wedding. Yakubets's new family ties may have added to his sense of invincibility: his bride's father, Eduard Bendersky, had been an officer in the Spetsnaz, Russia's military special operations forces.

Evil Corp adapted its enterprise and shifted to ransomware because that's where the money was. But Yakubets's criminal run was also a part of a harrowing shift in which ransomware evolved from a get-rich-quick scheme for hackers to a tool that nation-states could wield to harm adversaries.

Far from the "funny war" that the Apocalypse developer had waged with Fabian, ransomware was showing its potential as a weapon of actual cyber warfare. In 2017, U.S. government officials blamed North Korea for the devastating attacks caused by the WannaCry ransomware worm. WannaCry had infected the UK's National Health Service, among many other victims across 150 countries, before security researcher Marcus Hutchins famously found a kill switch that neutralized the unusual worm. It caused hundreds of millions of dollars in damages during its short rampage.

In November 2019, following years of investigations, the U.S. Department of Justice indicted Yakubets and a co-conspirator on computer hacking, bank fraud, and other charges related to Zeus and Dridex. While stopping short of attributing Evil Corp's attacks to the Putin regime, international law enforcement officials nonetheless uncovered that Yakubets had "provided direct assistance to the Russian government" while leading the criminal group. As of 2017, he was working for the Federal Security Service (FSB), a successor to the Soviet-era KGB.

By the following year, Yakubets was in the process of obtaining a license to work with the FSB's classified information. He was "tasked to work on projects for the Russian state, to include acquiring confidential documents through cyber-enabled means and conducting cyber-enabled operations on its behalf," the U.S. Treasury Department said.

Keith Mularski, who oversaw the FBI's investigation into Yakubets until he retired from his position as cyber unit chief in 2018, said that the Russian government uses cybercrimes like Evil Corp's ransomware as cover "when they're really trying to collect material from an intelligence gathering standpoint."

"He is doing the work of the state over there," Mularski said.

Yakubets was not taken into custody because Russia has no extradition treaty with the United States. The Treasury Department said at the time of the indictment that Evil Corp had illicitly earned at least $100 million from victims globally through the use of Dridex malware. Damages from its accelerating ransomware spree, though, went untallied. Citing connections to the FSB, the Treasury Department placed Evil Corp under sanctions. The announcement meant that ransomware victims who subsequently paid Evil Corp could face civil penalties, including fines, for supporting criminal activities.

But neither the indictment nor the sanctions put a stop to Evil Corp's reign. Knowing the sanctions would cause payments to drop off, the group came up with a work-around. It secretly tweaked Bit-Paymer's code and rechristened it WastedLocker. This way, victims couldn't be accused of running afoul of U.S. sanctions since the "new" ransomware wasn't yet linked to the group. Payments would continue unimpeded until security researchers could tie Evil Corp to the supposedly new strain.

Over the years, dogged analysis by researchers, including members of the Ransomware Hunting Team, repeatedly outed Evil Corp's connection to new ransomware strains. With similar persistence, the group rebranded its strains again and again, primarily using phishing emails to target sectors from manufacturing to health care to consumer goods, including a debilitating strike on the GPS device maker Garmin. Once, Fabian and Michael discovered that Evil Corp was disguising its ransomware as a rival strain known as Babuk or PayloadBIN.

"Looks like EvilCorp is trying to pass off as Babuk this time," Fabian tweeted in June 2021. "EvilCorp rebrands WastedLocker once again as PayloadBin in an attempt to trick victims into violating OFAC [U.S. Office of Foreign Assets Control] regulations."

Michael chimed in on Twitter later that day: "WastedLocker -> Hades -> Phoenix -> PayloadBin, all same malware/group behind it. Probably a few in-between don't care to recall at the moment."

Outed again, Evil Corp regrouped. In October 2021, a new ransomware, called Macaw Locker, hit two large targets: The U.S. division of the optical device manufacturer Olympus and Sinclair Broadcast Group, one of the largest American TV station operators. The ransom note, which featured a crude text-art picture of a parrot, directed victims to a site on the dark web. "Do not waste your time trying to recover the data-it is impossible," the site advised. "Send us a message in the chat window if you wish to buy a decryptor tool." Macaw Locker demanded tens of millions of dollars from each victim.

Fabian analyzed the code and determined that Macaw Locker was the latest reincarnation of Evil Corp. Lawrence Abrams interviewed him about the discovery and wrote an article for BleepingComputer, unmasking the sanctioned criminal enterprise once more and saving victims from inadvertently violating federal law. With a tinge of exasperation, Lawrence wrote:

> Now that Macaw Locker has been exposed as an Evil Corp variant, we will likely see the threat actors rebrand their ransomware again.
>
> This constant cat-and-mouse game will likely never end until Evil Corp stops performing ransomware attacks or sanctions are lifted.
>
> However, neither of those scenarios is likely to take place in the immediate future.

Lawrence had other reasons to feel overwhelmed by the malign persistence of ransomware attackers. To his amusement, and consternation, he knew criminals sometimes posted on his site. But a disturbing new tactic the Maze group first deployed on BleepingComputer took

Lawrence far beyond his comfort zone—and turned his site into a launchpad for one of the most drastic evolutions in ransomware.

It's not known where Maze was based or who was behind it. But just as other hackers fixated on Fabian, the Maze group was hung up on Lawrence. When Maze emerged in May 2019, Lawrence and Michael analyzed its code and spotted BleepingComputer's domain name in it. That October, Maze again tried to provoke Lawrence by including his email address in the code it used in attacks in Italy.

But the taunting soon turned into something far more sinister. Lawrence was finishing his work on a Friday evening in mid-November when an unexpected email came in just after 6:30. Signed by the "Maze Crew," the note described a trailblazing, not-yet-public attack that the group had carried out on Allied Universal, a California-based security staffing company with about 200,000 employees. In a Joker-like twist, Maze had downloaded mountains of data from Allied's network before encrypting its files and was using the stolen data as leverage. Maze told Allied it would leak the files if the company failed to pay the ransom. And although he didn't yet know how, Lawrence sensed the group was using him as a pawn in its vicious new scheme.

"We have also told them that we would write to you about this situation if they dont pay us, because it is a shame for the security firm to get breached and ransomwared," Maze wrote in the email to Lawrence. "We gave them time to think until this day, but it seems they abandoned payment process . . . If they dont begin sending requested money until next Friday we will begin releasing on public everything that we have downloaded from their network before running Maze."

To show they were serious, Maze sent Lawrence a batch of files—with titles like "Confidential Investigative Report," "Medical report_ assault," and "SEPARATION AGREEMENT"—that the group claimed to have stolen from Allied. Lawrence reviewed the contents, which appeared legitimate.

In subsequent emails, Maze told Lawrence that it always exfiltrated files for leverage and that in the Allied attack it had demanded 300 bitcoin (about $2.3 million at the time). Lawrence wrote back, asking how Allied and other victims could be sure the group would delete the stolen data if they paid a ransom. Maze's reply indicated that the Allied attack wouldn't be the last to leverage breached records.

"It is just a logic," Maze told him. "If we disclose it who will believe us? It is not in our interest, it will be silly to disclose as we gain nothing from it."

In other words, if Maze didn't hold up its end of the deal, future victims would find out and have no incentive to pay. Lawrence contacted Allied to warn the company about what Maze had told him. But perhaps viewing Lawrence as a member of the media rather than as a security researcher, a spokesperson sent a terse reply, saying Allied was "aware of a situation that may involve unauthorized access to our systems." Its internal IT staff and outside consultants were investigating the incident and reinforcing the company's cybersecurity, the statement said.

Desperate to share more details of this new threat with Allied, Lawrence tried again, but a spokesperson said the company would "not be providing any additional comment at this time." Nonetheless, over the days that followed, Maze continued to correspond with Lawrence about the attack. The group showed him proof that it still had access to the company's servers.

Then, for the first time, Maze directly urged Lawrence to contact Allied and suggested he write about the episode:

Ask them a question: would they like if next Monday [Maze] impersonate Allied Universal in a spam campaign[?] . . . LMAO.
I think you should write amazing article about this. Name it: "HOWTO: The easiest way for a security company to be f**ked up."

It dawned on Lawrence how he was being used. While he had previously contacted Allied as a courtesy, the communication also happened to be exactly what the hackers wanted in order to ratchet up the pressure on their victim. Now Maze had spelled out its agenda: enlist Lawrence and BleepingComputer to shame Allied publicly as a warning to victims who failed to come to the bargaining table.

Lawrence grew more and more uncomfortable with what was happening. He dismissed the idea of writing an article unless he learned that the company paid the ransom or that Maze had really leaked the files. He kept a close eye on his email and website, knowing Allied's Friday deadline to pay was approaching. Then, six days after receiving the initial email from Maze, Lawrence spotted a haunting post on BleepingComputer's forums. Maze had posted a description of the Allied breach and a link to almost 700 megabytes of leaked files that included termination agreements, contracts, medical records, server directory listings, and encryption certificates.

"We have already morning of Friday," the hackers wrote on the forum. "Yes, it is friday in asia. Forgot to mention that deadline is a friday by our local time, and not US."

For years, hackers had breached computer security systems and stolen information to sell on the dark web—but not for ransom. Lawrence had heard of threats to release data if a ransom was not paid, but as far as he knew, this was the first time that a hacker had actually followed through. Furious that Maze was using BleepingComputer to distribute stolen data, Lawrence deleted the post. He contacted law enforcement and once again attempted to reach Allied. After Lawrence removed Allied's data from his site, Maze reposted it on a Russian hacker and malware forum. On the forum, Maze again described the attack and the leaked data.

"They contacted us and after receiving of proofs about data leakage just disappeared," Maze wrote. "We gave them time to think and they made their decision. Really stupid decision as we think, as money we were asking was not really big considering reputational losses and consequences for their 'security' company."

The new dark web post didn't mention Lawrence but called out another member of the Ransomware Hunting Team, with a reference that made clear how closely Maze had been watching the team's social media accounts.

"P.S. Malwarehunterteam," Maze wrote. "I know you like to troll and talk about breaches. Guess what. We still have access to their systems."

That night, Lawrence put together an article, posting it shortly before eleven o'clock.

"This is an unfortunate story and one that BleepingComputer does not enjoy telling, but with Maze's actions it is important to be told," he told readers. "With this escalated attack, victims now need to not only be concerned about recovering their encrypted files, but what would happen if their stolen unencrypted files were leaked to the public."

When he had first written about Maze in May 2019, Lawrence had counseled readers to protect themselves "first and foremost" by having "a reliable and tested backup of your data that can be restored in the case of an emergency." Now that advice seemed futile. Backup files might save victims from encryption, but, as the Allied attack showed, not from massive data leaks. Even if victims had backups, they still would have to pay a ransom, or their confidential data would be posted on the dark web. This would mean public disclosure of intellectual property; police evidence; military secrets; private medical, educational, and employment records; and more.

"Double extortion" made ransomware more dangerous and unpredictable than ever. It also meant that ransomware attacks had to be treated as data breaches, with victims required to follow relevant state and federal laws to notify employees, clients, patients, and others whose data was compromised. With this added responsibility, the costs of recovering from an attack continued to rise, just as public trust in data privacy and security continued to erode.

Maze made no secret of the fact that BleepingComputer was its favorite media outlet. "We will have a good press release soon," Maze told the negotiator for one of its targets. "Read bleepingcomputer, we believe every media will post the info we gonna share ;)" The group kept trying to turn Lawrence into an accomplice and frequently sent him unsolicited emails. From a journalistic standpoint, he struggled with how to handle the communications. He felt a duty to be transparent with his readers, yet he didn't want to become a lever used by hackers to pressure and extort victims.

Maze went on to strike high-profile victims, including Canon, LG Electronics, and Xerox. In an attack on the City of Pensacola, Florida, Maze demanded $1 million in ransom. Then it told Lawrence that it had stolen files. He reported on the attack, and other media outlets followed his story, sometimes questioning whether Maze had filched as much data as it claimed. The group settled the debate about two weeks later when it released 10 percent of the files it claimed to have robbed from the city before encrypting its network. Again, Maze reached out to Lawrence, saying it leaked the documents as proof to the media of its claims.

"This the fault of mass media who writes that we don't exfiltrate data more than a few files," Maze wrote to Lawrence. "We've shown that our intentions are real."

Like many gangs that portrayed themselves as Robin Hoods, uplifting ordinary people by taking down big government or big pharma, Maze cloaked its greed in an anti-capitalist mantle. In 2020, its representative told Vincent D'Agostino, a negotiator for one of its victims, that Maze was "not that stereotyped picture of cartel with Yachts and private jets," adding that it was "not only the money" it wanted. Maze wanted to punish the "idiocracy" that failed to avert attacks. "The real criminals is government and corporates," the Maze representative said.

"Leaderships of companies do not spend money to security, storing the data recklessly," Maze wrote to D'Agostino, who heads cyber forensics and incident response at the cybersecurity firm BlueVoyant. "Government doesn't care about people as well, the people for them is only numbers . . . So if we want to speak with those people we need to speak to them using numbers as well, the best numbers they understand is losses."

The Maze negotiator seemed most frustrated that, despite its threats to leak stolen data, some victims, including Pensacola's city government, didn't pay the ransom. Maze believed that victim organizations refused to pay not because of a reluctance to reward criminals, but because they felt protected by their compliance with data breach notification laws.

"We can't even remember on how much we had companies who told us something like 'we made notifications and we do not care about publication,'" Maze told D'Agostino. "You see what it means? They used law to protect them from losses because of publication of data and now they do not care about clients. We do not like that, and we like to punishing all these companies."

In short order, other ransomware strains followed Maze's lead. By the end of 2020, more than two dozen groups were using the double-extortion tactic. Maze and most of the others created "leak sites" on the dark web where members of the public could view victims' names and stolen data, either for free or for a price. "Represented here companies do not wish to cooperate with us, and trying to hide our successful attack on their resources," Maze said on its leak site. "Wait for their databases and private papers here. Follow the news!"

Like Maze, REvil posted stolen data on a hacker forum before launching a leak site it called Happy Blog. There, it published names of victims as well as data it had stolen from them. Its high-profile victims included a law firm representing Lady Gaga and other celebrities, the money-exchange chain Travelex, and the American fashion brand Kenneth Cole. REvil shook the tech world when in April 2021 it published blueprints for Apple products, including an unreleased MacBook; the group said it had stolen the documents from the laptop manufacturer Quanta Computer, a key Apple supplier.

In the interview with Recorded Future, REvil's Unknown said that publishing files on the leak site was "absolutely gorgeous." With an air of invincibility, the hacker floated other possibilities for pressuring victims.

"I also think we will expand this tactic to persecution of the CEO and/or founder of the company. Personal OSINT [open-source intelligence], bullying. I think this will also be a very fun option. But victims need to understand that the more resources we spend before your ransom is paid—all this will be included in the cost of the service. =)"

Chicago data privacy attorney Michael Waters represented a plastic surgery group whose patients were similarly bullied. The data stolen in the double-extortion attack on the group included before-and-after photos of patients who had undergone breast augmentation surgery. The hackers contacted those patients by email and included personal photos in their messages. "They threatened to post them online unless payment was made," Waters said.

In addition to giving them leverage in negotiations, the shift to data breaches also emboldened gangs to become more creative in canvassing for targets. REvil breached insurance companies, intending to search for lists of their cyber policyholders. Knowing that such policies often covered ransom payments, REvil then targeted the companies they found. "Yes, this is one of the tastiest morsels," Unknown said. "Especially to hack the insurers first—to get their customer base and work in a targeted way from there. And after you go through the list, then hit the insurer themselves."

In another innovation, Maze formed what Lawrence dubbed a "cartel," banding together with other gangs to share a common data leak site. Maze told Lawrence in June 2020 that consolidating resources would lead to "mutual beneficial outcome, for both actor groups and companies . . . Organizational questions is behind every successful business."

That December, a year after Maze attacked Allied Universal, Lawrence wrote an article for BleepingComputer that revisited his early question about how victims could be sure their stolen data would be deleted after payment. The answer, he learned, was that they couldn't. REvil had re-extorted victims with threats to post data weeks after they paid for the files to be deleted. A handful of other groups had posted data from companies that had paid. Even Maze, despite its assurances, had mistakenly posted a victim's data on its leak site. In his first article about Allied, Lawrence had told readers that double extortion was something to "keep an eye on." Now he was telling them to expect the worst.

"There is no way for a victim to know for sure if a ransomware operation is deleting stolen data after a ransom payment is made," Lawrence wrote. "Companies should automatically assume that their data has been shared among multiple threat actors and that it will be used or leaked in some manner in the future, regardless of whether they paid."

By early 2021, alarmed by ransomware's higher profile and the gangs' increasingly harsh tactics, some smaller players were having second thoughts. One of these players was a hacker who went by the Russian version of the name Adrian on the messaging platform Telegram.

Adrian preferred to use a Russian name because his father was Russian and he wanted to sound intimidating. "The most dangerous hackers are from Russia," he said. But he was actually living in a Middle Eastern country where computer hacking was also common.

He grew up loving computers and playing video games like *Counter-Strike: Global Offensive* and *Fall Guys*. He graduated from high school but didn't go to college and never held a real job. He said he didn't leave the house often because "all of my world is related to computers." His interest in tech led him to join hacking channels on Telegram. From there, he entered the world of cybercrime, brute-forcing into servers secured with weak passwords.

In 2020, Adrian pivoted to ransomware because he otherwise "couldn't make money easily." Like many of his adversaries on the Ransomware Hunting Team, he taught himself cryptography, learning from books and videos online. He then developed his own ransomware strain, which he based on Phobos. He called it Ziggy after an iridescent snake discovered in Laos in 2016; the snake itself was named Ziggy Stardust in honor of late singer David Bowie's alter ego.

Although Ziggy's attacks helped him buy food and a new computer, Adrian said he was motivated more by politics than by money. He targeted users in the United States and Israel but demanded only a $200 ransom, an absurdly small amount compared to the seven- and eight-figure demands other groups were making. He split the proceeds with an affiliate who found the victims. MalwareHunterTeam, who had analyzed Ziggy with Michael, found an unusual "whitelist" of locations where the ransomware would automatically shut off rather than encrypt the target: Iran, Syria, Lebanon, and Palestine.

After about a year, during which he netted about $3,000 from victims, Adrian began feeling guilty and fearful. Law enforcement globally and in the United States had just disrupted a major ransomware-spreading botnet as well as the Netwalker strain. Another smaller ransomware developer, who was Adrian's mentor, had recently abandoned his own strain, called Fonix. Corresponding over Telegram, Fonix's creator told Adrian he was sad that he had hurt people. Adrian said he reflected on those words and prayed for guidance. He worried about what his parents and friends would think if they found out what he had done.

Adrian decided he wanted out. So, like everyone else interested in ransomware, he turned to BleepingComputer. There, he saw that demonslay335—Michael Gillespie—had already analyzed Ziggy. He found Michael on Twitter.

"Hello bro," he wrote to Michael. "How are you? I'm Ziggy ransomware main and i want to publish all keys. Can you help me and share decryption keys? I'm so sorry about what i did. Please help me bro."

Around that time, hackers from at least half a dozen strains had approached Michael, turning over private keys that he could use to develop decryptors. He was glad to take Adrian's keys, knowing it meant that victims of Ziggy could recover their files. But that didn't stop him from venting his characteristic, resigned irritation about the extra work being dropped on him on a Sunday. "Fucking ransomware authors closing shop on a weekend when I'm already busy," he said. Michael built the decryptor, which he released later that day. The next month, BleepingComputer reported that Ziggy was offering refunds to victims who'd paid a ransom. "They plan to switch sides and become a ransomware hunter after returning the money," the article said.

Lighter after his atonement, Adrian still worried about law enforcement coming for him. "I don't like to see people unhappy," he said. "It feels very bad. In our religion hurting people it is something named HARAM . . . But now i gave up. Am i criminal now?"

Adrian said that if the authorities don't catch him—and the odds are in his favor there—he wants to open his own IT shop where he can help people solve their computer problems, especially ransomware. Having made amends, and dreaming of using his skills for good rather than evil, Adrian pitied the unrepentant hackers who continued to spread ransomware.

"I think one day all of their creators will be sad about what they did," he said.

If anyone from the big ransomware gangs was feeling remorse, Fabian saw no evidence of it. Still, he wanted to make sure the Ransomware Hunting Team could capitalize on any second thoughts. In an unusual overture, Fabian opened a virtual confessional where hackers could come clean about their sins and repent by anonymously sending him decryption keys. Practically speaking, the confessional was an account on a messaging service favored by cybercriminals. In July 2021, he tweeted the details to his more than ten thousand Twitter followers.

"I have created an XMPP account to make it easier for people to anonymously send me key dumps," he tweeted. "So if you want to off-load your key database when you shut down your operation, feel free to contact me at fabian.wosar@anonym.im - no questions asked."

Fabian had asked for, and received, Sarah's blessing before sending out his tweet. "Why not?" she told him. "You might get something." Once he posted it, though, skeptics emerged immediately.

"Enjoy the spam," one follower replied. "It will be rough."

"Nothing so far," Fabian responded the next day. "I am actually questioning if it is working."

Another called him an "absolute madlad," slang for insane. "Really asked people to bombard him with spam," the follower wrote.

Undeterred, Fabian replied: "Whatever it takes to get some ransomware victims their data back."

Like a bored priest waiting on his side of the privacy screen, Fabian stood by patiently and hopefully for penitents to come forward. Sure enough, over the course of the first month, they began to trickle in. These sinners, however, didn't want absolution; they wanted revenge.

Most of Fabian's correspondents were hackers who claimed they were scammed out of money or otherwise wronged by their partners in crime. Others contacted him with information that could doom competitors. They provided Fabian with details of breaches and impending attacks, and they turned over decryption keys for those that had already taken place. The communication benefited both parties: Fabian helped targets prevent or recover from attacks, while the hackers sabotaged their foes—with low risk of being fingered.

In late August, a hacker connected to the ransomware group EL_Cometa reached out to Fabian. Previously known as SynAck, which had been attacking victims since 2017, EL_Cometa emerged in August 2021. Bitter infighting ensued, and the hacker, who identified vulnerable targets, felt cheated out of money by one of the group's partners. To settle the score, the hacker decided to undermine the whole operation. The hacker gave Fabian decryption keys for EL_Cometa's victims as well as log-in details for the cloud storage where their stolen data was kept.

In addition, the hacker gave Fabian details about targets whose systems had been compromised but not yet encrypted and proof of "backdoors"—secret entrance points left behind by intruders that allow for future access—placed in those networks to ensure continued access. These victims of impending attacks included the North Carolina–based turkey company Butterball.

The correspondent showed Fabian a detailed map of one of Butterball's networks and a screenshot of domain admin credentials that included comically easy passwords like Butterball1 and GObb1er. Working through the night, Fabian tried unsuccessfully to reach Butterball to warn them about what he'd learned. Around 1:00 a.m. London time, obsessed and frustrated, he vented on Twitter.

"I hate it when you know a company is about to be hit by ransomware but you can't get anyone there to listen to you or answer a call," he wrote, without naming Butterball or how he knew it was on the brink of disaster. "We know their security already failed them. Ransomware deployment is imminent. 1B+ US company."

Two days later, Fabian updated his followers. "We managed to reach the company and handed over the information we had to them," he wrote. "They were already in the process of taking appropriate actions, which is excellent news and kudos to their IT staff for catching on to the intrusion independently."

Butterball later notified "individuals whose personal information may have been accessed" that someone had hacked into its network and tried to upload files to a cloud server; the company said it detected the "suspicious activity" within an hour, halted the upload, and deleted the transferred files.

After sharing the breach details with Butterball, Fabian felt satisfied. The Ransomware Hunting Team had now contacted every victim named by the El_Cometa hacker.

"We managed to reach all of these victims and potential victims," Fabian wrote on Twitter. "We provided free decryption tools to the victims where the ransomware was already deployed and handed over all information dumps we obtained to their IT teams and [law enforcement agencies]. It's been a good week after all."

In the months that followed, new hackers messaged Fabian every few weeks. True to the role of confessor, Fabian cast no judgment. Granting hackers the space to open up about their transgressions without shame would, he believed, help them feel comfortable spilling their secrets. He also learned that the most efficient way to extract information was to make it clear that he was prepared to do the hackers' dirty work—letting them think "that they're taking advantage of me instead of the other way around," he said.

Now that Fabian was in regular contact with his adversaries again, he saw up close how the landscape had changed. He was dealing with hackers inside large gangs rather than with small, stand-alone operators. He understood that affiliates had no allegiance to their groups and vice versa. Money, and nothing else, established loyalty among his correspondents.

Yet some things, like a shared fascination with cryptography, hadn't changed at all. Sometimes, even as they sought revenge on their enemies, the hackers took a few moments to fish for Fabian's approval of their handiwork or to worship at his ransomware altar. Those messages reminded him of the banter he'd exchanged years earlier with Apocalypse, whose developer had called him "a god."

"People who create ransomware have a certain appreciation for the skills and knowledge to do what we on the Hunting Team do," Fabian said. "Coming to me, this is their way of showing respect."

Still, the pressure on Fabian, Michael, and their teammates from both hackers and victims was overwhelming. And the stresses of this not-so-funny war affected them—and their loved ones—in unexpected ways.

5.

THE PRICE OF OBSESSION

Even before the team was formally established, Michael realized that he, Fabian, MalwareHunterTeam, and the others needed more than a way to communicate among themselves. They also needed a website dedicated to cataloging ransomware, where victims could upload their encrypted files, identify which strain had attacked them, and learn whether their data could be recovered without paying hackers. Such a self-help site would benefit victims while freeing up the hunters to work on cracking new strains.

In the Nerds on Call office and at home, Michael began working on a solution. "I'm a programmer," he said. "What do I do? I automate."

With his typical just-the-facts approach, Michael named his site after its purpose. In March 2016, he launched ID Ransomware with an announcement on Twitter and BleepingComputer. "All too often after a ransomware attack, the first question is, 'what encrypted my files?', followed by, 'can I decrypt my data?'" he wrote. "This web service aims to help answer those questions, and guide a victim to the correct information relating to their infection."

The only frill he allowed himself was an epigraph from GI Joe: "Knowing is half the battle!" Otherwise, the home page was as straightforward as the name. It asked victims for an encrypted file and a ransom note—or, if there was no note, any email addresses or links provided by the attacker. It listed known ransomware strains and answered frequently asked questions. For example:

Can you decrypt my data?
No. This service is strictly for identifying what ransomware may have encrypted your files. It will attempt to point you in the right direction, and let you know if there is a known way of decrypting your files . . .

Is my data confidential?
. . . I cannot guarantee files are kept 100% confidential. The data is temporarily stored on a shared host, and I am not responsible for anything done otherwise with this data.

ID Ransomware took off immediately. Victims, researchers, law enforcement officers, and consultants all submitted encrypted files for analysis. When a previously unidentified type of ransomware was detected, Michael added it to his database. It was a monumental task. Within a month of its launch, ID Ransomware was receiving fifteen hundred submissions a day. Most of them came from countries other than the United States; volunteers worldwide eventually translated it into almost two dozen languages, from Swedish to Nepali. As a central clearinghouse, ID Ransomware also proved invaluable to team members, identifying newly discovered strains to analyze and decrypt.

Michael gave Lawrence full access to all the raw material that poured into ID Ransomware but made him promise not to use it to break news. Michael didn't want to inadvertently interfere with a law enforcement investigation. He was sharing the information with Lawrence as a colleague, not as a journalist.

"I'm itching to write some of these stories, and I don't, because I know that I can't," Lawrence said. "Sometimes I'm writing a story, and I'm like, 'Fuck, I know the answer to this question, and I can't say anything. Because I don't want to betray Michael's trust.'"

Nonetheless, the aggregated information gave him a first look at the ongoing evolution of ransomware. "[Michael] collects amazing data because so many people use it," Lawrence said. "He has tons of information. You can see statistics, trends, what kinds of attacks are happening and when."

Michael soon developed other free applications for victims. RansomNoteCleaner removed ransom notes left behind on a system after an infection—eliminating the time-consuming task of removing them manually—and CryptoSearch located encrypted files and made it easier to back them up, in the hope that a solution might someday be available.

ID Ransomware also cross-referenced victims' IP addresses with Shodan, a site that can show a computer's vulnerabilities. When Shodan found a weakness that could have allowed hackers in, ID Ransomware flagged it—and, like the notes Michael had stuck in his classmates' high school lockers, suggested fixing the problem.

Instead of the succinct web address he wanted, idransomware .com, Michael's site was located at the longer and less convenient idransomware.malwarehunterteam.com. The reason was personal: he was broke.

Although idransomware.com was available, and only cost a small sum up front, Michael couldn't buy it. Payment was required by check or credit card, but Michael had defaulted on his credit cards, and his bank had frozen his checking account. Instead, a sympathetic MalwareHunterTeam, all too familiar with poverty, allowed Michael to share a domain name for free.

Yet, shortly after its launch, Michael assured visitors that ID Ransomware "is, and always will be, a free service to the public." He added, "I do not ask for any money for my services. I do, however, highly recommend investing in a proper backup to prevent you from becoming a victim in the future . . . However, if I or this website have helped you, and you really do wish to give back, feel free to toss a dollar or two my way." Beneath this was a link for donations to help cover the costs of running the site.

Michael didn't consider, and couldn't have afforded, registering

ID Ransomware as a nonprofit, which would have enabled donors to deduct gifts from their taxes. Contributions were scarce. A surprisingly large donation of $3,000 through PayPal thrilled him, but the godsend proved to be a scam—probably revenge by hackers whose ransomware he had disabled—and PayPal demanded the money back. Michael couldn't repay it, and he had to switch to another service.

His principled refusal to charge victims for bailing them out took its toll. His Nerds on Call salary alone couldn't pay the bills. At Facet Technologies, the parent company of Nerds on Call, the young employees got plenty of experience and mentoring. What they didn't get was rich. As a lead technician in 2008, Dave Jacobs earned a starting salary of $20,000 a year. "That's even low for our area. But I lived with a roommate so I could get by on it." Facet was paying him $32,000 a decade later, when he left for Caterpillar.

Michael rarely groused about his salary and never asked for a raise; the raises he did receive were modest. He was promoted from technician to programmer and then to project manager, overseeing an offshore team that built websites and applications. He disliked the new role. Facet had absorbed another company's website-building division, and the newcomers' performance wasn't up to Michael's standards. "I did a lot of fixing their stuff," he said.

Even with a bigger title, he retained his old responsibilities. He was still programming and still running the shop, which meant answering phones and dealing with customers. The multitasking left less time for ransomware. But he lacked the self-confidence and motivation to look for a higher-paying job. He didn't like change, and Facet was the only employer he had ever known. He suffered from "impostor syndrome," the nagging insecurity that told him he didn't deserve wider recognition and a bigger job.

"The idea of him having to go through an interview and talk himself up, that's not him," Dave said. "That's not him at all."

Michael and Morgan had been struggling financially ever since their wedding, even with her income from nannying jobs. She chronicled their precarious state on Facebook. "I really hope we can afford our lifestyle lol," she wrote in March 2013. "Lol we just might have to live paycheck to paycheck for a bit . . . it's not like we even budget for clothes and extra stuff."

That month, they bought their home in Bloomington for $116,000 with a Federal Housing Administration loan for low-income borrowers. They "overextended themselves for the house a little bit," Dave said. "Everything you budget for the month may look great, but it's hard to account for the what-ifs and the surprises."

In June 2015, Morgan posted, "Does anybody have $1200 I can have?" The next month, they bought a used Nissan Pathfinder because Morgan insisted that they needed a car with a third row of seats to accommodate the kids she nannied. "Sometimes she gets things in her head that they think they need, and they really don't," Dave said. The monthly payment was $450.

"This is about what we can afford," Michael told Dave.

"Yeah, but dude, your other car is super old and you've got tons of problems with it. What if you have to get rid of that car and replace it before you get this paid off? In another year or two, you might have to be contending with a second car payment."

"Well, I'd kind of rather deal with the known."

"Dude, I'm telling you, it's a bad idea."

Sure enough, the other car soon broke down.

Brian and Jason, his bosses at Facet, knew he was hard up. If they wanted Michael to look presentable for a meeting with an important client, they paid for a haircut. "We paid for multiple haircuts" before Michael decided to grow a ponytail, Brian said. Brian also offered unheeded advice on sticking to a budget. "Some people have to figure it out on their own," he said.

Jason suggested renting out their furnished basement, which had a kitchenette, a bedroom, and a bathroom. Friends and relatives sometimes stayed there for nominal rent, but Michael and Morgan didn't want strangers as tenants.

To supplement his Nerds on Call salary, Michael took a second job as a newspaper carrier for *The Pantagraph*. Growing up, he had enjoyed delivering the *Pekin Daily Times* in his neighborhood after school. But *The Pantagraph* was a morning paper, and no routes were available near his house. He got up every morning at three, latched his bike to the back of his car, and headed to the *Pantagraph* building. There, he picked up 150 papers, folding and wrapping each one with rubber bands and bags. Then he drove fifteen miles north in the pitch dark to his route, parked, unhitched his bike, and rode from house to house. He left the newspaper in a box, on the porch, or wherever specified. After a couple of customers complained about him stepping on their lawns, he stayed on the walkways. When he finished his route, he returned home for a nap before going to Nerds on Call.

After paying for gas, rubber bands, and bags, he cleared only about $200 a month. He quit shortly before Christmas. He was too tired to hang on for the expected trove of holiday tips, and he was starting to worry about his health. He had noticed blood in his urine.

"It just beat him up so bad," Dave said. "He was just too exhausted and couldn't keep doing his day job."

Morgan was lonely. Consumed with his job and ransomware, Michael had little time for her.

They were temperamental opposites. Michael was rational, private, and ultra-focused, while Morgan was gregarious, emotional, and candid. But they depended on each other. He needed her to draw him out and connect him to other people and his own feelings. Amid her family turmoil and shifting moods, she needed his equanimity and steadfast support. They also enjoyed the same hobbies, like poking around at garage sales.

"I love my husband and the fact that I can be my complete self around him and I never feel judged or feel like I am anything but perfect in his eyes," she once wrote on Facebook. "I've never had anybody in my life give me so much confidence in myself."

But now he often stayed late at Nerds on Call, where he had a laptop on his desk and a higher-powered computer under it. He used both computers to crack ransomware. His colleagues would leave him to lock up. One evening, there was a blizzard. By the time he was ready to go home, he was snowed in, so he spent the night in the office, munching snacks from the receptionist's drawer.

"I felt like I never saw him," Morgan said. "We would be hanging out in the evening, and he would be like, 'Oh my gosh, I have to go do this.' And he would just disappear for hours."

While waiting for him to come home, she took care of the pets, watched television, scrolled social media, and drew in coloring books. Increasingly, she struggled with motivation. "A lot of times, when I wake up, I get into an existential crisis of what is the point," she said. "Like looking at my phone, what is the point, brushing my teeth, what is the point, taking a shower, what is the point. I can't get myself to do any of those normal everyday human things because I feel worthless."

To make new friends, she joined a local women's group, going along to dinner or a spa. What she yearned for most was to have a baby, but she struggled with infertility. So she lavished maternal affection on her cats, whom she called "my babies," and on the boy she nannied. "Little James wrote his first ever paper about me and him playing in the snow, I'm so touched, this makes me so happy!!" she posted on Facebook.

She sought to relieve her stress by indulging in an expensive habit: marijuana. Her sister, who was staying with them temporarily and working at a local Hardee's, was smoking pot with her friends, and Morgan decided to "give it a go, see what it's like." The first time, "it felt like this gleeful happiness, this carefree feeling of relaxation and actual focus, being able to do what I want to do," she said. "Weed gave me my life back."

At first, she only smoked on weekends. Then she progressed to evenings after her day's work as a nanny. She found her own supplier and bought a "half" every other week. "I would try to make those fourteen grams last, but it was very stressful." As her supply dwindled, she started to panic. "'What happens if I get triggered or have an episode, and I don't have any, and we don't have the money to get any?'"

Without a doctor's prescription for medical marijuana, Morgan paid street prices, shelling out as much as $2,000 a month. It wreaked havoc on their budget. "Next thing I know I go look at the account and there's five hundred dollars missing here, there's two hundred dollars missing there," Michael said. "Luckily, I had restrictions on how much you could pull out."

They raced like Olympic sprinters to spend their paychecks: he on bills, she on pot. "I didn't care about the utilities, I didn't care about the house, or the cars, or anything to be honest," Morgan said. "I was just more worried about killing myself and being in those dark places." Their marriage "depended on how quick I could get to the money before he'd use it on bills. He also knew the fallout of me not having weed, because then I would have breakdowns that I couldn't get out of."

Increasingly, they fell behind on bills. But it wasn't only the cost of cannabis that Michael objected to. He was a straight arrow, and Morgan was breaking Illinois law. Because he valued logical analysis and clear thinking, traits that enabled him to crack ransomware, being with someone with a hazy mind frustrated him. "He didn't really want anything to do with me," Morgan said.

He buried himself deeper in his work, which only stressed Morgan more. As a child, she had felt abandoned when her parents went out drinking. Now her husband's absences triggered similar anxieties. "There were definitely times where he would get wrapped up into work, and he just didn't think to text me," Morgan said. "And I would just be waiting and waiting and waiting and waiting for him to come home. And so I would call him freaking out, or he would come home and I would be threatening to hurt myself because I didn't feel like I mattered. And that wasn't the case, he wasn't cheating on me or doing something stupid.

"Or he would say, 'I'll be home in an hour.' And then an hour would go by, and then it would be two hours, and then it would be three hours, and I'm sitting here trying to decide, 'Well, should I message him, but I don't want to bother him because I don't want to be a burden.' So I would just have to be stuck with my feelings."

Finally, Morgan gave Michael an ultimatum. He either had to leave her or accept her smoking. "It was actually almost a deal breaker," she said. "I had reached the point where I couldn't stand him hating on me anymore. I finally found something that helped, and he couldn't accept it. Not only that, but he hated it, and he hated me for it."

At her insistence, he agreed to take one hit of a blunt. The experiment, conducted in their cluttered garage, did not go well. While Morgan smoked her usual quota, a single puff addled Michael. Uncharacteristically talkative and giggly, he chattered about his thoughts and feelings and how his brain worked. Then, as he glanced at a grill with a large fan on top of it, the two appliances magically transformed into a mythical winged creature.

"It's a fucking dragon!" he exclaimed.

He went back in the house and lay down, thinking he "had gone insane," he recalled. "I got completely freaked out that I would never return back to normal. I felt like I was trapped in *Inception*," he added, referring to the 2010 Leonardo DiCaprio movie about infiltrating the subconscious. "It scared me more than anything in my life."

Seemingly unable to have children, Morgan temporarily fulfilled her desire for a family. During the 2017 school year, she and Michael hosted an exchange student from Thailand. Tang stayed in their spare room and attended Bloomington High.

"That was one of the few options we had at that time for parenting," Michael said.

At twenty-five, Michael felt self-conscious about parenting a high schooler. Tang was on the school's soccer and bowling teams, and he attended all of her sports events. "That was just weird," he said. "I look like a teenager with a beard, trying to hang out with all these forty-year-old parents who have real teen kids."

Morgan relished her new role, and she enjoyed Tang's company. While Michael was at the office, she sat with Tang and helped her with homework. Morgan chaperoned her at the school's homecoming dance and conferred with Tang's teachers about her progress. "Parent teacher conferences went amazing!!!" she proclaimed on Facebook. "The general consensus is that Tang . . . is a very hardworking student that self advocates and even helps other students! We are so proud of her!!" She snapped photos of Tang during the first snowfall the girl had ever seen.

Outgoing and personable, Tang adjusted well to her new surroundings, going to concerts and a theme park and visiting Chicago with friends. Under the rules of the exchange program, she didn't pay rent. The extra mouth to feed compounded her hosts' financial troubles, which were becoming acute. The Gillespies were forced to rotate which utilities to pay, knowing that the others would be shut off.

Without electricity, Michael would empty the refrigerator, pack its contents in a cooler, drive to work, and store the food in the office fridge. Without heat, they spent more time away from home—Michael stayed late at the office, Morgan and Tang visited friends—and covered themselves with extra blankets at night. Without water for as long as three or four days, they couldn't flush the toilets; Michael peed in the backyard. He and Morgan used the water at work, and they stocked up on bottled water for the cats. Even when they found the money, restoring service wasn't easy. Because their credit cards and bank accounts were blocked, Michael had to bring cash to a utility office or money transfer service like Western Union.

This wasn't the opulent America of luxury cars, lush campuses, and swanky mansions that Tang had seen in movies and on television. Feeling sorry for her host family, she alerted her parents in Thailand. Reversing the usual direction of charity, the Thai family offered to bail out the U.S. family by paying the gas bill. The Gillespies declined. "I didn't let her parents do that," Michael said. He paid the bill, and the heat was turned on the next day, but it "was still pretty embarrassing."

Morgan's relatives blamed Michael for the couple's financial woes. They said Facet was taking advantage of him and suggested he find a more lucrative job, like being a corporate IT specialist. "They're always pressuring me," Michael said. "'You should work at State Farm, you could make three times as much.'"

At the least, his in-laws said, he should collect fees from ID Ransomware users. Even his staunchest champion, his wife's grandmother Rita, whom Michael calls "Granny," brought it up. "I try to not interfere in that area," Rita Blanch said. "Unless, being silly at times, when I would say to him, 'Babe, you need to charge, you could, like, be rich.'"

For Michael, the insinuation that he was a loser evoked unpleasant memories of high school days when classmates called him a weirdo behind his back. Still, he clung to his ideals and ignored his in-laws' advice. Despite the steep personal cost to him and to Morgan, he had no intention of charging ransomware victims or becoming a cog in a Fortune 500 bureaucracy. "Even if it was a two-hundred-grand starting gate, I don't want to work at State Farm in tier one support," he said. "Something I know I can fix, but it's not within my jurisdiction so I have to pass it along."

Michael also ignored signs of ill health. He knew he should seek help, but he was afraid. Any encounter with the healthcare system made him squeamish, especially if it had the potential to disrupt his life and put his ransomware fighting on hold. "The human body grosses him out," Morgan said. "If you start talking about a pulse or a heartbeat or eyeballs or blood, Michael starts getting fidgety."

Finally, worried about his increasing discomfort and loss of energy, Morgan made an appointment for him. In October 2017, a surgeon removed a tumor that was initially believed to be benign. But when the tissue sample came back, it turned out to be bladder cancer, which rarely affects young adults.

"Can everyone keep Michael in your thoughts please?" Morgan posted on Facebook. "Got some bad news today."

He took only two days off from Facet—one for the surgery, and one to recover. He didn't want to let his coworkers down.

"Poor guy, but he was a pretty good trouper through the whole cancer thing," Dave said. "He doesn't really outwardly show it a lot when he's super stressed about stuff."

Fortunately, the cancer was still at an early stage, and Michael was expected to recover fully. But the immunotherapy treatment that his doctor recommended was an ordeal. Every week for about two months, a nurse injected a liquid form of tuberculosis bacteria into his bladder. The bacteria activated immune cells, which attack cancer cells. Morgan had to hold him down and rub his foot to calm him. Then they would go home and wait an hour for him to urinate. Afterward, they bleached the toilet.

"Feeling scared," he confided to his Facebook friends following his first treatment in November. "Fucking worst thing I've ever done. Not looking forward to 5 more."

After the immunotherapy ended, the doctor gave him the good news that he was in full remission. Michael released his long-pent-up emotions in an uncharacteristic and memorable binge at the Facet Christmas party, held at a Peoria golf club. Michael, who rarely drank, went up to the bar.

"I don't really know what I like or what I want," he told the bartender. "Can you make me something kind of sweet?"

The bartender mixed him a Long Island iced tea, a potent cocktail with five kinds of alcohol: vodka, rum, tequila, gin, and triple sec. Michael gulped it down, and then another, and another, within half an hour.

"You can imagine the train wreck the poor guy was," Dave said. "The dude wanted to loosen up a little bit and he just doesn't know what his limit is. He didn't know what was in it. Just tastes pretty good."

Dave, sitting next to him, grabbed Michael's shirt collar so he wouldn't fall over. "You okay there, buddy?" Dave kept asking him. Morgan called Michael's father, who came and drove him home.

Michael wasn't the only team member who was so preoccupied with ransomware that it took a personal toll. Daniel Gallagher was also struggling. He was torn between the demands of his day job and his obsession with pursuing and shaming ransomware attackers.

Like Fabian and Michael, Daniel was diagnosed with ADHD as an adult and has a propensity to fixate on one task for an extended time. Also, because he has a trait known as grapheme-color synesthesia, he perceives letters and numbers as specific colors. For example, the letter *D* is gray-blue and the number 9 is burgundy. A series of numbers, he said, has "a certain feel. Fall colors, or cool or warm. So when I'm looking through lots of text or IP addresses, I perceive them in a certain color, so I can pick out what I'm looking for faster. I can scan through data and not actually read it, but it's easy enough for me to see a color go by. I think that's why I do really well in data analysis. The connections will just pop out. It's almost like a dopamine hit every time you make a connection." Many creative people—including famous artists, musicians, and scientists—have had the same type of synesthesia. The Nobel Prize–winning physicist Richard Feynman wrote that he saw mathematical equations "with light-tan j's, slightly violet-bluish n's, and dark brown x's flying around."

Daniel had two roles on the team. One was finding malware samples. He wrote what are known as YARA rules, directing VirusTotal to search its gigantic database of malware for samples meeting the criteria. He also created a tool to share samples automatically. "I started off like Red in *The Shawshank Redemption*, the man who can get you things."

The other role was his real passion. While Lawrence was fascinated by the attackers and Fabian mocked them, Daniel was determined to punish them. If other hunters suspected someone of creating ransomware, they let Daniel know. "He's the rabbit hole hunter," Michael said.

Daniel often denounced suspected cybercriminals on Twitter, where his avatar was a Grumpy Cat image. "I tend to shit post a lot." His aggressiveness incurred a backlash. "People had the impression of me that I was a bully or a jerk online, because there's been a few times on Twitter that I'll single somebody out," he said. "But there's always a reason behind the scenes. Someone just needs to be called out publicly, and kind of digitally slapped because they're just not understanding the effect they're having."

Born in 1981, Daniel had a nomadic childhood. His father—like Fabian's, an alcoholic—painted houses. His mother sometimes worked as a cashier but spent much of her time packing and resettling Daniel and his five siblings as the family moved from Texas to Florida to Massachusetts, chasing painting jobs. By the time he finished high school, Daniel had lived in seven states. Relocating so often, he found it hard to make friends.

An uncle gave him his first computer, an IBM, when he was eight, but his favorite hobby was tinkering with cars. He studied automobile technology at a vocational high school on Cape Cod and in his senior year won state and national contests in the field, demonstrating mastery of electronics. He later competed in autocross races, driving a Volkswagen GTI that he reprogrammed for more horsepower before buying a 2020 Audi RS3. "My passion is still to drive and race and have a fast car," he said.

After graduating from high school in 1999, he worked at a Cadillac dealership in Hyannis, Massachusetts. Four years later, after his parents divorced, he moved to a resort area in North Carolina's Blue Ridge Mountains, joining an older sister who had helped raise him. There were few jobs in his specialty, automotive electronics, so he waited tables in chic restaurants for almost a decade. Earning $1,000 a week in the summer and collecting seasonal unemployment in the winter, Daniel "got trapped in the good money" of the service industry. "I felt like I was wasting my brain," he said. "It wasn't what I was meant to do."

So he went to community college, earning an associate's degree and a certificate in cybercrime technology. He envisioned a law enforcement career but changed course after realizing that some cases, such as those involving child pornography, would exact a psychological toll. In 2012, a local hospital hired him as a network engineer to oversee cybersecurity. When the hospital was absorbed into Mission Health, he asked, "Who's doing my job?" The answer was nobody, so he invented a role: "I was the one-guy cyber defense team for about two years for a health system of about fifteen thousand employees. So it was nuts."

Daniel began to prioritize the threat of ransomware in 2016 with the proliferation of a strain known as SamSam, which was unprecedented in its reach. In an era of "spray and pray" tactics, when many gangs indiscriminately sought a few hundred or a few thousand dollars from individual computer users, SamSam targeted an organization's entire computer network and demanded tens of thousands of dollars in ransom. Over the next three years, SamSam would encrypt computer systems across North America and the UK, causing more than $30 million in losses to at least two hundred entities, including the cities of Atlanta, Georgia, and Newark, New Jersey, and the port of San Diego, California. SamSam hackers collected at least $6 million in ransom, and its code was unbreakable.

It especially ravaged hospitals, delaying appointments and treatments for patients nationwide. Although it spared Mission Health, Daniel thought, "If we're not careful, this could happen to us." He organized tabletop exercises, simulating a network shutdown.

Daniel did his best to pursue the SamSam attackers. "I had it out for them." Night after night, he tried to trace them on social media and the dark web, to no avail. The research whetted his appetite for ransomware hunting. He would leave his house at six in the morning, drive seventy miles to Mission's offices in Asheville, work a full day, return home in the evening, and look on social media for mentions of ransomware to investigate. Then he'd dive in.

One early success came after MalwareHunterTeam identified a new ransomware, called Exotic, in October 2016. Exotic appeared to still be under development, with three variants released in quick succession. The ransom note for one of the variants featured an image of Hitler and a Nazi flag. "You are infected by the Exotic virus," it said. "Pay or your files will be gone! Have a nice day :)"

Daniel was determined to track down the hacker, who went by the name EvilTwin online. EvilTwin had made "dumb mistakes in operational security," which allowed Daniel to trace his identity. On a beautiful fall Saturday afternoon, before heading outside to enjoy the North Carolina foliage, he reported his progress to the team.

"Pretty much have this little kid and his Minecraft buddies all fully identified," he wrote over Slack. "Names, and towns they live in. They are all like 15-16 as was pretty much expected." He said that the skiddies—script kiddies—lived in Grafing, Germany, a small town near Munich.

"Of course . . . Bayern," Fabian replied, referring to the German state. "Bayern is like the Texas of Germany. Lots of rich idiots, highly traditional and religious."

Sarah chimed in: "Will law enforcement really do much if they are 15/16?"

"Unfortunately I don't think so," Daniel replied. "The only thing you can really do with them is try and change their path. In my experience, that usually only works by rewarding or punishment and since there is no way I am rewarding these little brats, I want to convince them there could likely be punishment . . . So sometimes you can just let them know how exposed they are and hopefully it makes them start to question things before they do them."

Sarah suggested contacting EvilTwin's parents and other family members. Since the teen came from Germany, Fabian offered to draft a message.

Daniel was skeptical. "I have found even then you get parents who feel their children are angels and I am the bad guy for calling them out," he wrote.

Daniel let it go for a few weeks. But in mid-November, when he discovered that EvilTwin was experimenting with a different strain of ransomware, he decided he'd had enough.

"I'm just going to start calling them by their first names when I call them out on Twitter," he told MalwareHunterTeam. Then he did just that, tweeting at the hacker and addressing him by his first name: David.

After that, he sent David a private message. Daniel urged the teen to stop what he was doing—that it wasn't worth the risk of law enforcement coming for him. "Don't write ransomware," Daniel recalled telling him. "Write the stuff that stops ransomware." When the hacker balked, Daniel let him know he'd be passing along his information to European authorities. "You need to learn a lesson."

The hacker's account went dark. Almost three years later, in December 2019, Lawrence Abrams's weekly list of shout-outs lauded not only Ransomware Hunting Team members and other known security researchers but also a less familiar contributor for providing ransomware information to BleepingComputer. It was David. He had changed his hat color from black to white.

Recognizing the Twitter handle, MalwareHunterTeam complained to Lawrence that he was praising a known ransomware developer. Putting the pieces together, Lawrence came across Daniel's years-old Twitter roasts of the former skiddie and asked Daniel for more information.

"He was one of the kids I publicly called out for doing shady shit and told him to change his ways," Daniel replied. "I even told him that if he wanted to earn some actual respect, he should help take down ransomware instead of create it. If that is what he has been doing since then, we should be open to someone changing the path they were on."

"I agree," Lawrence said. "He has only been helpful with me."

"From what I have seen, they seem to be genuine in what they are doing," Daniel said. "Honestly, I feel kinda good about possibly being responsible in some way for getting them on the right path."

"Yeah, you should," Lawrence said. "He's trying to do good now."

In June 2017, Daniel set his eyes on a new target. Wazix, as the developer called himself online, was selling his new strain, TeslaWare, on dark web criminal forums. Wazix demanded $100 in Bitcoin and deleted victims' files if the amount wasn't paid within seventy-two hours. Lawrence analyzed a sample of TeslaWare and reported on BleepingComputer that it was "a complete mess, inefficient, and horribly slow." Its cryptography had "numerous flaws" and was easy to crack. Lawrence advised victims not to pay the ransom and to contact BleepingComputer for guidance on decryption.

Scouring the internet, Daniel discovered the hacker hadn't fully covered his tracks. He lived in France, and his real name was Jovan—to Daniel, a string of different colors, from the gray-purple *J* to the orange *n*. "If that name pops again somewhere else, I can just home in on that," he said.

Using his signature move, Daniel called him out on Twitter by his first name. "Now now Jovan. Does somebody need a nap?" Daniel tweeted at the hacker on July 17.

The hacker let out a series of expletive-laced tweets.

"Author of TeslaWare ransomware [WAZIX] is having a mental breakdown on Twitter," one security researcher commented.

After the hacker went dark, Ransomware Hunting Team member Jornt van der Wiel, a Dutch researcher for the Russian cybersecurity company Kaspersky, contacted the French police. "Ok they are interested," Jornt told the team. "I just need to gather all the info this evening."

The team was ecstatic. "Yes yes and fucking yes to all of this," Michael wrote.

"Hell yeah," Sarah said.

Fabian noted that Wazix's operational security "has as many holes as his ransomware it seems."

Jornt's police contact let him know that Wazix could be prosecuted even though he was a juvenile. But the investigator needed a "clear picture" of Wazix's activities, Jornt said, so that he could convince his boss and the prosecutor to open the case.

Despite the crush of his regular job, Daniel was on it. "This is amazing," he wrote. "Might take me a couple days with my current workload, but happy to assist!"

A few days later, Jornt came back with another update: "[The police] will most likely press charges against this guy," he said. "We are currently discussing with the police what for, exactly."

"Awesome," Sarah said. "Keep us in the loop if you can."

"Please let me know if I can assist," Daniel wrote. "I will rearrange my schedule if it means putting a criminal behind bars."

On August 22, after hearing from the French police, Jornt reported to the group, "Wazix has been arrested last week, hands on the keyboard . . . Thanks for your collaboration." The investigator asked the team to keep the arrest quiet since police were looking for Wazix's affiliates. They agreed.

Jornt congratulated his teammates. "Everybody here did an amazing job."

"I'm really surprised," Sarah said. "This is fast for law enforcement. But that's awesome."

Even as he chased hackers out of business, Daniel's hospital responsibilities and dogged pursuit of wrongdoers combined to push him to the brink of collapse. When a fast-spreading malware worm penetrated the Mission Health system in late 2016, Daniel worked seven straight eighteen-hour days, isolating sections of the company's network and stopping sixty-three infections. "That changed me. I got so burned out and never recovered."

Mentally and physically exhausted, he was losing weight. Overwork and his corresponding bad moods were also straining his marriage. "I knew if I kept pushing at the level I was, I would put myself in the hospital," he said. He left Mission Health in 2017 for a less stressful job teaching and developing online cybersecurity courses. A year later, he became a senior security analyst at a search engine company. He also scaled back his late-night detective work, despite feeling guilty that he might be letting his teammates down.

"I continually feel bad that I haven't been contributing and I'll apologize every once in a while. Everyone's like, 'You have your life.' Of course, if something big is happening you jump in there. There've been plenty of nights I'm on at 3 a.m. in the channel and sharing information. We're like a global company, so you get on at those times to be able to share intel."

Fabian was struggling, too, burdened by the pressure of being one of the world's premier ransomware breakers. He derived his self-worth from sharing expertise and saving victims. Years of enduring their demands, and their disappointment when he couldn't rescue them, weighed on him. One owner of an Ohio family business brought to the verge of bankruptcy by ransomware emailed Fabian for help from a hospital bed; the stress of the hack had given him a heart attack. At the time, the code was unbreakable, and there was nothing Fabian could do.

Another victim threatened to commit suicide unless Fabian could retrieve the data: "Please help me outtt or i gonna die . . . u are last hope for me."

Fabian posted a screenshot of the message on Twitter. "Requests like the one below are not okay," he wrote. "There are not a lot of things I am proud of, but I do feel proud of myself for still feeling compassion for every ransomware victim that reaches out to me. That is despite the years of abusive, demanding, and downright disrespectful requests I get from ransomware victims every single day."

Like patients given terminal diagnoses, "ransomware victims really go through all the seven stages of grief," Fabian later reflected. "Denial, bargaining, grief, depression, all these different steps until eventually they reach the point of acceptance."

He mentioned his own stress to his general practitioner, who gave him a pamphlet on mental health services. Two weeks after signing up for a consultation, he still hadn't heard back, and he went public with his hardship. "I had a particularly shitty month," he wrote on Twitter in July 2019. "You know, the kind of month that makes you want to light yourself on fire and burn down everything with you. Filled with rage and sadness, with no end in sight."

At the same time, he was becoming a public authority on ransomware, sharing his incendiary insights with the media. When he denounced cyber insurers for "keeping ransomware alive" by paying attackers, industry leaders, dismayed but impressed, asked him to speak at an October 2019 conference held at a five-star resort in Lisbon, Portugal. He was honored by the invitation and excited to attend. But when he arrived, he felt out of place. He stepped onto one of the hotel's sun-dappled balconies, standing beside potted trees to escape the crowd. "Everything is fancy," he said. "Everyone there was wearing suits, and there I was, sweaty in a T-shirt and jeans. I don't belong there."

When asked how his talk went, he replied, "OK, I guess. I don't really have a benchmark." He barely mingled with the other attendees, spending most of his time in his room at a more modest hotel. Alone, he ruminated about the victims who clamored for his help. He didn't sleep for four nights and began experiencing symptoms of psychosis. "I was having conversations with people who aren't really here."

By the time he returned to the UK, his Emsisoft colleagues had become aware of his distress and checked in on him online. Soon afterward, a doctoral student at Oxford University who had read about his work asked him to talk to a computer science class. Excited but nervous, and painfully aware of his lack of formal education, Fabian accepted. "Pretty sure I will go up in flames the moment I step into the room." But his outspoken views and obvious command of his subject enthralled the students. "Went 40 minutes over because people kept asking things," he said afterward. It was the solace that Fabian, ever eager to please, needed.

He drew added consolation from two cats he had rescued from a kitten breeding mill that summer. One had blue eyes and one green, so he named them Sapphire and Emerald. He sometimes brought them to a cat psychologist to help them deal with the emotional scars they had incurred before he saved them. He eventually found a therapist for himself, too.

The pressure from victims weighed on Michael as well as Fabian. "They just assume I'm Jesus," Michael said. "They assume I can break anything." Still, neither his exasperation with the constant badgering from victims nor his financial, marital, and medical woes deterred him from hunting ransomware. He and BloodDolly repeated their early TeslaCrypt triumph with other strains, notably WhiteRose. It hacked computers that used the Windows Server 2003 operating system, which by then was obsolete. Most of its victims were small European businesses that couldn't afford newer servers.

Most ransom notes are straightforward and succinct, informing victims their files have been encrypted and providing payment instructions. WhiteRose's note was a bizarre anomaly. Likened by Lawrence Abrams to "an assignment from a creative writing course," it sugarcoated the sordid reality with a lofty meditation on the beauties of nature:

> Behind me is an empty house of dreams and in front of me, full of beautiful white roses. In the garden environment, peace and quiet . . . Everything is natural. I'm just a little interested in hacking and programming . . . Believe me, my only assets are the white roses of this garden. I think of days and write at night: the story, poem, code, exploit or the accumulation of the number of white roses sold and I say to myself that the wealth is having different friends of different races, languages, habits and religions. Not only being in a fairly stylish garden full of original white roses.
>
> I hope you accept this gift from me and if it reaches you, close your eyes and place yourself in a large garden on a wooden chair and feel this beautiful scene to reduce your anxiety and everyday tension.
>
> Thank you for trusting me. Now open your eyes. Your system has a flower like a small garden; A white rose flower.

Perhaps WhiteRose's creator should have paid less attention to the garden and more to cryptography. The strain's method of generating random numbers was inadequate. Although WhiteRose contained protection against brute force attacks, Michael and BloodDolly were able to circumvent it and extract some keys.

Michael posted his decryptors for WhiteRose and other strains on BleepingComputer. But when victims tried to download them, antivirus software often flagged the tools as suspicious. Hearing about the problem on his site, and realizing that Michael was strapped, Lawrence spent $400 on a certificate letting users know they were downloading the decryptors from a trustworthy source.

"He's doing so much, how do you not support him if you can?" Lawrence said.

Then the Gillespies' finances hit bottom. In June 2018, their exchange student, Tang, returned to Thailand, reducing household expenses. But a month later, Morgan lost her job as a nanny, which had supplied about a third of the household income. She had missed too many days dealing with Michael's illness and her own ailments or spending time with Tang, and the family that employed her decided she was unreliable. "They didn't like that I wasn't there all the time," Morgan said. Even worse, because the family said it had grounds to fire her for misconduct, she wasn't eligible for unemployment benefits under Illinois law. Morgan interviewed for other nannying jobs, without finding the right fit.

The Gillespies ditched their home security system, saving $50 a month, but it wasn't nearly enough. They could no longer make the payments on the Pathfinder. They surrendered the car to the bank, which sold it at a loss at auction and forced them to make up the difference. They had to share their remaining car, a Hyundai Elantra. They missed four mortgage payments on their house and began to receive foreclosure notices.

Again, a fellow ransomware hunter came to the rescue. Noticing that Michael no longer seemed available on his home computer, Fabian asked what was going on. Haltingly, Michael admitted that his internet had been turned off and that he might lose his house.

Worried for his friend's well-being and for the team, which relied on Michael's around-the-clock work, Fabian began donating to ID Ransomware. He also arranged for Emsisoft to hire Michael part-time to create Emsisoft-branded decryptors. "You can't find people like Michael through a public message board," Emsisoft's Christian Mairoll said. "Fabian suggested to get him onboard better sooner than later, as his ID Ransomware website is very valuable in tracking ransomware activities . . . When hiring, we don't look so much for formal qualifications. There are so many self-educated talents out there and their skills are so much more mature than those of anyone who went through elite universities. It's the kind of people who live and breathe a specific field of expertise, and they are hard to beat."

The income enabled Michael and Morgan to catch up on their mortgage payments. "Gosh, that was an amazing feeling, walking into the bank and slapping down four thousand dollars and bringing it completely current," Michael said. They wouldn't have to displace their pets, give up their beloved bungalow, or say goodbye to the squirrels, groundhogs, and monarch butterflies that frequented their yard after all.

6.

STOPPING STOP

R ay Orendez stared at the screen of his desktop computer, so frustrated that he nearly punched the wall. In an instant, his livelihood had been destroyed, and there didn't seem to be anything he could do about it.

It was a typically steamy June day in Manila, capital of the Philippines. Occasional lightning crackled the sky, and bursts of rain pelted the windows. After dinner in his second-floor condo, the self-described "photographer by passion and heart, basketball enthusiast, loving father and husband, medical practitioner" retreated to his home office. To make ends meet, Ray worked two jobs. Besides being a full-time caregiver at a hospital, he was a self-employed photographer.

The office was cluttered with electronics, including his computer and Nintendo Wii and GameCube consoles; in his scant free time, Ray liked to relax by playing retro video games. He was planning to edit photos of the latest events he'd shot for clients, a "Wicked Wednesday" bash at a nightclub and a basketball camp and game. But when he tried, he couldn't retrieve the folders that stored his photos. He had lost access to his entire portfolio of hundreds of thousands of photos and videos he had taken since 2014.

"All of my photo documents from my desktop were corrupted, and I didn't know what to do," Ray recalled. "At that time I feel like I am gonna lose hope of recovering all my files."

Ray grew up in Manila. His mom is a biology teacher; his dad drives a three-wheeled bike taxi. When he was a high school senior, he didn't know what he wanted to do with his life. An aunt was a nurse, and his mother suggested he become one, too. So he majored in nursing at Jose Rizal University in Mandaluyong City.

After graduation, he took the national board exam for his nursing license. While awaiting the results, he happened to go to a birthday party where a friend was taking pictures with a Nikon camera. Ray was intrigued. He enrolled in a college photography course, and his mom bought him his first camera, a Nikon D5000.

He failed the nursing exam. Instead of becoming a licensed nurse, he took a job as a nurse's attendant at a public hospital, caring for adults and children, checking their vital signs, and changing babies' diapers. He liked helping people, but the job paid only minimum wage, so he decided to profit from his hobby. At night and on weekends, he began photographing all sorts of events: weddings, birthdays, baptisms, and basketball camps and tournaments. For a higher price he provided video, too. In the albums he prepared for clients, he often inscribed an apt biblical quotation. For a retirement party, he chose Proverbs 16:31: "Gray hair is a crown of glory; it is gained in a righteous life." Clients flocked to him, and soon Ray was earning more from his side business than from his day job.

Then, on that humid June night in 2019, Ray tried to download a video game without paying for it. Ironically, the game he was hoping to pirate featured a pirate avatar. "Sometimes being a pirate gives you some sort of karma," he said. In this case, the karma was bad. Not only were his files locked, but they were retitled with an unfamiliar extension, ".gerosan."

A note popped up on his screen: "All your files like photos, databases, documents and other important are encrypted with strongest encryption and unique key. The only method of recovering files is to purchase decrypt tool and unique key for you . . . Please note that you'll never restore your data without payment." The price was $980, more than Ray could afford. He tried to salvage the files by renaming them, but he couldn't.

Without his portfolio, Ray couldn't show his best work to prospective customers. Nor could he satisfy clients who needed to replace lost or damaged photos or wanted to order from his inventory.

"My world was shattered," Ray said. "I almost quit photography because of the stupid ransomware."

His wife, Mara Yan Orendez, told him to stop being hysterical. Not everything was lost. She had stored his irreplaceable, adorable photos of their curly-haired toddler, Maddie—whom Ray fondly calls "my favorite subject" and "my own personal kid model"—on her laptop.

And, Mara said, maybe somebody could help them. Calling the police, Ray thought, would be a waste of time, and he wasn't eager to tell them that he had pirated the software. Although his files were encrypted, he still had internet access. He googled until he came across BleepingComputer. There, he found a tool for cracking the .gerosan variant.

He clicked on the program, which instructed him to submit a sampling of encrypted files for analysis. It also spewed out the media access control (MAC) addresses associated with his computer. The series of numbers and letters meant nothing to Ray, but he sent them in a private Twitter message to the tool's creator, demonslay335.

"Sir, can you help me?" he pleaded. "I am from Manila, I was infected by the gerosan ransomware."

Less than four hours later, at 12:22 a.m. Manila time, Michael responded with a terse bulletin: "Got your key."

Ray's computer had been captured by STOPDjvu, the world's most prolific type of ransomware. While it has attracted little attention from antivirus companies, media outlets, or law enforcement, it has devastated hundreds of thousands of victims like Ray.

Of all the ransomware strains that the Ransomware Hunting Team has worked on, STOPDjvu was Michael's longest-running crusade. STOPDjvu cropped up in early 2018 and was soon wreaking havoc around the world. Michael's decryptor has been downloaded more than 2.5 million times, or more than a thousand times a day. In 2020 and 2021, files encrypted by STOPDjvu accounted for 80 percent of submissions to ID Ransomware and to Emsisoft. STOPDjvu so dominated the landscape that Emsisoft reported two sets of ransomware data—one that included STOPDjvu, and one that didn't.

STOPDjvu has more than 500 variants; Michael refers to the first 145 as "old STOPDjvu" and the rest as "new STOPDjvu." Old or new, they use similar ransom notes, and the email address that victims are asked to contact rarely changes. "I think it's always been the same group of attackers," Michael said.

With a business model based on a high volume of small payments, the group behind it demands a typical ransom of less than $1,000—well below the average ransom demand. Most of the victims are students or workers in Asia, South America, and Eastern Europe who, like Ray, accidentally infected their computers with STOPDjvu when they tried to pirate software. Often, they can't afford the ransom, and what they lose is crucial to their education or career—perhaps the only draft of a senior thesis or an engineering blueprint. But since they had intended to break the law themselves, they're unlikely to call the police, leaving law enforcement unaware of STOPDjvu's ubiquity. Because of STOPDjvu's low profile and small ransom amounts, stopping it is rarely a priority for police or cybersecurity firms, enabling the strain to spread unchecked. Once, Michael discovered the address of a STOPDjvu server and handed it to the FBI. "They didn't do anything," he said.

Michael didn't pay much attention to the very first variants of STOPDjvu. But when it "started blowing up on BleepingComputer," he said, he became "the only guy in the world working STOP." As the STOPDjvu panic peaked in mid-2019, he was besieged by twenty to fifty private Twitter messages a day from desperate victims like Ray Orendez. Others implored him on BleepingComputer to retrieve their theses, databases, or family photos.

Their ceaseless begging wearied him, and their carelessness in not backing up their files frustrated him. Someone in India, the country most often hit by STOPDjvu, tried to reach him by friending Morgan on Facebook. She was "freaked out," Michael said. "I called his ass out and blocked him."

Still, Michael dropped everything to help STOPDjvu victims. Even in the middle of dinner, if someone sent him the information he needed, such as a MAC address, he would jump up (much to Morgan's dismay), run to his computer, and plug in the data. Undoubtedly, he felt a grudging empathy for his legions of supplicants. Like them, he was living paycheck to paycheck; he couldn't have paid STOPDjvu's relatively small ransom, either. "They literally don't have the four hundred dollars, which I can relate to," he said.

As a teen, he, too, had pirated products that he couldn't afford to buy, like the Adobe Photoshop software that he taught during his days as a website moderator offering tutorials on graphic design. "I was smart about it," he said. "I didn't click on the first link I found."

Morgan once wrote a Facebook post praising "Michael's amazing computer skill and his ability to get any tv show/movie/book/music that I could ever have asked for." She added, "Like for real we've probably saved a million dollars."

In the battle against STOPDjvu, Michael wasn't completely on his own. Fellow Ransomware Hunting Team member Karsten Hahn also pitched in. He contributes to the team by finding and analyzing new types of ransomware, primarily through the VirusTotal database. Karsten was the first to identify about 70 percent of the known STOP-Djvu variants, and notified Michael whenever he did so.

Karsten, who is transgender, grew up in Soviet-controlled East Germany, near the Polish border, dreaming of being a superhero. As a child, Karsten loved to wear a Batman costume his mother had made. But when he wore the costume on a trip to the supermarket and attempted to rescue other kids, pretending that they were being attacked by gangsters, his mother was embarrassed. "She forbade me to wear the suit," he said.

Karsten's mother was a doctor; his father, an official in the Stasi, the East German secret police. After German reunification, the Stasi was disbanded, and its brutal reputation left Karsten's father with few job options. He worked in a warehouse and farmed Christmas trees.

When Karsten was eight, his parents divorced. Karsten later lived with his mother and her boyfriend, who was emotionally and verbally abusive to the teenager. "He made me doubt myself and my abilities all the time," Karsten said. "I felt stupid and worthless." Karsten suffered panic attacks and underwent years of psychotherapy.

"I always was into computers," Karsten said, but his mother and her boyfriend discouraged the interest. "I always got told, more or less, that girls don't do computers." Initially passing up college, he became a kindergarten teacher, but he wasn't cut out for it. "What you need to do that job is divided attention, and I am very focused in everything I do," he said.

Summoning his courage, he told his mother that he wanted to study computer science at a university. She acquiesced. "All of my kids are allowed to change their career direction once," she told him, offering financial support. At the Leipzig University of Applied Sciences, his master's thesis on malware analysis won a €1,000 prize in 2015 as the best computer science thesis in Germany. He started his own YouTube channel teaching malware analysis. Sarah White watched it and was so impressed that she nominated Karsten to join the Ransomware Hunting Team. One of the few members with a graduate degree, Karsten joined the team because its services are free. "That mindset is what appeals to me. If they would charge for that, I would not help them."

When he came out as transgender in 2016, Karsten was married and had a three-year-old son. "My mother cried for two years at least. For her, it was like her daughter was dying. My husband, he said he felt the same, like I am dying." They divorced, and Karsten became a single parent. He asked his employer if he could work from home so that he could drop off and pick up his son from school. The company, a German cybersecurity firm, didn't respond immediately. In the meantime, he explained his plight to Fabian, who offered him a job working remotely for Emsisoft at a higher salary. In the end, Karsten stayed at the German company after it adjusted his hours to accommodate him.

Like Michael, Karsten has seen his share of hard times, and he empathizes with STOPDjvu victims. He said they're unjustly blamed because they were trying to pirate software when they were attacked. "You have a prejudice against those people who do that, so you tend not to help them," he said. "But which people do that? Those are the poor people who cannot afford the software. Sometimes downloading an illegal program may be your only way out of poverty."

As Karsten identified STOPDjvu variants, Michael set out to reverse engineer them. He analyzes ransomware strains with the patience and skill of a doctor diagnosing a mysterious ailment. His examining table is his virtual machine, and the infected systems are his patients. Their symptoms: a ransom note, unfamiliar file names, and jumbled and seemingly random text. His tools, the equivalent of MRIs or CT scans, are software programs that help him see through the outer layers protecting the ransomware and into its underlying structure.

If the cryptography is solid, the ransomware is almost unassailable. Fortunately for the Ransomware Hunting Team, attackers sometimes make mistakes. That's because getting the cryptography right isn't their only priority. They also want encryption to be fast and unobtrusive, so that victims don't notice and thus don't block the ransomware while it's in the process of invading their computers. As a result, the attackers cut corners, writing their software code in a small number of bytes so it can encrypt a user's file faster. Or they neglect to erase a key from the host computer's memory, leaving it accessible until the machine is shut down.

Typically, ransomware alters the extensions at the end of the file name. It goes on to encrypt the files themselves, generally using a cipher, which is a type of algorithm with a set of instructions for changing one sequence of characters into another. A simple Caesar cipher, for example, replaces each letter in the text with another letter that is a given number of spaces later in the alphabet: an A may become a D, a B an E, and so on.

Ransomware gangs generally rely on either of two types of ciphers. In a "stream cipher," the key yields an ongoing stream of numbers that transform all of the text. A "block cipher" divides text into segments of equal length and encrypts them in different but related ways. Either way, an algorithm contained in the ransomware code performs a mathematical operation that combines the key with the original data to create an encrypted file.

Because the new file name or extension often serves as a kind of gang signature, it can help Michael figure out who he's dealing with. But his main focus is trying to recover the text. One of his first steps is to take the ransomware code itself, which Karsten or MalwareHunter-Team often unearth on VirusTotal, and run it on what are known as bait files. These files are designed to attract malware, but Michael uses them for a different purpose. Before being infected, they contain lots of zeros, making it easier for Michael to see how the encryption changes the numbers. A program called a hex editor represents that change more dramatically by transforming the binary code—zeros and ones—into a wider variety of numbers and letters. With the help of the hex editor, he can test the ransomware on bait files of different lengths to see if it encrypts them all in the same pattern, which could indicate that the attacker reused the same key for multiple files—a potential vulnerability.

When he comes across a new strain, he applies another program, CryptoTester, which checks how closely it matches known ransomware algorithms. Michael invented CryptoTester—and, with his usual disregard for personal gain, makes it available for free.

Opening another window on his machine, he takes a close look at the ransomware itself. Using "decompilers" and "disassemblers," Michael translates the ransomware into programming languages that "de-obfuscate"—one of his favorite verbs—various parts of its code. With skill and a certain amount of serendipity, he can learn how the decryption key is created, and whether and how it can be cracked.

"Let's try that magic trick again," he says, brightening as he moves closer to solving these puzzles.

The cryptography hiding the keys has evolved greatly since the AIDS Trojan. Joe Popp wouldn't recognize it. Popp used a basic form of what's known as symmetric encryption, in which the same secret key is used to lock and unlock the files. Conceptually, symmetric encryption is no different from the ciphers employed by spies for centuries to encode and decode messages, although the keys are more complex. The Nazis' Enigma code, which the British famously broke in World War II, relied on symmetric encryption.

The 1970s saw a major advance in cryptography—asymmetric encryption. This approach relies on a pair of mathematically related keys. Typically, a "public key," which is accessible to any observer, encrypts the files—but it does not unlock them. Only a different "private key" can do that. It's connected mathematically to the public key but is known only to its creator, and isn't necessarily kept in a server or even online.

The best-known asymmetric code is RSA, named after computer scientists Ron Rivest, Adi Shamir, and Leonard Adleman. Adleman won the prestigious Turing Prize, often referred to as the Nobel Prize of computer science, for developing the RSA algorithm, which makes clever use of prime numbers. In the early 1980s, "hybrid encryption" was created, adding another level of protection by combining symmetric and asymmetric encryption.

With the exception of the AIDS Trojan, though, all these cryptographic methods remained purely defensive. They were designed to shield national security communications, financial records, and other valuable information from enemies and thieves, and to ensure that the data was authentic. Then, at a 1996 conference, two Columbia University researchers, Adam Young and Moti Yung, presented a seminal paper showing how to use hybrid encryption for extortion.

Their idea was ingenious. Under their model, a hacker can infiltrate a computer and use a symmetric key to encrypt the victim's files—anyone who knew the key could later decrypt the files. The symmetric key, however, is formidably protected: it is randomly generated and presumably difficult to crack; it is also safeguarded a second time when it's encrypted by a public key embedded in the ransomware program. After a ransom is paid, the attacker uses the private key to decrypt the symmetric key, which in turn decrypts the files.

This hybrid approach has a clear advantage for hackers. Symmetric encryption is hundreds or thousands of times faster than asymmetric encryption. But because it encrypts and decrypts with the same key, symmetric encryption also tends to be more vulnerable. The Young-Yung hybrid model seemed to offer a desirable combination: the speed of symmetric encryption and the protection of asymmetric.

Intended to alert society to a potential criminal threat, their paper was a blueprint for ransomware attacks. It was dismissed by academics as "simultaneously innovative and somewhat vulgar," Young and Yung later wrote. But just as dynamite, originally meant for mining and construction, was soon applied to making bombs, so cryptography would be put to destructive purposes. With the arrival of digital currency—which, remarkably, Young and Yung also predicted—hackers could better deter tracking of ransom payments. Now Young and Yung's academic concept began menacing people and companies worldwide.

"We have observed that what we described over 20 years ago is the exact 'business model' used today in . . . the industry of ransomware," Young and Yung wrote in 2017.

Still, that model was not foolproof. Despite its multiple layers, hybrid encryption is only as secure as its symmetric key. The most common weakness that the Ransomware Hunting Team exploits is the attackers' faulty application of a standard cryptographic practice: using random numbers as symmetric keys.

If a key is a random and sufficiently large number, it can't be cracked. But it has to be very random—and very large. Half a century ago, a random symmetric key with 2^{56} zeros and ones was safe; no computer could process so many numbers in a reasonable amount of time. With today's supercomputers, a key needs at least 2^{128} binary numbers. A smaller key can be brute-forced by testing each possibility in turn. (Think of a car odometer with zeros across the screen, and flipping the numbers in order, starting with the farthest right, from zero to one.) Researchers sometimes employ multiple computers to brute-force a key, with each checking a different chunk of possibilities.

The hackers sometimes make the team's task easier by encrypting files with keys that aren't random. Because computers are deterministic machines, designed to leave nothing to chance, generating random numbers can be more challenging than it sounds. One method makes use of lava lamps by taking pictures of the heated wax bubbling inside the glass container and translating the seemingly chaotic movements into numbers.

Because lava lamps don't produce enough data on their own, the random numbers they generate are most effective as a starting point for what is called a pseudorandom number generator. These algorithms use an initial value, or "seed," to spawn a huge—but ultimately repetitive—sequence of numbers. Like blackjack dealers using multiple decks to prevent gamblers from gaining an advantage by counting cards, the ransomware developers hope that the sea of numbers spat out by their generator is vast and unpatterned enough to stymie code crackers. Sometimes it is. Some operating systems, including Windows, contain a built-in function to generate pseudorandom numbers that today's computers can't crack.

But sometimes the seed is predictable. One popular seed is the current time, measured in the number of seconds that have elapsed since January 1, 1970—a concept known as Unix time. By guessing that the attackers used the time method, hunters narrow the universe of possible seeds and random numbers to crack the code. It's just one of the ways that the hackers, despite the formidable arsenal of techniques at their disposal, fail to protect their keys.

Over and over, Michael probed STOPDjvu for weaknesses. As more "ridiculously desperate" victims inundated him, the strain consumed an ever-larger share of his waking hours, both at home and at work. "Only this strain, never had this with any other ransomware, ever," he said.

One vulnerability of STOPDjvu's symmetric encryption was its use of what's known as an offline key. Worried about protecting their encryption key, since it could also be used to decrypt files, the attackers didn't put it in the ransomware that initially infiltrated a target. Instead, when the ransomware was ready to encrypt the data, it notified the attacker's server over the internet to send the key. Sometimes, though, the ransomware was temporarily cut off from the internet—because the computer's antivirus software blocked the connection, the attacker was in the midst of switching servers, or there was just a glitch. In those cases, the malware defaulted to an offline key already embedded in the code. But, like a spare house key left under the front doormat, the offline key was far less secure.

Michael found a pattern in STOPDjvu's coding that indicated which files had been encrypted by an offline key while the ransomware was cut off from the internet. From there, extracting the key was easy. And while STOPDjvu created a unique online key for every computer it hit, it created only one offline key per variant. Sometimes multiple variants shared the same offline key. Each offline key that Michael retrieved could restore access for many victims.

Next, Michael devised an ingenious scheme to trick STOPDjvu's servers into giving him the online key. It started with a curious discovery: STOPDjvu, almost alone among ransomware strains, used the victim's MAC address to help generate the key. Since every item of hardware attached to a network has its own MAC address, STOPDjvu's creators could use that address to identify which key belonged to each of its many victims. When it was ready to encrypt, the ransomware program would send the victim's MAC address to the attacker's server, and receive the key in return.

This gave Michael an idea. If the ransomware program could use the MAC address to obtain the key from the server, why couldn't he? To hide his identity, he would make the request anonymously over Tor, a dark web browser. The server would mistake him for the ransomware seeking to encrypt more files and send him the key. Since STOPDjvu's cipher is symmetric, the key that the server expected to encode the files could also unscramble them.

Michael built a tool that automatically extracted MAC addresses from the victims' computers, as well as a bot that contacted the servers' URLs—which he had pulled from the malware—and harvested the keys. The servers weren't programmed to flag this activity as suspicious, and unlike humans with limited patience, they didn't get tired of repeated demands. Some victims had several MAC addresses, and the bot tried each in turn to see which of them would elicit the key.

One difficulty was that the attackers often covered their tracks by changing their servers' URLs and domain names. As a result, the server addresses that the bot contacted were sometimes outdated, and its requests bounced back. Michael had to act fast to plug the MAC address into the bot while it could still reach the server. "I had to hit that server real quick before they shut it down," he said. Sometimes he was too late. A victim would send him six addresses, and he wouldn't have time to try them all before the server switched directories. Still, in six months, what he called a "fun escapade" saved 375 people—including Ray Orendez—from paying ransoms.

Ray benefited from a fluke of timing. Only eight days earlier, Michael had updated the tool to grab the victim's MAC address. For Ray's computer, the tool identified five addresses. That Thursday morning at Nerds on Call, Michael popped them into the bot. It duped the server and obtained the online key, which Michael sent to Ray.

Ray still couldn't open some of his files. On Friday evening Manila time, he emailed Michael: "Sir, the password and ID didn't work."

Michael guessed that the dysfunctional files required an offline key, probably because the ransomware had temporarily lost contact with the server during the encryption. Just that week, by another fortuitous coincidence, Michael had unearthed the offline key for the variant that locked Ray's computer. The .gerosan extension on Ray's files signified that they had been disabled by version 101 of old STOPDjvu.

"Any files skipped were encrypted by the offline key," Michael replied. "I released the update yesterday."

"Got it sir, thanks so much for the help," Ray replied.

If there was no offline key, and the MAC address wasn't submitted to the server soon enough, Michael had a third option, one that capitalized on STOPDjvu's biggest flaw. By employing the same key to encrypt all of a computer's files, STOPDjvu violated what Ransomware

Hunting Team member Sarah White, in her 2019 talk titled "Pouring Salt into the Crypto Wound: How Not to Be as Stupid as Ransomware Authors," described as the "golden rule" of stream ciphers: "Never reuse a key!"

For this third method to work, victims had to supply Michael with only one "file pair," the original and the encrypted version of the same file. Although they had not backed up their systems—otherwise, they wouldn't need his help—many victims happened to have a clean copy of one of the corrupted files in their email or on their phone. Applying the logic-based operation "exclusive or," Michael could then compare the two files and derive the encryption key. Since STOPDjvu was symmetric, that key would also unlock the infected file. And since STOPDjvu broke Sarah's golden rule by using the same key to encrypt other data on the computer, that key would unlock all those files, even without the originals.

"People would say, 'All my data is encrypted,'" Michael recalled. "I'd say, 'I don't need all the backup, just one good before and after to break the rest of it.'"

In October 2019, he created a self-help portal that retrieved the key automatically when a victim uploaded a file pair. Reducing the constant demands from STOPDjvu victims freed him up to crack other ransomware strains.

Inevitably, as victims stopped paying, STOPDjvu's creators would realize that yet another variant had been cracked. They finally replaced the symmetric encryption used for "old STOPDjvu" with hybrid encryption—both symmetric and asymmetric. They used a stream cipher called Salsa20 to encrypt the files, and RSA, which is asymmetric, to encrypt the Salsa20 key. Today, Michael said, "ninety-nine percent of ransomware uses RSA in some way."

RSA's security relies on a mathematical conundrum. While any decent calculator can multiply prime numbers, even very big ones, no one has found a shortcut to doing the opposite: taking a large number and factoring it into its constituent primes. It's easy to factor 35 into the primes 7 and 5. But there's no simple way to figure out that 1,034,776, 851,837,418,228,051,242,693,253,376,923 equals 1,086,027,579,223, 696,553 times 952,809,000,096,560,291.

RSA's public key is a semiprime—the product of two prime numbers. Michael can find the public key. But he needs to know its two factors to calculate the private key. Unfortunately, STOPDjvu used RSA to generate prime numbers so enormous that when they were multiplied together, even the most powerful contemporary computers couldn't factor the product within a lifetime. Now, when Michael tricked the STOPDjvu server into sending him the key that was used to encrypt the files, he couldn't use that same key to unlock them. The "file pair" method no longer worked, either.

Only one flaw remained. Each STOPDjvu variant still relied on one default key when the target computer lost touch with the server. Because that key was generated by RSA, Michael could no longer retrieve it. But when someone who paid the ransom and received an offline key in return sent it to him, he could use it to rescue other victims of the same type of STOPDjvu.

"Even with new Djvu, if it's offline, the victim has hope," Michael said.

Through the methods he discovered—exploiting the offline key, confusing the attacker's server, comparing the file pairs—Michael had helped legions of STOPDjvu victims. Not all of them learned from their mistakes. Even after being burned by old STOPDjvu, they still pirated software and didn't save copies of their files. Several people whom he had bailed out were hit by new STOPDjvu or other strains, and they became upset when he explained that he could no longer help them because the ransomware had become more sophisticated. Michael brooded over their ingratitude. "Really peeves me when I've saved a victim from ransomware, and a year later they come to me with another one that's not decryptable," he said.

Ray Orendez was different. He knew he had gotten lucky, and he didn't want to tempt fate a second time. He stopped pirating software, and he announced on his Facebook page to prospective customers, "Pictures are stored in a flash drive."

During the pandemic, Ray put his business on hold, because the types of events and celebrations he photographed were canceled. He cared for patients with COVID-19 at his hospital job and contracted the disease himself; fortunately, his symptoms were mild. "This past two years was a hard-fought fight for us in the medical field," he said in 2021.

He remained thankful for his deliverance from STOPDjvu. "[Without Michael,] all of my photo portfolio in my desktop will be gone to waste because of that stupid virus," he said. "I am surprised he didn't charge me anything."

7.

RYUK REIGNS

W hile STOPDjvu plundered students and workers across much of the world, another gang was dramatically ramping up the threat of ransomware, crippling much bigger targets and demanding much larger sums. Based in Russia, this group—known as Ryuk—emerged in August 2018, six months after STOPDjvu.

Ryuk was in the vanguard of a ransomware revolution. It was one of the first gangs to routinely demand six-figure payments and to carefully select and research its targets. With Ryuk showing the way, ransomware groups realized that it was easier and more efficient to make $1 million by disabling one business with a thousand computers than by demanding $1,000 apiece from a thousand people with one computer each. Some gangs multiplied their destructive impact by targeting companies known as managed service providers, which handle IT for dozens of clients such as medical offices or local governments. The average ransom payment skyrocketed from less than $6,000 in the third quarter of 2018, when Ryuk arrived on the scene, to more than $230,000 two years later. "Ryuk continued to set records with ransom demands that are an order of magnitude larger than other types of ransomware," the ransom negotiation firm Coveware reported in April 2019. It was also one of the most active gangs, accounting for more than 20 percent of all ransomware attacks, excluding STOPDjvu, throughout 2019.

Ryuk targeted organizations with high revenues, weak cybersecurity, and an urgent need to resume operations. Just as STOPDjvu was attacking more home computer users than any other strain, so Ryuk devastated corporations, nonprofit groups, schools, and critical infrastructure, especially health care. One victim was the DCH Regional Medical Center, the only full-service hospital in Tuscaloosa, Alabama.

The water oaks lining its streets led Tuscaloosa to be nicknamed the "Druid City," after the pagan priests who worshipped the stately shade tree. Established with community funding in 1923 as Druid City Hospital (DCH), the 583-bed medical center is located just east of the University of Alabama's flagship campus. It features cancer and trauma centers and offers robotic surgery. "Every drunk university student comes through our doors, every little old lady comes through our doors," said Lisa Marie Cargile, a former nursing team leader there. It's also the hub of the DCH Health System, which includes a smaller hospital across the Black Warrior River in Northport and a hospital and nursing home in Fayette, thirty-five miles northwest.

Early on the morning of October 1, 2019, three months after STOPDjvu encrypted Ray Orendez's files, a ransomware attack froze computer service throughout the three DCH hospitals. Quickly recognizing the scale of the threat, DCH leaders declared an internal disaster. To contain the attack, DCH shut down most servers and virtual private network (VPN) connections. At an emergency 8:00 a.m. meeting, administrators canceled all nonessential events and assigned ancillary staff to support critical areas. The hospital notified the FBI and Secret Service, and Secret Service agents showed up that day.

DCH announced on its website that same morning that, "in the best interest of patient safety," it was closing the three hospitals to "all but the most critical new patients" and diverting local ambulances to other facilities. People scheduled for outpatient appointments or tests were instructed to call ahead. Those showing up for emergency care might be transferred to another hospital after being stabilized.

The hospital explained the reason for these drastic moves in language uncharacteristically direct for an institution that might still have to negotiate with its assailants: "The three hospitals of the DCH Health System have experienced a ransomware attack. A criminal is limiting our ability to use our computer systems in exchange for an as-yet-unknown payment."

At 2:22 p.m., the emergency preparedness coordinator for the Alabama Department of Public Health alerted three other hospitals, a nursing home, and an emergency management agency in the region to be ready to take DCH patients. "The 3 DCH system facilities are on diversion at the current time due to a ransomware attack," he wrote. "We need ALL hospitals in the district to update their current bed status since ill or injured people may be redirected to their facilities."

The DCH hospitals weren't the first in Alabama to be stricken by ransomware. Three months earlier, an attack had knocked out computer systems at Springhill Medical Center in Mobile, Alabama, including monitors at the nurses' station that displayed patients' vital signs. The hospital told the media that it had experienced a "network event" that "has not affected patient care." Actually, the attack eliminated vital protections, including electronic equipment at the nurses' station that monitored fetal heartbeats in the delivery rooms.

When Teiranni Kidd was admitted to Springhill on July 16, 2019, she wasn't told about the hack. The next day, when she was about to give birth, only a printout from a fetal heart monitor by her bedside showed that the fetus was in distress. That warning allegedly didn't reach the attending obstetrician; if it had, she could have delivered the baby by cesarean section.

"Fetal tracing information was not accessible at the nurses' station or by any physician or other healthcare provider who was not physically present in Teiranni's labor and delivery room," according to Kidd's subsequent lawsuit.

Kidd's daughter, Nicko Silar, was born severely brain damaged, and died in April 2020. Hers was the first death linked to ransomware. Springhill denied wrongdoing and said it stayed open after the ransomware attack "because the patients needed us and we . . . concluded it was safe to do so." The hospital has not identified the attacker, though *The Wall Street Journal* reported it was likely Ryuk.

Deprived of patient histories and other digital records, the DCH hospitals likewise floundered. Cancer patients couldn't receive radiation treatments for three days. Some surgeries and pain management procedures were postponed. In the nine days following the attack, from October 1 to October 10, 2019, ambulances were diverted to other facilities 237 times. The average number of patients seen daily in the emergency department compared to September dropped precipitously across all three hospitals.

Nurses struggled to verify that they were giving patients the right medicines in the correct dosage, without conflicting with or duplicating the drugs they were already taking. "It was hell," said Cargile, who was home on medical leave but in constant touch with her team. "Most of the younger nurses, anybody who had been a nurse less than ten years, had never done any paper charting at all. They were overwhelmed to say the least. My coworkers were being told it would take four to six months to get a new system up running and organized. In my opinion, paying the ransom was the only option the hospital truly had."

It didn't take long to identify the culprit. "Investigators have determined," DCH announced on October 2, "that the ransomware variant Ryuk was used to encrypt the files."

The name Ryuk refers to a demon character in a popular Japanese anime comic series. Its code was similar to an earlier strain, Hermes, which was linked to North Korea. A Russian group is said to have purchased the Hermes code on the dark web and refined it. For example, unlike Hermes, Ryuk didn't encrypt entire files, just enough to make them unusable, so it could save time and avoid detection. It also added the file extension ".ryk."

By May 2019, Ryuk had targeted more than a hundred U.S. and international organizations, primarily logistics and technology companies and small cities, prompting warnings from the FBI and the UK's National Cyber Security Centre. It didn't even exempt its own base of operations, Russia, which ranked as its sixth most frequent target worldwide in 2019. Ryuk dramatically reduced attacks in Russia in 2020, possibly because it was seeking or receiving the Putin regime's protection. In July of that year, a leader of the criminal organization that included Ryuk messaged a colleague about establishing an office "for government topics."

Payments to Ryuk were well above the average for all ransomware throughout 2019 and 2020. Its rule of thumb was that companies should surrender a tithe—or *desyatina* in Russian—of 10 percent of their revenue, a significant price but seldom enough to bankrupt them. Some businesses that paid couldn't recover their files because the decryptor supplied by Ryuk was flawed.

Initially, Ryuk specified its monetary demand in the ransom note. Later, it discontinued that practice, instead telling victims to contact an email address. It used five email providers, including ProtonMail, the secure Swiss service. When ProtonMail shut down Ryuk's network of twenty thousand accounts in October 2020, the gang switched to other platforms and to private chats over a portal. Although Ryuk sometimes bargained with victims, its replies were invariably terse— often fewer than ten words, or just a dollar figure.

Colder and more ruthless than other gangs, it spurned jokes and conversation. Only on a rare occasion did Ryuk stray from its usual brevity to explain why it was hammering Western businesses. "À la guerre comme à la guerre," it wrote to a victim, quoting a seventeenth-century French idiomatic expression: in times of hardship, make the best of what you have. The phrase is also the title of a 1920 essay by Vladimir Lenin, urging a war on poverty, hunger, and disease.

Michael first encountered Ryuk when someone uploaded to ID Ransomware a file encrypted by an unfamiliar strain that had just struck three large corporations, including two in the United States. The gang was demanding six-figure payments. He and the Ransomware Hunting Team immediately recognized that they were up against a dangerous adversary. Over the ensuing months, and in spite of glimmers of hope, Ryuk would become their white whale. As other big, profitable strains came and went, Ryuk remained a powerhouse, its frequent and damaging attacks reminding team members of the limits of their effectiveness.

Fabian actually had a head start. He had cracked the first version of Ryuk's North Korean precursor, Hermes. After Karsten Hahn came across Hermes in February 2017, Fabian decided to analyze it in a live-stream session. As he pored over the code and talked viewers through his analysis, he found a flaw. Not for the first time, the random numbers that the ransomware supposedly generated weren't random enough, so it was possible to brute-force the key. Michael wrote a decryptor based on Fabian's work.

Perhaps Hermes's developers were watching, too. They strengthened their random number generation in the next version. But Fabian found a slipup there: it was using the same key for multiple victims.

That same problem persisted once the Russians refashioned Hermes into Ryuk. In a small number of cases, when someone paid the ransom and received a key, the team could use it to unlock the files of other victims so they didn't need to pay. Word also reached the team that the FBI had independently discovered the same vulnerability. But Ryuk soon identified the flaw and began sending a different key to each paying victim.

As the team continued to track Ryuk, Fabian noticed that it appeared to have spun off a small renegade group. The team heard from about half a dozen victims of this offshoot. "Cowboy Ryuk," as Fabian christened it, was "completely unhinged," the opposite of the tight-lipped professional foe they had come to know. It spewed insults and profanity, destroyed files, and stole sensitive data, which it published even if a ransom had been paid. Cowboy Ryuk was easy for the team to spot because it used an older version of Ryuk's code, along with its own ransom notes and file extensions. Its cryptography was sophisticated but sloppy, as if it didn't care whether the keys that it sent to paying victims worked or not, and it lasted only a brief time.

Ryuk's emergence reflected another development that escalated the ransomware threat. Besides attacking big targets for big money, it was part of a larger criminal enterprise. A single organization deployed not only Ryuk but also two notorious types of malware, TrickBot and Emotet, which were originally known as "banking Trojans" because they were developed to penetrate financial accounts. Under its quasi-corporate chain of command, workers were hired for various tasks—from human resources to writing code to developing phishing emails—based on their skills. The TrickBot-Emotet-Ryuk organization had about four hundred online user names, but the actual number of members was considerably smaller, as some went by multiple aliases. About half of the names belonged to the Ryuk subgroup.

TrickBot and Emotet conducted preliminary research to help the gang craft phishing emails that targets would click on. Then they infiltrated computers in people's homes, businesses, and government offices either via the phishing emails or via Remote Desktop Services (the Windows component that allows users to access other computers), and gained administrative credentials. In this way, they created a worldwide botnet of millions of infected computers.

TrickBot and Emotet prowled unnoticed inside these systems, looking for damaging information to steal. Through paid accounts with business research services like ZoomInfo and Owler, they gathered data on their targets' revenues to determine whether to launch a ransomware attack and how high to set the demand. Once the espionage was complete, they unloaded their Ryuk payload, usually in the middle of the night in the victim's time zone so that the ransomware could spread more widely before detection. The code carried instructions to delete or encrypt backup systems and to disable antivirus protections.

Deep within the recesses of the dark web, the gang monitored and directed its ongoing campaigns on secret control panels. Updated daily by the cybercriminals, the panels listed targets ranging from a police department in Texas to an urban school district in California, including their IP addresses, the number of devices connected to their networks, their passwords, the email addresses of affected users, and the purpose of the campaign—for example, to steal data or collect a ransom. Green, yellow, and red traffic lights indicated the status of the attack. Next to many entries were comments, such as *razbor*, a Russian word meaning "examining." Another comment, "crypt," meant that the victim was already or about to be encrypted by the ransomware strain for which TrickBot provided a gateway. Usually, it was Ryuk.

Alex Holden, a Russian-speaking native of Ukraine who founded Hold Security in Milwaukee, Wisconsin, turned the tables on Trick-Bot. To avert attacks on corporate clients, he and his thirty analysts in the United States and Central Europe infiltrated the organization like human malware. Posing as fellow hackers, choosing from more than three thousand false identities with invented criminal histories, they gained access to the control panels. They also conversed with members of the gang and learned how they operated.

"A lot of cybercriminals are lonely," Holden said. "They want to talk to someone who understands."

Most of his analysts were women, but they pretended to be male, the gender of most people working for TrickBot, Emotet, and Ryuk. "It is about building a kinship," Holden said. A software program checked their Russian-language messages to make sure that the word endings had the right gender, to avoid accidental slipups.

While probing for information, analysts appealed to the hackers' senses of smell, touch, or taste. "These sensors will signal 'truth' to your brain," Holden said. For example: "I am sitting right now at a kitchen table, but I can't concentrate. I had too much vodka last night, my head is heavy, my mouth feels like an ashtray from cheap smokes. My wife is yelling, and my kids are running around. All I want is to sleep but I need to get this access. Or some more vodka."

Sometimes, the analysts were so convincing that Ryuk asked them to collaborate on attacks. They demurred, on the pretext that their services were in great demand and they were too busy committing other cybercrimes.

Like other ransomware operations, Ryuk in some cases delegated responsibilities and risks to affiliates. But it kept more of the ransom money than the developer's customary fifth or third. One group of cybercriminals broke into an insurance company in Nevada and began "exploring options with ransomware," Holden said. When Ryuk asked for half of the profits, the gang grumbled that Ryuk was extorting them as well as the company but went ahead anyway.

One of the few data points missing from the control panels was whether the victim had cyber insurance. But the crooks were well aware that insurance payouts supplied a hefty share of their profits. "There's a running joke in the Ryuk gang," Holden said. "The ransom note should include the option 'Bill my insurance.'"

Victims who paid the ransom were regarded as valued customers. The gang wanted to fulfill its side of the bargain and was distressed by the glitches in the keys that it sent. Once, Ryuk's boss notified his contacts that he had good and bad news. The bad news: Ryuk's decryptor had a potential bug. The good news: The gang was rolling out a new tool anyway. His tone reminded Holden of a CEO reluctantly acknowledging a product defect.

Like any legitimate corporation striving to compete in a crowded market, the Trickbot-Emotet-Ryuk organization was always looking to expand. In August 2020, Ryuk began collaborating with another Russia-based ransomware gang, Conti. As it collected hundreds of millions of dollars from victims, Conti paid commissions to a Trick-Bot boss named "Stern."

Conti displayed a sophisticated understanding of the gaps in U.S. law enforcement's approach to ransomware. "With the public and private sector, everything is very decentralized, and now they are trying to change this, but so far without success," one Conti member wrote to another. "In the event of an attack, in theory, it is necessary to appeal to the government, but it is not entirely clear to whom." The hacker then described the roles of the FBI and the Department of Homeland Security as well as local police departments.

The partnership was fruitful, as Conti launched a series of lucrative attacks under the TrickBot umbrella. TrickBot's managers plowed profits back into the business. Between April and August 2021, TrickBot reinvested $25 million, acquiring physical office space and hardware and hiring more workers, Holden said. Its managers discussed whom to attack, and how to improve efficiency and maximize revenues. "It is necessary to press harder, bother with calls, annoy partners, cover in the media," Stern's assistant, Mango, wrote to him in 2021.

"I propose to organize the work in such a way that by the time of the lock we have a full report on the analysis: top management, contacts, their personal data, what we will find, partners, their contacts and, most importantly, a strategy for how to press, what is permissible for which targets . . . We just need to put ransoms more realistically and stand firm."

Vitali Kremez, one of Michael's frequent collaborators, was preoccupied with Ryuk. He analyzed the malware and, like Alex Holden, burrowed into the gang's structure and finances.

Vitali grew up in Belarus. After dropping out of college, he immigrated to the United States, where he worked construction jobs and played guitar in bars before joining the Manhattan district attorney's office as a cyber analyst. He next joined Flashpoint, a New York–based firm that specialized in investigating cybercrime. Vitali scrutinized malware and eavesdropped on conversations in hacker forums to connect the dots between cyberattacks and the gangs behind them.

Vitali met Michael on Twitter, and they began working together in 2019 on the GetCrypt strain of ransomware. Armed with Vitali's research, Michael brute-forced the strain and wrote a decryptor. Their skills were complementary. "I'll dissect and analyze how the malware evades detection and what services it targets," Vitali said. "He was more niche focused on the cryptography."

Later in 2019, Vitali left Flashpoint for a rival company, Sentinel. He then led his own boutique firm, AdvIntel. At Lawrence's invitation, and with other members' approval, he joined the Ransomware Hunting Team in March 2020.

For Vitali, the TrickBot-Emotet-Ryuk nexus posed the ultimate challenge. He and another researcher traced sixty-one Bitcoin wallets where Ryuk was believed to deposit profits. They found that the gang, through an intermediary, cashed out most of its Bitcoin on two exchanges in Asia. Another significant chunk of its loot flowed through a laundering service that exchanged it for local currency or another digital currency.

After years of studying Ryuk, Vitali noted that one conclusion was "painfully clear": "The criminals behind Ryuk are very business-like and have zero sympathy for the status, purpose, or ability of the victims to pay."

Stumped by Ryuk, the FBI sent victims to the Ransomware Hunting Team. When Ryuk attacked OrthoVirginia in early 2021, Terri Ripley, chief information officer for the orthopedic care provider, called an FBI cyber agent in Richmond. The agent asked whether the organization had good backups. She said no; the backups were infected, too.

After they hung up, the agent emailed her with a referral—the FBI had little else to offer. "Not sure if you checked, but there is a third party providing the ability to check for [decryptors] of Ryuk," he wrote, sharing a link to ID Ransomware. "If you see a message, 'this ransomware may be decryptable under certain circumstances . . .' it should point you to a [contact] who may be able to assist with decryption."

Terri's team formally logged the attack with the FBI's Internet Crime Complaint Center. OrthoVirginia's CEO, she said, "called the FBI every day at lunchtime. There was no help, nothing they could do. Just 'We have your information, we'll reach out.'"

Once OrthoVirginia learned that Ryuk's ransomware was unbreakable, it began negotiating with the hackers. But, despite its encrypted backups, it ultimately chose to rebuild its system rather than pay the ransom.

■ ■ ■

Like OrthoVirginia, DCH found itself at a dead end. On October 5, 2019, the hospital system surrendered. "We worked with law enforcement and IT security experts to assess all options and execute the solution that was best for our patients," it announced. "This included purchasing an encryption key from the attacker to expedite system recovery and help ensure public safety." The amount of the payment was not disclosed, but a demand in the mid–six figures would have been typical of Ryuk at the time.

Five days later, DCH resumed normal operations. But it wasn't done paying for the attack. DCH faced further financial demands from its own patients, in the form of a new type of lawsuit targeting hospitals victimized by ransomware attacks.

Lawsuits over data breaches have been common for years. But it was often hard to prove that people were injured financially or otherwise by the theft of their information. As ransomware attacks on hospitals mounted, lawyers at the Chicago firm Mason Lietz & Klinger had an idea. They could expand the standard data breach lawsuit to encompass a more tangible harm: disruption of medical services, even when no data was revealed.

"That's something we coined to get around the argument that there's no harm from data exfiltration," Gary Klinger said.

By the end of 2020, the firm had brought about thirty lawsuits against hospitals and other entities hit by ransomware, alleging negligence in failing to prevent the attacks. In what some might regard as blaming the victim, a lawsuit filed in federal court and transferred to Tuscaloosa County Circuit Court accused DCH of endangering patients' health and exposing their personal information by failing to monitor its computer network and systems properly. "As a consequence of the ransomware locking down the medical records," the complaint stated, patients "had to forego medical care and treatment or had to seek alternative care." DCH responded that the plaintiffs did not prove any negligence or harm and that the case should be dismissed.

Among the plaintiffs was seven-year-old Gabryella McCraw. On October 5, she suffered an allergic reaction. Her eyes were swollen shut, and there were red marks all over her face. Her legal guardian, Sheneka Frieson, took her to Northport Medical Center.

There, a nurse told them about the Ryuk attack and said that although the hospital had agreed to pay the ransom, it still could not see most patients. Gabryella would have to wait four to five hours for treatment. As a result, according to the lawsuit, "it took three days for Ms. McCraw's swelling to go down."

In June 2021, DCH settled with the patients for an undisclosed sum. Meanwhile, the criminal syndicate at the root of their difficulties was ensconced in Russia, beyond the reach of the American justice system.

8.

THE FBI'S DILEMMA

Investigating cybercrime was supposed to be the FBI's third-highest priority, behind terrorism and counterintelligence. Yet, in 2015, FBI director James Comey realized that his Cyber Division faced a brain drain that was hamstringing its investigations.

Retention in the division had been a chronic problem, but in the spring of that year, it became acute. About a dozen young and mid-career cyber agents had given notice or were considering leaving, attracted by more lucrative jobs outside government. As the resignations piled up, Comey received an unsolicited email from Andre McGregor, one of the cyber agents who had quit. In his email, the young agent suggested ways to improve the Cyber Division.

Comey routinely broadcast his open-door policy, but senior staff members were nevertheless aghast when they heard an agent with just six years' experience in the bureau had actually taken him up on it. To their consternation, Comey took Andre's email and the other cyber agents' departures seriously. "I want to meet these guys," he said.

He invited the agents to Washington from field offices nationwide for a private lunch. As news of the meeting circulated throughout headquarters, across divisions, and into the field, senior staff openly scorned the cyber agents, dubbing them "the 12 Angry Men," "the Dirty Dozen," or just "these assholes." To the old-schoolers—including some who had risked their lives in service to the bureau—the cyber agents were spoiled prima donnas, not real FBI.

The cyber agents were as stunned as anyone to have an audience with Comey. Despite their extensive training in interrogation at the FBI Academy in Quantico, Virginia, many were anxious about what the director might ask them. "As an agent, you never meet the director," said Milan Patel, an agent who attended the lunch. "You know the director, because he's famous. But the director doesn't know you."

You also rarely, if ever, go to the J. Edgar Hoover Building's seventh floor, where the executive offices are. But that day, the cyber agents—all men, mostly in their midthirties, in suits, ties, and fresh haircuts—strode single file down the seventh-floor hall to Comey's private conference room. Stiffly, nervously, they stood waiting. Then Comey came in, shirt sleeves rolled up and bag lunch in hand.

"Have a seat, guys," he told them. "Take off your coats. Get comfortable. Tell me who you are, where you live, and why you're leaving. I want to understand if you are happy and leaving, or disappointed and leaving."

Around the room, everyone took a turn answering. Each agent professed to be happy, describing his admiration for the bureau's mission.

"Well, that's a good start," Comey said.

Then sincerity prevailed. For the next hour, as they ate their lunches, the agents unloaded.

They told Comey that their skills were either disregarded or misunderstood by other agents and supervisors across the bureau. The FBI had cliques reminiscent of high school, and the cyber agents were derisively called the Geek Squad.

"What do you need a gun for?" SWAT team jocks would say. Or, from a senior leader, alluding to the physical fitness tests all agents were required to pass, "Do you have to do pushups with a keyboard in your backpack?" The jabs—which eroded an already tenuous sense of belonging—testified to the widespread belief that cyber agents played a less important role than others in the bureau.

At the meeting, the men also registered their opposition to some of the FBI's ingrained cultural expectations, including the mantra that agents should be capable of doing "any job, anywhere." Comey had em-braced that credo, making it known during his tenure that he wanted everyone in the FBI to have computer skills. But the cyber agents be-lieved this outlook was misguided. Although traditional skills, from source cultivation to undercover stings, were applicable to cybercrime cases, it was not feasible to turn someone with no interest or aptitude in computer science into a first-rate cyber investigator. The placement of nontechnical agents on cyber squads—a practice that dated to the 1990s—also led to a problem that the agents referred to as "reeduca-tion fatigue." They were constantly forced to put their investigations on hold to train newcomers, both supervisors and other cyber agents, who arrived with little or no technical expertise.

Other issues were personal. To be promoted, the FBI typically re-quired agents to relocate. This transient lifestyle caused family heart-ache for agents across the bureau. One cyber agent lamented the lack of career opportunities for his spouse, a businesswoman, in far-flung offices like Wichita. The agents told Comey they didn't have to deal with "the shuffle" around the country for professional advancement because their skills were immediately transferable to the private sec-tor and in high demand. They had offers for high-profile jobs paying multiples of their FBI salaries. Unlike private employers worried about staying competitive, the FBI wasn't about to disrupt its rigid pay scale to keep its top cyber agents.

Feeling they had nothing to lose, the agents recommended changes. They told Comey that the FBI could improve retention by centralizing cyber agents in Washington instead of assigning them to the fifty-six field offices around the country. That made sense because, unlike in-vestigating physical crimes like bank robbery, they didn't necessarily need to be near the scene to collect evidence. Plus, suspects were often abroad.

Most important, they wanted the bureau's respect.

Comey listened, asked questions, and took notes. Then he led them to his private office. They glanced around, most of them knowing they were unlikely to be granted such access to power again. Comey's desk featured framed photos of his wife and children, and the carpet was emblazoned with the FBI's seal. The agents had such respect for the bureau that they huddled close so that no one had to step on any part of the seal.

Perhaps the most striking feature of the office was the whiteboard that sprawled across one of the walls. On it was an organizational chart of the bureau's leadership with magnets featuring the names and headshots of FBI executives and special agents in charge of field offices. Many were terrorism experts who had risen through the hierarchy in the aftermath of the September 11, 2001, attacks.

Comey was sympathetic to his visitors and recognized the importance of cyber expertise to the FBI's future. At the same time, he wasn't going to overhaul the bureau and alienate the powerful old guard to please a group of short-timers.

"Look, I know we've got a problem with leadership here," Comey told the cyber agents as they studied the whiteboard. "I want to fix it, but I don't have enough time to fix it. I'm only here for a limited amount of time; it's going to take another generation to fix some of these cultural issues." But the agents knew the FBI couldn't afford to wait another generation to confront escalating cyberthreats like ransomware.

Although attacks were becoming more sophisticated, bureau officials told counterparts in the Department of Homeland Security and elsewhere in the federal government that ransomware wasn't a priority because both the damages and the chances of catching suspects were too small. Instead of aggressively mobilizing against the threat, the FBI took the lead in compiling a "best practices" document that warned the public about ransomware, urged prevention, and discouraged payments to hackers.

To FBI leadership, ransomware was an "ankle-biter crime," said an agent who attended the meeting with Comey.

"They viewed it as a Geek Squad thing, and therefore they viewed it as not important," he said.

■　■　■

Many of the issues the FBI cyber agents raised during their meeting with Comey were nothing new. In fact, the bureau's inertia in tackling cybercrime dated all the way back to a case involving the first documented state-sponsored computer intrusion.

In 1986, Cliff Stoll was working as a systems administrator at the Lawrence Berkeley National Laboratory when his boss asked him to resolve a 75-cent shortfall in the accounting system the lab used for charging for computing power. Stoll traced the error to an unauthorized user and ultimately unraveled a sprawling intrusion into computer systems of the U.S. government and military. Eventually, the trail led to German hackers paid by the Soviet Union's intelligence service, the KGB. Stoll immortalized his crusade in the 1989 book *The Cuckoo's Egg*. In the course of his investigation, he tried seven times to get the attention of the FBI but was rebuffed each time.

"Look, kid, did you lose more than a half million dollars?" the FBI asked him.

"Uh, no," Cliff replied.

"Any classified information?"

"Uh, no."

"Then go away, kid."

Stoll later spoke with an air force investigator who summed up the FBI's position: "Computer crimes aren't easy—not like kidnapping or bank robbery, where there's witnesses and obvious losses. Don't blame them for shying away from a tough case with no clear solution."

It wasn't until almost a decade later that the federal government took its first significant step to organize against cyberthreats. After the 1995 bombing of the Alfred P. Murrah Federal Building in Oklahoma City, the Clinton administration called together a dozen officials from across the government to assess the vulnerability of the nation's critical infrastructure. Since essential services such as health care and banking were moving online, the committee quickly turned its attention from physical threats, like Timothy McVeigh's infamous Ryder truck, to computer-based ones.

The group helped establish what became known as the National

Infrastructure Protection Center (NIPC) in 1998. With representatives from the FBI, the Secret Service, intelligence agencies, and other federal departments, the NIPC was tasked with preventing and investigating computer intrusions. The FBI was selected to oversee the NIPC because it had the broadest legal authority to investigate crime.

Turf battles broke out immediately. The National Security Agency and the Pentagon were indignant about reporting to the FBI about sophisticated computer crimes that they believed the bureau was incapable of handling, said Michael Vatis, then a deputy U.S. attorney general who led the effort to launch the center.

"They said, 'Oh, no, no, no. It can't be the FBI,'" Vatis recalled. "'All they know how to do is surround a crime scene with yellow tape and take down bad guys. And they're notorious for not sharing information.'"

Meanwhile, infighting over resources roiled the FBI. "You had a lot of old-line people arguing about whether cybercrime was real and serious," Vatis said. "People who came up through organized crime, or Russian counterintelligence. They were like, 'This is just a nuisance from teenagers. It's not real.'"

At the time, only a couple of dozen FBI agents had any experience or interest in investigating computer crime. There weren't nearly enough tech-literate agents to fill the scores of new job openings in the NIPC. Needing warm bodies, the FBI summoned volunteers from within its ranks, regardless of background. Among them was the New Orleans–based agent Stacy Arruda. During her first squad meeting in 1999, as her supervisor talked about "Unix this, and Linux that," she realized she was in over her head.

"Arruda, do you have any idea what I'm talking about?" the supervisor asked her.

"Nope."

"Why are you nodding and smiling?"

"I don't want to look stupid."

It was an easy admission because most of the new NIPC agents were similarly uninformed about the world they would be investigating.

When the bureau ran out of volunteers to join the NIPC, agents were "volun-told" to join, Stacy said. That's what happened to Scott Augenbaum. He said he was assigned to the NIPC because he was the only agent in his Syracuse, New York, office "who had any bit of a technology background," meaning he "could take a laptop connected to a telephone jack and get online." He was disappointed by the assignment because it was "not the cool and fun and sexy job to have within the FBI." His friends in the bureau teased him. "They told me, 'This cyber thing is going to hurt your career.'"

Following the September 11, 2001, terrorist attacks, FBI director Robert Mueller created the bureau's Cyber Division to fight computer-based crime. The division took over the NIPC's investigative work, while prevention efforts moved to DHS, which was established in November 2002. The DHS, however, put the computer crime prevention mission on hold for years as it focused instead on deterring physical attacks.

To ramp up the new division, the FBI put a cyber squad in each field office and launched a training program to help existing agents switch tracks. It also benefited from the "patriot effect," as talented computer experts who felt a call to service applied. Among them were Milan Patel and Anthony Ferrante, two of the agents who would attend the meeting with Comey.

Fresh out of college, Anthony was working as a consultant at Ernst & Young on 9/11. From his office in a Midtown skyscraper, he watched the towers fall. In the days that followed, he resolved to use his computer skills to fight terrorism. While pursuing a master's degree in computer science at Fordham University, he met with an FBI recruiter who was trying to hire digital experts for the new Cyber Division. The recruiter asked Anthony what languages he knew.

"HTML, JavaScript, C++, Business Basic," he answered.

"What are those?" the perplexed recruiter responded. "I mean, Russian, Spanish, French."

It wouldn't be the last time Anthony felt misunderstood by the bureau. When he arrived at Quantico in 2004, he found himself in a firearms class of about forty new agents-in-training. There, the instructor asked: "Who here has never shot a gun?"

With his gaze cast downward as he concentrated on taking notes, Anthony raised his hand. The room became silent. He looked around and saw he was the only one. Everyone stared.

"What's your background?" the instructor asked.

"I'm a computer hacker," Anthony said.

On a campus that recruits jokingly referred to as "college with guns," his answer was not well received. The instructor shook his head, rolled his eyes, and moved on.

Milan arrived at the FBI Academy in 2003 with a college degree in computer science from the New Jersey Institute of Technology. From Quantico, he was assigned to a cyber squad in New York, where his new boss didn't quite know what to do with him. The supervisor handed him a beeper, a Rand McNally map, and the keys to a 1993 Ford Aerostar van that "looked like it was bombed out in Baghdad," Milan said. Another agent set him up with a computer running a long-outdated version of Windows.

"Oh my God, this is like the Stone Age," he thought.

As time went on, Milan discovered how cumbersome it was to brief supervisors about cyber cases. Since many of them knew little about computers, he had to write reports that he considered "borderline childish."

"You had to try to relate computers to cars," he said. "You're speaking a foreign language to them, yet they're in charge, making decisions over the health of what you do."

Milan realized that most of his Cyber Division colleagues, like Stacy and Scott, didn't have a technical background. Some agents ended up in the Cyber Division because it had openings when they graduated from Quantico, or because it was a stop on the way to a promotion. In a popular move, many senior agents and supervisors pursued a final assignment in the division before becoming eligible for retirement at age fifty, knowing it made them more attractive to private-sector employers for their post-FBI careers.

"On a bureau cyber squad, you typically have one or two people, if you're lucky, who can decrypt and do network traffic analysis and programming and the really hard work," Milan said. "And you've got two or three people who know how to investigate cybercrime and have a computer science degree. And the rest—half of the team—are in the cyber program, but they don't really know anything about cyber." Some of those agents made successful cases anyway, but they were the exception.

Despite the internal headwinds, Milan worked on some of the bureau's marquee cybercrime cases. He led the investigation into Silk Road, the black-market bazaar where illegal goods and services were anonymously bought and sold. As part of a sprawling investigation into the dark web marketplace, law enforcement located six of Silk Road's servers scattered across the globe and compromised the site before shutting it down in October 2013. Ross Ulbricht, of San Francisco, was later found guilty on narcotics and hacking charges for his role in creating and operating the site. He is serving two life sentences plus forty years in prison.

Milan was nominated for the FBI Director's Award for Investigative Excellence; he became a Cyber Division unit chief, advising on technology strategy. Then, shortly after the Dirty Dozen meeting with Comey, he left the FBI for a higher-paying job in the private sector.

Anthony was selected for the FBI's Cyber Action Team, which deployed in response to the most critical cyber incidents globally. As a supervisory special agent, he became chief of staff of the FBI's Cyber Division. After the meeting with Comey, Anthony remained in the FBI for another two years. He left in 2017 to become global head of cybersecurity for FTI Consulting, where he worked with companies victimized by ransomware.

He kept tabs on the bureau's public actions in fighting the crime. Despite occasional successes, he said in 2021 that he was disappointed by the small number of ransomware-related indictments in the years that followed Comey's 2015 gathering.

"They would work cases, but those cases would just spin, spin, spin," Anthony said. "No, they're not taking it seriously, so of course it's out of control now because it's gone unchecked for so many years . . .

Nobody understood it—nobody within the FBI, and nobody within the Department of Justice. Because they didn't understand it, they didn't put proper resources behind it. And because they didn't put proper resources behind it, the cases that were worked never got any legs or never got the attention they deserved."

Beverwijk is a city of 41,000 people near the coast in the Netherlands, about twenty miles northwest of Amsterdam. In the seventeenth century, wealthy merchants built estates there. These days, it is mostly known for De Bazaar Beverwijk, one of Europe's largest ethnic markets, boasting dozens of food stalls and more than two thousand vendors hawking Arabian spices, Turkish rugs, clothing, antiques, and more. The small beach resort just west of Beverwijk is known locally for its favorable surfing conditions, and sunbathers there enjoy the widest sand beach in the Netherlands.

Beneath the glittering North Sea is a less well known attraction, one that has lured ransomware gangs from across the globe—and spurred Dutch law enforcement to be proactive and innovative in fighting them. Beverwijk is a landing station for one of the transatlantic fiber-optic cables connecting the United States to Europe. Due in part to the gradual slope of its shores, the Dutch coast is a popular area for landing the submarine fiber-optic cables that contribute to the country's fast internet speeds. Hackers, frustrated by slow and unreliable connectivity where they live, have flocked—digitally to the Netherlands to set up the servers they use to commit crimes.

Legal conditions were also favorable. Internet providers weren't liable for the contents of the servers they hosted. Hackers, who benefited from strong privacy laws, could buy server space without exposing their identities. As if that weren't enough, cybercriminals had worst-case-scenario reasons to put their infrastructure in the Netherlands, too. In a dark web forum that was reminiscent of an underworld version of Yelp, hackers ranked the conditions of prisons globally—and Dutch jails got top marks.

The Dutch National Police and the Ministry of Justice felt

compelled to respond to the steady stream of hackers setting up shop in the Netherlands. Leaders in the Ministry of Justice gave the National Police a stand-alone budget to organize a new High Tech Crime Unit (HTCU). Underscoring its importance, it was located in the National Police's headquarters, just southeast of Utrecht. Since its launch in 2007, the unit has earned a global reputation as one of the world's leading cybercrime-fighting organizations.

From its start, the HTCU was strikingly different from the FBI's Cyber Division. Early leaders like Marijn Schuurbiers treated the unit like a start-up and used Nike's slogan—"Just do it"—as a mantra. Marijn has a university degree in informatics and spent several years as a regular cop. He knew that most traditional police officers, when it came to cyber skills, "could never compete with young people who studied specifically [computer science] and did nothing else all of their lives." So, rather than taking the FBI approach of teaching advanced cyber skills to existing law enforcement officers, the HTCU hired tech experts with no policing background. HTCU leaders also established a guideline that these computer specialists must make up half the staff. The HTCU wanted them to shape the culture of the unit and knew that would happen only if they had a strong collective voice. The computer scientists quickly asserted themselves, protesting a rule that traditional police coordinators lead investigations. Yielding to their objections, the HTCU changed the policy, putting digital investigators in coordinating and decision-making positions.

Each cyber expert was paired with a traditional law enforcement officer, and they worked cases as a team. In the brightly lit office overlooking a highway in the front and a garden in the back, the partners were given back-to-back or side-by-side desks so that they could compare notes at any time. They interviewed suspects together. It was a stark departure from other parts of the national police force, where digital experts often sat in separate offices, disconnected from daily operations.

"You had someone who was more trained in interrogation techniques with someone who could just punch through the bullshit if the suspect tried to talk their way out of something," said John Fokker, who later became digital coordinator of the HTCU team focused on ransomware. "The old school with the new school made it work."

When the unit started with a staff of thirty-two, computer experts were required to pass police exams. They became sworn law enforcement officers, carrying guns and badges. But some talented digital recruits couldn't pass the physical fitness tests or didn't want to use weapons—and leadership realized they didn't really need to. Ever agile, the HTCU changed the requirements, allowing computer experts to join without passing traditional police exams. But they left the job titles unchanged: digital staff remained eligible for promotion to nearly any job in the HTCU.

"There was no real distinction," John said of the members of his ransomware-focused squad. "The digital guys on my team, who didn't have a gun, sometimes even outranked their colleagues who were conventional police officers. There was mutual respect."

In 2013, as the FBI struggled with the makings of a Cyber Division brain drain, the HTCU went on a computer scientist hiring spree. Aiming to expand its staff from sixty to ninety, it embraced an unconventional approach that was unfathomable to FBI recruiters: it held a security competition known as Capture the Flag. The contest would simulate a real-world digital crime, and Dutch citizens would be invited to solve it on their own time, using their own computers. The challenge was designed to test participants' abilities in programming, digital forensics, malware analysis, reverse engineering, and cryptography. Those who successfully completed the challenge would be invited to apply for a job.

Pim Takkenberg, then the HTCU's team leader, proposed the competition after learning that one of the UK's intelligence agencies had used a similar contest to recruit computer experts. He believed it would accomplish two goals. First, it would weed out candidates who lacked the advanced technical skills the HTCU wanted. Second, it would help spot diamonds in the rough—introverts like Michael

Gillespie, who lacked formal training or whose talent didn't jump out from their résumés.

But the competition could succeed only if enough people took part. Pim had been a regular attendee at "Hack Talk" tech nights held at cultural centers around the Netherlands. Hundreds of people with a passion for computers—from tinkerers and video game enthusiasts to technical analysts and cybersecurity experts—sipped beer while listening to guest speakers, panel discussions, and live music. Pim suggested the HTCU sponsor a similar event to launch what he called the "online cybercrime game." The event, held at a venue in The Hague that coincidentally was called Trojan Horse, drummed up buzz for the challenge. More than a thousand people attended in person, and even more watched the kickoff as it was livestreamed.

Ultimately, the HTCU had twelve hundred applicants for the thirty vacancies. During interviews, candidates—some of whom may have otherwise been uncomfortable talking up their skills or experience—were animated in discussing how they solved the challenge. The unit was particularly interested in applicants who took unusual approaches.

As they were finishing up the hiring spree in late 2013, the HTCU doubled down on a crime that the FBI at that time dismissed as an ankle-biter issue. It established several new squads, including one that would focus on ransomware.

Many people on the autism spectrum are un- or underemployed. Often they can't find jobs that accommodate their needs, or they come across poorly in interviews because they avoid eye contact or miss social cues. But, as several Ransomware Hunting Team members demonstrate, neurological differences can be associated with exceptional abilities in mathematics, problem-solving, and concentration. Marijn believed that diversifying the HTCU's staff was a continuous process—and the unit was already embracing unconventional recruitment methods. So when an opportunity arose to hire autistic tech specialists, he and his colleagues paid attention.

The proposal came from Peter van Hofweegen, director of ITvitae, an organization in the Netherlands that trains and coaches technically inclined people with autism. A youthful looking man in his early sixties who wears bold black-framed glasses and billowing scarves, Peter cofounded ITvitae in 2013. The school accepts autistic applicants who don't fit into traditional education and work settings. Harnessing their remarkable talent, Peter and his colleagues help the trainees refine their skills and specialize in areas such as data science or cybersecurity. Then they connect them with employers who are eager for their technical skills.

Over the years, as he reached out to prospective employers in search of placements for his students, Peter was unwilling to take no for an answer. His persistence led to lucrative offers for them from well-known corporations and cybersecurity firms. When a student named Tom expressed a desire to work for the HTCU, Peter resolved to make it happen, even though he had never previously sent anyone from ITvitae to work there.

But Peter knew that placing students with the elite HTCU would be a stretch. Tom didn't finish high school. Another candidate he had in mind, Mark Coumans—who'd be finishing his training before Tom— had dropped out of college. Both had spotty employment records. Typically, they wouldn't make the cut for the HTCU, even considering the unit's unconventional hiring process. Yet both Mark and Tom had extraordinary abilities that Peter was convinced could help fight cybercrime.

Mark, who was diagnosed with autism as an adult, had worked in IT as a young man. But for ten years before joining ITvitae, he was out of the workforce. During that time, he felt fulfilled as the full-time caretaker for his young children and coach of their soccer teams. Much like Sarah White, he became engrossed in niche topics, such as how to optimize performance in long-distance running.

None of that qualified Mark for a career as a cyber investigator. Still, with his characteristic perseverance, Peter implored the HTCU to set Mark's résumé aside and talk with him. "We just need one believer," Peter thought. "One person who sees value in our way of working."

Concerned about whether the HTCU could provide extra attention that people with autism might need, even broad-minded Marijn had his doubts about Peter's pitch. But an HTCU program coordinator named Yvonne Horst was a believer. At her urging, the HTCU agreed to give Mark a six-month trial internship.

Mark started as a junior data science intern at the HTCU at the same time as three professional data scientists hired by the unit. His new colleagues had university degrees and career experience at major companies such as accounting giant KPMG. Mark's inexperience starkly contrasted with their advanced skills. "My six-month introductory course at ITvitae is not comparable to four years of university studies," he conceded.

After four months, Yvonne called Peter with a progress report about Mark.

"I'm very sorry, but Mark cannot stay," she told him. "We'll finish the six months, and then you will have to find something else for him."

On a Friday afternoon, not long after, Yvonne called HTCU team members to help identify the owner of a suspicious van believed to be involved in a serious threat. All they had to go on was a grainy image of the van, which had an unusual logo on its side. Many investigators picked up on the logo, running reverse image searches to try to identify it. "If everybody's doing the same thing, either everyone will shout, 'I found it' at the same time, or nobody will shout at all," Mark recalled.

So he went in a different direction. He zeroed in on the make and model of the van and other defining features, which allowed him to narrow it down to a limited number of vehicles registered in the Netherlands with those same characteristics. He worked through the weekend and presented his findings to Yvonne that Monday. Ultimately, the threat was deemed less serious than initially suspected. But supervisors were nonetheless impressed by Mark's approach and his determination.

A short time later, when a colleague from a national crime squad asked Yvonne if someone from her team could help on a long-dormant cold case, she suggested Mark. With an ability to hyperfocus similar to that of some members of the Ransomware Hunting Team, Mark studied the case file. Conducting open-source research, he put together a report on the case that identified a possible suspect whom the police had not previously considered. While the police have kept details of the case confidential, the HTCU was so taken by Mark's work that it reversed its decision to let him go.

Yvonne called Peter with the news, explaining that "something incredible has happened."

"Mark is special," she said. "We have work for him."

The HTCU hired Mark as an open-source intelligence researcher, putting to use his innate ability to go deep on a single topic. In the years that followed, he would become a full police officer. He wasn't required to pass the physical fitness tests. "I'm not going to be in a position where I have to chase a suspect," he said. He was filled with pride as he worked on the HTCU's biggest cases, including ones that ultimately resulted in ransomware arrests.

ITvitae sent Tom to work at the HTCU a year after Mark. Then the floodgates opened. The Dutch National Police eventually became one of the top employers for graduates of ITvitae. Mark and Tom worked in the elite HTCU. However, the Dutch National Police also sought candidates to work in its ten regional cyber squads, which handled more routine cases. Over time, ITvitae sent about two dozen additional students to work on those regional squads. Some handled tedious yet essential tasks such as reviewing crime-scene footage from security cameras, and were able to home in on small details that others might have missed. Others worked as data scientists or digital investigators.

"If Mark did not advance the cold case, then Tom wouldn't have fulfilled his dream to work at the police, and twenty-five others probably wouldn't have had the opportunity," Peter said, his voice quaking with emotion. "They are misfits. But they are very, very important to have at your organization."

■ ■ ■

By 2012, FBI leadership recognized that most crimes involved some technical element—the use of email or cell phones, for example. So that year, it began to prioritize hiring non-agent computer scientists to help on cases. These civilian cyber experts, who worked in field offices around the country, did not carry weapons and were not required to pass regular physical fitness tests. But respect for the non-gun-carrying technical experts—the kind of appreciation that John Fokker of the HTCU described—was lacking. This widespread condescension was reflected in a nickname that Stacy Arruda, the early NIPC agent who went on to a career as a supervisor in the Cyber Division, had for them: dolphins.

"Someone who is highly intelligent and can't communicate with humans," said Stacy, who retired from the FBI in 2018. "When we would travel, we would bring our dolphins with us. And when the other party started squeaking, we would have our dolphins squeak right back at them."

If agents like Milan and Anthony had a hard time winning the institutional respect of the FBI, it seemed almost impossible for the dolphins to do so. They worked on technical aspects of all types of cases, not just cyber ones. Yet, despite the critical role they played in investigating cyber cases—sometimes as the sole person in a field office who understood the technical underpinnings of a case—these civilian computer scientists were often regarded as agents' support staff and treated as second-class citizens.

Randy Pargman took a circuitous route to becoming the Seattle field office's dolphin. In many ways, Randy and Michael Gillespie are kindred spirits—soft-spoken, self-described nerds with an understated passion for public service. Randy came to love computers the same way Michael did, through ham radio and from his grandmother.

As a kid in California, Randy regularly hung out with his grandma, who was interested in technology. She bought magazines that contained basic code and helped Randy copy it onto their Atari video game console. It was his introduction to computer programming. Later, as a teenager, Randy was drawn to a booth of ham radio enthusiasts at a county fair and soon began saving up to buy his own $300 radio. It was the early 1990s, before most home users were online, so Randy was thrilled when he used the radio to access pages from a library in Japan and send primitive emails.

After high school, Randy put his radio skills to work when he became a Washington State Patrol dispatcher. Although it wasn't a part of the job description, he created one computer program to improve the dispatch system's efficiency and another to automate the state's process for investigating fraud in vehicle registrations. The experience led him to study computer science at Mississippi State. In the summer of 2000, while still in college, Randy completed an FBI internship, an experience that left him with a deep appreciation for the bureau's mission. So, following brief stints working for the Department of Defense and as a private-sector software engineer once he graduated, he applied to become an agent. He was hired in 2004, around the same time as Milan and Anthony.

Like those two agents, Randy was shocked by the digital Stone Age he found himself in upon arriving. At the FBI Academy, a computer instructor gave lessons on typing interviews and reports on Word-Perfect, the word processing platform whose popularity had peaked in the late 1980s. To Randy, even more outrageous than the FBI's use of WordPerfect was the notion that agents would need instruction on such a basic program. The first week of class, the instructor delivered another surprise.

"Okay, who are the IT nerds in here?" he asked.

After Randy and a classmate raised their hands, the instructor addressed them directly.

"You're not going to be working on cybercrimes. You're going to be working on whatever the bureau needs you to do."

The other tech-savvy recruit later confided to Randy that he was dropping out of the FBI Academy to return to private industry. "This is not what I thought it was going to be," he said.

Randy was similarly torn. He believed in the FBI's mission but wanted to work solely on cybercrime. Like Anthony, he didn't have experience with guns, and he was unsure about how he would handle that aspect of the job. He faced a reckoning when an FBI speaker led a sobering session about the toughest aspects of working for the bureau, from deadly force scenarios to the higher-than-average rates of suicide and divorce among agents.

After consulting with FBI counselors and a bureau chaplain, Randy decided he didn't want to become an agent. Instead, he stayed in the FBI as a civilian, working as a software developer at the FBI Academy. Eight years later, when the FBI launched the computer science track, Randy eagerly applied. He became the Seattle field office's dedicated computer scientist in October 2012.

"This is why I had gotten into the FBI to begin with," Randy said. "I can concentrate just on cybercrime investigations and not have to deal with the whole badge and gun."

Once Randy got to Seattle, he began to dream big. His vision: The FBI could model its Cyber Division after one of the world's most successful computer crime-fighting law enforcement organizations, the Dutch HTCU. He knew how traditional and hidebound the bureau was, how different from the HTCU and its innovative culture. But, ever idealistic, he hoped that the HTCU's remarkable track record would persuade the FBI to adopt elements of the Dutch approach.

Randy had long been familiar with the HTCU's reputation for arresting hackers and disrupting their infrastructure. When he met a Dutch officer through an FBI program for midcareer professionals, he asked her the secret to the HTCU's success. Her response was straightforward: the HTCU was effective because it paired each traditional police officer with a computer scientist, partnerships that had been a founding priority of the unit.

The density of computer science experts in the HTCU astounded Randy, who thought it was brilliant. He suggested the Dutch approach to managers in the FBI's Operational Technology Division, which oversaw the new computer science track. They laughed.

"We can't get funding for that many computer scientists," one contact told him. "That would be crazy."

Randy acknowledged that, since the FBI's Cyber Division was

much larger than the Dutch Police's HTCU, establishing a one-to-one partnership was a stretch. Yet the FBI's setup all but ensured that its drastically outnumbered computer scientists would not find a collective voice, as the tech experts had done in the HTCU. As Randy dug into cyber investigations in Seattle, he learned that the bureau's staffing imbalance was straining its cyber experts, both civilian computer scientists and technically advanced agents like Milan and Anthony.

Many of the cyber agents Randy worked with in Seattle had prior careers as accountants, attorneys, or police officers. To get acquainted with the digital world, they took crash courses offered by the SANS Institute, the bureau's contractor for cybersecurity training; popular offerings included Introduction to Cyber Security and Security Essentials Bootcamp. From an institutional perspective, learning on the job to investigate computer crime was no different from learning on the job to investigate white-collar or gang crime. But FBI leadership didn't take into account something that Marijn Schuurbiers of the Dutch Police knew from the HTCU's start: it's not easy to teach advanced computer skills to someone who has no technical background.

Cyber agents routinely came to Randy with basic tasks such as analyzing email headers, the technical details stored within messages that can contain helpful clues.

"This is easy, you need to learn how to do this," Randy told one agent. He produced the IP address from the headers.

"What does that mean?" the agent responded. "What is this IP address?"

Randy had to make the time to help because, if he didn't, the agent might do something embarrassing, like attempt to subpoena publicly available information "because they just didn't know any better."

In the FBI, investigations into specific ransomware strains were organized by field office—for example, Anchorage, Alaska, investigated complaints related to Ryuk while Springfield, Illinois, investigated those involving a strain called Rapid. From time to time, Randy learned of victim complaints to the Seattle office about emerging ransomware strains. Since cases weren't assigned directly to computer scientists, he pushed the agents to take them on.

"Oh boy, here's one that nobody is working," he told one colleague. "Let's jump on this."

"That sounds amazing," the agent responded. "But I'll be so busy with that case that I won't get to do anything else."

In the early days of ransomware, when hackers demanded no more than a few hundred dollars, the FBI was uninterested because the damages were small—not unlike Cliff Stoll's dilemma at Berkeley Lab. Later, once losses grew, agents had other reasons to want to avoid investigating ransomware. In the FBI, prestige springs from being a successful "trial agent," working on cases that result in indictments and convictions that make the news. But ransomware cases, even with the enthusiastic support of a computer scientist like Randy, were long and complex, with a low likelihood of arrest.

The fact that most ransomware hackers were outside the United States made the investigative process challenging from the start. To collect evidence from abroad, agents needed to coordinate with federal prosecutors, FBI legal attachés, and international law enforcement agencies through the Mutual Legal Assistance Treaty (MLAT) process. Seemingly straightforward tasks, such as obtaining an image of a suspicious server, could take months. And if the server was in a hostile country such as Iran or North Korea, the agents were out of luck. Aware of this international labyrinth, even some federal prosecutors discouraged agents from pursuing complex cyber investigations.

During Randy's time as Seattle's computer scientist, the field office took on a number of technically sophisticated cases. He was especially proud of one that led to the Justice Department's indictment of hackers accused in the notorious Fin7 attacks, which breached more than a hundred U.S. companies and led to the theft of more than fifteen million customer credit card records. But during his seven years in Seattle, the office never got a handle on ransomware.

"If you spend all of your time chasing ransomware, and for years you never make a single arrest of anybody, you're seen as a failure," Randy said. "Even if you're doing a ton of good in the world, like sharing information and helping protect people, you're still a failure as an investigator because you haven't arrested anybody."

Despite its own inaction, the FBI feuded with the other federal agency responsible for investigating ransomware: the Secret Service. Although the Secret Service has been guarding presidents since 1894, its lesser-known mission of combating financial crimes dates back even longer—to the day in April 1865 that Abraham Lincoln was assassinated. Before heading to Ford's Theatre, Lincoln signed legislation creating the agency and giving it the mandate to fight counterfeit currency. As financial crime evolved, and moved online, the Secret Service and the FBI squabbled over cases. Although it, too, had a federal mandate to fight computer crime, the Secret Service was sometimes bigfooted by the FBI, said Mark Grantz, who was a supervisory special agent for the Secret Service in Washington.

"They'd say, 'Yeah, we've got a case on that already. We were looking at him five years ago. Give us everything you've got and we'll go from there.' That was their MO," Mark said. It left him wondering: "You haven't touched that case in five years, why are you asking me for my case file?"

Grantz led an investigation into a ransomware attack in January 2017, eight days before Donald Trump's inauguration. The strike disabled computers linked to 126 street cameras in a video surveillance system monitoring public spaces across Washington, D.C., including along the presidential parade route. Instead of paying the five-figure ransom, the district scrambled to wipe and restart the cameras, which were back online three days before the swearing-in. Assisted by other law enforcement organizations, the Secret Service traced the hack to two Romanians, who were arrested in Europe, extradited to the United States, and found guilty on wire fraud charges—an uncommon U.S. law enforcement success against ransomware operators.

Other Secret Service investigations sometimes stalled because agents had to rotate away for protective detail. "That's where it gets frustrating," Mark said. "You'd train someone. They'd do digital forensics for five years. They'd get really good at it. And then you'd send them off to do presidential detail."

■ ■ ■

Randy Pargman also grew frustrated by the FBI's reluctance to engage meaningfully with private-sector cybersecurity researchers. When the FBI did connect with experts in the private sector, sensitive information typically flowed only in one direction—to the bureau.

Following large cyberattacks against U.S. targets, the FBI routinely affirmed its commitment to public-private partnerships to help prevent and gather intelligence on such strikes. But some agents believed the rhetoric was hollow, comparing it to public officials' offering "thoughts and prayers" after mass shootings. The reality was that many people in the FBI had a deep distrust of private-sector researchers.

"There's this feeling among most agents that if they share even a little bit of information with somebody in the private sector, that information will get out, broadcast over the internet—and the bad guys will definitely read it, and it will destroy the whole case," Randy said.

Even though he couldn't work on ransomware cases, Randy found ways to feel fulfilled in his job, including by helping organizations defend themselves against impending cyber intrusions. He examined malware command-and-control servers obtained through the MLAT process, then alerted potential victims to imminent attacks. "That was a really good feeling because we stopped a ton of those intrusions," he said. FBI leadership rewarded his efforts: Randy earned both the FBI Director's Award for Excellence in Technical Advancement and the FBI Medal of Excellence.

But he grew tired of his subordinate role as an "agent helper," and he thought about how things would be different if the FBI were more like the Dutch HTCU. In the bureau, he couldn't be promoted since Cyber Division leadership roles were open only to agents. And while agents could retire at fifty with full pensions, he had to wait until age sixty-two, and would receive less money. In 2019, Randy resigned from the FBI, telling his supervisor he wanted to be in a role where he could enact changes rather than just suggest them.

"I love working for the FBI," he told his supervisor. "It's very meaningful and fulfilling. But there is no leadership spot for me to go to, only because I'm not an agent. So you cannot be upset that I'm going to get a job where I can be a leader, and make changes, and create a team to do big things."

The Dutch word for computer intrusion is *computervredebreuk*. It translates to "computer peace disturbance" and is similar to the Dutch term for a physical domestic disturbance. True to their language, the HTCU regarded ransomware as an assault. From the time he received his posting as digital coordinator for the team focused on ransomware in 2014, John Fokker was passionate about investigating what he considered "one of the most severe cybercrimes you can commit." At the time, the victims were mostly on home computers; they lost photos or university theses. "My mom and dad could have been the victims," John said.

John was already a digital investigator in the Dutch National Police when he passed the Capture the Flag competition to join the HTCU, which had gained attention as a hot assignment. His squad didn't have to wait long for its first big case. In late 2014, a Swedish IT employee for IKEA found his computer files locked by a ransomware strain called CoinVault. It demanded about $200 and spread through pirated software, attacking victims in Europe and the United States. The Swedish victim traced the infection to a hacked server in the Netherlands and contacted its owner, a small telecom company, which then reported the hack to the HTCU. When investigators examined the server, they found it was full of keys that could decrypt CoinVault victims' files.

One of the first steps of the investigation followed a guiding principle of the HTCU: engage with private-sector researchers, like members of the Ransomware Hunting Team. The unit's leaders believed establishing such partnerships could help with both leads and expertise. "They all had a piece of the puzzle, and if you didn't bring it together, you couldn't see the whole picture," Pim said.

In investigating CoinVault, the HTCU called Jornt van der Wiel, the Netherlands-based Kaspersky researcher and future Ransomware Hunting Team member. After obtaining the CoinVault keys, investigators asked Jornt—whom Marijn knew from conferences they'd both attended—to create a decryption tool that victims could use to unlock their files. They also wanted his help analyzing the ransomware's code in their effort to track down the hackers.

When Jornt dug into the ransomware samples, he found two user names embedded in the code. "Nobody's that stupid," he thought. Just in case, he passed the information to the HTCU, which invited him to headquarters to compare notes. Jornt reassured John that he would wait until the investigation's conclusion to discuss it publicly. "We won't publish any blog posts," Jornt said. "We won't tweet anything without your consent."

With that understanding, John told Jornt what the HTCU had learned—the kind of two-way information sharing that Randy longed to see in the FBI. The hackers had made a mistake: they had connected to the ransomware-spreading server from their parents' IP address instead of through a VPN. The IP address was registered to the surname Jornt had found in the code. The HTCU developed the case and eventually caught two suspects, Dutch brothers, who confessed to the crime and were convicted. It was among the first arrests of ransomware operators.

After the arrests, Kaspersky updated the CoinVault decryptor to include the fourteen thousand new keys the brothers turned over. Then the Dutch Police coordinated with Kaspersky, Europol, and the California-based antivirus company McAfee to create a website where the public could download the CoinVault and other new ransomware decryption tools for free. The No More Ransom website, launched four months after Michael's ID Ransomware, became another popular place to find free decryptors.

Despite its success, the HTCU wasn't immune to the challenge of retaining talented cyber investigators who felt the pull of the private sector. Pim Takkenberg left in 2013 after fourteen years in the police, and John Fokker left in 2018 after six years. Both Pim and John continued to work in cybersecurity and regularly shared intelligence with their old team, which eventually grew to 170 members. In his job as manager at Utrecht-based Northwave, Pim oversaw an advanced cyber training program for ITvitae students.

The HTCU also grappled with how to catch criminals located in hostile countries. To cope, the unit used a strategy it called off-center targeting. While investigating ransomware operators, it also regularly seized ransomware servers in the Netherlands, disrupted ransomware-spreading botnets, and notified victims of impending attacks—"anything to make the hackers' return on investment lower," said Matthijs Jaspers, who oversees the unit's partnerships with the private sector. For example, after Jornt and the Ransomware Hunting Team analyzed a strain called WildFire that had targeted victims in the Netherlands in 2016, he shared the findings with the HTCU. The unit seized the hackers' command-and-control server and recovered about 5,800 decryption keys. That's when the team, impressed by Jornt's skills and contacts, invited him to join.

The HTCU's off-center targeting gained global attention in January 2021, when a worldwide band of private researchers collaborated with the unit to disrupt Emotet, one of the notorious botnets that facilitated Ryuk attacks. With the researchers' help, global authorities—led by the HTCU and including the FBI—hijacked hundreds of Emotet command-and-control servers to take down the botnet. Law enforcement also distributed an Emotet uninstaller to victims' systems.

After the Emotet disruption, with swagger earned through success, the HTCU directly addressed hackers in English- and Russian-language messages it posted on popular dark web forums:

> Emotet was one of the most prolific botnets of the past decade. It ultimately failed to escape the reach of the Netherlands Police and its international partners. Hosting criminal infrastructure in The Netherlands is a lost cause.
>
> We feed on underground information sources and the cybersecurity industry . . . Everyone makes mistakes. We are waiting for yours.

When it came to ransomware, the FBI didn't have a lengthy roster of achievements to boast about. To be more effective, it needed to overhaul its outmoded approach to cybercrime. Instead, clinging to its cultural standards, the bureau tried to turn traditional law enforcement officers into tech specialists while passing over computer scientists who could not meet its qualifications to become agents. "Is the person who can do fifteen pull-ups and run two miles around the track in under sixteen minutes the same guy that you want decrypting ransomware?" Milan Patel said. "Typically people who write code and enjoy the passion of figuring out malware, they're not in a gym cranking out squats."

The FBI wanted its cyber agents to be athletic college graduates with relevant job experience, who also had to be willing to shoot a gun, relocate their families, and pivot away from investigating cybercrime as needed.

Michael Gillespie certainly wouldn't make the cut. But the FBI needed his expertise. So it made him an informant.

9.

THE G-MAN AND
THE DOLPHIN

It was the kind of overture that Michael Gillespie had been half expecting after the immediate success of ID Ransomware. But he was still taken aback in 2016 when an FBI agent named Mark Phelps asked to meet with him.

Michael didn't feel he could refuse. But he explained that he was overwhelmed with work at Nerds on Call and with the Ransomware Hunting Team, and Mark would have to accommodate his schedule. They chose a time after the end of Michael's workday and decided to meet at a Panera Bread restaurant five hundred feet from his office.

On the night of the meeting, as he crossed the five lanes of traffic that separated Nerds on Call's strip-mall parking lot from Panera's, Michael became nervous. He hadn't considered the significance of talking with the FBI and realized he didn't know what to expect. He grew paranoid, as though the purpose of the meeting were to arrest him for some unknown crime. It was the same feeling he had whenever he drove past a police car: a wave of anxiety, even though he knew he wasn't violating any law.

Mark and another FBI employee, Justin Harris, greeted him at the restaurant. They told him that they were paying for his meal. But with little appetite, and afraid to upset the FBI by overspending, he only ordered an apple. When the trio sat down, Mark explained the reason for the meeting. He was a cyber agent, and Justin was a computer scientist. They had come across Michael's website, and they wanted to know what information he might have that could help the FBI investigate ransomware. Michael was relieved to hear that they planned to tap his expertise, not nail him for some inadvertent offense.

Mark and Justin asked if Michael's analysis of information he gathered on ID Ransomware could help identify attackers. Michael knew hackers worked hard to cover their tracks, but he also believed he could, in some cases, identify the IP addresses of their servers. He told them that if he could help, he would.

As they wrapped up their discussion, Mark asked to meet again. Dazzled by the prospect of working with the FBI, and humbled that they had sought him out, Michael agreed. A short time later, he signed on to become an FBI informant. "Informants . . . may receive compensation in some instances for their information and expenses," according to the FBI. The bureau gave him a secret code name, to be used on official documents that could end up in court. All Michael will say about the alias is that it is "very fitting." Whenever he signed his code name, he guarded his privacy by disguising his handwriting.

Special Agent Phelps and his new source came from similar roots. Mark's family was also midwestern, blue-collar, and religious. Mark's parents, Ron and Jane, married in 1972, when both were teenagers. Born in 1981, Mark grew up in Indiana. The family's two-bedroom house was less than a half mile from the Indianapolis Motor Speedway, which has hosted the famous Indy 500 since 1911.

Ron Phelps spent nearly fifteen years in Local #20 Sheet Metal Workers Union, where his father—Mark's grandfather—and other relatives worked. Then he took a new job as sales and project manager for a central Indiana roofing contractor. In 2001, he became president of a start-up roofing and sheet metal company called Horning. Employing about 90 people, Horning aims to "supply good jobs for hard working people," according to Ron's LinkedIn page. Over his career,

Ron worked on projects including the Conseco Fieldhouse (now the Gainbridge Fieldhouse)—home of the NBA's Indiana Pacers—and the Indianapolis Zoo.

As a child, Mark entertained his parents with card and magic tricks. At Speedway High, the clean-cut teenager with neatly combed hair and a wide smile played center on the Sparkplugs' football team and participated in the National Honor Society and the science club. He played trumpet in the school's stage band, which won first place in a statewide competition in his senior year.

Mark, like Michael, had a high school girlfriend he would later marry. A year older than Mark, Shawn Dillard participated in many of the same extracurricular activities, including band, theater, and Students Against Destructive Decisions (SADD). As her mother had done more than two decades earlier, Shawn enrolled at Purdue University to study veterinary technology. Mark majored in computer science at Indiana University–Purdue University Indianapolis. In July 2004, after both had graduated from college, the Speedway sweethearts were married by an evangelical pastor in Indianapolis.

Mark worked briefly at the FBI before finding a job as a software engineer with Raytheon. But he dreamed of returning to the FBI as an agent, and he knew the age cutoff to become an agent was thirty-seven. After nearly a decade at Raytheon, he applied to the bureau and was accepted, taking a pay cut to join.

The bureau sent him to Peoria, Illinois, around 2015 to investigate cybercrime. He and Shawn bought a four-bedroom house in the nearby village of Dunlap. Known locally for its school district, Dunlap was popular with agents, who called it the "FBI 'hood." The lush backyard of their hip-roof colonial provided plenty of space for their golden retriever, Nugget. Shawn obtained her state veterinary technician's license and later found work as a pet insurance claims analyst for Nationwide.

A teetotaler whose favorite book is the Bible, Mark found ways to connect with his Christian beliefs. He and Shawn made a pilgrimage to the Bald Knob Cross, a 111-foot structure in the Shawnee National Forest, a four-hour drive south from Peoria. Visible for more than

7,500 square miles when illuminated at night, the imposing cross is the setting for events ranging from Easter Sunday services to the annual Blessing of the Jeeps.

Sharing a passion for CrossFit, the popular fitness regimen known for its cult-like following, Mark and Shawn joined a local gym. Mark posted photos on Facebook of his workout achievements. In one, he shows a handwritten outline of his routine: "1 mile run; 100 pull-ups; 200 push-ups; 300 squats; 1 mile run." Alongside it are photos of himself—muscular with close-cropped brown hair and outfitted with a teal bandana, sunglasses, and a tactical vest. In another, he and a smiling Shawn stand in front of their garage, flexing their exposed biceps. "Tank top toooooooozday! Show dem gunz!" he captioned it.

Peoria is one of five outposts of the FBI's field office in Springfield, the state capital. A small field office with about 140 agents and support staff, Springfield handles all types of cases, from public corruption and national security to drug trafficking and child predators. Its investigations have led to convictions of three sitting or former Illinois governors. One of its most famous cases took place in the early 1990s. After being tipped off by undercover informant Mark Whitacre, the Springfield office investigated the agricultural giant Archer-Daniels-Midland for price fixing. ADM paid a $100 million criminal fine. Three former executives went to prison, including Whitacre, who embezzled $9.5 million from the company while assisting the FBI. The saga was chronicled in the 2009 film *The Informant!*, with Matt Damon in the title role.

Even its cyber agents are sometimes pulled in other directions. "Mark's not just doing cyber—I mean, he's literally doing, like, drug busts, too," Michael said. "It's a lot harder to actually get results and put someone in cuffs for cyber stuff."

Springfield's territory encompasses vital government research facilities and infrastructure. One of the world's fastest supercomputers is housed at the National Center for Supercomputing Applications at the University of Illinois at Urbana-Champaign, which handles myriad classified projects. Scott Air Force Base, about twenty-five miles east of St. Louis, Missouri, is home to the U.S. Transportation Command, which coordinates military transport globally.

"Between NCSA and TRANSCOM, we had great partners as well as great potential targets for hostile intelligence services and criminal groups," said Weysan Dun, who was special agent in charge of the office from 2003 to 2007. "That's one reason we were very active in cybercrime."

Dun said agents at smaller field offices like Springfield sometimes get an "inferiority complex," wrongly thinking that the best cases are found in the biggest cities. He tells them that Springfield is a "small office that roars."

The Springfield office had cyber agents in outposts across its territory, including Mark in Peoria. Supporting them was the Springfield office's dolphin. Justin Harris studied computer science, first at a community college, then at the University of Illinois, Springfield, earning a master's in 2014. Later that year, he joined the FBI.

Like his counterpart Randy Pargman in Seattle, Justin helped with all kinds of investigations, not just cyber cases. Justin's FBI colleagues knew he was spread thin. One called him "completely overworked."

"He gets pulled into everything," the agent said. "The guy's really good. But there needs to be like ten of him in Springfield alone."

Michael began seeing Mark and Justin—or someone less tech savvy when Justin was busy—every few months. Michael looked forward to the encounters. Despite the FBI's few ransomware indictments, the mystique of working with the bureau excited him. It was an antidote to the grind of fixing broken hard drives at Nerds on Call and to the onslaught of personal crises he faced at home.

They would meet at a Red Robin hamburger joint or at a Denny's, places that had Wi-Fi and were relatively quiet. No longer limiting himself to a piece of fruit, Michael came to enjoy dining on the FBI's dime. At Denny's, he ordered a $12 skillet instead of the $2 biscuit and gravy he usually got. Once, Mark splurged, taking him to a Peoria steakhouse where a filet cost about $30—or, as Michael thought about it, the same as a tank of gasoline. They ordered fried calamari as an appetizer, his first time trying it. Though Mark didn't realize it, the repast was a few days before Michael's birthday. "Thank you for the birthday meal," Michael told him.

Their conversations were so enjoyable for Michael that he almost forgot he was sitting with a government agent. "We're just guys hanging out, eating, talking about ransomware," he said. Reality set in when Mark, needing to discuss something confidentially, would escort Michael to the parking lot, where they would sit in the agent's car. Or when Mark would slide a document across the table for Michael to sign to acknowledge he was providing the bureau with information of his own free will.

As time went on, Michael grew more comfortable around Mark. He shared his troubles—his cancer, Morgan's job loss, the looming foreclosure on his house. Mark listened empathetically before diving into ransomware. He relayed that he wasn't receiving a paycheck when they met during the thirty-five-day federal government shutdown that ended in January 2019, and he occasionally mentioned upcoming CrossFit events, but he revealed little else about himself. "We mostly talked about me," Michael said.

Although Mark was his main contact, it was Justin who had a deeper understanding of Michael's findings. While he appreciated Mark's willingness to learn—eventually the agent even took classes in reverse engineering—Michael was grateful for Justin's presence during tech-heavy discussions. Michael often felt more of a connection with Justin, who could speak his language.

Michael and Justin bemoaned their work predicaments, which had striking similarities. Facet and the FBI sometimes saddled them with basic tasks instead of the challenges they craved. Justin's job was like "any small-to-medium-sized business where you do whatever someone throws on your desk," Michael said. "We talked about how we both had that same situation, where we have this higher skill set— I'm trying not to sound elitist, it's kind of an awkward balance. But if

I'm in the middle of doing some really hard-core technical stuff, and I am the only one in the office that can even do that—and then I get called up front to sell someone a flash drive—that totally throws me off. I come back to my desk, and I'm like, 'What the hell was I doing?'"

At the office, Michael confided in Jason Hahn and Dave Jacobs about the FBI meetings. "IIe was proud of what he did and wanted to tell someone about it," Jason said. But he didn't mention it right away to other Ransomware Hunting Team members. He was aware of their low regard for the FBI's work on ransomware.

Around 2013, three years before Mark began cultivating Michael, an FBI agent in New York asked Lawrence Abrams to become a source on ransomware. The agent explained that Lawrence would get an identification number so that, if he provided information, the number instead of his name would appear in any investigative paper trail.

On hearing the proposal, Lawrence had the opposite reaction of Michael—he was immediately uncomfortable. "I know I watch a lot of movies, but I just feel like I'm going to go missing someday," Lawrence told the agent. He declined the offer. "Send me a subpoena, I'll give you any information you need."

Fabian's own disillusionment with the FBI began when he found a "very hot lead" on the developer of the ACCDFISA strain—the phony agency that purported to remove child pornography from computers for a price. Fabian, who had collaborated with Lawrence for the first time in cracking ACCDFISA, tried to reach an FBI contact but learned that the agent had been reassigned and no longer investigated cybercrime. He spoke with another agent, who wasn't helpful.

His doubts were reinforced in 2016 when he and another researcher identified two servers, one based in the United States and the other in the Netherlands, that were spreading a ransomware strain called ASN.1 in the United States and in Europe. They uncovered the hackers' real IP address as well as their web hosting service, bringing them tantalizingly close to identifying the attackers.

The elated researchers were eager to pass the information to people who could act on it. So in November 2016, they drafted a report outlining their evidence and sent it to a contact at the FBI.

The response disappointed them. The FBI contact asked basic questions that reflected a startling ignorance of ransomware. He wanted to know, for example, how command-and-control servers work, the significance of IP addresses, and whether the screenshots in their report could be enlarged.

"TBH im a bit amazed," the other researcher emailed Fabian. "All this stuff is imho already more than obvious, but still they somehow want it in the report."

Fabian agreed. He was hoping the FBI would "seize the server and help the ransomware victims" by retrieving keys to unlock encrypted files. But it seemed the contact scarcely knew what a server did.

Fabian also sent the tip to John Fokker of the Dutch National Police, since one server was in the Netherlands. Fokker recognized the value right away.

"Great news," John responded. "We are eager to start things up an[d] try to seize the server."

Fabian followed up with an eight-page report detailing his evidence. ASN.1 shut down a few weeks later.

In addition to their meetings, Michael emailed regularly with Mark, passing along tips. Mark usually thanked Michael for his information but rarely told him how it was being used. Michael accepted this one-way communication as FBI protocol.

The FBI needed the information Michael collected on ID Ransomware. The site received thousands of submissions a day—about the same number of ransomware complaints the FBI got in an entire year. Many victims, especially businesses, were reluctant to report ransomware to the FBI, fearing the bureau would slow down the recovery process or make the attack public. They were also afraid agents might rummage through their dirty laundry. Even if victims did contact the FBI, it was often weeks after the incident, when clues had gone cold.

Michael gave the FBI a possible fast track to victims by providing IP addresses that uploaded files to his site. From time to time, Michael came across a business victim identified by name in a ransom note as he monitored submissions. If it was a U.S. company, he sometimes dashed off the information to Mark so that the FBI could get in touch with the victim and monitor the attack as it unfolded.

He turned over other details gleaned from ransom notes, such as Bitcoin wallet numbers and hacker email addresses, which the FBI could use to trace money in the ransomware economy and track attackers. More broadly, the site's raw statistical data helped the FBI assess how prevalent and damaging a particular strain was at any given time. "They ask me a lot about statistics," Michael said. "How hard is the U.S. getting hit by this strain or that strain?"

Then there was Michael's technical input. He analyzed so much ransomware that he could quickly spot patterns in the code. When a new ransomware strain resembled an existing sample, it could mean that the hacker groups were connected.

Michael also played a role in the FBI's investigation of SamSam, which led to one of the U.S. Department of Justice's first indictments of ransomware developers. In November 2018, the department charged two Iranian men with fraud for allegedly developing and deploying the strain. The suspects remained at large, likely in Iran.

Michael wondered how much help he was; Mark never discussed it with him. But after the case was over, Mark acknowledged with a brief nod that Michael's information had proven useful.

One day in early 2018, Brian and Jason, Michael's bosses at Facet, pulled him aside. They told him the FBI had invited them to the Springfield headquarters for a tour. As the day approached, Jason suggested that Michael dress up for the occasion. "Make sure you look your best, Mike," Jason told him.

Nonetheless, Michael was wearing his normal work khakis and a coat on the winter morning that Jason, Brian, and Brian's wife drove to Springfield. An FBI employee greeted the group and began showing them around the impressive, corporate-style office. Set back from the street, the sprawling, low-slung building featured a central rotunda and a full-color FBI seal formed from an array of stones on the front entrance floor. Eventually, their guide invited them to attend an "all-employee meeting" in a large conference room. They approached the room, shuffling through a throng of people gathered outside.

"I hope you're good in front of big crowds," someone said, nodding at Michael.

As he entered the conference room, dozens of FBI employees erupted into applause. Michael had followed Brian into the room, but suddenly Brian was walking toward the back while he was being shepherded toward the front. He saw his name projected on a screen.

"Hey, they're talking about you!" someone shouted.

Michael was speechless as Sean Cox, special agent in charge of the Springfield office, handed him a certificate as its honoree for the 2017 FBI Director's Community Leadership Award. Created in 1990, the prestigious award honors individuals and organizations for providing "tremendous support" in combating crime, terrorism, drugs, and violence and "outstanding contributions to their local communities through service." Each of the FBI's field offices selects someone to receive it. At Mark's recommendation, Cox had chosen Michael. It was Cox's idea to make it a surprise.

Finally processing what was happening, Michael smiled broadly and shook Cox's hand. He shared a few words expressing his gratitude.

Cox invited the visitors for a chat in his office. Uncharacteristically, Michael's face seemed to be stuck in a smile. Later that day, he excitedly told Morgan the news, which soon circulated among his in-laws. Rita Blanch, Morgan's grandmother, sent out a group text message to family members. They were stunned. "What? Our Michael?" one replied.

He bought a suit and invited his parents to Washington, where he would formally receive his award during a ceremony at FBI headquarters. He was disappointed when they begged off because they were in the midst of moving to Florida. Michael then asked Brian and Jason to join him instead. Proudly, they accepted. The FBI covered Michael's travel expenses while Brian—knowing Michael's financial hardship—

paid Morgan's. Around the office, employees joked that Brian and Jason had an ulterior motive. "They went with him to try to nerf anybody trying to recruit him," Dave Jacobs said. "He would be very difficult to replace."

The Gillespies arrived early at the FBI's Hoover Building on a sunny April morning. The award ceremony began, and honorees from each field office approached FBI director Christopher Wray individually to receive their awards. They were chosen for their work fighting the opioid crisis, teen violence, human trafficking, poverty, and hate crimes. Michael, the youngest, was one of two recipients that year who battled cybercrime.

Wearing a dark suit that swallowed his slender frame, Michael beamed with pride as he accepted his award and shook hands with Wray. In a press release, the FBI cited Michael for creating ID Ransomware and for "having cracked and decrypted multiple ransomware strains himself." It continued with a nod to the Ransomware Hunting Team: "Michael is plugged into a network of leading cybersecurity experts with whom he collaborates to analyze the malware and discover means of decryption so that victims can avoid paying ransom and recover their data."

When they returned to the Normal office, Jason and Michael sat down to talk. Even if the FBI didn't recruit him, as Dave and their other colleagues predicted, the ceremony made Jason realize Michael had outgrown Nerds on Call.

"Mike, we all know what your love is," Jason told him. "We can see it's in ransomware. We know that's what you want to do. We're here to support it and to help you get there. But we're not the business for your kind of work."

At home, Michael mounted a new wooden shelf over a doorway. On it, he placed the glass plaque engraved with his name, alongside a framed certificate signed by Wray. He reflected on his conversation with Jason. He wanted to work on ransomware all the time, but it was hard for him to imagine a professional life without Nerds on Call.

■　■　■

In the summer of 2019, the FBI observed that ransomware attacks were becoming more sophisticated and costly. Health-care organizations, industrial companies, and the transportation sector were bearing the brunt of the attacks. In September of that year, the bureau convened its first-ever Ransomware Summit in an auditorium at Carnegie Mellon University in Pittsburgh. Insurers, lawyers, and employees of antivirus companies and incident response firms joined representatives from the Department of Homeland Security, the Secret Service, and the Justice Department at the invitation-only event.

Mark invited Michael. The FBI flew him to Pittsburgh, put him up in a hotel, and gave him a daily stipend to be a "subject matter expert." On the first day of the summit, Michael gave a thirty-minute talk just for FBI agents, starting with an in-depth discussion of the Rapid strain, which the Springfield office was responsible for investigating.

He followed up with a presentation about ID Ransomware. He introduced agents to the site, so that they could encourage victims to consult it, and to its gold mine of data, which they could use in their own investigations.

For the first two days, Michael wasn't allowed into any other sessions, which were reserved for FBI personnel. Viewing the agenda, he realized that he could have contributed to the discussion. "I could see what office was working on which ransomware. I know some stuff about that one, I've analyzed that one. I wonder if they came to the same conclusions on that one. Every single one of them."

His exclusion came as a disappointment. Instead of comparing notes on ransomware, Michael sat in his hotel room. He ventured out only to treat himself, using the FBI's stipend, to a gourmet milkshake from the Milk Shake Factory just down the street from his hotel. Unaccustomed to being away from home, he missed his wife.

His mood brightened when he met Lawrence for the first time. Although the FBI didn't cover Lawrence's travel expenses, he came in from New York to meet Michael. "I've been working with him for so many years now, that to finally meet him was really the main reason I was going," Lawrence said,

Once the summit's events opened to the select private-sector attendees, Mark used the downtime after formal sessions to introduce Michael to other cyber agents—identifying them not only by name but also by field office and which ransomware strain they focused on. Michael held court as agents and researchers sought his analysis. He was so in demand that he didn't have time to chat with everyone who wanted to talk to him.

That wasn't always true at night, when Michael was invited out for drinks and dinner. While he enjoyed some parts—such as hearing a federal prosecutor describe behind-the-scenes details of a success-ful case—he couldn't schmooze about non-cyber topics he knew little about. One night, Lawrence bought him a drink, but Michael felt dizzy after one sip. He switched to water and tried to stay awake as someone droned on about blockchain technology.

During the day, he took part in a panel discussion alongside John Fokker, the former HTCU team leader, and a researcher from cyber-security software company Trend Micro. Michael described ID Ran-somware, and an audience member later asked whether his site had a privacy policy.

Hacker email and Bitcoin addresses found in files uploaded there "may be stored and shared with trusted third parties or law enforce-ment," according to a disclaimer on the site. "I'm not a legal person, but to me that's good enough," he said.

Lawrence, who attended the panel discussion, wasn't so sure. Some users might go to ID Ransomware specifically because they don't want to involve law enforcement. Yet Michael offered up their IP addresses and more.

Lawrence worried that his younger teammate hadn't thought through the consequences of sharing that kind of information. "There's so much liability here," Lawrence said. "I think he is putting himself in quite a bit of harm's way with this. There's definitely reper-cussions if a company wants to go after him. Even if his privacy policy states all of this, and even if he would win in a lawsuit, he can't afford to cover a lawsuit. The reality is, he is too trusting."

■ ■ ■

At the summit, Lawrence raised another delicate issue with his FBI contacts. He was well aware that, from time to time, Michael and other researchers used the attackers' own tactics against them. They would hack into a gang's command-and-control server, extracting keys so that victims could recover files without paying a ransom.

For example, just a few months before the summit, Michael discovered a vulnerability in a server used by the MegaLocker ransomware gang. MegaLocker attacked home users and companies worldwide, charging up to $1,000 for a decryption key. The weakness allowed Michael to get into the server and harvest victims' keys.

Michael posted on the BleepingComputer forums: "Victims please do not pay." A site moderator noted that "our experts are working on a way to decrypt Megalocker encrypted files."

"Oh, you, you are not good people," MegaLocker clapped back in Russian. "And I think, why did the clients stop writing? And here it is." Wrongly suggesting that there was no way to recover without paying a ransom, MegaLocker added, "Why entertain people with vain hopes?"

Though he was doing so for a good cause, Michael was skirting the Computer Fraud and Abuse Act of 1986, the federal law that prohibits intentionally gaining access to a computer without authorization. Such activities have contributed to a gulf between the FBI and some top-flight researchers. The FBI took a dim view of "hacking back," and many researchers simply didn't trust the bureau not to investigate them.

Lawrence understood both viewpoints. When he saw members of the Ransomware Hunting Team "doing shit that's iffy," such as hacking back, he tried to discourage them, though often to no avail. "Stop what you're doing," he urged them. "You don't know what's being investigated currently. And you don't know what's going to happen afterwards. It's not worth risking, legally, your life to get a few keys off a server. Report it to someone and let them deal with it."

At the same time, he pointed out to his FBI contacts at the Pittsburgh summit that the bureau's rigidity was hampering its fight against ransomware. The Dutch HTCU and Europol were regularly announcing arrests and takedowns, "but the FBI gets a 'partnered with' mention instead of taking a leading role," he said. "We get people all the time that want to give you information that are scared to do so because they're afraid you're going to go after them."

He was taken aback by an agent's response: "The reality is they shouldn't do it because they are breaking the law."

"We both know that, but this is the kind of person you need to help on these investigations."

The agents suggested that Lawrence act as intermediary between the researchers and the FBI. But that might mean establishing a more formal arrangement, which he had decided against years earlier. He still didn't want to.

Michael passed information about MegaLocker's servers, and the exchange on the forums, to Europol and the FBI. As far as he knew, neither the FBI nor European law enforcement moved to shut down the servers.

He was frank with Mark about his tactics. Perhaps because he was so straightforward, and they had a strong relationship, Mark did not admonish him. Nevertheless, Michael decided against attempting to hack into any other MegaLocker servers. "I was already in very gray-hat territory with what I did," he said. But he continued to collect keys from the server he was already inside. In May 2019, he released a decryptor.

"That's kind of an interesting thing with my relationship with the FBI," he said. "They kind of wink-wink, we're telling you not to, but can't stop you.'"

After Michael, the FBI honored a second member of the Panera trio: Justin Harris. In early 2021, Christopher Wray gave Justin a Citation for Achievement, recognizing his work providing "incident triage expertise" to a victim of a computer intrusion. A redacted copy of the award, posted on LinkedIn by a retired Springfield agent and former colleague, indicated that the attack involved elections in 2018. "Justin did more than his share in this case and others," wrote Christopher Trifiletti, who worked on it alongside Justin before retiring. "Justin has heard me say this in small rooms too many times, and it embarrasses him every time, so let me say it in this large space," Trifiletti added. "In 20 years of recruiting good people for the FBI, Justin is my best recruit ever."

"If I ever become famous, Chris is going to be my PR person," Justin replied. "Even in retirement you found [a] way to embarrass me . . . I'm just fortunate to have a career I enjoy, encourages learning, and facilitates continuing education."

Mark Phelps became preoccupied with politics. The pandemic and the 2020 presidential campaign led him to embrace alt-right advocacy. He stewed over lockdowns and mask mandates, which he described to Facebook friends as "baby steps to tyranny."

"This thing is not as bad as it is made out to be! Let's get back to normal!" he wrote in July 2020. In another post, he expressed frustration that lockdown restrictions infringed on his personal liberty. Quoting Assistant Attorney General Eric Dreiband, he wrote, "There is no pandemic exception to the U.S. Constitution and its Bill of Rights." He shared an article from *WND*—formerly *WorldNetDaily*, a far-right news and opinion website known for promoting conspiracy theories—with the headline "Coronavirus Could Be 'Exterminated' If Lockdowns Lifted."

He supported President Donald Trump's decision to keep houses of worship open during the pandemic and defended him against critics. "How are the same people who say Trump oversteps his bounds and authorities by sending feds to help stop violence in cities say that Trump didn't do enough to 'stop COVID'?" he wrote. He also echoed Trump's false argument that voting by mail fosters voter fraud. Three months before the election, Mark posted a meme: "If you won the PowerBall would you mail in the ticket? Or would you go in person? Why is that? (remember this when you vote)."

Support for Trump was common among FBI agents and across law enforcement. But after Joe Biden was declared the winner of the 2020 election, and Trump falsely blamed his loss on voting fraud, Mark's posts became increasingly extreme. Undermining the bureau's own efforts to stem the spread of disinformation, one of the posts linked to a

YouTube video supposedly showing poll workers interfering with ballots. Facebook's independent fact-checkers flagged the video as false.

"We have been told that this election was the most secure election in American history," Mark wrote on December 12, 2020. "That is a lie. It was in no way free or fair. Do not look for nor expect truth from the main stream media or politicians. Seek the truth yourself. It takes way more effort than it should, but it is there. This is not all about republican vs democrat. This is about our republic and our constitution that many have sworn to support and defend. Pray for truth and justice. Many need those prayers right now."

On January 6, 2021, rioters urged on by Trump stormed the U.S. Capitol in a deadly attempt to disrupt the joint session of Congress assembled to formalize Biden's victory.

In a post that he "borrowed from a friend who stole from a friend," Mark equated the assault on the citadel of American democracy to the Black Lives Matter protests that had swept the country the previous summer. In a comment on the post, one of Mark's Facebook friends raised a question. "Any possibility antifa was involved today?" the friend wrote, referring to far-left protesters whom Trump had blamed for inciting violence. "Very good chance," Mark replied.

Wray, the FBI director, later testified before the Senate Judiciary Committee that there was no evidence of left-wing involvement.

An acquaintance spotted Mark's Facebook post and believed it could be viewed as a violation of the Hatch Act, which prohibits federal employees from engaging in some political activities such as posting "a comment to a blog or social media site that advocates for or against a partisan political party" or group. Concerned about the public perception of such remarks by a federal law enforcement officer—and trying to save Mark from himself—the acquaintance called the FBI, suggesting the agent be instructed to take the post down.

Months later, the post was still up, but the spotter was unsurprised. "Here's the thing," the person said. "I don't know that Mark's that concerned, because his skill set translates well to a bigger salary somewhere else."

Michael wasn't friends with Mark on Facebook and didn't know about the posts. "Actually I didn't even know he supported Trump," he said. But he was increasingly disillusioned with the FBI. In February 2021, he cracked a new ransomware strain that seemed very familiar. As he analyzed it, he realized that its encryption method and file format closely resembled those of Rapid. He tipped off Mark, who thanked him, but Michael heard nothing more.

"That is always the elephant in the room," Michael said. "The FBI didn't give you shit back. Just a one-way tunnel. They keep talking about how they're trying to make that better. But for various reasons, they can't."

10.

SHAKING DOWN A CITY

O n the morning of Tuesday, May 7, 2019, Bernard "Jack" Young was eagerly anticipating the crowning moment of his career. Two days later, he would be inaugurated for a job that he had once coveted but that he'd almost given up wishing for: mayor of Baltimore. He'd grown up as one of ten children in a working-class family on Baltimore's East Side. His father operated towing equipment, and his mother was a housekeeper at the Holiday Inn. For spending money, he collected deposits on soda bottles and caught worms to sell as bait. Without finishing college, he worked his way up from clerk to manager in Johns Hopkins Hospital's radiology department, while also embarking on a political career as an aide to a city councillor and an active member of local Democratic clubs. He became a councillor himself in 1996, and council president in 2010.

It looked as if he wouldn't rise any higher. But then a pay-to-play scandal engulfed Mayor Catherine Pugh. Local organizations had paid a total of $860,000 for her self-published *Healthy Holly* children's books, even though thousands of purchased copies were never printed or delivered. Pugh took a leave of absence on April 1, 2019—she eventually pled guilty to fraud and conspiracy charges, and was sentenced to three years in federal prison—and Jack took over as acting mayor.

Now the word "acting" had been removed from his title, and he was soon to be sworn in. But the accidental mayor immediately faced an enormous and unfamiliar threat. When he logged on to his phone and city-issued laptop, something was missing. Normally, he was deluged with emails, but he hadn't received any new messages overnight, and he couldn't send any either. Shortly after 7:00 a.m., he called the city's chief information officer, Frank Johnson. "Something's wrong with the system," Jack told Frank. "You need to check it out."

Frank's staff was already checking. Baltimore's elected officials and employees had been complaining since shortly before midnight that they couldn't open their city emails and files. Around 5:00 a.m., a technician looked into their complaints but couldn't access the system remotely. At first, the problem was thought to be a power outage or networking issue, easily fixable. But an engineer dispatched to the city's data center on Lexington Street couldn't log in. Even the "break glass" access codes, named after the method of pulling a fire alarm in an emergency, didn't work.

Jack headed to his city hall office, where Frank called him around 9:00 a.m.

"Mr. Mayor, I just want to inform you that our system has been compromised by ransomware," Frank said. "And they're asking for a ransom."

Jack's first reaction was optimism. "We can fix this," he thought. But the more he looked into it, the more downcast he became. Although its 911 system had been hit by ransomware the year before, Baltimore had no formal plan for responding to a cyber disaster. "I finally figured out that we had an antiquated system that wasn't prepared for this kind of attack."

A note from the intruders began popping up on employees' screens. "Your network targeted by RobbinHood ransomware," it read. "We're watching you for days and we've worked on your systems to gain full access to your company and bypass all of your protections ... We won't talk more, all we know is MONEY." The gang demanded 13 bitcoin (about $75,000 at the time) within four days. Then the price would rise $10,000 per day.

The ransomware knocked the city's print shop offline, thwarting arrangements for Jack's inauguration: a contractor had to be hired to print the programs. But that was the least of the new mayor's problems. The attack brought much of his government to a standstill. It stymied a wide array of public services and revenue sources, from parking tickets to water bills, in addition to private business deals, such as home sales, that required city approval or records.

Instead of hosting a reception after the inauguration, as he had expected to do, Jack went straight to work. "I was like, 'Why me? Why did this happen when I became mayor?'" he recalled. "Not that I wanted it to happen to anyone, but it was something that, honest to God, I had sleepless nights." The attack "was the thing that worried me the most," even with "the shootings and murders and everything going on."

Across the country, other mayors faced similar challenges. As ransomware scaled up, gangs began targeting municipal governments, which often have porous and outdated cybersecurity defenses. The attack on Baltimore was one of more than a hundred that year on state and local governments, about twice as many as in 2018.

The mayors wrestled with a dilemma as old as ransom itself: To pay, or not to pay?

In a 1911 poem, "Dane-geld," Nobel laureate Rudyard Kipling advised against yielding to extortion. Alluding to the failed policy of Ethelred the Unready, a tenth-century English king, of paying Danish invaders to stop raiding his country's coast, Kipling wrote, "If once you have paid him the Dane-geld / You never get rid of the Dane."

Baltimore and other U.S. cities attacked by ransomware were as unready as Ethelred. The federal government was of little help; the FBI advised against paying ransoms but rarely caught the hackers or seized their profits. And the U.S. Department of Homeland Security, which is responsible for protecting the nation's cybersecurity, couldn't decide whether helping cities recover from ransomware attacks was part of its job.

Mayors had to weigh the immorality and shame of rewarding criminals against the financial and human costs of defiance, from prolonged disruptions in operations to resources diverted from vital projects. If they could restore services quickly with backups, they could afford to resist. But many small municipalities, from Valdez, Alaska, to West Haven, Connecticut, had no choice but to pay.

In March 2018, Atlanta became the first major American city to be victimized by ransomware. The SamSam attack disabled many online services; people couldn't apply for city jobs or pay water bills and traffic tickets. Atlanta police lost years of dashboard camera footage from patrol cars. But Mayor Keisha Lance Bottoms spurned the $51,000 demand. "It was counterintuitive to me to pay to get your own stuff back," she said. Two factors made her decision easier. The city's backup files were intact, and Atlanta had purchased cyber insurance three months before, which covered part of the $20 million cost of recovery.

For similar reasons, an earlier RobbinHood victim refused to pay. Hit the month before Baltimore, the City of Greenville, North Carolina, had backed up all its files just a day or two before the incident, and insurance paid for most of the cleanup.

With patchwork defenses and no insurance, Jack Young was in a weaker position than Bottoms or Greenville mayor P. J. Connelly. He had a financial incentive to cave. If Baltimore didn't pony up the relatively small ransom, it would have to spend far more money and time recovering files. Services could be stalled for untold weeks or months.

But what sort of example would Jack set by rewarding criminals? And if he did pay them, would they keep their promise? All over the city, from the Inner Harbor to Pimlico, Reservoir Hill to O'Donnell Heights, residents debated what their new city leadership should do.

In the late 2010s, Baltimore had one of the highest violent crime rates of any U.S. city. In 2019, the year of the ransomware attack, 348 people were murdered there, 30 more than in New York City, which has a population 14 times larger.

The city lurched from one crisis to another. More than 16,500 buildings were vacant and abandoned. Corroded pipes leaked sewage and natural gas, century-old water mains burst, and cases of lead paint poisoning were on the rise. Almost 54 percent of Baltimore public schools received one or two stars, the lowest ratings on Maryland's 1–5 scale, compared with only 6 percent of schools in the rest of the state.

Small wonder, then, that Baltimore administrators had for years considered other problems more pressing than cybersecurity. A warning from the city's IT office that its outdated servers were "a natural target for hackers" and that "extortionists are an increasing threat" went unheeded. Different parts of the system weren't walled off properly, so malware could spread easily. Turnover at the top undermined long-term planning. From 2012 to 2017, Baltimore's IT office cycled through six acting or permanent heads.

The city wasn't completely unprepared. Martin Okumu, director of IT infrastructure, had begun backing up files on the cloud. "It was my initiative; I had to fight for the money," he said. "I was moving data onto Amazon Web Services for four or five months before the attack, anticipating possible threats. You go to sleep every night knowing that something like this could happen."

In 2014, Gayle Guilford became the city's first chief information security officer, with two part-time engineers on loan from other duties. She scrounged for funding and free expertise wherever she could find it. Whenever Phyllis Schneck, DHS's cybersecurity chief, spoke at a public event, Gayle showed up. She waited until the talk was over, approached Schneck, proffered a business card, and said, "I know you do vulnerability assessments. I'd like you to do one for Baltimore." Eventually, DHS contacted Gayle. Its assessment identified both "critical and noncritical issues," she said. "We were one of the first cities in the country to participate in the program."

Gayle also hounded the city's chief financial officer for money to buy threat detection equipment.

"How can you prove to me it's needed?" he asked.

She explained that cyberattackers were "hitting you every single second of every day," and proved it by lugging to his office an eighteen-hundred-page printout of attempted intrusions into Baltimore's system. He gave her $150,000.

"My team always called me the bag lady," Gayle said. "I was never too proud to beg."

Unfortunately, the installation of the cyber threat intelligence system and other software was still in progress at the time of the RobbinHood attack. Gayle was also working on a cyber insurance application, but until the threat detection tools were in place, the city couldn't pass the assessment required for the policy.

The March 2018 ransomware attack on Baltimore's 911 dispatch system should have been a wake-up call. A city troubleshooting team left a port, or channel to the internet, exposed to hackers, who penetrated a server. But the damage "wasn't as big as it could have been," Gayle said. "It was in a place that couldn't bring down the system or corrupt the data." The city isolated the threat and restored backups within twenty-four hours.

The successful response may have given some officials too rosy a view of the city's readiness. "Not for one instant" was 911 down, Mayor Pugh boasted to a conference of mayors in June 2018. "We immediately switched to a manual system, and so we were out of operation less than five minutes . . . There was really no harm done to the system."

At another conference that same month, Baltimore city solicitor Andre Davis heard his Atlanta counterpart describe how the recent SamSam attack had hobbled municipal services there. But when Andre returned home, Atlanta's experience slipped his mind. He didn't call the mayor or chief information officer to ask whether Baltimore could suffer the same fate. He was too busy leading a national search to replace the city's police commissioner, who had resigned after being charged with failing to file federal tax returns.

The bearded former federal appeals court judge called the lapse one of his biggest failures and greatest regrets. "If I had been nearly as smart as I thought I was as a city attorney," Andre said, "I would have returned from that two-day conference and the first thing I would have done that Monday morning would have been to call our chief of IT and say, 'Hey, I just learned in some detail what happened to Atlanta. Are we covered?' I didn't do that. When the ransomware attack happened in 2019, I was like, 'God, how can I not have raised a red flag?'"

The Atlanta attack alarmed Frank Johnson, Baltimore's chief

information officer. At a meeting on Capitol Hill, he handed a thick report to a legislative aide to Democratic congressman C. A. "Dutch" Ruppersberger, whose district includes part of Baltimore. It laid out the city's vulnerabilities and potential fixes. Frank explained that he was trying to persuade city leaders to fund the recommendations but that he was competing with other departments and priorities.

The next year, when Baltimore was attacked, the aide called Frank to ask what had gone wrong.

"I couldn't sell the plan," Frank answered.

Whether due to coincidence or the hackers' intentionally exploiting a window of vulnerability, the attack took place during a transition in city government that went well beyond a new mayor. There was also a new city council president, with Brandon Scott replacing Jack Young. And Frank Johnson had a new deputy, Todd Carter. Todd hadn't expected to return to full-time work so soon. After a thirty-year career handling information technology for utility companies, he had semi-retired to look after his mother, who was having hip surgeries and suffered from Parkinson's disease. But he noted, "If you've ever cared for a mother with dementia, it drives you crazy yourself." Baltimore, his hometown, was seeking a deputy chief information officer, and a friend recommended Todd. He arranged for someone to help his mother during the day.

On May 6, 2019, he received his ID card and went through orientation. Nothing prepared him for his second day. When he arrived at the Baltimore City Information & Technology (BCIT) office in the Harry S. Cummings Building on East Fayette Street, kitty-corner from city hall, the computers were sitting idle. The phones worked, but voicemail and email didn't. Baltimore police and FBI and Secret Service agents were striding through the halls. Todd's boss and coworkers huddled in one emergency meeting after another.

Todd joined those meetings and learned about the attack. "There was an unspoken belief that the security team could solve it," he said. "They would work their magic, and we would move on." But then the number of servers and workstations found to be infected climbed from twenty to forty into the hundreds. "It became clear that someone had violated us. Someone was sneaking into our home and going from room to room."

At one emergency meeting, the directors of BCIT and other city agencies decided to order employees to unplug their computers. The move was designed to block any further spread of the ransomware, since no one knew whether the malware was still moving through the network or where it might be heading. But the shutdown had the disadvantage of making it harder to trace the virus's path. Then staffers began frantically calling federal agencies and private security companies for help.

"No one in the city, including me, had ever been through an incident response like this," Todd said. "It was obvious to me that no one really knew what to do. Everyone was in shock."

Although the city never revealed how RobbinHood breached its defenses, insiders say that the gang exploited a fundamental flaw in the city's cybersecurity: fragmented management. It infiltrated an unauthorized server that was run by a Department of Public Works employee and relied on an old Oracle database system to manage records and programs. "It was an application that wasn't up to date," a former administrator said. "The system wasn't patched, and the bad guys knew it wasn't."

DPW was one of several city departments that managed their own servers, applications, and desktops. As a result, standards, policies, expertise, and backups varied. But since most of the departments were on the same network, a virus that penetrated any of them could spread to the others. The exceptions included the police department, which had a separate network and was largely unaffected. The cybersecurity assessment undertaken by DHS to appease Gayle Guilford had covered only BCIT and the Health Department, so it missed the DPW vulnerability.

Little was known about the culprit, RobbinHood. Milwaukee

researcher Alex Holden discovered conversations on the dark web pointing to a twenty-nine-year-old escapee from a Turkish prison who liked to fantasize about crossing the Black Sea to the port of Odessa, in Ukraine, to meet girls. After buying a ransomware kit and scanning the internet for potential targets, the ex-con brought a code resembling RobbinHood's to what is called an obfuscation service. He paid the service to disguise the ransomware from antivirus software and mentioned he was planning a big attack. The timing fit with Greenville and Baltimore, and Holden shared the information with federal law enforcement. Other experts, though, disputed the theory.

Whatever RobbinHood's identity or country of origin, the hacker's cryptography was solid. As usual, the Ransomware Hunting Team scrutinized the unfamiliar strain. MalwareHunterTeam tracked down a sample of RobbinHood's code on VirusTotal, the malware database. Vitali Kremez, who would soon join the team, examined how the ransomware disabled antivirus protections and moved from one computer to another. After it finished encrypting files, he found, it created four different ransom notes and sometimes displayed a cheerful farewell: "Done, Enjoy Buddy :}}}"

Lawrence Abrams described Vitali's findings on BleepingComputer. "Unfortunately, at this time no weakness has been found in the ransomware, and there is no way to decrypt files for free," he wrote.

Jack Young's immediate instinct was to stand up to RobbinHood. If the city were to pay the ransom, "what guarantee is there that we'll get the keys to unlock all of our systems?" he said. "Or they'll come back again. I wasn't falling for that."

His top advisers agreed. At a meeting the next day in Jack's office, Frank Johnson, Andre Davis, two FBI agents, and a couple of cybersecurity contractors hired by the city urged the mayor to reject the ransom demand. Johnson assured the mayor that BCIT had robust backups, though he couldn't vouch for city agencies with separate IT operations. The FBI was emphatic: yielding to cyber extortion would only encourage more attacks.

"You pay these guys, maybe you get your records back, maybe you don't," Andre chimed in. "Maybe they come back with a new intrusion, and a couple of weeks later they attack again."

Andre urged the mayor to leave the lines of communication with the hacker open and not to tip his hand. Letting RobbinHood think that the city might pay could deter a second attack or elicit useful information about vulnerabilities or stolen data. But Jack had no interest in pretending to negotiate and announced his position publicly.

The hardships imposed on the residents of Baltimore by the Robbin-Hood attack, and Jack's refusal to pay the ransom, soon became apparent. The biggest concern was the housing market.

In Baltimore, no home sale could become final without a blue "lien sheet" from the city listing any outstanding property taxes, water bills, and housing code or environmental violations. Since RobbinHood had encrypted this data, the city couldn't issue up-to-date lien sheets. Worried about being on the hook for undetermined fees, underwriters stopped insuring deals in Baltimore, and housing sales slowed dramatically.

Property sales are an important economic engine for any city, and the impasse hurt all the parties involved. Sellers needed to be paid so they could purchase new homes. Buyers were in limbo. The city was forfeiting the taxes it collected from each sale, totaling an average of about $90 million a year. And in the midst of a typically busy spring, Baltimore's fifty title companies, which check that the seller legitimately owns the property and then issue title insurance for it, lost their income stream.

In May 2019, Cotton Duck Title Co. in Baltimore's Hampden neighborhood handled only ten sales, down from its usual forty. "We were dead in the water," said Dan Harvey, president of the company, which is named after a brand of heavy canvas fabric that used to be manufactured in Hampden for boat sails and work clothes. "We had to explain to people all day long that we can't tell them when they're going to close on their house. Realtors wanted answers. Buyers and sellers wanted answers. Lenders outside Maryland were saying, 'What's the problem?'" The number of residential units sold in Baltimore decreased in fiscal 2019 for the first time in seven years, due at least partly to the ransomware attack.

Cars were almost as big a headache as houses. RobbinHood disrupted the impound lots where cars were towed if they had been abandoned, blocked traffic, or parked in front of a hydrant. The inventory of cars towed in the two weeks before the attack was unavailable. Operations were hampered for three months as city workers manually checked in each car, taking photos and logging the information. People scoured the lot on Pulaski Highway, which was crammed to capacity, to find their cars. Normally, unclaimed cars were auctioned off, but the city canceled auctions for May and June to give owners a chance to retrieve their vehicles, delaying sales of at least six hundred vehicles.

Parking enforcement stalled, too. A few years before the attack, Baltimore's transportation enforcement officers had switched from writing citations by hand to issuing them with an electronic device. The ransomware disabled the new system, and the officers went back to writing paper tickets—more than fifty thousand in May, June, and July. But the city lacked the staff to enter all of them manually into a database so that people could pay them. The city halted its scofflaw program, which booted cars with multiple unpaid citations, and made sure that people who had been unable to pay their tickets didn't face late fees or have their licenses suspended.

Water billing had also gone digital. In 2016, the city installed smart meters in homes to record water consumption. Now more than a hundred servers with water billing records were useless, and DPW couldn't process the data or generate monthly bills. All it could do was urge residents to put money aside or come to the office and pay as much money as they wanted credited to their accounts.

The repercussions reached beyond Baltimore's boundaries. Since the city owned the reservoirs that supplied suburban Baltimore County, it also handled the county's water service, including maintenance and billing. So residents of the county, which had a larger population than the city, didn't get their bills either.

Since the average water bill in Baltimore had more than doubled from 2010 to 2018, some hard-pressed residents welcomed the sudden halt to water charges as a reprieve. But when DPW began mailing out bills again on August 7, three months after the ransomware attack, some charges were startlingly large. A 10 percent rate increase, approved in January 2019, had taken effect during the hiatus despite protests from the advocacy group Food and Water Watch. "We called on the city not to institute the increase, and they ignored it," said Rianna Eckel, the group's senior Maryland organizer.

Also, without monthly bills to act as a warning, leaks left unfixed for three months resulted in gargantuan usage readings. Leakage appeared to explain why one resident's $1,012.63 bill showed him using 527 gallons a day. "I'm a working stiff," he told a local television station. "I don't have $1,000 to throw at a water bill."

Bumbling and heading up blind alleys marred the city's early response to the attack. Gayle Guilford's priority was determining where the ransomware had entered the system so that she could trace its path from computer to computer. But some city hall staffers interfered. Jumping to the conclusion that the crime had been an inside job, they instructed her to investigate two people whom the city had fired. Gayle quickly realized that they couldn't have been responsible. Still, she had to consult her team, watch security footage, and report both suspects to the FBI. With such distractions, it took two days to pinpoint the compromised DPW server where the attack originated.

"It was a living hell," Gayle said.

Her boss, Frank Johnson, was overwhelmed. His marketing mantra, "People, Process, Product," was no substitute for the technical expertise he lacked. Around noon on May 7, a few hours after the attack was attributed to a strain of ransomware, Eric Costello, a city council member, attended an emergency meeting in the BCIT offices. "Frank was freaking out," Eric recalled. "He didn't seem to be asking the right questions."

So Eric, a former senior IT analyst for the federal government, asked Frank and his staff, "Do we have a prioritized list of systems for recovery?"

Nobody answered. "People looked at me like I had two heads," he said.

Frank was also telling cybersecurity contractors that they could spend as much city money as they needed to restore service. Eric warned him several times against offering them a blank check. "It's encouraging predatory behavior," Eric said. "They'll sell you the sun, moon, and the stars, when all you need is an asteroid rock." Overall, the city would dole out more than $4 million to vendors.

Facing the prospect of an expensive and painful recovery, some business owners and politicians began urging Jack to change his mind and pay RobbinHood. With the housing market in limbo, title executives were especially outspoken. Although Cotton Duck's Dan Harvey agreed with the mayor's stance, he said that others in the housing industry expressed the opposite opinion: "'You're going to spend eighteen million dollars when you could pay seventy-five thousand dollars and move on? You're crazy!'"

Title companies, real estate agents, and home builders discussed pooling their money and paying the ransom. They told the mayor that if giving taxpayer money to criminals was politically taboo, they could take care of it privately.

"We said to Jack, 'You can posture yourself any way you want,'" recalled Al Ingraham, chief executive of the Greater Baltimore Board of Realtors. "'But there may come a time when your computer people say it's going to be a year to restore service. In that case, you may have to pay the ransom.'"

Jack declined the offer. "I wanted to help them, but I wasn't gonna pay," he said.

Bill Henry, a city councillor, expressed misgivings. At a hearing, he said constituents were asking why the city didn't pay the "comparatively small" ransom and upgrade cybersecurity at the same time.

"I don't have an answer," Henry said.

While Henry understood that capitulating could spur attacks on other cities, people were "losing their livelihoods day after day because we wouldn't pay the ransom," he said. "Our responsibility is to Baltimore city. The way I looked at it, paying [seventy-five thousand dollars] for a chance to recover our data was probably worth it."

Baltimore's ex-mayor Sheila Dixon told a radio host that she would have paid RobbinHood. "I would write the check and give them the money so that we can get things back up and running," she said.

Jack said that he didn't take Dixon's criticism seriously. She had resigned as mayor in 2010 after being convicted of embezzling gift cards donated to the needy and pleading guilty to perjury in a separate case. Her scandal-ridden departure had elevated Jack to city council president, just as he would later owe his position as mayor to Pugh's wrongdoing.

A national columnist joined the critics. Pointing out that Baltimore "could have done much more to protect itself" from attack, Yale Law School professor Stephen L. Carter argued on Bloomberg Quint that negotiating with hackers "is not always a bad thing," adding, "The victim might reasonably decide that avoiding large losses at small cost is the wiser response . . . But here's another unpleasant truth about the real world: Sometimes the bad guys win."

A mysterious Twitter account taunted Jack. Posting a sample of documents that it said were stolen from Baltimore's network during the attack, it threatened to leak sensitive financial and personal information. "If you don't like to see all of them in the darknet, tell to mayor!" it said. It was unclear whether the account was connected to the hackers; at a minimum, the people behind it were familiar with the dark web address listed in the ransom note. In the end, they didn't act on the threat, and city officials denied that a data breach had occurred.

With most city services still down, constituents began writing to Jack, urging him to pay the ransom. He briefly wavered. "In order to move the city forward," he told one interviewer, "I might have to think about it."

But he held firm, and many Baltimoreans rallied behind him. They were fed up. His predecessor, Pugh, had extorted hundreds of thousands of dollars from local institutions. Now a hacker was holding the city hostage.

"A lot of people were saying, 'We shouldn't be paying a criminal,'" one resident remembered. "'We've been paying a criminal for years.'"

Baltimore was in danger of becoming an anarchist's paradise. But two lawyers with a knack for managing crises and resolving turf squabbles helped restore order.

A former logistics officer in the U.S. Marine Corps, Melissa Ventrone served seven months in Afghanistan in 2010. After retiring from the military in 2016, she joined the Chicago office of the law firm Clark Hill PLC. As a leader of Clark Hill's cybersecurity, data protection, and privacy team, she helped hospitals, police departments, and other victims minimize fallout from ransomware attacks.

At 6:00 a.m. on Wednesday, May 8, she got a call from a contractor she knew. The vendor had recommended her to Baltimore officials, and Frank wanted her to take over as incident response commander. By 6:00 p.m., she was checking in to a hotel near city hall.

Melissa began working from 7:00 a.m. to 10:00 p.m. every day out of a BCIT conference room, supervising the cleanup and recovery of computer systems and prioritizing which servers needed to be rebuilt or replaced first. She corralled the city government's different fiefdoms into collaborating with the central IT office. "That's where my military experience came in," she said.

Like Melissa, Sheryl Goldstein had also toiled in a war-ravaged country where the internet was rarely available. After NATO intervention ended the grisly war between Serbian forces and the Kosovo Liberation Army in 1999, Sheryl helped rebuild Kosovo's legal system. "We've become very dependent on technology," she said, "but the world can work without phone or email."

Back home, Sheryl got to know Baltimore's government from the inside during a five-year stint as director of the mayor's office of criminal justice, essentially serving as the police department's chief of staff.

"If you do public safety in Baltimore, you're handling a crisis every day," she said. "I'm a fixer." She was working at a private foundation when, about a week after the ransomware attack, Jack brought her back to the mayor's office. Her title was deputy chief of staff for operations; her mission was to restore city services to normal operation.

As she had done in Kosovo years before, Sheryl walked around and talked to people. This helped her assess the harm that RobbinHood had done, especially to the housing market. "People sold houses before the internet," she reminded everyone. "There must be a way."

With her prodding, Baltimore officials and industry leaders reached a deal. Baltimore would approve a sale if the seller signed an affidavit promising to pay all public taxes, assessments, and charges that turned out to be due on the property once the city regained access to its records. Some underwriters still grumbled that they were inadequately protected. "[Can the city] pull the rug and leave us hanging?" one wondered. Nevertheless, property sales resumed on Monday, May 20.

Baltimore's teamwork salvaged another unglamorous but vital service: granting building permits. Because the attack knocked out almost all the other departments that had to approve major projects, their staffers gathered each day in front of half a dozen computers in a third-floor conference room at the Department of Housing and Community Development, which had its own IT operation and had been spared major damage. Because the visitors were able to log in to the permit system and sign off on projects, the department collected about $2 million in permit fees, and contractors and developers avoided costly delays.

"We were the one working place in the whole city," said Jason Hessler, deputy commissioner for permits.

While Melissa and Sheryl pushed to get Baltimore back on track, federal officials bickered about whether and how much they should help.

Soon after the ransomware attack, the same assistant to Representative Ruppersberger who had discussed the city's preparedness with Frank Johnson contacted DHS's Cybersecurity & Infrastructure

Security Agency (CISA). The aide asked CISA, which had been established just six months before, to give Baltimore whatever assistance it requested. CISA couldn't afford to ignore Ruppersberger's office. As a member of the House Appropriations Subcommittee on Homeland Security, he had authority over the DHS budget.

Although Baltimore's representatives didn't know it, their request reignited a long-running dispute within DHS. The department tried to help state and local governments prevent ransomware attacks, but CISA director Christopher Krebs wanted his agency to expand into another role: aiding in the recovery. He believed that the federal government underestimated ransomware's threat to national security and its connection to foreign regimes. "From the government's perspective, it was shitware," Krebs said. "Ransomware hackers were not seen as sexy GRU, FSB higher-order cyber concerns," he said, referring to Russia's intelligence services. Increasingly, state and local governments hit by ransomware were seeking federal assistance in containing the damage, and Krebs was eager to provide it.

Jeanette Manfra, CISA's assistant secretary for cybersecurity, disagreed with her boss. An army veteran with nearly a decade of experience at DHS, Manfra was a pragmatist who believed incident response was a high-cost, labor-intensive endeavor best handled by the private sector.

"Every single time something happens in their community, they're yelling at DHS, 'What are you going to do about it?'" Manfra said. "We tell them, 'Your state and local authorities need to address it.' They don't like that answer."

Whenever ransomware struck a city or a public school system, Krebs wanted CISA to be there. Each time, Manfra bristled. "What are we going to do?" she asked during one meeting. "Bring a new load of computers to every school in the country? You can't do it."

Krebs admitted CISA's limitations but worried about the optics of doing nothing. "We're the cybersecurity agency," he said. "We're supposed to be helping state and locals, and we're nowhere to be seen in these events? To me, that just didn't sit right."

When Baltimore was attacked, they had a particularly heated

argument. Manfra told Krebs that there was nothing CISA could do. "I can't just drive racks of new machines to them," she told him. "Their network's gone. I can't give them money. They're already doing what they need to be doing."

She suspected that local politicians were looking for a scapegoat. "They don't really want anything from us," she told Krebs. "They're just trying to put the blame on us." She argued that CISA had more urgent priorities. "Do you want me to take people off election risk assessments to go try to help the city of Baltimore?"

If need be, yes, Krebs yelled. He wanted DHS advisers to help Baltimore's chief information security officer understand the steps toward recovery and to be a source of "trusted, strategic advice" from an organization that wasn't trying to sell something.

Krebs called the mayor, and CISA staff soon contacted Baltimore's IT administrators. But, in contrast to the state of Maryland, which immediately provided technicians to help configure replacement laptops and workstations, CISA didn't send a team until the summer. The tepid response disappointed Sheryl Goldstein, who felt that DHS should have an incident response team, as Krebs had envisioned. "Every city has to hire a Clark Hill or other vendors to get through this, when it's become a big national problem," she said. "In this crisis moment, you're on your own, trying to figure it out."

Ruppersberger was also frustrated. "I believe the federal government needs to do more to help municipalities better protect their networks," he said in a press release less than a month after the RobbinHood attack.

Krebs saw the criticism as an opportunity not to "let the crisis go to waste." He called Ruppersberger and said that if DHS was going to add ransomware to its priorities, it required more money. During federal budget markups, Ruppersberger added a $10 million appropriation for state and local CISA personnel. The money helped the agency hire state-level advisers for elections and cybersecurity.

Opposed to Krebs's vision for CISA and lured by a higher-paying job, Manfra left DHS for Google. For his part, Krebs was unceremoniously fired by Donald Trump after he rejected the president's claims of widespread voter fraud in the 2020 election.

After leaving CISA, Krebs was more sympathetic to Manfra's viewpoint. She raised a "legitimate question of whether we could actually do anything," he said. "We didn't have the personnel, or the resources, nor the mandate to get out there and fix people's networks for them. They need to be making the investments; we are not equipped to go fix their problems. If we did, there would be a bit of a moral hazard where everybody's just gonna say, 'Fuck it, if we have a problem, CISA will come in and fix it for us.'"

As DHS dithered, the U.S. Attorney's Office for the Eastern District of North Carolina oversaw the criminal investigation into RobbinHood, staying in touch with Baltimore city solicitor Andre Davis. In the early fall of 2019, there appeared to be a breakthrough.

"There was a good period of time when my hopes were raised," Andre said. "I remember a couple of conversations with the U.S. attorney. 'Man, I hope this works.'" But, as of December 2021, no charges had been filed.

RobbinHood launched more attacks, boasting in its ransom note about its greatest hits: "It's impossible to recover your files without private key and our unlocking software. You can google Baltimore city, Greenville city and RobbinHood ransomware."

In the meantime, Baltimore was digging out. Where backups were available and uncorrupted, technicians recovered encrypted files. They examined computers of ten thousand employees, swapping out at least three thousand that were compromised. They replaced 335 servers that had been encrypted or "impacted," meaning that the ransomware was present but hadn't taken over; about 400 other affected servers were decommissioned. And, rather than adopt a piecemeal approach, the city comprehensively upgraded cybersecurity, isolating key systems and network segments, rebuilding applications and databases, increasing monitoring, and requiring more complex passwords.

The task was Herculean, and the cost was steep, totaling an estimated $18.2 million: $10 million for recovery and prevention, and $8.2 million in lost or delayed revenue. In October 2019, Baltimore paid an annual premium of $835,000 for $20 million worth of cyber insurance coverage; the premium rose to $950,000 the next year.

Also in October 2019, Frank Johnson resigned. His deputy, Todd Carter, was named interim chief information officer. In February 2020, his position became permanent.

The ransomware crunch, Todd felt, had prepared him for the challenge. "Most IT professionals haven't gone through anything like this," he said. "What better way to learn about your new team than to see it perform in a crisis?"

Frank became senior vice president for sales and marketing at Seculore Solutions, a Maryland cybersecurity firm that had been one of the vendors hired by Baltimore in the wake of the attack. The city paid the company more than $900,000 for network monitoring.

Gayle Guilford was supposed to receive the city's Richard A. Lidinsky Award for excellence in public service five days after the ransomware attack, but she postponed the ceremony because she had too much work. Instead, it was bestowed in September 2019. Eight months later, she retired. She's listed with other award recipients on a plaque in Baltimore City Hall's rotunda. "I Serve the City," the inscription reads. "I Serve the People."

In June 2019, two Florida cities, Riviera Beach and Lake City, paid ransoms of $600,000 and $460,000, respectively. The next month, the U.S. Conference of Mayors unanimously adopted a resolution sponsored by Jack Young against paying ransoms. "Paying ransomware attackers encourages continued attacks on other government systems, as perpetrators financially benefit," the resolution read. It wasn't binding, and many cities still bowed to hackers' demands. Florence, Alabama, for instance, paid DoppelPaymer almost $300,000 after the gang shut down the city's email in May 2020 and threatened to post or sell stolen data.

Jack Young vowed for months not to seek reelection, then changed his mind. But the flip-flop alienated voters, the pandemic stymied much of his agenda, and he was criticized for verbal gaffes. The ransomware attack was no longer foremost in their minds, and they didn't reward him for standing up to RobbinHood. In June 2020, he finished fifth out of twenty-four candidates in the Democratic primary, with 6.2 percent of the vote.

After a quarter century in public office, Jack was at loose ends. Under Baltimore's ethics law, he couldn't lobby or consult with the city for a year. So he spent the interval baking. Following recipes he had learned as a boy by watching his grandmother, he made doughnuts, cookies, biscuits, rum cakes, and other treats.

While he baked, he reflected on one of the "proudest moments" of his career—defying RobbinHood. "People wrote in, advising me on what I should do and what I shouldn't do, but I made up my mind. As a matter of principle, and also a matter of caution, I was not paying criminals for hacking into a government system."

11.

THE EXTORTION ECONOMY

O f all the hedge funds that dominated Wall Street in the first decade of the twenty-first century, few if any made more money and exuded more swagger than SAC Capital Advisors. Year in and year out, it averaged a remarkable 30 percent return on investment. Its cutthroat culture reflected the ethos of its relentless, temperamental founder, Steven A. Cohen, one of the richest people in America. Despite whispers that Cohen owed his uncanny stock-picking to inside information, "young traders longed to work for him, and rich investors begged to put their money in his hands," Sheelah Kolhatkar wrote in a 2017 book about SAC. With bonuses pegged to the profits they generated, SAC's top portfolio managers could earn tens of millions of dollars a year.

From his seat as an SAC analyst managing a high-yield and dis-tressed debt portfolio in 2006, Bill Siegel watched his coworkers with a combination of horror and amusement that he likened to being in a depraved cartoon. Boyishly charming, with dark hair that over the years would be flecked with gray, Bill didn't fit the standard profile of an SAC highflier: he wasn't an ex-jock or an Ivy League graduate, and he wasn't ferociously competitive. The son of two lawyers, he grew up in Washington, D.C., and attended Sidwell Friends, the private high school known for educating the children of U.S. presidents from

Theodore Roosevelt to Barack Obama. Then he studied business at the University of Michigan, where he spent much of his time partying.

In contrast to Bill's previous job managing investments for union retirement funds, where helping to reduce blue-collar workers' financial worries gave him a sense of fulfillment, SAC's "selfish pursuit of money" for the already rich gnawed at him. Bill was disgusted when news broke in 2007 that a top portfolio manager had sexually harassed a male subordinate, forcing him to take black-market estrogen pills and wear women's clothing. Bill realized that managers who made big money for SAC could get away with almost anything. One day, over lunch with a small group of like-minded coworkers, he announced, "This place is crazy."

At the same time, he was growing physically ill. A sudden onset of acute ulcerative colitis, likely exacerbated by the stress of his job, left him in crippling pain. He took escalating courses of drugs, culminating in a regimen of various immunomodulators, biologics, and corticosteroids. Still, he showed little improvement. "The drugs were killing me, and if I went off the drugs, I would die," he said.

As the subprime mortgage crisis plunged the U.S. financial system into chaos, the performance of Bill's group tanked, and SAC fired him in early 2008. Even at the time, he saw his dismissal as cathartic. "It was a head-clearing moment where the world's priorities line up and choices are clear," he said. Subsequent developments reinforced his views. A federal investigation would force SAC to plead guilty to insider trading charges and pay a record $1.8 billion penalty. Cohen himself would escape criminal charges, though he would be banned from managing other people's money for two years; he would later rebrand himself as the owner of the New York Mets.

After leaving SAC, Bill had surgery to remove his large intestine, which ultimately allowed him to live pain-free. Feeling like himself again, he proposed to his girlfriend and got married. He dived into the realm of start-ups, honing his entrepreneurial drive and business instincts. Eventually, as an industry sprang up to serve—and profit from—victims of an emerging cyber threat called ransomware, Bill would become one of its most pivotal players. He would transform and professionalize the fledgling specialty of ransomware negotiation, fostering a surge in insurance coverage of ransom payments and exposing "data recovery" firms that purported to help victims but actually exploited them. The data he collected and the blogs he wrote would become go-to resources for anyone seeking to participate in or analyze this new extortion economy. And he would work closely with the Ransomware Hunting Team, sharing information and tips with its members, and letting clients know when Michael Gillespie or Fabian Wosar had broken the strain that crippled them.

Yet all this success would make Bill uneasy. As he grew more influential, something about his personality didn't allow him to fully enjoy it. What if all he'd done only made the ransomware epidemic worse?

Bill first became familiar with a vital element of ransomware transactions—digital currency—when he worked at SecondMarket, a popular marketplace for buying and selling shares in companies such as Facebook prior to their initial public offerings. SecondMarket's founder and CEO, Barry Silbert, was one of the earliest and most active investors in Bitcoin, which would make him a billionaire. Silbert spread the cryptocurrency gospel to colleagues. "It's the future," he told Bill, who was fascinated by Bitcoin's potential for disrupting the financial system.

In 2016, Bill left his job to become chief financial officer of Security-Scorecard, which provided corporations with cyber risk assessments of their vendors. There, he talked regularly with chief information security officers of Fortune 500 companies who used SecurityScorecard's product. They described the cyber threats they faced and the steps they were taking to mitigate risk. It wasn't long before a couple of them mentioned a maneuver that surprised him: they were creating shell companies in the Cayman Islands to stockpile Bitcoin.

"Why are you doing that?" he asked.

"It's because of ransomware," one replied. "If we have to pay a ransom, we need to be able to do so quickly."

Bill was intrigued. He knew the process of setting up a shell company, and of handling and accounting for millions of dollars' worth of Bitcoin, would be "a pain in the ass" for a publicly traded corporation—something they'd only do if they really thought they needed to. He called friends who had left SecondMarket to work at Digital Currency Group, a firm founded by Silbert that invested in Bitcoin and blockchain companies. Bill wanted to know if anyone had heard of corporations holding Bitcoin reserves in case of a ransomware attack.

"Hey, is this a thing?" he asked.

"Oh yeah, it's a thing, and we know because we get calls every day," a contact told him.

Some of the businesses calling Digital Currency Group wanted more than a Bitcoin stockpile; already hit by ransomware, they wanted the firm to pay the Bitcoin ransom on their behalf. Digital Currency turned them away. Paying ransoms was outside the scope of its business, and it was afraid of running afoul of government regulations.

But where Digital Currency saw risk, Bill sensed opportunity. Commuting on the Metro-North train from his home in Westport, Connecticut, to SecurityScorecard's Manhattan office, he often sat beside Alex Holdtman, a product manager at a cyber disaster recovery company and a former colleague at SecondMarket. The friends passed time on the train by spitballing start-up ideas. Most of them, they agreed, stank. But in early 2018, Bill proposed one that they thought had potential: handling ransom payments.

Their backgrounds seemed perfect for the new venture, and their strengths were complementary. Alex, who had studied computer science and math at the University of Connecticut, could analyze malware and write software. Bill was a charismatic dealmaker familiar with the realm of start-ups, who also had experience working with businesses small and large—their prospective client pool. Both were familiar with Bitcoin and had worked in cybersecurity. Their timing was similarly fortuitous. As they discussed their business idea, Ryuk was preparing to usher in a new era of large corporate targets and routine six-figure ransoms.

Eager to become entrepreneurs, Bill and Alex quit their stable jobs at growing companies. They started researching online, seeking statistics on the number of companies hit by ransomware annually. What they found seemed to indicate that ransomware was a large and growing problem, but the data mostly came from unreliable surveys. They learned that companies struck by ransomware had few places to turn for basic information about what to do next. For many victims, it wasn't even clear whether paying a ransom was legal. The lack of reliable information meant that companies struck by ransomware would likely be receptive to the kind of services that Bill and Alex wanted to offer.

They gradually refined their concept. They believed managed service providers were sufficiently worried about ransomware attacks to keep them on retainer. If those fears became reality, Bill and Alex would handle the ransom negotiation and payment. At the same time, they would gain credibility by collecting information from their cases in a database to analyze ransomware trends.

"There was an opportunity to stand in the middle of the car accident with our measuring stick and watch the accident happen," Bill said. "Then we could clean up after the accident, and have our nice clean data set of what actually happened."

Their wives were anxious about the new venture. Bill, with three kids, and Alex, then with one—he and his wife later had a second child—weren't just giving up job security. Since they had no outside investors, they were spending their savings to launch their company, which they christened Coveware.

Bill and Alex were undeterred. They learned that some strains of ransomware could be decrypted with free tools available on Bleeping-Computer and elsewhere—and that they should check before paying a ransom for clients. But when they googled the phrase "how to decrypt ransomware," those sites weren't the first to come up. Instead, two U.S. firms, Florida-based MonsterCloud and New York–based Proven Data Recovery, consistently appeared at the top of the search results.

The partners talked to businesses that used MonsterCloud and Proven Data to recover from ransomware attacks. Those sources described how the data recovery firms, for a fee, helped them recover without paying ransoms. Bill and Alex were suspicious. They'd learned from sites like BleepingComputer that the strains mentioned by these victims had not been cracked. The only option for recovering locked files would be to pay a ransom.

But there was scarcely a mention of ransom negotiation or payment on the firms' websites. Bill researched their spending on Google AdWords, the pay-per-click program that allowed users to buy ad space at the top of search results. MonsterCloud and, to a lesser extent, Proven Data were spending thousands of dollars to reserve space on results pages for keywords that included all the most common ransomware strains. So when an IT administrator from a company struck by Dharma entered "Dharma" into Google, MonsterCloud would be the first result, increasing the likelihood that it would get the victim's business. Bill and Alex also talked to former Proven Data employees, who confirmed that the company was paying ransoms without telling clients.

Bill and Alex realized that Proven Data and MonsterCloud were their competitors. The data recovery firms paid attackers for a fee, as Coveware intended to do. The difference was that Proven Data and MonsterCloud refused to admit it.

"There we were, kind of horrified, that a company would just be essentially acting in a predatory, usurious manner to a company that had literally just gotten killed by ransomware," Bill said.

Even ransomware gangs, eager to proclaim solidarity with victims, were warning about duplicitous data recovery firms. "Decryption of your files with the help of third parties may cause increased price (they add their fee to our) or you can become a victim of a scam," the Phobos group wrote in its ransom note.

This deceit was old news to the Ransomware Hunting Team. In late 2016, Fabian had come across MonsterCloud, Proven Data, and several other data recovery firms based in the UK and Australia that claimed to have broken ransomware strains that he and the team hadn't. He was skeptical.

"Everything the ransomware did has been analyzed by other

researchers," he said. "It's incredibly unlikely they were the only ones to break it."

To test his suspicions, Fabian devised an experiment that he dubbed Operation Bleeding Cloud, after MonsterCloud and the notorious Heartbleed software vulnerability that was publicly disclosed in 2014. He and Sarah White tweaked an existing ransomware variant and used it to infect their own test files. Then they emailed Monster-Cloud, Proven Data, and the other firms, posing as a victim who didn't want to pay a ransom.

Fabian sent sample encrypted files to the firms along with a fake ransom note that included an email address to contact the attacker—himself—for instructions on how to pay. Each note also contained a unique ID sequence for the fictitious victim, so Fabian could later identify which firm had contacted him even if it used an anonymous email account. The firms eagerly agreed to help recover the files.

"They all claimed to be able to decrypt ransomware families that definitely weren't decryptable and didn't mention that they paid the ransom," Fabian said. "Quite the contrary actually. They all seemed very proud not to pay ransomers."

Soon, the email accounts that he'd set up for the imaginary attacker began receiving emails from anonymous addresses offering to pay the ransom, he said. He traced the requests to the data recovery firms, including Proven Data and MonsterCloud.

"The victims are getting taken advantage of twice," he said.

Proven Data boasted on its website that it was "the first company in the world to assist victims of ransomware." A more accurate statement would be that it was a pioneer in pretending to help ransomware victims, while actually misleading them.

Two brothers, Victor and Mark Congionti, established Proven Data around 2011 at Mark's house in White Plains, New York; years later, as the company expanded, it moved to an office in nearby Elmsford. Neither brother knew much about coding. Mark was a substitute math teacher. Victor had a more technical background—he had worked as an IT security analyst for an insurance company—but his passion was electronic dance music. On a roommate-search website, he described himself as a "foodie," "fitness junkie," and "party person."

At first, Proven Data specialized in recovering information from broken hard drives, cameras, and other hardware. Around 2015, its business model shifted. As ransomware proliferated and calls poured in from prospective clients seeking help releasing their encrypted files, Proven Data began promising to help victims by unlocking their data with the "latest technology." In essence, the firm told clients that it could do what Michael and Fabian did: decrypt ransomware. It couldn't. Instead, it obtained keys from attackers by paying ransoms and charged clients the amount of the ransom plus a fee.

Its staff relied on "canned responses" that gave clients two options for data recovery. The first was paying the ransom. The second was unlocking the files using Proven Data's technology. Unbeknownst to clients, the second option didn't exist. If they chose it, Proven Data paid the ransom anyway.

Some clients became suspicious. After its networks were frozen by ransomware in June 2016, the City of Safford, Arizona, hired Proven Data. The company's case manager, Brad Miller, told the city in an email that engineers had analyzed a sample file and found there was a "high chance for data recovery" by "using our streamlined process and latest technology." Miller acknowledged that Proven Data's price "can be high" and suggested that the city's insurance "may cover the cost."

Proven Data had no employee named Brad Miller. It was an alias that the company assigned to the overseas freelancers it hired. "Their names can be complex," Victor Congionti said. "We used this alias to simplify things . . . We did not view it as deceptive. It was for convenience."

A week later, Proven Data told Safford that the "decryption process has completed successfully." Then the city discovered that some files remained locked. Proven Data opened a new case and insisted on charging the city once more. Safford acquiesced—its insurer ultimately reimbursed most of the total bill of $8,413—but systems administrator Cade Bryce wondered why the city had to pay twice if Proven Data already had the solution.

"If their algorithms did the first one, why couldn't they do the second?" Bryce asked himself.

In mid-August, Proven Data gave up. "We haven't had any luck decrypting this remaining variant and contact to the hackers has not yielded any results as well," it said in an email.

The likely explanation was that Proven Data had paid the ransom, but bugs in the ransomware had permanently damaged the files. Sam Napier, the city's IT administrator, shared the company's admission of failure with Bryce. "I think you were right about them working with the hackers and adding a fee," Napier wrote.

The FBI's office in Anchorage, Alaska, was also skeptical of Proven Data's apparent success in decrypting ransomware. It began investigating Proven Data after a strain called DMA Locker infiltrated the files and backups of Leif Herrington's real estate brokerage in Anchorage in April 2016. The ransom note demanded 4 bitcoin (then worth about $1,680).

Herrington called the FBI. At first, the bureau didn't care. "There's thousands of these going on every day," it told him. "We don't have the resources to do anything."

Herrington's son looked into the attack, discovered there was no known way to decrypt the files, and suggested his father pay the ransom. After unsuccessful attempts to do so on his own and through a local IT firm, Herrington called Proven Data. It told him that its proprietary software would unlock his files for $6,000, and didn't mention paying the ransom.

Herrington's IT consultant, Simon Schroeder, gave Proven Data a sample infected file for evaluation. A couple of days later, Schroeder granted remote access to Proven Data and watched as it unlocked a set of files in forty-five minutes.

The firm cleared the files so quickly that Schroeder suspected it had paid the ransom. Although Herrington was back in business, he called the FBI again. This time, the bureau was intrigued. When an agent came to the real estate office, Herrington encouraged the FBI to investigate whether Proven Data was working with DMA Locker. The agent told Herrington that if Proven Data was misrepresenting its methods and expertise, it might be breaking the law. And if it paid ransoms, it was effectively keeping the gangs in business.

The FBI confirmed this hunch. It found several hundred emails between Proven Data and addresses associated with DMA Locker attacks. It also traced 4 bitcoin flowing from a Proven Data account to the online wallet that DMA had designated for payment. An email from the hacker's address thanked Proven Data for the payment and included instructions for decrypting Herrington's files.

Proven Data "was only able to decrypt the victim's files by paying the subject the ransom amount," an FBI affidavit stated.

The bureau spoke with the Congionti brothers. Mark conceded that, at the time of the attack, there was no known way to unlock the files without paying the hacker.

Victor later acknowledged that the company paid Herrington's ransom. "It was the only option to get his data back," he said. "We regret that he felt misled ... There was obviously a misunderstanding as to how we would solve his problem."

The FBI never brought charges against Proven Data. But the recollections of a former Proven Data staffer, Jonathan Storfer, who negotiated some of its later payments to DMA Locker, substantiate Herrington's worries about cooperation between the company and the hacker.

Proven Data used its real email addresses with DMA Locker. Storfer wondered if the attacker was a British soccer fan, because his emails contained references to Manchester United, such as the username "John United" and another honoring former team manager Alex Ferguson. The ransom price was set in British pounds, an unusual currency in ransomware circles, to be paid in Bitcoin.

"DMA was actually a very good, nice negotiator for the most part,"

Storfer said. "He was very clear, straightforward [and communicated in] very proper English. And he had a tool that worked impeccably well, and he would even troubleshoot for you."

The DMA Locker hacker was so familiar with Proven Data's Bitcoin wallet numbers that he would send a decryption key as soon as he saw the transaction on the blockchain, the electronic public ledger. Normally, attackers waited for Proven Data to send confirmation that the ransom had been paid before sending a key.

"One of the weird benefits was that he knew our wallets enough that every time we sent him a payment, he would send us a key before we could send a transaction ID," Storfer said. "He would literally sit on the blockchain, and just be like, 'Oh yeah, Proven, let me give you guys some keys.'"

When the hacker decided to retire from the ransomware business, he let Proven Data know—and proposed one last deal. "Hey, I'm shutting down service," he told Storfer. "Do you have any other clients that need keys? I'm doing this super discount for any of them."

It was, Storfer said, "one of the benefits of being friendly with—the biggest air quotations—the hackers."

The sociable Storfer had an unkempt beard and an aversion to physical exercise. An accomplished amateur chef, he collected cookbooks, often watched *The Great British Bake Off*, and could spend a week curing duck prosciutto. "I'm obsessive about food in general," he said.

In 2017, he was a year out of college and looking online for a job close to his Westchester County home when he spotted an opening for an office manager at Proven Data. He'd never heard of the company, but he applied and was hired. He thought he would be scheduling meetings, sending out packages, and accepting deliveries. But prior jobs at retail stores and restaurants had honed his customer service skills. After a short time at Proven Data, he was given the title of client solutions manager, at a starting salary of about $41,000 a year, and assigned to negotiate with hackers.

By then, Proven Data had ditched the scripts that purported to offer clients the choice to pay the ransom or not. Instead, Storfer took a "don't ask, don't tell," approach to informing clients that Proven Data would pay their ransoms. If they didn't ask, he said nothing; if they asked, he told the truth. "It was more of a lie by omission," he said.

As a negotiator, Storfer reduced the ransom price by bonding with the attackers. He quickly learned never to use the word "hacking." Instead, he assumed that those he was dealing with thought of themselves as businesspeople. "Look, we can't afford this at this time," Storfer would say. "Do you mind providing your product at a lower rate?"

Often, the victims who contacted Proven Data had already berated their attackers. So Storfer's ingratiating approach was a refreshing change and sometimes reaped discounts, which Proven Data passed along to clients. "They're doing a job where everyone hates them, so feeling like they were respected made them work with us," Storfer said. "We were able to get a five-thousand-dollar ransom lessened to three thousand dollars because they knew we could deliver it exactly when we said we were going to get it to them."

Once the attackers agreed to lower the ransom for one client, it was easier to persuade them to reduce it for others. Storfer would tell them, "'Look, we have another client who you may be able to help. Can you provide this pricing?' Their response is: 'Sure thing.'"

Though successful, these tactics made Storfer uncomfortable. "It's one of the weird kind of gray areas that I never felt comfortable with—that I had to interact and almost befriend these individuals," he said. He became a familiar figure to the hackers, who would "want to verify that we worked with them before . . . I'm using terms like 'working with them,' but it's the skin-crawliest way to describe it, because we truly hate them. And it was something that we would openly talk about [at Proven Data:] how creepy and crawly we felt in general to have to put yourself on their side and empathize with these individuals to get them to work with you. Because you kind of have to shed your skin afterwards."

Despite Storfer's best efforts, sometimes the hackers behaved erratically. Proven Data would pay the requested ransom, but they would not respond. At such times, Storfer would share the attacker's email address and details of the snub with other hackers in the same gang.

Then the hacker "would come back and say, 'Sorry, I've been on a coke binge for three weeks,'" Storfer said.

The most notorious gang with which Storfer forged a mutually beneficial relationship was SamSam. Proven Data paid ransoms to SamSam for more than a year. "We were very open [with them,] and we would essentially announce ourselves," Storfer said.

As he developed a rapport with the hackers, Storfer was able to negotiate extensions on payment deadlines. "Hello, this is Proven Data, please keep this portal open while we contact and interact with the customer while moving forward," Storfer would say. SamSam would then remove the timer on the portal. "They would respond quicker and in many cases would be able to provide things a little bit easier."

Eventually, the attackers began recommending that victims work with the firm. "SamSam would be like, 'If you need assistance with this, contact Proven Data,'" Storfer said. Some clients wondered about this endorsement. "Clients would ask us why, and we would have to respond to that, which was not really a fun conversation."

These prior understandings posed a legal risk. The hackers' confidence that Proven Data would pay the ransom could be seen as evidence of a criminal conspiracy. "That does seem like you are working for the other side," said Bart Huffman, a Houston lawyer specializing in privacy and information security. "You are facilitating the payment at the recommendation of SamSam, in the manner suggested by SamSam."

Proven Data "never had a 'close relationship' with SamSam attackers," Victor Congionti said, without denying Storfer's account. "Our contact with attackers is limited to minimizing the attack on the customer . . . Anyone can reach out to a hacker and tell them to keep the portal open longer."

That wasn't the only thorny aspect of dealing with SamSam. Sam-sam Kandi happens to be the name of an Iranian village, and the gang was eventually discovered to be operating from Iran. One of Proven Data's final payments to SamSam—for 1.6 bitcoin (about $9,000 at the time)—was sent in November 2018. The payment moved from Proven Data's Bitcoin wallet to one specified by the attackers, and ultimately to one linked directly to the Iranian hackers.

Twelve days after Proven Data made the payment came the indictment of the two Iranians who allegedly developed SamSam. The U.S. Treasury Department banned payments to two Bitcoin wallets connected to the attackers, citing sanctions on the Iranian regime.

Victor Congionti said that Proven Data did not know the hackers were affiliated with Iran until they were indicted. "Under no circumstances would we have knowingly dealt with a sanctioned person or entity," he said.

By the time of the indictments, Storfer had left Proven Data. After working there for a year and a half, his conscience had begun weighing on him, especially once the FBI began questioning Proven Data employees in the Alaska case. "I would not be surprised if a significant amount of ransomware both funded terrorism and also organized crime," he said. "So the question is . . . every time that we get hit by SamSam, and every time we facilitate a payment—and here's where it gets really dicey—does that mean we are technically funding terrorism?"

Storfer was tired of justifying his line of work to family and friends, some of whom teased him for answering late-night hacker emails. "Do I miss ever having to explain what my job is to anyone else? No. Having that conversation and trying to explain, 'Oh, what do you do?' Oh, I negotiate with hackers for a living . . . It is a very weird business."

Familiar with Storfer's negotiating expertise, Bill Siegel sought to recruit him to his new company. Storfer was tempted, but in the end he left the industry. "I just decided that I wanted to get out of the space because I felt uncomfortable," he said. The realm where Proven Data, MonsterCloud, and Coveware operated "is the Wild West. They set their own rules."

■ ■ ■

Proven Data and its rival, MonsterCloud, were alike in many ways. Both claimed to have assisted thousands of ransomware victims. Both offered other services besides data recovery, such as sealing breaches to protect against future attacks. Both used aliases for their workers to communicate with clients. Both charged substantial fees on top of the ransom amounts. And just as Proven Data boasted a 98 percent success rate, MonsterCloud "guaranteed" victims that it would remove ransomware.

MonsterCloud was, if anything, more brazen than Proven Data in pretending that it didn't pay ransoms. "Don't Pay the Ransom," its website asserted. "Paying-up is a risk you don't want to take. Let our experts handle the situation for you."

The website featured a promotional video by John Pistole, a former deputy director of the FBI under Robert Mueller. "Police departments, government agencies, hospitals, small businesses, and Fortune 500 firms trust MonsterCloud to help recover from attacks and protect against new ones," Pistole said in the video. "MonsterCloud's proprietary technology and expertise protects their professional reputations and organizational integrity."

However, Pistole acknowledged in a 2019 interview that Monster-Cloud didn't rely on "proprietary technology and expertise" to decrypt files. "The model I'm used to is, you pay the ransom," he said. "That's the business model as I understood it last year when I did my initial look at it after meeting Zohar . . . Based on my experience and knowledge, ransom is paid and they facilitate the best practices moving forward."

"Zohar" was Zohar Pinhasi, who scripted Pistole's testimonial. A former IT security intelligence officer for the Israeli military, Zohar moved to the United States in 2002. The following year, he cofounded a Florida company called PC USA Computer Solutions Providers, which backed up clients' files on the cloud. Zohar established MonsterCloud in 2013 and, like Proven Data's founders, eventually pivoted to ransomware recovery from other tech services.

Zohar had a narrow face, a shaved head, and an affluent lifestyle. He drove one new Mercedes after another and owned two houses in South Florida, including a five-bedroom waterfront home in Hallandale Beach.

Over lunch at Shalom Haifa, a restaurant near MonsterCloud's storefront office in Hollywood, Florida, Zohar said MonsterCloud received up to thirty calls a day. It had twenty employees in South Florida, as well as extensive global contacts, including on the dark web.

The firm's secrecy sometimes alienated potential clients. Tim Anderson, an IT consultant based in Houston, reached out to MonsterCloud in January 2019 after the ransomware strain Nozelesn attacked one of his clients and the hackers demanded a $7,000 ransom. MonsterCloud wanted $2,500 for an analysis and up to $25,000 for actual recovery. Anderson requested an explicit technical description of how MonsterCloud would unlock the files, but the firm demurred.

"I immediately smelled a rat," Anderson said. "How do I know they're not taking the twenty-five thousand dollars and paying the ransom guy seven thousand of it? The consumer doesn't know what's going on."

He declined MonsterCloud's services, and his client hired another company to pay the ransom.

MonsterCloud buttressed its credibility with testimonials from law enforcement officials such as Pistole, who served as the FBI's deputy director from 2004 to 2010. Pistole then headed the Transportation Security Administration under President Barack Obama before leaving government in 2015 to become president of Anderson University in Indiana. MonsterCloud paid Pistole through a speaker's bureau and named him a "founding member" of its "Cyber Security Advisory Council." If the advisory council had other members, they weren't listed on MonsterCloud's website.

Zohar also brought Pistole into another company he ran, Skyline Comfort LLC, which aimed to put massage chairs in airports. For a few minutes' massage, passengers would pay a fee, which Skyline would split with the airport authority. Pistole's role was to connect Zohar with airport officials in return for payment if the company became profitable. Skyline dissolved in 2021.

MonsterCloud's website displayed promotional videos not only from Pistole but also from several rural police departments that had been hit by ransomware. They received free service from Monster-Cloud in exchange for their praising testimonials. The taxpayer-funded departments spurned the notion of rewarding hackers with a ransom payment—negotiating with criminals is anathema to law enforcement—so MonsterCloud's promise of a technological solution was alluring. The firm also benefited from the local police's unfamiliarity with ransomware decryption. Unaware that in most cases the only way to recover is by paying the hackers, the police generally believed MonsterCloud's assurances that its proprietary technology could save them. (More tech-savvy forces that saw through Monster-Cloud may have liked being able to deny that they paid the ransom.)

In May 2018, the ransomware strain Mr.Dec struck the Lamar County, Texas, sheriff's office. "You are unlucky!" the attacker wrote. "The terrible virus has captured your files!"

With no backups, the only way to recover from Mr.Dec at the time was to pay the ransom. But Lamar County network administrator Joel Witherspoon didn't know that. When county officials hired MonsterCloud, Witherspoon made it clear that Lamar County would not pay the 1-bitcoin ransom (then worth about $8,000). MonsterCloud told him they "had a team of specialist engineers working on it."

"I don't think they would ever pay [the ransom]," Witherspoon said.

Without knowing he'd been misled, he said MonsterCloud "did an excellent job" retrieving the department's files. He was especially impressed by his primary contact there, Zack Green. "Zack's title, dear God, it's a mile long title," Witherspoon said. "He seems to know a lot." The titles on Green's email signature—none of which are formal industry credentials—included "Ransomware Recovery Expert," "Cyber Counterterrorism Expert," "Cyber Crime Prevention Expert," and "Cyber Intelligence Threat Specialist."

Actually, nobody named Zack Green worked at MonsterCloud. Zohar acknowledged that Green was an alias, but he declined to say for whom. "We go based on aliases, because we're dealing with cyberterrorists," he said.

In their testimonial, Witherspoon and other Lamar County administrators touted MonsterCloud's services. "If we were not able to recover, we would have been set back quite a few years," Witherspoon said in the video. "Man, these people really know what they're doing . . . We did not lose any data."

The Trumann, Arkansas, police department was another satisfied customer. In November 2018, Dharma ransomware crippled the department, which had two dozen officers serving a population of eight thousand. The attack froze decades' worth of data, including case notes, witness statements, affidavits, and payroll records. Frantically searching for a solution on Google, the department's IT manager came across MonsterCloud.

Two of MonsterCloud's selling points impressed Trumann police chief Chad Henson: the first was "how friendly they are to law enforcement and to government entities," and the second was that they wouldn't pay the ransom. "I'm the one in the seat, the one charged to safeguard the department," Henson said. "To turn around and spend taxpayer money on a ransom—that is absolutely the wrong decision. It is the nuclear option. But with MonsterCloud, we can just remove that option."

So Henson called MonsterCloud and explained his plight. "Don't worry about it," they told him. "We are pretty sure we can get everything back."

MonsterCloud restored the department's files within seventy-two hours, and waived its $75,000 fee in return for a testimonial. It assured Henson that it did not pay the hacker.

Perhaps the chief should have scrutinized Trumann's contract with MonsterCloud more closely. The fine print authorized the company to pay the ransom, and without the police department's knowledge. Calling MonsterCloud's recovery method a "trade secret," the contract said that the firm would not explain the "proprietary means and methods by which client's files were restored." If "all possible means of directly decrypting client's files have been exhausted," it added, MonsterCloud would try to recover data by "communicating with the cyber attacker." Since there was no known way of decrypting Dharma at the time, paying the hacker would have been Monster-Cloud's only recourse.

In an interview, Zohar defended his business stoutly. "Our goal is to restore the data and help the customer," he said. "If we need to walk to the moon on broken glass, we will. We don't care how, what, where, whatever. Our goal is to get the data out."

Asked if MonsterCloud paid ransoms, he dodged the question. "We work in the shadows," he said. "How we do it, it's our problem. You will get your data back. Sit back, relax, and enjoy the ride."

Bill Siegel and Alex Holdtman designed their new company to be as transparent as Proven Data and MonsterCloud were duplicitous. By being open about its dealings with hackers, they believed Coveware could upend the ransomware recovery industry. Rather than guarding its technique as a trade secret, Coveware would document every step of the negotiation process with screenshots and share the details with clients. When prospective customers were affected by strains already broken by the Ransomware Hunting Team or other researchers, Bill and Alex would direct them to the free decryption tools without charging.

"We felt like, at a minimum, we can disrupt these scummy operators," Bill said.

With no experience or training in ransom negotiation, the founders practiced the fake-it-till-you-make-it credo they knew from the start-up world while they learned on the job. As chief technology officer, Alex wrote case management software that streamlined and standardized incoming data. Bill, the CEO, copied a move that had been successful at SecondMarket. Their former employer, by releasing quarterly reports based on its data, had become a de facto authority on pre-IPO trading. Likewise, Bill launched a blog on Coveware's website

in hopes of establishing the new company as a trusted source for prospective clients, law enforcement and the media on ransomware.

Titled "Introducing Coveware!," his very first post, in May 2018,
took direct aim at firms like Proven Data and MonsterCloud. Bill described conversations with IT professionals about the aftermath of
ransomware attacks—and about how they were victimized twice, first
by the hackers and second by the data recovery firms.

"We expected to hear about frustrating situations and anxiety-
ridden periods of recovery," he wrote. "We were not anticipating the
murky class of 'service providers' (a term we use generously) whose
treatment of ransomware victims is both usurious and predatory.
These stories made us angry . . . It motivated us to build a better
experience—and that is what we've done."

Addressing what he called "the elephant in the room," he acknowledged that he expected "criticism and scrutiny." Although paying
ransoms was legal, except to entities under federal sanctions, the FBI
discourages it. The new business defied the bureau's guidance.

"Coveware makes it easier for businesses to pay," Bill wrote. "Popular refrains involve a utopian vision of every afflicted business and
person, ceasing to pay, and the problem disappearing for good. While
we understand and appreciate these refrains, we deem the implemen-
tation unrealistic."

Bill assured his readers, "We also have no intention of profiting off
of the payment of ransomware." He may have been deluding himself as
much as his readers. He added that Coveware's data collection would
"help the security community build and deploy better security tools."

Bill and Alex had quickly dropped the idea of a subscription model
after finding that managed service providers weren't willing to pay a
retainer for a hypothetical response to an attack that might or might
not happen. Instead, they worked with companies that had already
been attacked. In the summer of 2018, they took on cases without
charging fees as they learned how to deal with hackers. The first
month, Coveware had three cases, including a Texas junkyard that recovered its files after Bill negotiated down the ransom demand. The
next month, it had a dozen clients. By October 2018, Coveware had

handled enough cases to put together statistics for its inaugural quarterly report, which explained that the average ransom demanded of its
clients was $5,974 and the most common strain afflicting them was
Dharma.

"Through our negotiations it is clear that hacker groups are taking
detailed notes on the size and type of the machines they encrypt along
with the size of the organizations," Bill wrote. "Ransom amounts are
scaled accordingly."

Bill continued to write blog posts, which in turn helped Coveware
rank higher on Google search results and attracted new clients who
otherwise might have hired MonsterCloud or Proven Data. He connected with Lawrence Abrams, who agreed to share Coveware's posts
on BleepingComputer. As more victims sought help, Bill and Alex began charging for their work. They established flat fees—ranging from
$1,500 to $7,500, depending on how complex they thought the case
would be—which they quoted up front.

MonsterCloud took notice of Coveware's traction. The same month
the upstart released the quarterly report, MonsterCloud posted a blog
of its own, hypocritically attacking Coveware for paying ransoms—as
if the Florida firm weren't doing the same.

"The company Coveware provides negotiation services where the
ransom amount is discussed with the cybercriminals," the Monster-
Cloud blogger wrote with feigned abhorrence. "Bill Siegal [sic]—
Coveware's Chief Executive Officer and co-founder—has described
the company's vision as 'pragmatic'. Siegal believes that some businesses do not have any option other than initiating the ransom procedure with the cybercriminals."

The MonsterCloud blogger downplayed Coveware's early success
in dealing with hackers as "beginner's luck," wrongly insinuating that
most hackers don't provide a key after receiving a ransom. "Other cybercriminals groups are unlikely to begin the ransomware removal
process after receiving ransom," the blogger wrote.

The blogger warned that paying ransoms could have "bigger im-
plications in the future . . . Any ransom payment enables the cybercriminals to profit and continue their campaigns. As a result, this

dangerous industry can be promoted and flourished rapidly through such payments."

Bill had anticipated that righteous critics would consider him an enabler. But he was indignant that the first pundit to make such a judgment publicly profited from doing the very same thing.

In December 2018, just as he and Alex began taking salaries for the first time since starting Coveware, Bill felt emboldened to write another post about what he called "ransomware payment mills." Under the headline "Beware of Dishonest Ransomware Recovery firms," Bill warned readers about the "excessive fees charged" by companies that "advertise guaranteed decryption without having to pay the hacker." Such firms, he wrote, just pay the ransom without the client's knowledge.

In early 2019, ProPublica, a nonprofit organization focused on investigative journalism, learned that a new business called Coveware was paying ransoms and called Bill. He mentioned his blog post about his unsavory competitors. Four months later, in May, ProPublica published an investigation into the data recovery industry. Titled "The Trade Secret," it revealed how firms like MonsterCloud and Proven Data promised high-tech solutions to ransomware but almost always just paid the hackers, without telling clients.

Bill felt vindicated. Evidence of his competitors' duplicity was laid bare for the public. And the growth of his business, and of ransomware itself, exploded.

Payment negotiation firms were only a small part of the burgeoning extortion economy. The ransomware threat was also a boon for cybersecurity companies, as businesses fearing a first or repeat attack fortified their defenses. Sometimes, though, the customers were buying a false sense of security. The products varied in quality and required updates as ransomware evolved. Ultimately, they depended on human competence and were only as effective as the IT staff who implemented and monitored them.

Ransomware insurance was another booming field. As ransomware became more targeted, and demands climbed, American companies and public entities began to view attacks as inevitable. To cope, they increasingly took out cyber insurance policies.

At first, many insurers had been reluctant to cover cyber disasters, in part because of the lack of reliable actuarial data. When insurers cover traditional risks such as fires, floods, and auto accidents, they price their policies based on authoritative information from national and industry sources. But there were no equivalent sources for assessing cyber risk. Despite this uncertainty, dozens of carriers embraced cyber coverage, a booming sector in an otherwise low-growth industry. By 2019, cyber insurance was an $8 billion market in the United States.

Hoping to protect policyholders from attacks, some cyber insurers required them to undergo rigorous security assessments as a condition of coverage, the same way fire insurance companies require commercial buildings to have sprinklers. Insurers developed a streamlined system for handling the explosion in ransomware claims, coordinating cadres of lawyers, consultants, negotiators, and other vendors. They typically provided policyholders with a toll-free number to call as soon as an attack was detected. Recognizing the possibility of future lawsuits related to the incident, the number often connected the victim with a lawyer to maintain confidentiality from the start. The "breach coach" attorney then walked the victim through the recovery process, including the hiring of insurer-approved vendors that became flooded with insurance-referred, ransomware-related work.

With its transparent approach, and its reams of data appealing to the actuarial mind, Coveware became a mainstay for insurers. Its business soared, and Bill hired more employees to keep up. He increasingly found himself on the phone with insurers who wanted Coveware to negotiate ransoms in the aftermath of attacks on their policyholders. One such call came in June 2019, when Ryuk struck Lake City, a municipality in rural northern Florida with a population of about twelve thousand.

Initially, Lake City had hoped to restore its systems without paying a ransom. IT staff was "plugging along" and had taken server drives to a local vendor who'd had "moderate success at getting the stuff off of it," according to city spokesman Michael Lee, a police sergeant. However, the process was slower and more challenging than anticipated.

Lake City contacted its insurer, the Florida League of Cities, which shared the risk for cyber coverage with the insurance giant Beazley. The attack had deleted the city's backup files. As local technicians worked to recover them, Beazley requested a sample encrypted file and the ransom note so that Coveware, its approved vendor, could open negotiations with the hackers. The initial ransom demand was 86 bitcoin (about $700,000 at the time)—a price Beazley deemed too high. But when Bill talked the hackers down to 42 bitcoin (about $460,000), the insurer agreed to cover it.

Lake City mayor Stephen Witt gathered the city council in an emergency session to decide whether to pay the ransom, leading a prayer before polling the council members. "Our heavenly father," Witt said, "we ask for your guidance today, that we do what's best for our city and our community." Without deliberating, the mayor and the council unanimously approved paying the ransom. The city wanted to resume normal services as quickly as possible, and the cost of a prolonged recovery from backups would have exceeded its $1 million coverage limit.

Lake City fronted the ransom amount to Coveware, which converted it to Bitcoin, paid the attackers, and obtained the decryption tool. The Florida League of Cities then reimbursed the city for the ransom and other recovery expenses, minus a $10,000 deductible.

"Our insurance company made [the decision] for us," said Lee, the city spokesman. "It really boils down to a business decision" for the insurer. "How much is it going to cost to fix it ourselves and how much is it going to cost to pay the ransom."

Lee acknowledged that paying the ransom would spur more attacks, but he said Lake City trusted Beazley's judgment: "The insurer is the one who is going to get hit with most of this if it continues. And if they're the ones deciding it's still better to pay out, knowing that means they're more likely to have to do it again—if they still find that it's the financially correct decision—it's kind of hard to argue with them because they know the cost-benefit of that. I have a hard time saying it's the right decision, but maybe it makes sense with a certain perspective."

Lee was correct that, at the time, paying the ransom made financial sense for insurers. Recovering files from backups could be arduous, time-consuming, and unpredictable. It potentially left insurers on the hook for costs ranging from employee overtime to public relations efforts to ongoing fees for data recovery consultants. Hiring Coveware or a similar firm to negotiate payment instead often led to a quick resolution. Consequently, insurers routinely approved ransom payments—contingent on "proof of life," a term borrowed from kidnap ransom negotiations and referring to evidence from the hacker that a sample file could be decrypted. Policyholders usually dropped their qualms about negotiating with criminals when they realized it could speed up their return to normal operations.

"Time is of the essence for the business, or the municipality," Jeremy Gittler, who managed the cyber portfolio for the insurer AXA XL in the Americas, said at an FBI ransomware summit in September 2020. "And time is of the essence, frankly, for the bottom line of the carrier because we also cover any sort of business interruption, so you want to get the business up and running as soon as possible."

The propensity of insurers to pay ransoms frustrated Ransomware Hunting Team members who were trying to cut off the flow of money to hackers. Shortly after Lake City paid its ransom, Fabian Wosar consulted for a U.S. corporation attacked by ransomware. After determining that restoring files from backups would take weeks, the company's insurer offered to cover the $100,000 ransom so it could avoid paying ongoing business interruption costs as the policy required. The victim agreed, but the decision backfired when the decryptor obtained from the hacker didn't work properly. Fabian repaired the decryptor, and the insurer covered his work.

"Paying the ransom was a lot cheaper for the insurer," Fabian said.

"Cyber insurance is what's keeping ransomware alive today. It's a perverted relationship. They will pay anything, as long as it is cheaper than the loss of revenue they have to cover otherwise."

The industry didn't dispute this. Loretta Worters, spokeswoman for the Insurance Information Institute, a nonprofit industry group based in New York, compared ransom payments to auto insurance fraud. Insurers will pay a fraudulent claim filed by a policyholder who sets a car on fire to collect auto insurance, for example, when it's cheaper than pursuing criminal charges, she said.

"You don't want to perpetuate people committing fraud," Worters said. "But there are some times, quite honestly, when companies say: 'This fraud is not a ton of money. We are better off paying this.'"

As ransomware claims surged in 2019, industry insiders like Worters began to wonder about the long-term consequences of approving record-setting ransom payments. "When you pay out to these criminals, what happens in the future?" she said. Attackers "see the deep pockets" of the insurance industry, and if they think they can extract more money from victims because of it, "they're going to ask for more," she said.

Her fears soon became reality. Hackers began targeting insured victims, demanding unprecedented eight-figure ransoms. Beazley, for one, ended 2019 with 775 ransomware incidents, up 131 percent from the prior year. Before encrypting victims' systems, Beazley found, hackers ran keyword searches for terms such as "insurance." Then the hackers located their targets' policies and scanned the documents for coverage limits, setting ransom demands accordingly.

One Beazley customer was hit with a $3 million demand. When its negotiator told the hackers it was a small organization that couldn't afford such a high price, the hacker replied by naming the victim's cyber risk manager, saying the manager had "taken care of the company" with cyber insurance. As proof, the hacker sent the negotiator a copy of the policy. "Sure enough, we checked that, that it was in fact the policy," Kimberly Horn, then a global cyber and tech claims team leader at Beazley, said at the FBI summit. "And the $3 million demand was commensurate with the limits."

In another case, handled by Travelers, the attacker got onto a private conference call between the victim and its incident response team. The hacker was "listening to the negotiation process, which certainly didn't help the situation," Tim Francis, who oversaw cyber product management at Travelers, said at the summit. "That's rare, but you can understand how that can happen, when they're in the network, and they know the phone numbers. They see a calendar invite to a meeting, and lo and behold, [they join in]."

Having cyber insurance became almost a requisite for publicly traded U.S. companies, which regularly sought Bill Siegel's services. By late 2019, Coveware was handling ransomware incident response for as many as six public companies a month.

The U.S. Securities and Exchange Commission requires public companies to report "material" events that reasonable investors would want to consider in decisions to buy and sell stock. But Bill, ever devoted to transparency, noticed that many companies failed to report ransomware attacks to the SEC, or described them in vague terms. They feared that public acknowledgment would harm their reputation, alarm investors, and drive down their share price.

"They specifically avoid saying it," he observed. "It scares people . . . Any company that uses a phrase like 'malware that encrypted' or 'malware that caused system disruption or downtime' is likely referring to ransomware."

Always cognizant of public opinion, and realizing who ultimately paid his bills, Bill used Coveware's blog to reject the notion that cyber insurance was fueling ransomware, calling such an assertion "far fetched." He shifted the blame to organizations that failed to secure their networks. "Ransomware attacks happen because there is a large population of enterprises with extremely weak security defenses," he wrote. "The number of targets is large, and the cost of conducting an attack is extremely low."

■ ■ ■

Initially, Fabian Wosar and Michael Gillespie were skeptical of Coveware. Although it was open about its methods, unlike the data recovery firms, Coveware was in the same line of work. That was the opposite of the team's mission. But Bill did not give up courting them. He admired the team and recognized that a strong relationship was good for Coveware's reputation. Soon enough, he bonded with Fabian over their mutual distaste for MonsterCloud and Proven Data. He won Michael over by emphasizing that Coveware had a social conscience and regularly shared data with FBI agents. If victims couldn't afford his services, Bill said, he wanted to help them for free, like the Ransomware Hunting Team. "A point that we always bonded on was doing the right thing first without worrying about the money," Bill said.

Bill didn't become a full-fledged team member, and he wasn't invited to join its private Slack. But, over a separate channel, he discussed issues affecting Coveware clients with Fabian and Michael. For instance, in October 2019, he reached out over Slack about a new strain that had crippled an asset management firm. The firm had contacted MonsterCloud, which requested $85,000 to recover the files without paying the hackers. Then, seeking a second opinion, the management company called Coveware.

Bill explained to the victim that there was no known way to retrieve the files without paying a ransom, and he warned the prospective client about MonsterCloud. The firm scoffed at him. But Bill still wanted to help. He consulted Michael, who was already in the process of analyzing the ransomware strain because a BleepingComputer user had sought his help with it on the forums. The user had paid the ransom, but the decryptor obtained in return wasn't working.

Less than twenty-four hours after Bill reached out, Michael cracked the ransomware and built a free decryptor. Coveware called the asset management firm with the good news.

"Hey, I just sent you a free decryptor tool for that," the Coveware negotiator said. "Turns out it's a pretty simple one. Check your inbox."

That's when they heard the "sound of the guy's stomach falling out of his ass," Bill said, because it was too late. The firm had already paid MonsterCloud $85,000.

A year later, on Thanksgiving Day 2020, the Russian ransomware giant REvil struck a construction-engineering firm in upstate New York. Desperate for help, the firm searched on Google and found MonsterCloud. Reassured by its pledge to recover the encrypted files using proprietary technology, the firm engaged MonsterCloud, which demanded a retainer, the ransom note, and two sample encrypted files. Unbeknownst to the firm, MonsterCloud immediately contacted the hackers. The company sent along two sample files so that the hackers could unlock them as "proof of life." The hackers decrypted the files and returned them to MonsterCloud. Then MonsterCloud sent the freed files to the engineering firm, purporting to have released them using its own software.

Next, also without the client's knowledge, MonsterCloud started negotiating with REvil. The gang demanded $200,000, and Monster-Cloud counteroffered with $10,000. After MonsterCloud offered a few incremental increases, the hackers let the negotiator know they'd done their research on the engineering firm. "You have reported an annual income of $4 million," they wrote. "We are not expect small money from you."

The hackers behind REvil resented being lowballed. "After those kinds of tricks," the group's leader later told an interviewer, "the price tag only goes up . . . Nobody likes hagglers, especially show-offs."

MonsterCloud and the hacker finally settled on $65,000. Monster-Cloud then contacted the engineering firm, quoting a fee of $145,000 to recover the files.

But the firm, frustrated by MonsterCloud's lack of responsiveness, had separately sought assistance from GroupSense, a Virginia-based cybersecurity company that, like Coveware, handles ransom payments. When the GroupSense representative logged on to REvil's dark web portal to begin negotiating, he discovered a transcript of negotiations that had already taken place and a timer indicating three days had passed since discussions began.

GroupSense put together what had happened, explaining the situation to the unsuspecting clients. Ultimately, the firm attempted to rebuild its system from backups and old emails. GroupSense's CEO,

Kurtis Minder, however, was disgusted by the incident and couldn't let it go. Not long after, he called John Pistole, the former deputy director of the FBI and MonsterCloud advisory council member, to tell him the story. Although Pistole had previously heard about MonsterCloud's misrepresentations from ProPublica, he acted surprised on the call. "Wow, I didn't know that's going on," he told Minder. "That's awful." Pistole then asked Minder if he was interested in hiring him.

Minder contacted the FBI and spoke with an agent. "I just don't know if this is illegal," the agent told him. "And I don't think that the numbers are big enough for the FBI to care."

Finally, Minder filed a complaint with the Federal Trade Commission, alleging that MonsterCloud had deceived the engineering firm by saying it was "doing the decryption in house," while actually paying the threat actors—and netting an $80,000 profit," Minder wrote. "This strikes me as fraud. I do not want this company doing this to other victims."

The FTC declined to say whether it was investigating the complaint.

Bill Siegel was crushing Zohar and the Congionti brothers in business referred by insurance companies. At the same time, soaring ransom demands were making his competitors' ruse less feasible. Purporting to crack a strain, while actually paying the ransom and charging it to clients, was harder to pull off with multimillion-dollar demands. MonsterCloud and Proven Data responded differently to the predicament. Unlike Zohar, Victor Congionti was repentant. He acknowledged that Proven Data's willingness to pay ransoms "was not always clear to some customers," and said its disclosure policy had "evolved over time." He said Proven Data was now "completely transparent." Reflecting its newfound candor, the company asked clients for written authorization to reach out on their behalf to the hackers. "Our engineering team has determined that there is no available option other than to pay the ransom," Proven Data notified victims in such cases. "We will be leveraging our prior experience in handling

this specific ransomware variant to achieve the highest level of success. If we do not receive the decryption keys or cannot decrypt your
files, you will not be billed our service fee, but the ransom amount is
non-refundable." Proven Data also helped clients assess the risks of
negotiating with hackers by letting them know if the gang that attacked them had in the past failed to bargain in good faith or had supplied a faulty decryption key.

The company also started to crack ransomware for real. In April
2020, the owner of a managed service provider that had been infected
with ransomware hired Proven Data. Since many businesses depended on the MSP to host their data, there appeared to be no choice
but to pay the $800,000 ransom as soon as possible. The client was
"minutes away" from making the payment when an encryption analyst at Proven Data discovered a flaw in the hackers' cryptography. He
cracked the code and recovered the files.

Proven Data shared its breakthrough with law enforcement and
with Michael Gillespie. Like art students showing their paintings to
Picasso, the company was eager to impress one of the world's premier
ransomware hunters. Under the moniker "TechGuru11," a Proven
Data analyst contacted Michael over BleepingComputer. "There is
a new one we saw last week . . . that was able to be brute forced," he
wrote. Once TechGuru11 supplied more details, Michael recognized
the strain as a variant of DeathHiddenTear. He had cracked earlier
versions, but the hackers had fixed the vulnerability. Michael tested
Proven Data's new decryption method, and it worked. "I was able to
break one key just a bit ago for a victim who had the same variant you
had," he wrote to TechGuru11.

By late 2020, both Coveware and ransomware itself had grown beyond
anything Bill Siegel could have imagined during his Metro-North train
rides with Alex Holdtman. The company had hired ten employees, including one in Hawaii to take care of negotiations during overnight
hours on the East Coast. Coveware was handling 130 cases a month,
more than any other negotiation firm.

Bill regularly tapped the expertise of the Ransomware Hunting Team, comparing notes about new strains. He also reached his goal of becoming an authoritative source of information on ransomware, even testifying before Congress on the topic. Coveware's quarterly reports became staples of mainstream media coverage and were even referenced on one gang's website: REvil cited Bill's analysis that paying them resulted in successful decryption. Bill responded by notifying law enforcement and by emphasizing in a blog post that he did not condone criminals using Coveware's data to "coerce victims into paying."

Coveware had become a leader in ransomware negotiation. But its success forced Bill to face a question that he had turned over in his mind: "Do you actually create the problem?" No matter how transparent and aboveboard Coveware was, it provided a morally ambiguous service that he helped legitimize. SAC Capital Advisors, where Bill worked early in his career, had abandoned ethical standards on its way to becoming the world's most profitable hedge fund. Bill had fostered a far different culture at Coveware. Yet it, too, profited by systematically engaging in ethically compromised transactions. Its business model enriched both Coveware and the criminals—who, like Steve Cohen, seemed beyond law enforcement's reach.

By the spring of 2021, demand for Coveware's services was so overwhelming that, to keep up with it, Bill would have had to triple his staff. Instead, he ended up "turning away more work than we accept" because "I want to retain the lining of my stomach."

As ransomware surged, the American cybersecurity industry flourished. Cyber response firms that previously handled data breaches and electronic scams followed the gravy train of insurance payouts for ransomware response. There's "really good money in ransomware" for the cyberattacker, recovery experts, and insurers, said Bret Padres, then CEO of Crypsis, a prominent Virginia incident response firm. Routine ransom payments had created a "vicious circle . . . It's a hard cycle to break because everyone involved profits: We do, the insurance carriers do, the attackers do."

The state of the cyber incident response industry reminded Bill of a satirical motivational poster—the kind that a malcontented office worker might hang in a cubicle. The one befitting the cybersecurity industry featured a tight shot of two people shaking hands and the word "CONSULTING" in capital letters. Beneath it, the caption: "If you're not a part of the solution, there's good money to be made in prolonging the problem."

Bill wasn't about to walk away from a thriving business, and instead fell back on other ways to deal with the qualms he felt about his industry's role in the rise of ransomware. He regularly took on pro bono work for victims who couldn't afford his services. And, showing that Coveware is "perfectly comfortable with ransomware going away," he collaborated with contacts at the FBI. "Helping businesses matters, helping law enforcement matters," he said. "Those things make me feel good."

The Ransomware Hunting Team recognized the paradox. "It's a weird situation for Bill," Lawrence Abrams said. "He's facilitating ransomware payments. You could say he's part of the problem. But think of how much his intelligence is helping law enforcement."

The 2019 book *Kidnap*, by Anja Shortland, which analyzed the economics of traditional ransom, reassured Bill that Coveware's mission was justified. Shortland concludes that kidnapping for ransom will never go away and that professional negotiators can reduce spiraling demands and make the process safer and more predictable. Bill told employees to buy the book and expense it to Coveware.

Bill was elated when he could help victims without paying a ransom—when one victim's decryption tool worked on another victim's files, or when he could direct clients to free tools developed by the team. But those examples were the exception among his cases, and the hackers' offensive seemed unrelenting.

"You can have individual wins," Bill said. "But there's no grand slams, there's no touchdowns, and the waves just keep coming."

12

LAWRENCE'S TRUCE

O n a bleak St. Patrick's Day in 2020, with holiday festivities canceled as COVID-19 swept across the United States, Lawrence Abrams messaged his contacts in the ransomware gangs. Led by Ryuk, the gangs had been steadily attacking bigger targets and demanding bigger ransoms. Then came the pandemic. By increasing society's dependence on computers, it played into the attackers' hands. A reign of terror loomed, with hospitals especially vulnerable because they were deluged with patients and their cyber-security was often weak. So Lawrence asked the hackers to spare hospitals and other medical facilities for the duration of the pandemic.

He appealed to them as ordinary, decent people with parents, children, and partners they loved. How would you feel, he asked, if a member of your family was infected with COVID-19 and couldn't receive lifesaving treatment because the local hospital was hit by ransomware?

He didn't bother to run his idea by the Ransomware Hunting Team or by other security researchers on a Slack channel he'd joined to brainstorm ways to protect essential services from cybercriminals. "This was all me."

The next morning, Lawrence awoke to a flurry of replies. Responding first, the DoppelPaymer gang agreed to his proposal. DoppelPaymer said that they "always try to avoid hospitals, nursing homes, [and

911 call centers], not only now." If they hit a hospital by mistake, they would "decrypt for free."

Still, realizing that Lawrence would make their pledge public on BleepingComputer, DoppelPaymer warned other victims against posing as healthcare providers to avoid paying a ransom: "We'll do double, triple check before releasing decrypt for free."

As if it were a legitimate tech company, the Maze gang followed the well-worn corporate PR strategy of circumventing the media and addressing the public directly. "We also stop all activity versus all kinds of medical organizations until the stabilization of the situation with virus," it wrote on its dark web site.

Two other groups—Nefilim and CLOP—also promised not to attack hospitals, nursing homes, and other medical facilities. "We work very diligently in choosing our targets," Nefilim messaged Lawrence. "We never target non-profits, hospitals, schools, government organizations."

Gathering the responses, Lawrence wrote an article for Bleeping-Computer under the headline "Ransomware Gangs to Stop Attacking Health Care Orgs During the Pandemic." Its lead art was a rendering of a dove interlaced with an EKG readout forming the word "PEACE" in capital letters.

Undercutting this optimism, the Netwalker gang spurned Lawrence's proposal. Ignoring numerous examples to the contrary, Netwalker insisted that no ransomware group would hack into a hospital. But if "someone is encrypted" by accident, Netwalker continued, "then he must pay for the decryption."

REvil did not respond to Lawrence's overture. In a later interview with another outlet, REvil leader Unknown acknowledged that "the crisis is palpable," and that victims "are not able to pay the same amounts as before." But Unknown added ominously that pharmaceutical companies were "doing just fine" and deserved "more attention." In a statement posted on Emsisoft's blog, Coveware and Emsisoft echoed Lawrence's plea. "While we will never condone criminal behavior, we understand why financially motivated cybercrime exists."

We also know you are humans, and that your own family and loved ones may find themselves in need of urgent medical care," they wrote. "Please do not target healthcare providers during the coming months, and if you target one unintentionally, please provide them with the decryption key at no cost as soon as you possibly can. We're all in this together, right?"

Lawrence was satisfied. He felt that he was helping frontline workers and COVID-19 patients and that his faith in the hackers' humanity had been validated. "For the most part, they all resoundingly said, 'We will not target health care.'"

But some Ransomware Hunting Team members wondered if Lawrence had been gulled. "It was a good idea but you can never trust a threat actor's word," Sarah White said. Other observers were also skeptical. To some, Lawrence's attitude was reminiscent of Stockholm syndrome, in which hostages develop an emotional bond with their captors.

Aaron Tantleff, a Chicago lawyer who advised ransomware victims during the pandemic, including medical facilities, read Lawrence's article and discussed it with colleagues and clients. "In my mind, this was hysterical," he said. "Hackers with a heart of gold."

As Lawrence sought the détente, Michael Gillespie was contemplating a life-changing career move. Bill Siegel at Coveware met Michael in person at the FBI's Pittsburgh summit in 2019. Soon afterward, Bill and his colleague Alex Holdtman told Fabian that they were looking for an expert to build and fix decryptors. Fabian recommended Michael. "I knew Michael needed a new job because of his financial situation," Fabian said. Bill agreed that it sounded like a good fit.

Fabian then encouraged Michael to apply to Coveware. "He was like, 'I don't know.' He has a lack of self-worth and self-esteem. He always worried he wouldn't be good enough. I had to kick him. I was certain it was going to be a good move," he said. "It would solve so many of his problems."

Bill interviewed Michael over Zoom, the videoconferencing service that would become a staple of pandemic life. On March 19, six days after President Trump declared COVID-19 a national emergency, Michael accepted Bill's job offer. Coveware tripled his salary and fully covered his health insurance, a benefit the Gillespies appreciated, given their frequent medical scares. Michael would finally have the chance to work full-time on "any and everything ransomware," including creating decryptors and guides for victims.

"I still get to release free decryptors through Emsisoft," he said on the day he accepted the job. "It's just I'll be doing more custom tools mostly for individual victims." Bill shipped a $2,000 laptop—which Michael called "my new toy"—and a twenty-seven-inch monitor, "huge upgrades" for his home workstation. Although Coveware was based in Connecticut, the job would be fully remote, regardless of the pandemic, so Michael and Morgan could stay in their beloved Bloomington, Illinois, home.

Unexpectedly at ease with his departure from Facet, Michael worked his final week from his house, as the company followed the Illinois governor's stay-at-home order. The Gillespies, like millions of other Americans, had to get used to the lifestyle imposed by the pandemic. "Gonna take some adjustments for Morgan to not keep bugging me while I'm home," Michael said. He started at Coveware on March 30.

Michael's move to Coveware made sense for both sides. Bill gained a talented researcher and cemented his relationship with the Ransomware Hunting Team. Also, Coveware could expand beyond its fraught original business of negotiating ransoms. It now had a staffer who could crack ransomware and create decryptors for clients so they wouldn't have to reward criminals. And if the strain was uncrackable, and the decryptor that the attackers provided to Coveware clients in return for payment didn't work well, Michael could repair it, as Fabian was already doing from time to time for Coveware clients. For Michael, his obsession was now his occupation. He could take a break to update ID Ransomware or check his Twitter mentions for victims to rescue. Coveware wouldn't suffocate him like the big corporations where his in-laws wanted him to work.

The higher salary gave him financial security for the first time. After the Gillespies paid off their credit card debt, they had enough left to hire a housekeeper and a dog walker. Morgan could afford to see a chiropractor and a holistic therapist, who used tarot cards, crystals, and astrology. She also joined a gym, where she swam. Illinois had legalized marijuana, and she began patronizing dispensaries. In the morning, she often had an edible to whet her appetite.

Michael quickly proved his worth to his new employer. A victim facing a multimillion-dollar demand from a new gang, Ragnar Locker, had hired Coveware. On his third day of work, Michael cracked the strain. He found that Ragnar Locker, like old STOPDjvu, violated Sarah's rule against using the same key to lock multiple files; one key unlocked all the files on a computer drive. As before, Michael required an original and an encrypted file so he could compare them and extract the key. This time, though, he didn't need to ask the victim for the files. Coveware's team provided them. That was a perk he relished: "I don't have to talk to a victim too often."

Impressed, Bill asked Michael to give a presentation at Coveware's weekly virtual show-and-tell. "They were curious about how I do what I do," Michael said.

One Friday afternoon, occasionally interrupted by cats crawling across his desk, Michael dazzled his new colleagues by demonstrating how bait files could reveal a key within the bewildering array of encrypted data. As he zoomed out, he showed the key stream of numbers and characters recurring in a telltale diagonal pattern. Even his less tech-savvy viewers were impressed. Bill invited him back for an encore to dissect more triumphs.

The information gathered by ID Ransomware also proved valuable to Coveware. Once, when a client paid the ransom, the hackers' negotiator demanded more money instead of providing the key.

Since ID Ransomware extracted hacker email addresses from ransom notes submitted by victims, Michael poked around in his database and found other contact information for the gang. Coveware sent a transcript of the earlier negotiations to a new address, showing that the ransom had been paid. The strain's developer replied, saying the negotiator who had tried to re-extort the client was not an official partner and assuring Coveware that the person would be punished. The developer then provided the key without any additional payment.

After solving Ragnar Locker on his third day at Coveware, Michael helped three or four of its victims. Then the hackers fixed their vulnerability by creating a different key for every file. Ragnar Locker became one of the pandemic's most fearsome cyber gangs. It carefully chose its targets and identified each victim by name in the ransom note.

In July 2020, Ragnar Locker shut down the travel management firm CWT's operations and stole sensitive files. The hackers demanded $10 million. CWT's negotiator protested, citing the disappearance of corporate travel during quarantine.

"You hit us at the wrong time with COVID virtually eliminating our revenue streams," the negotiator wrote, counteroffering $3.7 million. "I understand that you probably saw a large revenue number online, but please take into consideration that we have made way less than our normal revenue since the pandemic started. No one has been traveling so our sales have plummeted to a scary level . . . I completely understand that this is a business for you, but right now I'm tasked with trying to keep our business afloat."

"This is the market and you have been offered an adequate price," Ragnar Locker replied. "Unfortunately, the amount you offered is not enough to close our deal with you." The two sides settled on $4.5 million in Bitcoin for the key and deletion of the stolen data. Once CWT paid, Ragnar Locker offered advice on avoiding more attacks, including changing passwords, reducing user privileges, and having "3 system administrators working 24 hours."

Ragnar Locker joined the Maze cartel, with each gang's leak site displaying data stolen by the others. Ragnar Locker tried to pressure an Italian beverage vendor, the Campari Group, to pay a ransom by posting Facebook ads threatening to expose its files. The gang charged the ads to a Chicago disc jockey's hacked Facebook account. "We can confirm that confidential data was stolen and we talking about huge volume of data," one ad asserted.

Michael cracked dozens of other ransomware strains during the pandemic, bailing out victims in the United States and beyond, from a construction company in Phoenix, Arizona, to a public university in Guadalajara, Mexico.

Among the individuals he rescued was Chris Cyrulewski, an automotive designer for Koenigsegg, the Swedish company that makes some of the fastest and most expensive automobiles in the world. "You won't get into one for less than two million dollars," he said. Chris, who shares five patents, has contributed his combination of engineering skill and an artist's eye to numerous show cars. He also helped develop an amphibious airplane, the ICON A5, which is featured in the 2010 Tom Cruise movie, *Knight and Day*.

A native of Michigan, where his father, uncle, and grandfather all worked as engineers for General Motors, Chris lived in Sweden with his wife and three daughters. Normally, he worked at Koenigsegg headquarters, but during the pandemic he spent Mondays and Fridays in his home office. It featured a model of the Koenigsegg Jesko, a supercar that could reach speeds of 330 miles per hour. As he fine-tuned his designs, he sparked his imagination by listening to Frank Herbert's *Dune* series; when he finished the seventh and last novel in the sci-fi cycle, he started over at the beginning.

On a November Monday in 2020, Chris was sitting at his desk, digitally sculpting an exterior body panel. Then, right in front of him, one of *Dune*'s themes—never trust computers—proved true. Chris tried to listen to the audiobook, but when he clicked on it, it wouldn't play. He noticed that the file names were different, too; the extension now included ".encrypt." A note instructed him to contact an address on the dark web and pay an unspecified amount of Bitcoin to decrypt his files.

Alarmed, he rejected that option. He didn't want to reward criminals, and he was scared of going on the dark web. After some research, he learned that he'd been hit by a new ransomware strain, Solve. It encrypted network-attached storage devices, which connect backup files to a network. Chris stored most of his projects and family photos on his NAS. Although he also backed up his work to a cloud-based server, he had no way to retrieve most of the photos. "There were a great many personal things I would be regretful to lose."

Chris started deleting encrypted files that he didn't need or had copied. Then, combing through the Solve thread on BleepingComputer, he saw a post by another victim saying that demonslay335 had provided a key. Chris messaged Michael, asking for the decryption tool. "I have been holding on to a few important files just in case this happens," Chris wrote.

"You will first need to find the largest encrypted file and its original that you can," Michael replied. "I will only be able to decrypt files up to the size of the pair you provide."

"That's not a problem," Chris answered.

Michael then sent the decryptor with instructions. "Just Awesome," Chris wrote. "It's black magic to me but it works. Decrypting as I write this email." As a token of his thanks, he offered Michael a Koenigsegg hat or sweater. Michael declined the swag.

On a single weekend in the winter of 2021, Michael cracked three ransomware types. Sarah White drew his attention to one of them. "Not sure if you saw this," she messaged him on the team's Slack that January, linking to a researcher's tweet about a new ransomware.

Michael recognized the file extension. The same ransomware, known as Lorenz, had attacked a Coveware client, an auto body shop, demanding $1.5 million. Coveware was negotiating with Lorenz, which had lowered its price to $500,000.

Analyzing the sample, Michael realized that Lorenz's method of generating random numbers was too weak to protect the key. "I whipped up a quick proof of concept, really ugly brute-forcing tool." After unlocking some files that the client provided, he told the case manager to stop negotiations.

The case manager was relieved. "This guy's negotiating like an amateur," he said.

"Yeah, it was definitely the work of an amateur," Michael answered.

Another ransomware strain that Michael cracked that weekend invoked the pandemic in its name—DEcovid19—and ransom note. "I am the second wave of COVID19," the note said. "Now we infect even PC's."

While Michael escaped COVID-19, at least three of his teammates weren't so fortunate.

As a loner and hermit, Fabian considered himself at low risk. He had been staying home and social distancing long before everyone had to. Even his food was delivered to his apartment. "I didn't know my lifestyle was called quarantine," he joked. Still, he caught the virus—twice. The first time, he was bedridden for a week. He speculated that he was exposed when he chatted with a neighbor while taking out the trash. By the second time—when he apparently contracted the virus from an unmasked man who was coughing as he delivered groceries—he was vaccinated, and the symptoms were mild.

The illness barely slowed his ransomware hunting. He cracked one strain after another during the pandemic, often in collaboration with Michael. One was Zeppelin, which preyed on hospitals and energy companies from the United States to Algeria. Although Zeppelin fixed the problem that Fabian discovered, most affiliates kept using the old, vulnerable version rather than paying the developer for the update. As a result, many victims continued to benefit from Fabian's decryptor.

Early in the pandemic, a romantic relationship brightened Karsten Hahn's life. In September 2020, he and his partner visited an "escape room," where patrons solve clues to find their way out. Inside the last riddle, he hid a ring. "Now I am engaged to this wonderful man!" he tweeted, and team members replied with their congratulations.

But then, in January 2021, Karsten fell ill and was diagnosed with COVID-19. The symptoms lingered. Six months later, his chest and throat still hurt, and he often felt fatigued. At Essen University Hospital, a doctor told him that he was improving and that "it just needs time and patience." Encouraged, Karsten and his fiancé bought an apartment together and forged ahead with wedding plans.

Sarah White also had a bout with COVID, while another teammate continued to struggle with finances. MalwareHunterTeam asked Fabian for a loan to buy a house. Fabian said he wasn't comfortable with loaning the money, but he offered instead to increase his teammate's hours at Emsisoft so that MalwareHunterTeam could save up. Fabian also assured MalwareHunterTeam, who complained about corruption in Hungary's government, that if he wanted to leave his homeland, Emsisoft would pay to move him elsewhere in Europe.

But MalwareHunterTeam wasn't open to other solutions. "He can see and accept only one way of doing something," Sarah said.

Daniel Gallagher set up a PayPal fundraiser to appeal for donations to his friend:

> For years now, MalwareHunterTeam has been selflessly expending their personal time and resources to help others by hunting malware and tracking criminals. They have tirelessly been at the forefront of notifying both individuals and companies about critical malware events. All of this done without any direct compensation.
>
> Unfortunately, they now find themselves in a challenging personal situation and have reached out to the infosec community for help. So it is now our time to give back!

Forty-six well-wishers contributed a total of $4,111.48. Daniel gave the most, $1,000, and Lawrence chipped in $200, writing, "Thanks

MHT for all you do." MalwareHunterTeam responded by accusing the Twitter-verse of stinginess, given that the goal was $20,000.

"Last donation was over 5 days ago," MalwareHunterTeam tweeted in March 2021. "So can we say now that of the 118k followers (of course not counting very poor people, ones who have no PayPal, etc), less than 50 people think that our hard work in the past years worth even a 1$donation?"

Lawrence's COVID-19 truce with the hackers began to unravel almost immediately. Even the groups that had agreed to it, like Maze, seemed to back away, interpreting the terms as narrowly as they could.

On March 18, 2020, the same day that it promised to "stop all activity versus all kinds of medical organizations," Maze posted the personal data of thousands of former patients of Hammersmith Medicines Research, a London company that refused to pay ransom. Hammersmith ran clinical trials for drug companies and later would test a coronavirus vaccine. When Lawrence sought an explanation, the hackers said that they had attacked Hammersmith on March 14, prior to the truce. "They basically said, 'We locked them before this, we have not broken our pledge. This is not a new victim.' So I'm not gonna judge on that," he said.

Still, Lawrence urged them to take down the data, but they refused. On BleepingComputer, he acknowledged that the Hammersmith attack raised doubts about the hackers' commitment to the truce. "We will have to see if they keep this promise, which to most has already been broken," he wrote.

Only direct patient care was off-limits for Maze. Once, the gang ensnarled the computer network for a small U.S. hospital's storage, equipment, and parking. The infected files contained data such as key codes that doctors and nurses used to drive into the garage. When the hospital requested a free decryptor, citing the truce, Maze balked. The auxiliary services "didn't qualify for a get out of jail card," said Aaron Tantleff, the Chicago cybersecurity lawyer. Because the files weren't crucial, the hospital spurned the $35,000 ransom demand. Insurance covered the remediation costs.

Maze's narrow interpretation of the truce set the pattern. Over the ensuing months, participants mostly abided by its letter—but not its spirit. For example, they continued to target manufacturers of medicines and equipment vital to treating COVID-19 patients. They rejected Lawrence's request for a cease-fire on drugmakers, whom they scorned as profiteers exploiting the crisis. "[Pharma] earns lot of extra on panic nowdays, we have no any wish to support them," DoppelPaymer said.

DoppelPaymer, which had been the first gang to accept Lawrence's proposal, attacked Boyce Technologies, Inc., a company producing three hundred ventilators a day for desperately ill COVID-19 patients in New York hospitals. The gang encrypted Boyce's files and posted stolen documents such as purchase orders.

Beyond drawing such fine distinctions, the truce participants were bound to make mistakes. In September 2020, DoppelPaymer paralyzed thirty servers at University Hospital in Düsseldorf, Germany, forcing cancellation of outpatient and emergency services. The gang, which apparently intended to hit the affiliated Heinrich Heine University instead, provided a free decryptor. Still, some things can't be undone. After being redirected to a hospital twenty miles away, delaying her treatment for an hour, a seventy-eight-year-old woman died. As panic escalated throughout Western Europe, authorities weighed charging the hackers with negligent homicide.

"She may have died due to the delayed emergency care," Germany's senior public prosecutor told the media. They ultimately closed the investigation, unable to prove that timelier treatment would have saved her life.

While truce participants tried, however halfheartedly, to leave patient care alone, other gangs that had rebuffed or ignored Lawrence's overtures routinely assaulted hospitals and health services.

Contradicting its insistence to Lawrence that it would never attack a hospital, Netwalker hit one medical facility after another. Netwalker "specifically targeted the healthcare sector during the COVID-19 pandemic, taking advantage of the global crisis to extort victims," according to the U.S. Department of Justice.

"Hi! Your files are encrypted," its ransom note read. "Our encryption algorithms are very strong and your files are very well protected, you can't hope to recover them without our help. The only way to get your files back is to cooperate with us and get the decrypter program . . . For us this is just business."

In June 2020, Netwalker attacked a Maryland nursing home chain and breached the private records of almost 48,000 seniors, which included Social Security numbers, birth dates, diagnoses, and treatments. When the company rebuffed the ransom demand, the gang dumped a batch of data online.

That same month, Netwalker stole data from and shut down several servers at the University of California–San Francisco's epidemiology and biostatistics department, demanding a $3 million ransom.

"We've poured almost all funds into COVID-19 research to help cure this disease," the university's negotiator pleaded. "That on top of all the cuts due to classes being canceled has put a serious strain on the whole school."

Netwalker's representative was skeptical: "You need to understand, for you as a big university, our price is shit. You can collect that money in a couple of hours. You need to take us seriously. If we'll release on our blog student records/data, I'm 100% sure you will lose more than our price."

Netwalker scorned counteroffers of $390,000 and $780,000: "Keep that $780k to buy McDonalds for all employees. Is very small amount for us . . . Is like, I worked for nothing." After six days of haggling, they compromised on $1.14 million, and UCSF received the decryption tool.

The Ransomware Hunting Team was unable to crack Netwalker. "It's one of the most sophisticated ransomwares now, very secure," Michael said.

But in a rare success for that time, the FBI disrupted Netwalker's operations and took down its most profitable affiliate. Although Net-walker's developers were based in Russia, the alleged affiliate, Sebastien Vachon-Desjardins, was a Canadian citizen living in the province of Quebec. An IT technician for the Canadian government's purchasing agency and a convicted drug trafficker, Vachon-Desjardins apparently hooked up with Netwalker by answering an ad that a gang member named Bugatti posted on a cybercriminal forum in March 2020. The ad explained how to become a Netwalker affiliate and asked applicants about their areas of expertise and experience working with other ransomware strains.

"We are interested in people who work for quality," Bugatti wrote. "We give preference to those who know how to work with large networks."

Vachon-Desjardins and his co-conspirators committed dozens of ransomware attacks in 2020, raking in at least $27.7 million, according to court documents in the United States and Canada. Vachon-Desjardins kept 75 percent of the profits, with the rest going to Netwalker. He also worked as an affiliate for other gangs such as REvil, Ragnar Locker, and Suncrypt.

During a conversation in November 2020 with Bugatti, Vachon-Desjardins referred to an attack on a public utility as his "latest big hit."

"I hit them hard bro," he wrote. "Very locked." He added that he would visit Russia soon, but the trip didn't materialize. In December, Vachon-Desjardins was indicted on computer fraud charges in federal court in Florida, where one of his first victims, a telecommunications company, was headquartered. When Canadian authorities, who were also investigating him, searched his cryptocurrency wallets in January 2021, they found $40 million in Bitcoin—the largest cryptocurrency seizure in Canadian history. He was arrested and extradited to the United States.

By mostly avoiding direct attacks on patient care, the ransomware gangs that agreed to Lawrence's truce may have forgone some revenue. They compensated for this by attacking another vital and vulner-able sector: schools.

Before the pandemic, schools infected with ransomware could still hold in-person classes. But once they went online to avoid spreading COVID-19, ransomware could shut them down, increasing the pressure to pay. School closures and cancellations associated with ransomware tripled from 2019 to 2020.

Three truce participants ravaged schools. Maze penetrated and posted data from the nation's fifth- and eleventh-biggest districts, Clark County, Nevada, and Fairfax County, Virginia. DoppelPaymer disrupted schools from Mississippi to Montana. After the school district in rural Chatham County, North Carolina, rejected DoppelPaymer's $2.4 million ransom demand, the gang posted stolen data online that included medical evaluations of neglected children. Nefilim was among the ransomware strains that targeted K-12 schools the most in 2020.

Also among the leaders in school attacks was a major gang that had ignored Lawrence's proposal: Ryuk. On Tuesday evening, November 24, 2020, in the middle of a school board meeting and two days before Thanksgiving, a Ryuk attack that school officials described as catastrophic took down websites, networks, and files of the nation's twenty-fourth-largest district, Baltimore County, whose 115,000 students were attending classes online.

Like the City of Baltimore eighteen months before, the county schools were susceptible to attack. A state legislative audit completed in February 2020 found that servers weren't properly isolated and, "if compromised, could expose the internal network to attack from external sources."

The ransomware attack closed schools for three days and reverberated for months. The school system couldn't generate student report cards, and it struggled to supply transcripts for seniors applying to college and graduates seeking jobs. With payroll records inaccessible, the district had to determine staff pay based on canceled checks and obtain permission from the Internal Revenue Service to extend the deadline for filing and generating W-2 tax forms. Teachers couldn't make deposits in or withdrawals from their retirement accounts.

The attack disabled laptops belonging to about 20 percent of teachers—those who were online and connected to the schools' network that night. One was Tina Wilson, a seventeen-year veteran of the district and sixth-grade language arts teacher at Catonsville Middle School, who was taking an evening course to become a school librarian and also checking her email. When she could finally log on, a week later, her files were frozen, and they had a new extension: .ryk.

She had lost her lesson plans. So on the first day back she read *The Maze Runner*, a young adult science fiction novel, to her students. They were scrambling, too. She had assigned them to write research papers on how to prepare for natural disasters, but they couldn't get into the database she had suggested.

"What bothered me is that the district had loopholes in the system that they had never fixed," Tina said.

Unlike the City of Baltimore, the suburban district tried to negotiate with the hackers. "They had to try to find a way to bring classes back as soon as possible," said Joshua Muhumuza, then a Dundalk High School senior and the student representative on the school board. But the county government, which funds the district, warned of "legal, financial and reputational consequences to an independent decision by BCPS to pay the ransom. Those consequences will be wide-ranging and long-lasting." School officials apparently heeded the admonishments. Although the district hasn't discussed the matter publicly, one insider said that it didn't pay. A year after the attack, estimated recovery costs had reached $9.7 million, of which insurance was expected to reimburse up to $2 million.

Ryuk was closely associated with the Conti gang. In March 2021, Conti attacked the school district of Broward County, Florida, the nation's sixth largest, and demanded a $40 million ransom. Negotiations dragged on for two weeks, with the district's representative professing "shock and horror that anyone thinks a taxpayer-funded school district can afford this kind of money!" Conti rebutted by emphasizing the district's $4 billion budget—"Don't play with us, your chiefs have this required amount in Bitcoins"—and anticipating "your possible losses from lawsuits from both your staff and your students from the leakage of their personal data."

Conti eventually reduced its price to $10 million. The district refused to go above $500,000, and discussions broke down. The gang then posted almost 26,000 stolen files online. Despite its threats, most of the data was mundane—employee mileage reports, travel reimbursement forms, construction invoices, and utility bills—and unlikely to draw attention or prompt lawsuits.

For Ryuk, attacking schools was a sideshow. After crippling the DCH Regional Medical Center in Tuscaloosa, Alabama, and other hospitals in 2019, it doubled down on healthcare attacks in October 2020, sowing anxiety and confusion among patients and providers across the United States.

The timing suggests that Ryuk was avenging one of the biggest and most damaging actions taken against ransomware.

Since 2018, Microsoft's Digital Crimes Unit—consisting of more than forty full-time investigators, analysts, data scientists, engineers, and attorneys—had been investigating TrickBot, the Russian malware that delivered Ryuk into victims' computers. Concerns that the Putin regime might use TrickBot to disrupt the 2020 U.S. presidential election added urgency to the task, though the fears would prove unfounded.

Microsoft investigators analyzed 61,000 samples of TrickBot malware, as well as the infrastructure underpinning the network of infected computers. They discovered how TrickBot's command-and-control servers communicated with the computers, and they identified the IP addresses of those servers.

Microsoft then parlayed this evidence into an innovative legal strategy. Contending that TrickBot's malicious use of Microsoft's code was violating copyright, the company obtained a federal court order to dismantle the botnet's operations. In October 2020, with the help of technology companies and telecommunications providers around the world, Microsoft disabled IP addresses associated with TrickBot, rendered the content stored on its command-and-control servers inaccessible, and suspended services to the botnet's operators. Within a week, Microsoft succeeded in taking down 120 of the 128 servers it had identified as TrickBot infrastructure.

Before going to court, Microsoft had telegraphed its plans to law enforcement contacts. Word reached U.S. Cyber Command, which was established in 2010 and oversees Department of Defense cyber operations. Reflecting the U.S. military's new, more aggressive cyber strategy, Cyber Command mounted its own offensive against Trick-Bot. Without identifying itself, it penetrated the botnet, instructing infected systems to disconnect and flooding TrickBot's database with false information about new victims.

TrickBot's hackers were impressed by the then-unknown assailant's expertise. "The one who made this thing did it very well," a coder told the syndicate's boss. "He knew how bot worked, possibly saw the source code and reverse engineered it . . . This appears to be sabotage."

These triumphs, however, proved temporary. Ryuk paused only a week to restructure operations before launching an assault on hospitals. "I was super surprised that the actors behind TrickBot decided to use the limited infrastructure they had left to try to attack the most vulnerable systems out there during a pandemic," said Amy Hogan-Burney, general manager of Microsoft's Digital Crimes Unit.

One early victim in this onslaught was Dickinson County Healthcare Systems in Michigan and Wisconsin, which Ryuk hit on October 17. "Salute DCHS," the ransom note read. "Read this message CLOSELY and call someone from technical division. Your information is completely ENCODED." Giving an address at ProtonMail, Ryuk advised, "Get in touch with us." DCHS's electronic systems were down for a week, and its hospitals and clinics had to rely on paper records.

On October 26, Alex Holden learned that Ryuk was about to strike more than four hundred healthcare facilities in the United States, including hospitals and clinics. "They are fucked in USA," one Ryuk hacker wrote to another. "They will panic."

Holden immediately shared the information with the Secret Service, including indications that the malware had penetrated some hospital networks. Based in part on his tip, the federal government warned of "an increased and imminent cybercrime threat to U.S. hospitals and healthcare providers."

Along with federal officials, Microsoft, and major cybersecurity firms, Holden quickly alerted the targeted hospitals to fortify their defenses. As a result, he said, at least two hundred locations averted attacks and the impact wasn't as widespread as feared. TrickBot managers tried to figure out where they had gone wrong. But not all the facilities in danger could be identified in time, and Ryuk succeeded in penetrating dozens of them, including several rural hospitals that were bearing the brunt of COVID-19's impact in their areas.

For instance, Holden got wind that Ryuk was targeting domain names that included the prefix "SL." But he couldn't connect the initials to any particular facility until an attack devastated Sky Lakes Medical Center in Klamath Falls, a rural city in southern Oregon, twenty-five miles north of the California border. At eight minutes after noon on October 26, a Sky Lakes employee in support services received an email that purported to contain "Annual Bonus Report #783." The employee, who had worked at the community hospital for less than a year, wondered if the message was related to a recent meeting she'd had with human resources. She clicked on a link, and her computer froze, which annoyed her, but she didn't report it.

Not until more than thirteen hours later, in the early morning of October 27, did the hospital's information technology staff learn, in a phone call from clinicians, that the system was slow. It took two more hours, and a failed attempt to reboot, before they realized that ransomware had hit Sky Lakes. Ryuk had spread throughout the network, compromising every Windows-based machine.

At a time when COVID-19 was surging after a summer lull, Sky Lakes doctors and nurses lost access to electronic records and images for more than three weeks, curtailing treatments, reducing revenues, and increasing chances for medical errors. "This was a huge blow," said John Gaede, director of information systems at Sky Lakes. "Our clinical staff, our doctors and nurses, had to go to a paper process for twenty-three days."

Sometimes, patients who needed emergency care couldn't remember what medications they were taking. Instead of checking an electronic database, the hospital pharmacist had to call the other pharmacies in Klamath Falls and ask what their records showed. Doctors' ability to diagnose illness was also hampered. Ordinarily, oncologists detect breast cancer by comparing a patient's new mammogram to older ones, but those older images weren't available.

Sky Lakes sent some cancer patients to Providence Medford Medical Center in Medford, Oregon, a seventy-mile drive over the Cascade Mountains. Several patients took camper trailers and stayed in Medford overnight, but Ron Jackson commuted.

Ron and Sherry Jackson had been married for fifty-five years and had two sons, four grandsons, and two step-grandchildren. Before retiring, the couple had worked at the Oregon Institute of Technology, a public university in Klamath Falls—Sherry in the accounting office, Ron as a carpenter and an operator of heavy equipment. They enjoyed camping and other outdoor activities. Then, in September 2020, Ron had a seizure and couldn't remember common words like "squirrel." He was diagnosed with glioblastoma, the aggressive brain cancer that killed U.S. senators Ted Kennedy and John McCain.

After Ron's tumor was removed on October 7, his doctors recommended a thirty-day regimen of radiation and oral chemotherapy. His treatments were still being scheduled at Sky Lakes when the Ryuk attack disabled the hospital. Ron's doctor called and gave him a choice: he could wait for radiation services to reopen, and there was no telling how long that would take, or he could go to Medford. Since the doctors had told Ron that he needed treatment as soon as possible, he and Sherry opted for Medford. Although the hospital there was willing to provide housing, the Jacksons demurred, because they felt obliged to help Ron's ninety-seven-year-old mother in Klamath Falls with groceries and doctors' appointments. They also declined offers from friends and family to chauffeur them.

"We're not used to asking for help," Sherry said. "We're used to giving help."

Ron had always done the driving, but the surgery had affected his vision. So for seventeen days, until he could resume treatments at Sky Lakes, Sherry drove their Jeep Grand Cherokee over the mountains to Medford, sometimes through ice and snow. "It was a white-knuckle drive," she said. "Ron was holding on tight."

Because roadside restaurants were closed for the pandemic, the Jacksons occasionally had to relieve themselves in the woods. "Sometimes those water pills didn't make it to Medford," said Ron, who was taking diuretics to offset the fluid retention that is often a side effect of chemotherapy.

Still, he and Sherry agreed with the hospital's decision not to pay the ransom. "We feel the hospital could be hit again by the same group for more money and again stop Ron's treatments," Sherry said. "How could you trust that they would not continue to come back over and over again?"

Once Sky Lakes replaced the 2,500 infected computers, and the system was operating again, all the paper records accumulated in the weeks while it was down still had to be entered into the system manually—a slow, laborious process. The hospital had prudently invested in a new backup system six months before the attack, and by March 2021, it had recovered almost all its files. Out of 1.5 million mammogram films, just 880 were missing when all was said and done.

Although Sky Lakes is insured, its policy "won't even come close to covering all of our losses," which were between $3 million and $10 million, said a hospital administrator. Retracing what had gone wrong, Gaede and two other managers interviewed the employee who had accidentally exposed Sky Lakes to Ryuk. They felt that, since a vigilant workforce is a primary defense against cyberattack, it was crucial to understand why she hadn't obeyed warnings to be on the lookout for suspicious emails.

They told her that she would not be punished and that they just wanted to learn from her experience. But as they gently questioned her in the second-floor meeting room, the enormity of her mistake dawned on her, and she went pale. Not long afterward, she quit her job.

The assaults on Sky Lakes and other hospitals made Lawrence's truce look hollow. Some of the most powerful ransomware gangs didn't care whom they hurt, or how badly. Nevertheless, he didn't regret his proposal.

"I don't know whether my email has had any effect or not," Lawrence said in December 2020, with the pandemic still raging and the gangs striking often. "But it thrust them more into the spotlight. And it made it harder for them to go after these types of organizations without looking like bigger scumbags than many people consider them to be already."

13.

PIPELINE TO TOMORROW

I n December 2020, a Coveware client hit by a ransomware strain called DarkSide sought Michael Gillespie's help. The company had paid the ransom, but the decryption tool supplied by DarkSide was slow to unlock the frozen files. Could Michael speed things up?

For Michael, this was business as usual, the kind of request that he handled routinely at his new job. He had no inkling that DarkSide would become one of the highest-profile strains ever or that by shutting down a vital piece of American infrastructure, the gang would catapult the ransomware threat to the top of the agenda at White House press conferences and a presidential summit.

Michael had trouble extracting the key, which was stored in the hacker's decryption tool in an unusually complex way. He messaged Fabian Wosar, who was able to isolate it. The teammates then began testing the key on other files infected by DarkSide. Michael checked files uploaded by victims to ID Ransomware, while Fabian used the VirusTotal database.

That night, they shared a discovery. "I have confirmation DarkSide is re-using their RSA keys," Michael wrote to the Ransomware Hunting Team over Slack.

"I noticed the same as I was able to decrypt newly encrypted files using their decrypter," Fabian replied less than an hour later, still working at 2:45 a.m. London time.

Michael and Fabian used the key to recover files from Windows machines. "We were scratching our heads," Fabian said. "Could they really have fucked up this badly? DarkSide was one of the more professional ransomware-as-a-service schemes out there. For them to make such a huge mistake is very, very rare."

The team celebrated quietly, without seeking publicity. Looking for DarkSide victims, Sarah contacted firms that handle digital forensics and incident response. "Hey listen, if you have any DarkSide victims, tell them to reach out to us, we can recover their files and they don't have to pay a huge ransom."

DarkSide took a break during the Christmas season. Michael and Fabian expected that when attacks resumed, their discovery would help dozens of victims. Instead, the team was blindsided by an ally in the fight against ransomware. On January 11, 2021, the cybersecurity firm Bitdefender, based in Romania, said it was "happy to announce" that it had developed a free decryption tool that victims of DarkSide could download.

The publicity was self-defeating. It ensured that the DarkSide gang would hear about and correct the vulnerability that Michael and Fabian had spotted before Bitdefender. As a result, while Bitdefender's tool helped a smattering of existing victims hit by the flawed ransomware, it would be useless for future targets.

The team immediately recognized that its discreet campaign to rescue victims was doomed. In a Slack channel used by the ransomware response community, someone asked why Bitdefender would tip off the hackers. "Publicity," Sarah responded. "Looks good. I can guarantee they'll fix it much faster now though."

The very next day, the gang acknowledged the "problem with key generation" and estimated that up to 40 percent of keys were affected. "This problem has been fixed, new companies have nothing to hope for," DarkSide posted. "Special thanks to BitDefender for helping fix our issues. This will make us even better."

■   ■   ■

It wasn't the first time that an antivirus company had trumpeted a solution that the Ransomware Hunting Team had beaten it to. The Bitdefender incident and others like it exposed the lack of coordination, communication, and agreement among the private-sector groups hunting ransomware about how to identify and communicate with victims without alerting the enemy.

From the team's perspective, antivirus companies eager to make a name for themselves sometimes violate an unwritten precept as old as espionage: don't let your opponents know what you've figured out. The team tries to prolong the attackers' ignorance, even at the cost of contacting fewer victims. Eventually, as payments drop off, the cyber-criminals are likely to realize that something has gone wrong, but the team wants to delay that reckoning as long as possible.

To be sure, such secrecy sometimes requires heartbreaking trade-offs. During World War II, the British Secret Intelligence Service learned from decrypted communications that the Gestapo was planning to kidnap and murder a valuable double agent in Lisbon, Johann-Nielsen "Johnny" Jebsen, code-named ARTIST. Jebsen's handler, Charles de Salis, requested permission to warn Jebsen, but was refused for fear of cluing in the enemy that its cipher had been cracked. Jebsen was indeed abducted and murdered. "[De Salis] regretted his silence for the rest of his life," according to intelligence historian Nigel West.

Marketing departments at cybersecurity firms are eager to promote the company brand and attract clients by touting a new decryption tool. But as ransoms have soared and gangs have grown wealthier and more technically adept, such publicity is likely to backfire. Today, ransomware creators "have access to reverse engineers and penetration testers who are very, very capable," Fabian said. "That's how they gain entrance to these oftentimes highly secured networks in the first place. They download the decryptor, they disassemble it, they reverse engineer it, and they figure out exactly why we were able to decrypt their files. And twenty-four hours later, the whole thing is fixed."

Bogdan Botezatu, Bitdefender's director of threat research, said that, without publicity, word of potential salvation won't reach enough people: "Most victims who fall for ransomware do not have the right connection with ransomware support groups and won't know where to ask for help unless they can learn about the existence of tools from media reports or with a simple search."

Bitdefender itself was not aware of the Ransomware Hunting Team's breakthrough. "We don't believe in ransomware decryptors made silently available," he said. "Attackers will learn about their existence by impersonating home users or companies in need, while the vast majority of victims will have no idea that they can get their data back for free."

Fabian and Michael acknowledged that, as the hackers sifted through compromised networks, they might have come across emails in which victims discussed a flaw discovered by the team in the ransomware. And sooner or later, as victims stopped paying, DarkSide would have recognized its mistake.

Nevertheless, Fabian said, "It's especially painful if a vulnerability is being burned through something stupid like this."

To its credit, Bitdefender has a long track record of assisting victims. It has worked behind the scenes with law enforcement and over the years has released eighteen free decryptors, saving individuals and businesses more than $100 million in ransom.

Bitdefender was especially effective in countering GandCrab, a notorious and pervasive ransomware gang that liked to taunt security researchers by including their names in the code. After European law enforcement penetrated GandCrab's command-and-control servers, Bitdefender developed decryption tools for several versions of the strain, helping numerous victims recover data without paying ransom. In May 2019, GandCrab's developers announced their retirement, claiming to have earned a total of $2 billion in ransom payments.

DarkSide, the gang that had ridiculed Bitdefender for "helping fix our issues," may have indirectly traced its origins to GandCrab.

Some security researchers believe that GandCrab rebranded as REvil, which emerged as GandCrab was leaving the scene. In turn, DarkSide employed some members of the REvil gang. "It is highly likely that DarkSide copied the business model and 'rules' from Gand-Crab," researcher Alex Holden said.

As DarkSide explained in August 2020, announcing its launch in a press release on the dark web, "We are a new product on the market, but that does not mean we have no experience and we came from nowhere."

Holden's research showed that DarkSide's operatives included a ransomware developer, a penetration tester to identify vulnerabilities in networks of potential targets, and a spokesperson for hacker forums and media. At least one of them was based on the south side of Moscow. Unlike REvil, which spurned Lawrence's truce, DarkSide recognized the public relations benefit of renouncing attacks on medical facilities during a pandemic. Although DarkSide emerged too late to participate in the original détente, it promised to spare hospitals, nursing homes, and makers and distributors of COVID-19 vaccines. It also exempted funeral homes, morgues, and crematoria, presumably because they were overwhelmed with coronavirus deaths, as well as government agencies, universities, and schools. Nor, as a matter of self-preservation, did DarkSide attack Russia or other members of the Commonwealth of Independent States, which is made up of former Soviet republics.

That still left plenty of targets for DarkSide in the Americas and Europe. The group chose them carefully. For instance, the hackers attacked one company during a week when they knew it would be vulnerable because it was transitioning its files to the cloud and didn't have reliable backups. Among DarkSide's higher-profile victims were the Dixie Group, a Georgia carpet maker; the Office Depot subsidiary CompuCom; and Toshiba Tec, a European business unit of Toshiba. DarkSide justified such attacks by saying, "We only attack companies that can pay the requested amount, we do not want to kill your business." DarkSide's "name and shame" wall on its dark web site identified dozens of victims that it was pressuring to pay and described the confidential data it claimed to have filched from them.

To infiltrate networks, the gang relied on advanced methods such as "zero-day exploits," which immediately took advantage of software vulnerabilities before they could be patched. Once inside, they moved swiftly, looking not only for sensitive data to use as leverage but also for the victim's cyber insurance policy so that they could peg their demands to the coverage. After two to three days of poking around, DarkSide would encrypt the files.

"They have a faster attack window," said Christopher Ballod, associate managing director for cyber risk at Kroll, the business investigations firm, who advised half a dozen DarkSide victims. "The longer you dwell in the system, the more likely you are to be caught."

Typically, DarkSide's demands were "on the high end of the scale," $5 million and up, Ballod said. DarkSide's representatives were shrewd bargainers. If a victim said it couldn't afford the ransom because of the pandemic, DarkSide was ready with data showing that the company's revenue was up, or that COVID-19's impact was factored into the price. One new twist: If publicly traded companies didn't pay the ransom, DarkSide threatened to share information stolen from them with short sellers who would profit if the share price dropped upon publication.

In November 2020, DarkSide adopted a ransomware-as-a-service model. Affiliates received 75 to 90 percent of the ransom, with DarkSide keeping the remainder.

DarkSide's grasp of foreign affairs was less advanced than its approach to negotiations. Around the same time that it adopted the affiliate model, it posted that it was planning to safeguard stolen information in "Iran or unrecognized republics," so that law enforcement or companies like Microsoft couldn't take down the servers. DarkSide apparently didn't realize that an Iranian connection would complicate ransom payments from victims in the United States, due to American sanctions. In October 2020, the Treasury Department's Office of Foreign Assets Control posted an advisory stating, "Companies that facilitate ransomware payments to cyber actors on behalf of victims . . . may risk violating OFAC regulations" if the actors were on a sanctions list or located in embargoed countries like Iran and North Korea.

Many cyber insurers had second thoughts about covering payments to DarkSide. With their insurers unwilling to reimburse the ransom, none of Ballod's clients paid DarkSide, despite concerns about exposure of their data. Bill Siegel's company, Coveware, stopped negotiating with the gang.

Trying to contain the fallout, the hackers walked back their statement, saying they had considered Iran as only "one of the POSSIBLE locations for storing data," and that they couldn't find a hosting provider there. In a childish tit for tat, they declared that they wouldn't cooperate with Coveware, and would recommend other data recovery companies to victims.

After World War II, demand for gasoline and other oil products soared. But getting them from refineries to consumers posed a problem. Existing pipelines were inadequate, and oil tankers were subject to the vagaries of weather and longshoremen's strikes. The solution, dubbed "the biggest plumbing job in history," rivaled the Panama Canal in ambition and magnitude. In 1962, in the largest privately financed construction project in the United States at the time, a consortium of nine oil companies began building a three-foot-wide pipeline from Houston to New York harbor. It was called the Colonial Pipeline because, of the fourteen states it passed through, nine were among the original thirteen colonies. Pipe was laid across Lookout Mountain in Tennessee and on the bottoms of many rivers, including the James and the Delaware.

The pipeline would ultimately stretch 5,500 miles and carry more than 100 million gallons a day of gasoline, heating oil, diesel, aviation fuel, and other oil products from twenty-nine Gulf Coast refineries to the East Coast. A subsidiary of Koch Industries has been the pipeline's biggest stakeholder since 2002.

From its inception, the Colonial Pipeline Company used computers to generate schedules for oil shipments. "Embracing computer

technology became a Colonial hallmark," according to a history com-
missioned by the company. Its view of oil spills was less enlightened.
The industry attitude that "a little oil on the ground" was nothing to
worry about was out of step with the growing movement to protect the
environment. In 1996, a corroded stretch of pipe, which the company
hadn't bothered to replace, ruptured in South Carolina, causing what
was then the sixth-biggest spill in U.S. history. The company pleaded
guilty in 1999 to criminal negligence and was fined $7 million. It also
paid $13 million in settlements to landowners and the state of South
Carolina.

Described in the corporate history as "a low point for a chastened
company," the Reedy River spill had a lasting impact on Colonial's culture. First, it inculcated a cautious, safety-first approach, epitomized
by the slogan some employees sported on T-shirts: IF IN DOUBT, SHUT IT
DOWN. Colonial adopted a policy that anyone in the organization had
the power to shut down the pipeline. Colonial closed down the entire
pipeline for the first time on December 31, 1999, for fear of power
surges from any computer glitches related to the Y2K transition, and
again during Hurricane Katrina in 2005. It hoped its proactive stance
would avert federal intervention. "The concern was about being dic-
tated to," a former company official said.

Colonial boosted IT spending by 50 percent from 2017 to 2021.
But when the Transportation Security Administration, which is part
of the Department of Homeland Security and oversees pipeline safety,
contacted Colonial in 2020 to schedule a voluntary cybersecurity review, the company begged off. Its excuses were that it was undergoing
a COVID-19 lockdown and moving to a new headquarters. No TSA assessment took place until it was too late.

Just before 5:00 a.m. on May 7, 2021, a Colonial employee found a
ransom note on the company's network. DarkSide had frozen the
company's billing and administrative systems and stolen personal information such as health insurance data and Social Security numbers.

The gang had exploited an outdated VPN that wasn't supposed to be active and was guarded by only a single password rather than the additional protection of multifactor authentication. The password was available on the dark web, probably because a Colonial employee had used it with another account that was hacked.

The company adopted the cautious approach that had been its hallmark since the Reedy River spill. Fearing that backup systems had been corrupted, and that the gang would affect or even seize control of operational equipment such as sensors, valves, and pumps, a supervisor shut down the pipeline. The flow of 45 percent of all fuel consumed on the East Coast abruptly stopped.

A vital artery was blocked, and the nation reeled. As gasoline prices rose, panicked drivers began topping off their tanks, prompting gas lines not seen since the oil shortages of the 1970s. As buyers stockpiled, the U.S. Consumer Safety Products Commission issued a warning against filling plastic bags with gasoline. The combination of reduced supply and higher demand shuttered gas stations across the Southeast. Almost two-thirds of stations in North Carolina were without fuel, and almost half in Virginia, Georgia, and South Carolina. The crisis affected aviation, too. Facing jet-fuel shortages, some flights were rerouted.

The devastating blow to America's critical infrastructure established ransomware in the national consciousness as a serious threat. FBI director Christopher Wray said there were "a lot of parallels" to one of the biggest and most traumatic disasters in U.S. history—the September 11, 2001, terrorist attacks. The Colonial shutdown brought home to ordinary Americans just how big a threat ransomware was. It was now disrupting their daily lives and the necessities and comforts they took for granted.

Colonial's disaster preparedness plan did not envision a ransomware attack. With no other recourse, Colonial paid DarkSide a $4.4 million ransom for a key to unlock its files. "It was the hardest decision I have ever made in my 39 years in the energy industry," Colonial CEO Joseph Blount told Congress. "I know how critical our pipeline is to the country, and I put the interest of the country first." The key that DarkSide provided to Colonial worked "to some degree," Blount said, and the shutdown ended after six days.

Colonial didn't end up on the hook for the entire $4.4 million. Before paying, Blount consulted the company's cyber insurer, which indicated it would cover the ransom. The company still expected to spend months, and tens of millions of dollars, recovering all its business systems.

Just as DarkSide failed to recognize the downside of an Iranian connection, so it appeared taken aback by the furor its pipeline attack had caused. "We are apolitical, we do not participate in geopolitics," it posted on its site three days after the attack. "Our goal is to make money, and not creating problems for society."

Fuming, Bill Siegel blamed Bitdefender. "It would be so much more impactful if the bad guys just kept using the insecure version and everyone knew not to pay them." The Ransomware Hunting Team, its efforts in vain, was furious, too. The team coined a term for the premature exposure of a weakness in a ransomware strain. They called it "pulling a Bitdefender."

The DarkSide saga illuminated a fundamental paradox. By cracking ransomware, the Ransomware Hunting Team and others, like Bitdefender, have rescued untold millions of victims from paying ransoms and thwarted countless criminals. Without the team to detect flaws in ransomware strains, any hackers, no matter how shoddy their code, could terrorize victims and force them to pay.

But the hunters' brilliance had an unintended consequence. By identifying flaws that hackers like DarkSide then fix, the team functioned as product testers for the ransomware gangs. Its discoveries forced the hackers to upgrade their cryptography and make the strains tougher or impossible to decode. Due to these improvements, as well as the increasing technical savvy and specialization of many hackers, ransomware overall became more secure. Michael and Fabian could still crack many emerging types of ransomware. But, reflecting the shift, they and Sarah began devoting more time to helping victims who paid the ransom recover faster and more smoothly than they would using tools provided by the hackers.

Like decrypting ransomware, this task furthered the team's goal of aiding victims. But it also served the interests of attackers by making victims who paid the ransom happier with the outcome. In addition, it led the team down a path that would test its commitment to a fundamental tenet of its mission: helping people for free.

The new enterprise started with a request from Bill Siegel. In 2019, he and Coveware had a problem. Companies hit by Ryuk were hiring Coveware to negotiate ransoms so they could recover their data and resume operations. But the decryption tool that the gang supplied in return was slow and faulty. Bill approached Fabian. "Listen, the Ryuk decryption tool is absolutely awful," Bill said. "We need something better." Fabian extracted the key from the Ryuk ransomware decryptor and created a faster and more reliable one.

The improved Ryuk decryptor was so successful that Bill asked what else Fabian could do. "We have a bunch of other ransomware families that are also awful," Bill told Fabian. "Can you create decryption tools for those as well?" Fabian agreed.

Eventually, Fabian, Michael, and Sarah built a universal decryptor. Unlike the decryptors they had built for specific ransomware strains over the years, the universal decryptor, with some tweaking, could work with any key—whether the Ransomware Hunting Team had obtained it themselves by cracking the strain or the hackers supplied it after receiving the ransom. The teammates put those keys into their own tool, Unidecrypt. Victims could then run the tool to recover their files. Coveware and Emsisoft licensed the technology from a company that Fabian and Sarah founded and offered the use of the tool to victims. Emsisoft's price was $5,000; Coveware's, $3,500. "It was a tick box on their à la carte menu," Fabian said.

Fabian, Michael, and Sarah believed this was ethically defensible, as did Lawrence. The clients were mostly major corporations that had paid millions of dollars in ransom and could easily afford a few thousand for improved decryption software. Since the universal decryptor sped up data recovery by 70 percent on average, Fabian called it "an absolute no-brainer" for victims. "They pay five thousand dollars after already paying a couple of million in ransom. But they will get their systems back a week ahead of time."

Still, as ingenious as the universal decryptor was, selling their services undercut the hunters' idealistic credo. The compromise became more glaring on the memorable weekend in 2021 when Michael cracked three strains. The Coveware client attacked by Lorenz was spared from enriching the criminals, but it paid a fee for essentially the same service that the team had previously provided for free. When they had time, Michael and Fabian still created free decryptors for some especially prolific strains and posted them on the Emsisoft website.

Bill downplayed the ethical dilemma raised by the Lorenz case. "The clients whose ransomware you can actually crack, it's less than ten percent," he said. "It's one, maybe two variants a month. We're typically seeing twenty to thirty variants a month."

Despite his misgivings about the ransomware response industry, there was so much unmet demand for Coveware's negotiating services that in late 2021 Bill began recruiting additional staff for new openings. An Australia-based "director of incident response" would be expected to "negotiate with cyber criminals," "manage financial operations associated with" ransom payments, and interact with "our partners in law enforcement."

At the same time, Bill did his best to raise the industry's standards by giving Coveware clients accurate and rapid data so they could make informed choices. While some competitors worked for weeks on cases without learning how hackers penetrated a system and what they did once inside, Coveware developed a tool that answered such questions within minutes. Beyond the forensic issues, the tool forecast how the negotiation was likely to unfold. And, by looking for damage to files that couldn't be fixed by decryption, it protected victims from paying the ransom in vain.

Bill maintained a sense of levity by compiling a "coffee table book" of the most outrageous remarks made by hackers during negotiations.

For example, in November 2021: "Our leadership has a birthday today and he can give you a discount."

Catastrophe is often the fastest route to reform. After the Colonial shutdown, the TSA tightened oversight of pipeline operators, ordering companies to designate a point person to report attacks and to review their systems and identify and patch any gaps. It imposed escalating penalties for violators. The era of voluntary compliance appeared to be over.

So did the era of the U.S. government underestimating the ransomware threat. Just before the pipeline chaos, the Department of Justice created the Ransomware and Digital Extortion Task Force to coordinate ransomware investigations and prosecutions. In the wake of the Colonial attack, President Biden issued an executive order to improve federal cybersecurity, and the Justice Department raised ransomware to the same priority level as terrorism.

The government task force had an ambitious mandate reminiscent of the Dutch HTCU's off-center targeting: to investigate all aspects of ransomware and its support structure, from cryptocurrency exchanges to botnets. The aim was "to ensure we track all ransomware cases regardless of where it may be referred in this country, so you can make the connections between actors and work your way up to disrupt the whole chain," said John Carlin, principal associate deputy attorney general.

The heightened focus on ransomware quickly paid dividends. Now that ransomware was an administration priority, FBI agents and computer scientists felt empowered to pursue it. After somehow gaining access to the private encryption key linked to DarkSide's Bitcoin account, the FBI was able to retrieve about half of Colonial's payment to the hackers—one of the rare instances of ransom money being recovered.

A week after the pipeline attack, DarkSide said it was shutting down, citing "pressure from the U.S." It could no longer connect to its website, blog, and payment server.

"The affiliate program is closed," DarkSide told its partners in a statement written in Russian. "Stay safe and good luck."

No sooner had the furor over the Colonial shutdown begun to quiet down than another major attack raised the national anxiety level all over again. REvil disabled the U.S. division of Brazil-based JBS, the world's largest meat processor, which paid an $11 million ransom. The pair of attacks by Russia-based gangs prompted President Biden to press Vladimir Putin at a June 2021 summit meeting to stop ransomware attacks originating from his country. A growing body of evidence tied Russia to ransomware. One cluster of ransom payments was traced to Moscow's tallest skyscraper, the Federation Tower East in the financial district. But Putin brushed Biden off.

Two weeks after the summit, over the Fourth of July weekend, REvil attacked Kaseya, a global company that makes IT management software. Because Kaseya's clients handle IT for many businesses, nonprofits, and government agencies, up to fifteen hundred organizations were affected.

At the time of the attack, the FBI had penetrated REvil's infrastructure and had obtained the decryption key. But it didn't let Kaseya know, for fear of tipping off the hackers before it could identify them. While victims languished, the REvil gang realized that its platform had been compromised. Its spokesman and leader, Unknown, shut it down and disappeared. Without Unknown, REvil resurfaced in September 2021, but it closed again in October.

The FBI waited almost three weeks to share REvil's decryption tool with Kaseya. Through Chris Krebs—the former director of the Cybersecurity & Infrastructure Security Agency, who had become a consultant—Kaseya reached out to Fabian to ask whether he could ensure that the tool was safe and effective.

"Just hypothetically, if you were to be given a ransomware threat actor tool for a popular ransomware family, and it was from a secret sauce but that sauce was one hundred percent trustworthy, could you help them?" Krebs asked Fabian.

"Yeah, we do that all the time," Fabian said. He had handled so many REvil cases that it only took him ten minutes to extract the key and put it into his universal decryptor, which he then secretly distributed to Kaseya customers.

Disturbed by the Kaseya attack and Russia's continued laissez-faire approach to ransomware, Biden got back in touch with Putin. He warned the Russian president in a July 9 phone call that the United States regarded ransomware as a threat to national security. If Russia didn't respond, the United States would.

"I made it very clear to him that the United States expects, when a ransomware operation is coming from his soil, even though it's not sponsored by the state, we expect them to act if we give them enough information to act on who that is," Biden said afterward. He said that he was "optimistic" that Russia would clamp down on ransomware. But the White House didn't invite Russia to a ransomware summit that it hosted virtually with representatives from thirty countries.

The government's ransomware task force continued to make inroads. In November 2021, the Department of Justice announced it had charged Yaroslav Vasinskyi of Ukraine and Yevgeniy Polyanin of Russia with deploying REvil against businesses and government offices in the United States. The Justice Department also seized $6.1 million in alleged ransomware payments to Polyanin. While Polyanin remained at large, Vasinskyi, who was allegedly responsible for the Kaseya attack, was arrested in Poland and was extradited to the United States. He pleaded innocent in a federal court in Texas in March 2022.

Also facing extradition was Denis Dubnikov, a Russian entrepreneur who was indicted for allegedly helping Ryuk launder payments from U.S. victims. Dubnikov was reportedly a founder of EggChange, a cryptocurrency exchange on the twenty-second floor of Moscow's Federation Tower East. At the FBI's request, Dutch authorities arrested him in Amsterdam in November. Through one of his companies, Dubnikov disputed the charges, calling them "unreliable."

■   ■   ■

As the government got tougher on ransomware, so did the cyber insurance industry. Early on, when demands were lower, it made financial sense to pay the ransom and move on, rather than shoulder the costs of a prolonged recovery from backups. But that attitude ultimately drove up cyber insurers' costs because hackers made ever-higher demands based on their confidence that the insurer would pay. As ransoms soared into the tens of millions of dollars, the economics shifted. Insurers could no longer take for granted that paying a ransom would be the less expensive option.

Due to higher ransom demands and more frequent attacks, underwriting losses increased substantially in 2020 and 2021 over prior years. Insurers responded by tightening coverage terms and doubling or even tripling premiums. In May 2021, the same month as the Colonial Pipeline shutdown, Paris-based AXA became the first global insurer to stop writing cyber insurance policies that cover ransom payments, although the shift applied only to customers in France. About a week later, possibly in retaliation, AXA's Asia division was hit by ransomware. The U.S. insurer American International Group said in August 2021 that it was reducing limits on cyber coverage to address "the rising threat associated with ransomware." Toward the end of the year, Lloyd's of London, which underwrites about one-fifth of the global cyber insurance market, advised members of its syndicate against taking on cyber business.

European cybersecurity regulators had an additional tool to bolster defenses against ransomware attacks. The 2018 General Data Protection Regulation (GDPR) required companies located in European Union countries or doing business there to improve cybersecurity, report data breaches within seventy-two hours, and delete data that is no longer needed. Violators could be fined as much as 4 percent of revenue.

While the GDPR sought to protect sensitive information, it handed ransomware gangs that succeeded in exfiltrating personal data another pressure point. If companies balked at paying, the attackers would snitch on them to EU authorities. Hackers who had breached a company's defenses knew the inadequacies of its cybersecurity better than anyone.

"In case of refusal to pay, we will contact the ... GDPR and notify them that you store user data in an open form and is not safe," one gang warned in its ransom note. "Under the rules of the law, you face a heavy fine or arrest."

Even with the government's new emphasis on ransomware, the FBI didn't undertake fundamental reforms to expand its roster of cyber experts. Its reluctance to adapt disappointed some former agents. "I think the next generation of cyber people in the bureau should be the type of people who want to be cyber first, and not agents at all," said Milan Patel, one of the agents who attended the 2015 meeting with Comey. "The bureau needs expertly trained technical programmers, cybersecurity engineers, that know how to write code, compile, dissect, and investigate—and it has nothing to do with carrying a gun."

Still, the FBI was flexible on one key issue: it was increasingly willing to cooperate with private researchers. In an October 2021 speech, Director Christopher Wray noted that the bureau had established the Office of Private Sector at headquarters, put private-sector coordinators in every field office, and formed teams within the cyber and counterintelligence divisions to work with industry. "We're up against some daunting threats posed by nation states, cybercriminals, and toxic combinations of the two," Wray said. "And we can only prevail with the help of our partners throughout the private sector."

Collaborating with the private sector offered advantages—and pitfalls. The government has the power to seize servers and subpoena data, while private companies have a deep and talented bench. Partnerships could combine these strengths. But the FBI needed to choose collaborators carefully and set clear expectations for them. Some companies put profit ahead of the public good. Others, like Bitdefender, publicized breakthroughs that they might have been better advised to keep secret. In this minefield, the bureau liked to work with people it knew and trusted, like the ex-dolphin from its Seattle office, Randy Pargman.

In his new job as vice president of threat hunting and counterintelligence at the cybersecurity company Binary Defense, Randy routinely came across information about impending cyber intrusions, and he connected with other researchers who did, too. They all wanted the intelligence they gathered to reach the people who needed it.

Randy admired the Ransomware Hunting Team and Michael's website, ID Ransomware. Channeling them, he developed an independent, all-volunteer website that he called Aunt Beast, after a character from the 1962 Madeleine L'Engle novel, *A Wrinkle in Time*. He chose the name in part because Aunt Beast "extends kindness to save strangers in dire need."

While Aunt Beast was not publicly accessible, members could invite anyone else they trusted. Its original handful of cybersecurity researchers brought in other industry colleagues and IT specialists. Those interested in defending their networks logged their organization's range of IP addresses into the site, while those with information regarding impending attacks logged intelligence about which IP addresses were in hackers' crosshairs.

When there was a match, Aunt Beast automatically notified the target organizations by email, text, or other forms of contact. It told them, for example, which IP addresses were attacking theirs, or that a known ransomware server was communicating every five seconds with their IP address to determine where their network was vulnerable.

Randy realized that his former employer could be helpful. Upon seizing a ransomware command-and-control server, for example, law enforcement could identify within the server's logs the IP addresses targeted for attack. Then they could add those addresses to Aunt Beast. Any matches would be notified without the authorities even needing to make a call. Randy hoped authorities would use Aunt Beast to "knock out notifications in seconds." Once the Justice Department's Ransomware Task Force was formed, he began sharing access to Aunt Beast with the FBI, the Secret Service, and DHS, as well as with the Dutch HTCU.

Randy views proactive notification as the "hugest opportunity to solve a big problem." Hackers' main advantage, he said, is their invisibility in victims' networks. But once targets learn of the attackers' presence, they can "kick them out."

"This information is actionable," Randy said. "You can put it to work, and you can actually stop these threat actors."

There was one drawback. Unless they were part of Aunt Beast, organizations couldn't necessarily be warned about an imminent attack because IP addresses don't always indicate a recognizable domain name. For that reason, Randy worked hard to broaden participation.

By February 2022, users had logged more than fifty-seven million IP addresses into the database, and the number was growing rapidly. The following month, warnings from Aunt Beast enabled operators of critical industrial control systems to thwart impending cyber attacks. Randy realized that Aunt Beast had "grown too big for me to be the single point of failure," and he turned his creation over to a global organization that coordinates cyber incident prevention. "It needs a team and a full-time system admin to keep the servers up and running," he said.

The ransomware landscape was constantly changing, and many big strains that the Ransomware Hunting Team battled had closed down. But as often as not, they resurfaced with different names yet the same characteristics. Just as Maze was shutting down in September 2020, for instance, a ransomware strain called Egregor sprang up. Its code and ransom note were similar to Maze's, and many former Maze affiliates flocked to Egregor. In February 2022, the developer of those strains released decryption keys for them on the BleepingComputer forums. In a way it was ironic. The same gang that had tried so hard to manipulate Lawrence Abrams then chose his site to walk away from ransomware.

Two months after DarkSide shut down, a user named BlackMatter posted on a popular dark web forum, seeking to purchase access to corporate networks in the United States, Canada, Australia, and Great Britain that had more than $100 million in annual revenue. Less than a week later, BlackMatter ransomware launched its dark web leak site. "Dear companies," the group wrote. "We recommend paying ransom, otherwise your data will be downloaded by competitors or hackers."

In its "About Us" section, BlackMatter wrote, "We are a team that unites people according to one common interest—money."

Within days, the Ransomware Hunting Team found and analyzed BlackMatter's code. "The initial rumors that BlackMatter could be a repaint of the DarkSide operation were quickly confirmed," Fabian blogged. "The very first BlackMatter version turned out to be almost identical to the last DarkSide version."

When Fabian set up his messaging account as a confessional for cybercriminals in July 2021, he hoped to establish a line of communication between hackers and the Ransomware Hunting Team. He did not anticipate that it would also result in more reliable contact between the team and the U.S. government.

For years, Fabian had struggled to get the government's attention. The Butterball incident—when a hacker came to Fabian's confessional with evidence of an impending attack on the turkey company— changed that. In his desperate attempt to warn Butterball, Fabian reached out to someone he knew at CISA, who took his information seriously. That person then connected him with an FBI agent in Pittsburgh, which was known as a hub for successful cyber investigations. As a member of the bureau's Cyber Initiative and Resource Fusion Unit, the agent worked with the private sector to make and advance cases. Fabian was elated to secure a reliable contact who "has been working on ransomware and cybercrime for many years and isn't going to be transferred out anytime soon."

After Butterball, the team began to connect regularly with both CISA and the FBI. CISA communicated with team members over

Slack. The new collaborators even bonded over the frustrations they encountered while working with the FBI. "The moment I started talking, they were like, 'Yeah, we know,'" Fabian said, recalling the conversation. "'It's like a black hole, stuff disappears in there.'" The FBI still wouldn't join Slack, but the Pittsburgh agent introduced Fabian to colleagues in other field offices who focused on specific ransomware strains.

As the team decrypted emerging types of ransomware, it could immediately and discreetly spread the word to the FBI and CISA. "We have a vulnerability for this new ransomware family that we just found," Fabian would tell them. "If you see any victims, please refer them to us, or reach out to us so we can exchange details about the vulnerability and see whether or not we can help."

BlackMatter gave the team a chance to demonstrate the value of collaboration. Following weeks of analysis, Fabian discovered a vulnerability in BlackMatter's ransomware and told CISA and the FBI about it. "Hey listen," he recalled telling his contacts. "If you have any BlackMatter victims, we can help them. They don't have to pay a ransom."

The FBI was interested, but, Fabian said, "they're still very much the FBI." His contact was reluctant to pass along Fabian's contact details to victims for fear that "it may look like the FBI is endorsing [Emsisoft], and the FBI can't endorse a private company." The agent told Fabian he would consult with a legal expert within the FBI and get back to him.

A day later, the agent called Fabian back; the FBI would give BlackMatter victims his contact details. The FBI provided a "long list of things we are and are not allowed to do," Fabian said. "This list of things we are not allowed to do is way longer." For example, the team was not allowed to advertise that the FBI had recommended them; it wouldn't have done that anyway, Fabian said. The bureau's hesitant cooperation paid off. It referred multiple victims, including a furniture company, to the team, which helped them recover without paying ransoms.

Two victims referred by the bureau told Fabian they had been "on the fence about reporting to the FBI in the first place because they thought nothing's going to come of it," he said. "It would just be another headache, and you would still have to pay the ransom or rebuild everything from scratch." For them, the team's services were a revelation.

"Now there's really something in it for victims to go to the FBI," Fabian said. "Victims report ransomware incidents to authorities, who may in return provide them with crucial intelligence from parties like us to recover their files without caving to criminals' demands. I see that as the biggest incentive you can give to victims."

For CISA, a partnership with the Ransomware Hunting Team provided a meaningful way to assist victims in the aftermath of a ransomware attack—the kind of help that former director Chris Krebs had longed to provide. Fabian said that the agency was "absolutely instrumental" in expanding the team's reach to BlackMatter victims, including Crystal Valley, a Minnesota-based farm supply cooperative that was left unable to mix fertilizer or fulfill orders for livestock feed. Along with Iowa-based New Cooperative, it was the second major agricultural business that the team saved from paying a ransom in September 2021.

That month, Coveware paid Fabian and Sarah's company about $140,000, as Bill's clients clamored to use the universal decryptor for quick recovery from BlackMatter. Clinging to their ideals, Fabian and Sarah didn't charge healthcare victims and others who couldn't afford to pay. As Bill had anticipated, a close relationship with the Ransomware Hunting Team was enhancing Coveware's reputation.

By mid-October, BlackMatter realized that it had a problem, and it fixed the vulnerability that the team had been exploiting. Still, by then, the team had saved fifty victims from collectively paying about $100 million to BlackMatter. Fabian reflected that "having an organization like CISA or the FBI, not even vouch for us, but at the very least say, 'Yes, these are legit people,' is so helpful for our outreach. We are just random dudes on Twitter—why would we be legit?" Weeks later, citing "pressure from the authorities," BlackMatter announced it was shutting down. Its affiliates shifted existing victims to another gang's site to continue negotiating ransom payments.

■ ■ ■

The ransomware battle was escalating on both sides. The attackers were getting savvier. Their cryptography was improving, and they were picking targets more shrewdly and with a surer political sense. To avoid drawing unwanted attention, they were mostly attacking rich but uncontroversial victims that could afford large ransoms but weren't as vital as Colonial to the basic functioning of society. The FBI noticed that some gangs were "redirecting ransomware efforts away from 'big-game' and toward mid-sized victims to reduce scrutiny."

One such attack hit close to home for the Gillespies. In December 2021, ransomware "thwarted admissions activities and hindered access to all institutional data" at Lincoln College, a predominantly Black 157-year-old liberal arts college in rural Illinois with a branch campus in Normal. Struggling financially and unable to project future enrollment, Lincoln shut down permanently in May 2022.

By early 2022, the U.S. government was taking the threat seriously. It was deploying both investigative resources and diplomacy to combat ransomware worldwide, and it was finally working with the Ransomware Hunting Team and other private groups. A new federal law required owners of critical infrastructure to report to CISA if they had been breached or paid a ransom. Separately, the SEC proposed a rule requiring publicly traded companies to report ransomware and other cybersecurity attacks within four days.

The United States also pressed Russia for help pursuing cyber-attackers based there. But the Kremlin seesawed between cooperation and obstruction, depending on its most urgent foreign policy interests. Even when it cracked down, it chose targets selectively. It apparently didn't pursue Evil Corp leader and FSB worker Maksim Yakubets, nor other notable cybercriminals indicted by the United States.

In October 2021, Russia sought to placate the Biden administration by prosecuting TrickBot, which had recovered from Microsoft's and Cyber Command's takedown a year earlier. But the case in Moscow was "set up to fail," Alex Holden said, and was soon closed or delayed when the Russian military buildup on the Ukraine border raised tensions with the United States.

Emotet, which had been quiet since the Dutch HTCU's takedown almost a year before, resurfaced in November 2021, borrowing Trick-Bot infrastructure to rebuild its botnet. Members of the TrickBot-Emotet-Ryuk group began joking that if the U.S.-Russia relationship became any more strained, ransomware would be legalized in Russia and they would have to declare the payments on their taxes.

In January 2022, Russia appeared to clamp down again. Acting on what it said was "the appeal of the competent U.S. authorities," its domestic intelligence service dismantled REvil, which had already been dormant for three months. The FSB not only arrested fourteen gang members but also seized a number of computers, twenty luxury cars, and 426 million rubles (more than $5 million). One of the suspects had reportedly been responsible for the Colonial Pipeline attack. The REvil arrests alarmed the TrickBot-Emotet-Ryuk organization. Ryuk's forums on the dark web shut down, and some of its leaders left for the associated Conti group or appeared to quit ransomware altogether.

The following month, Russia invaded Ukraine. The brutal aggression sparked worldwide outrage, forced millions of Ukrainians to flee their homeland, and made Putin a pariah outside his country. The Conti gang quickly announced its "full support of Russian government" and said that it would use its "full capacity to deliver retaliatory measures in case the Western warmongers attempt to target critical infrastructure in Russia or any Russian-speaking region of the world."

This proclamation of solidarity with the Putin regime soon backfired. It prompted a Ukrainian researcher who had penetrated Conti to leak more than sixty thousand internal messages sent as recently as February 2022. The unprecedented glimpse inside a ransomware gang's operations shed light on the group's structure, finances, day-to-day operations, and attitudes. The leaks indicated that a Conti member had intelligence on Ukrainian border activity a week before the invasion. "I already figured that S [TrickBot's Stern] is in service of Pu," another Conti employee wrote. With its leadership and secrets exposed, Conti reduced its attacks and lay low. In May 2022, the U.S.

Department of State offered a $10 million reward for information identifying and locating Conti leaders.

As the United States and European nations rallied around Ukraine, there was widespread speculation that Russia would retaliate with cyberattacks. Russian prosecutors appeared to drop the case against the REvil attackers and considered a deal that would draft them to fight Ukraine on the cyber front.

With Russia's economy battered by Western sanctions, it seemed likely that some former tech workers might compensate for lost jobs and income by turning to ransomware. If so, they might shroud their nationality because fewer ransomware victims may be inclined to reward Russian gangs. Unwilling to pay the Putin-geld, Western businesses, schools, hospitals, and government agencies disabled by ransomware would need the Ransomware Hunting Team more than ever.

Michael Gillespie's ransomware hunting and his relationship with the FBI had to take a back seat to his new responsibilities at home. In August 2020, he drove Morgan to an appointment with her gynecologist. While Morgan was at the office, a nurse instructed her to take a pregnancy test. Morgan rolled her eyes but complied. A few minutes later, the nurse burst into the examining room.

"You're pregnant!"

Overcome with emotion, Morgan rushed out to tell Michael, who had been waiting in the car. But he wasn't there. It was a scorching day, and he had walked to a grocery store to cool off. He returned to the car and saw Morgan walking toward him. When she got in, he started telling her what he had bought at the store. She threw the test at him.

"What? Huh?"

For many years, Morgan had dreamed of becoming a mother. At long last, when she had almost given up hope, she found herself pregnant. But she also knew that her diabetes and obesity raised the risk of complications or even miscarriage.

The couple immediately began preparing for the baby's arrival. They bought a royal-blue Dodge Caravan to accommodate their growing family, and Michael converted an upstairs bedroom to a nursery. From the sheets, bedspread, and mobile on the crib to the curtains, framed sheet music, and I JUST CAN'T WAIT TO BE KING sign on the walls, the decor was themed after *The Lion King*.

But, as Morgan had feared, it was a difficult pregnancy. She was frequently nauseous, required extra doctors' appointments, and at one point was hospitalized. Michael devoted himself to her care, even putting off meetings with the FBI.

On Monday, March 15, 2021, almost seven weeks before her due date, Morgan went to the hospital for a series of tests, which indicated that she was developing preeclampsia, a complication that can be serious or even fatal. Since delivery of the baby is "the most effective treatment" for preeclampsia, and since the fetus's heart rate was decreasing—a sign of decreased blood flow to the placenta—doctors decided to deliver the baby by cesarean section.

"Having a baby today," Michael messaged a Coveware colleague at 8:18 a.m. on March 17. "Going dark." At 12:40 p.m., Michael sat beside Morgan in her room at Carle Foundation Hospital in Champaign, Illinois. He nervously patted her head to comfort her until it was time for her spinal block, and he was asked to leave her room.

As Michael waited in the recovery room, he received an email from Mark Phelps, his FBI contact, about a ransomware strain called Tripoli. He drafted an email saying he would be unreachable for a while because his wife was about to give birth. He sent the note as he walked back to the operating room. Four minutes later, their son was born.

Morgan and Michael named him Lukan Atlas Gillespie. Morgan had picked the name long before. Lukan reminded her of *luce*, which means "light" in Italian, and Atlas was the Greek god who holds up the heavens on his shoulders. "Strength of light is what I was thinking," she said.

Michael switched his Slack emoji to a baby, and later to one of a dad feeding a bottle to an infant. He announced the new member of the family in a succinct tweet: "Gillespies++," using the programming symbol for adding one. He added, "break."

"Congratulations, Michael," Fabian responded. "I hope both the mum and the little future ransomware hunter are well. Enjoy fatherhood :)" Sarah added her congratulations. Emsisoft sent a parenting book and a stuffed kiwi bird, the national symbol of New Zealand, where Emsisoft is based. One of Michael's coworkers at Coveware knitted a scarf, hat, and sweater for Lukan.

Although his birth weight of eight pounds, three ounces was above average for a full-term baby, Lukan was immediately whisked to the hospital's neonatal intensive care unit. Morgan remained at Carle for five days. "I ended up voluntarily checking out because I was going crazy in the hospital," she said.

Once home recovering from her C-section, she was plagued by headaches and muscle pain. She and Michael visited Lukan in the hospital, an hour to the southeast, whenever she felt up to it. But the trip was hard for Morgan both physically and emotionally. A mother not yet allowed to nurture her newborn, she felt in limbo. By March 24, when the baby was a week old, Michael still hadn't held him. He preferred for Morgan to hold Lukan "whenever we have the chance, to calm her anxiety," he explained. "She's having a rough time being away from him, but yet she can't stand not being home for long."

Michael returned to work, saving the rest of his paternity leave for when the baby could come home. "How's the kiddo doing?" Sarah messaged him one day.

"Kiddo is taking about half a bottle now before passing out—have to tube feed the rest," Michael replied. "He has to consistently take the whole bottle before he can come home. Momma is like 95% healed, but she just had her first Covid vaccine and is having super bad headaches and soreness from it."

"I've heard the side effects for the vaccine can be rough," Sarah sympathized. "Hope it's not too long before he can go home."

Lukan was finally released from the hospital on May 14. He slept in his parents' room, and they didn't get much sleep. "It's a bit crazy," Michael reported. "He's on feed every 3 hour schedule. And we have to tube feed him whatever he doesn't finish from the bottle. So by time diaper change to wake him up, try bottle feed, then gavage the rest, have maybe an hour to spare before the whole cycle starts again."

When Morgan's diabetes or other ailments flared up, Michael took over with the baby. On paternity leave from Coveware, he bonded with his son. He pushed Lukan in the stroller through nearby Miller Park, enjoying the quiet and the shade, ambling past the playground, the bandstand, the Southern Pacific caboose, the lagoon where fishermen caught bass and catfish.

Since Michael didn't have time to identify new variants of STOPDjvu, which was still attacking thousands of victims a month, MalwareHunterTeam took over for him. But Michael found it hard to step away completely from ransomware. He monitored social media and Coveware's Slack channel on his work phone. Sometimes, by telling Morgan that he was "feeding the cats," he grabbed a few minutes away from baby duty to hunt ransomware.

On Lukan's fourth day home, Michael read that a new strain called EpsilonRed had attacked a Coveware client, encrypting the business's files and backups. Named after a telepathic Russian soldier in the Marvel comics who could breathe in outer space and had four flame-throwing tentacles, EpsilonRed penetrated hospitality businesses and other industries by exploiting vulnerabilities in Microsoft Exchange servers.

Fabian was already examining EpsilonRed, and Michael couldn't resist taking a look, too. While at his computer to print out logs of Lukan's feeding and diaper changes, he analyzed the strain and noticed a flaw. Its code contained zeros in a recurring pattern. When the pattern was broken, and the zeros did not repeat as expected, the substitute characters included part of the key.

EpsilonRed used a different key for each file format, and Michael couldn't find all the keys for the client's regular files. But he extracted keys for the backups and server, enabling the client to unlock and clean the backups and restore its system from them. It didn't have to pay a ransom.

As he devoted himself to fatherhood, he worried about losing his identity and prowess as a ransomware hunter. "I feel like I'm the most unproductive I've ever been in my life."

So he especially relished this triumph. It wasn't every day that he discovered a ransomware weakness that his team member, friend, and mentor had overlooked. "I was a little bit proud of that one," he said. "Fabian missed it at first. Even on paternity leave, I broke ransomware."

NOTES

INTRODUCTION: "ARE YOU INDEED A BARBARIAN?"

4 *Matthew, an affable Englishman*: At Matthew's request, we are withholding his surname and the school's name.

5 *"The history of civilization"*: George Orwell, "You and the Atomic Bomb," *Tribune*, October 19, 1945.

10 *an estimated four million victims*: Data from Emsisoft, tracking successful decryptions by Emsisoft-branded decryption tools (based on current tracking and past estimates).

12 *"I have fourteen"*: John Pearson, *All the Money in the World* (London: William Collins, 2017), 176.

12 *named after Caesar*: Christopher McFadden, "11 Cryptographic Methods That Marked History: From the Caesar Cipher to Enigma Code and Beyond," Interesting Engineering, July 3, 2018, interestingengineering.com/11-cryptographic-methods-that-marked-history-from-the-caesar-cipher-to-enigma-code-and-beyond.

13 *Iranian hackers are believed*: Bitcoin wallet analysis by Chainalysis. Author interview with Kim Grauer and Maddie Kennedy, March 12, 2021.

1. THE MAN WHO INVENTED RANSOMWARE

20 *"would end up being a CPA"*: Wally Guenther, "Neighbors Express Surprise at Arrest," *Plain Dealer* (Cleveland, OH), February 3, 1990.

20 *"the most important book"*: Joseph L. Popp, *Popular Evolution: Life-Lessons from Anthropology* (Lake Jackson, TX: Man and Nature Press, 2000), xviii.

21 *"Basically, all of the seminal papers"*: Author interview with Robert Sapolsky, June 12, 2000.

21 *"greater damage"*: Joseph L. Popp and Irven DeVore, "Aggressive Competition and Social Dominance Theory: Synopsis," in *The Great Apes*, ed. David A. Hamburg and Elizabeth R. McCown (Menlo Park, CA: Benjamin/Cummings, 1979), 323.

21 *"Life is merely an artifact"*: Popp, *Popular Evolution*, 1–2.

22 *"speculative stories"*: Stephen Jay Gould, "Sociobiology: The Art of Storytelling," *New Scientist* 80, no. 1129 (November 16, 1978): 531.

22 *"I went to places"*: Joseph L. Popp, "The Primates of Eastern Africa: An Adventure Book" (unpublished manuscript, 2006). Courtesy of Timothy Furlan.

23 *"Gnu dung is a palindrome"*: Author interview with James Malcolm, June 8, 2020.

28 *"the difficulties and inconvenience"*: Christopher Evans, "Mind Games: AIDS, Extortion and the Computer Crime of the Century," *Plain Dealer Sunday Magazine* (Cleveland, OH), April 18, 1993.

28 *"Any time the Kenyan government"*: Evans, "Mind Games."

31 *"restoration can be"*: Jim Bates, "Trojan Horse: AIDS Information Introductory Diskette Version 2.0," *Virus Bulletin*, January 1990, virusbulletin.com/uploads/pdf /magazine/1990/199001.pdf, 5.

31 *"While the conception"*: Bates, "Trojan Horse," 6.

34 *"Elizabeth Ketema"*: Deposition of John Austen, "Re: The Extradition of Joseph Lewis Popp from the United States of America," U.S. District Court, Cleveland, Ohio, Case No. 1:90-00055X, July 6, 1990.

34 *white, bearded*: Evans, "Mind Games."

34 *"alarmist"*: Statement of Dr. Gwyneth Lewis, "Re: The Extradition of Joseph Lewis Popp from the United States of America," U.S. District Court, Cleveland, Case No. 1:90-00055X, March 26, 1990.

36 *"Dr. Popp has been poisoned"*: Evans, "Mind Games."

37 *mentally competent*: Stipulation Accepted by Magistrate Joseph W. Bartunek, U.S. District Court, Cleveland, Case No. 1:90-00055X, March 12, 1990.

37 *"I would say"*: John S. Long, "Witness Claims Man Who Sent Computer Virus Discs Deluded," *Plain Dealer* (Cleveland, OH), March 2, 1990.

38 *"was entitled to the delivery"*: Magistrate's Order, U.S. District Court, Cleveland, Case No. 1:90-00055X, February 2, 1990.

38 *constitute a felony*: U.S. District Judge Ann Aldrich, Memorandum and Order, U.S. District Court, Cleveland, December 20, 1990.

38 *"His recent antics"*: Edward Wilding, "Popp Goes the Weasel," *Virus Bulletin*, January 1992, 2.

38 *"severely mentally ill"*: Kevin Harter, "Popp to Be Returned; Will Be in U.S. Soon, Lawyer Says," *Plain Dealer* (Cleveland, OH), November 27, 1991.

39 *"very sick man"*: Evans, "Mind Games."

40 *"It's a strange case"*: Evans, "Mind Games."

2. THE SUPERHERO OF NORMAL, ILLINOIS

43 *Lincoln appointed*: Britannica, s.v., "David Davis: United States Jurist and Politician," britannica.com/biography/David-Davis.

43 *proposed the 1858 debates*: "The Lawyers: Jesse W. Fell (1808–1887)," Mr. Lincoln & Friends, mrlincolnandfriends.org/the-lawyers/jesse-fell/.

44 *honored his late niece*: Lisa Ellesen, "Gage, Dorothy Louise," McLean County Museum of History, mchistory.org/research/biographies/gage-dorothy-louise.

45 *before-and-after photos*: Kaley Johnson, "Meth Addiction 'Poster Girl' from Pekin Dies at 55," *Belleville News-Democrat*, July 29, 2017.

47 *declared bankruptcy*: Bankruptcy Petition 08-83512, U.S. Bankruptcy Court, Central District of Illinois (Peoria), December 30, 2008.

47 *Bionicle*: BS01 WIKI, s.v. "Bionicle," last modified November 24, 2021, biosector01 .com/wiki/BIONICLE.

49 *"extreme and repeated"*: Petition for Dissolution of Marriage, Beth Ann Blanch v. Robert E. Blanch, Tazewell County Circuit Court, Case 03D-693, December 26, 2003.

49 *pay $200 a month*: Marital Settlement Agreement, Beth Ann Blanch v. Robert E. Blanch, Tazewell County Circuit Court, Case 03D-693, August 9, 2004.

49 *attend Pekin schools*: Joint Parenting Agreement, Beth Ann Blanch v. Robert E. Blanch, Tazewell County Circuit Court, Case 03D-693, August 9, 2004.

51 *regional headquarters*: "Pekin Wasn't Always a Welcoming Place," *Pekin Daily Times*, June 21, 2013.

51 *"Don't let the sun"*: James W. Loewen, *Sundown Towns: A Hidden Dimension of American Racism* (New York: The New Press, 2018), viii.

51 *"Chinks"*: Jason Ruff, "The True Story of a Proud Little City and Its High School Mascot," *Teton Valley News*, May 30, 2019.

3. THE HUNTERS GATHER

63 *six computer stations*: Salem4Youth, salem4youth.com/educational/valor-high-school/.

67 *"the most indispensable man"*: Sir Arthur Conan Doyle, "The Adventure of the Bruce-Partington Plans," 1908, accessed via Project Gutenberg, gutenberg.org/ebooks/2346.

71 *bought farmland*: Rosalie Chan, "How a Tech CEO Runs His 40-Employee Company from a Farm in New Zealand," *Stuff*, January 21, 2019, https://www.stuff.co.nz/technology/110052135/how-a-tech-ceo-runs-his-40employee-company-from-a-farm-in-new-zealand.

71 *fake customer support*: "CryptoLocker Ransomware Infections," Cybersecurity & Infrastructure Security Agency, November 5, 2013, cisa.gov/uscert/ncas/alerts/TA13-309A.

75 *Radamant*: Lawrence Abrams, "Radamant Ransomware Kit for Sale on Exploit and Malware Sites," BleepingComputer, December 28, 2015, bleepingcomputer.com/news/security/radamant-ransomware-kit-for-sale-on-exploit-and-malware-sites/.

75 *"I am not really sure"*: Monika, "Strong Indications That Ransomware Devs Don't Like Emsisoft," Emsisoft blog, December 29, 2015, blog.emsisoft.com/en/20954/strong-indications-that-ransomware-devs-dont-like-emsisoft/.

79 *"Project closed"*: Lawrence Abrams, "TeslaCrypt Shuts Down and Releases Master Decryption Key," BleepingComputer, May 18, 2016, bleepingcomputer.com/news/security/teslacrypt-shuts-down-and-releases-master-decryption-key/.

81 *originated in Malaga*: Kate Fazzini, "Alphabet Cybersecurity Group Chronicle Is Expanding to Spain with a Growing Team of Virus Hunters," CNBC, December 7, 2018, cnbc.com/2018/12/07/alphabet-chronicle-cybersecurity-arm-expands-to-malaga-spain.html.

83 *"social deduction"*: Secret Hitler, secrethitler.com.

83 *image of Jigsaw's*: Lawrence Abrams, "Jigsaw Ransomware Decrypted: Will Delete Your Files Until You Pay the Ransom," BleepingComputer, April 11, 2016, bleepingcomputer.com/news/security/jigsaw-ransomware-decrypted-will-delete-your-files-until-you-pay-the-ransom/.

84 *dozens of variants*: Linas Kiguolis, "Jigsaw Ransomware Virus. 48 Variants Listed. 2021 Update," 2-spyware.com, March 8, 2021, 2-spyware.com/remove-jigsaw-ransomware-virus.html.

4. THE FUNNY WAR

85 *If the default language*: Sarah, "Apocalypse: Ransomware Which Targets Companies Through Insecure RDP," Emsisoft blog, June 29, 2016, blog.emsisoft.com/en/22935/apocalypse-ransomware-which-targets-companies-through-insecure-rdp/.

85 *Fabiansomware*: Haylee, "Fabiansomware: When Hackers Lose It," Emsisoft blog, September 2, 2016, blog.emsisoft.com/en/22935/apocalypse-ransomware-which-targets-companies-through-insecure-rdp/.

88 *"Fabian, please, don't crack me!"*: Joe Tidy, "Hated and Hunted: The Perilous Life of the Computer Virus Cracker Making Powerful Enemies Online," BBC News, March

2019, bbc.co.uk/news/resources/idt-sh/hated_and_hunted_the_computer_virus
_malware_ransomware_cracker.

88   *"Crack me again"*: Tidy, "Hated and Hunted."

88   *"They've taken the time"*: Tidy, "Hated and Hunted."

88   *"lay of"*: Tidy, "Hated and Hunted."

89   *The Russian chairman*: Alexander Bratersky, "Investor in German Shipyard Shot
     Dead in Moscow Cafe," *Moscow Times*, October 2, 2011, themoscowtimes.com/2011
     /10/02/investor-in-german-shipyard-shot-dead-in-moscow-cafe-a9885.

92   *CTB-Locker*: Dark web ad provided by John Fokker, principal engineer and head of
     cyber investigations for the Advanced Threat Research team at McAfee.

92   *Dark web forums became rife*: Author interviews with John Fokker, March 11 and
     May 12, 2021; and examples of job ads he provided.

92   *Cobalt Strike*: Author interviews with John Fokker, March 11 and May 12, 2021; and
     examples of job ads he provided.

93   *"Get ready for an interview"*: Dark web ad provided by John Fokker.

93   *$1 million in such an account*: Lawrence Abrams, "REvil Ransomware Deposits $1
     Million in Hacker Recruitment Drive," BleepingComputer, September 28, 2020,
     bleepingcomputer.com/news/security/revil-ransomware-deposits-1-million-in
     -hacker-recruitment-drive/.

93   *"It seems like"*: Dmitry Smilyanets, "'I Scrounged Through the Trash Heaps . . . Now
     I'm a Millionaire': An Interview with REvil's Unknown," The Record by Recorded
     Future, March 16, 2021, therecord.media/i-scrounged-through-the-trash-heaps-
     now-im-a-millionaire-an-interview-with-revils-unknown/.

95   *Underworld ancillary*: Author interviews with John Fokker.

96   *"headache to this"*: Panel discussion on Day 4 of the FBI Cyber Division Ransom-
     ware Summit, September 2020.

96   *The cybercrime mastermind*: "Maksim Viktorovich Yakubets," FBI Most Wanted,
     fbi.gov/wanted/cyber/maksim-viktorovich-yakubets.

96   *malware spree*: "Russian National Charged with Decade-Long Series of Hacking
     and Bank Fraud Offenses Resulting in Tens of Millions in Losses and Second Rus-
     sian National Charged with Involvement in Deployment of 'Bugat' Malware," U.S.
     Department of Justice, press release, December 5, 2019.

97   *Bugat*: "Russian National Charged."

97   *As a joke*: Author interview with Keith Mularski, managing director at Ernst &
     Young and former FBI cyber unit chief, October 28, 2021.

97   *basements of Moscow cafés*: Tweets by the UK's National Crime Agency (@NCA_UK),
     December 5, 2019, twitter.com/NCA_UK.

97   *Videos circulated online*: Tweets by the UK's National Crime Agency.

97   *Yakubets was married*: Sergei Dobrynin and Mark Krutov, "In Lavish Wedding Pho-
     tos, Clues to an Alleged Russian Cyberthief's FSB Family Ties," RadioFreeEurope/
     RadioLiberty, December 11, 2019, rferl.org/a/in-lavish-wedding-photos-clues-to
     -an-alleged-russian-cyberthief-fsb-family-ties/30320440.html.

98   *Spetsnaz*: "'V' for 'Vympel': FSB's Secretive Department 'V' Behind Assassination
     of Georgian Asylum Seeker in Germany," Bellingcat, February 17, 2020, bellingcat
     .com/news/uk-and-europe/2020/02/17/v-like-vympel-fsbs-secretive-department
     -v-behind-assassination-of-zelimkhan-khangoshvili/.

98   *blamed North Korea*: Thomas P. Bossert, "It's Official: North Korea Is Behind
     WannaCry," *Wall Street Journal*, December 18, 2017.

98   *indicted Yakubets*: "Russian National Charged."

98   *"provided direct assistance"*: "Treasury Sanctions Evil Corp, the Russia-Based
     Cybercriminal Group Behind Dridex Malware," U.S. Department of the Treasury,
     press release, December 5, 2019.

99   *Citing connections*: "Treasury Sanctions Evil Corp."

99   *Garmin*: Sergiu Gatlan, "Garmin Outage Caused by Confirmed WastedLocker Ransomware Attack," BleepingComputer, July 24, 2020, bleepingcomputer.com/news/security/garmin-outage-caused-by-confirmed-wastedlocker-ransomware-attack/.

100 *"Now that Macaw Locker"*: Lawrence Abrams, "Evil Corp Demands $40 Million in New Macaw Ransomware Attacks," BleepingComputer, October 21, 2021, bleepingcomputer.com/news/security/evil-corp-demands-40-million-in-new-macaw-ransomware-attacks/.

101 *BleepingComputer's domain name*: Lawrence Abrams, "Maze Ransomware Says Computer Type Determines Ransom Amount," BleepingComputer, May 31, 2019, bleepingcomputer.com/news/security/maze-ransomware-says-computer-type-determines-ransom-amount/.

101 *attacks in Italy*: Lawrence Abrams, "Maze Ransomware Attacks Italy in New Email Campaign," BleepingComputer, October 29, 2019, bleepingcomputer.com/news/security/maze-ransomware-attacks-italy-in-new-email-campaign/.

101 *Lawrence was finishing*: The section describing Maze's use of BleepingComputer to launch the double extortion tactic is drawn from the following article: Lawrence Abrams, "Allied Universal Breached by Maze Ransomware, Stolen Data Leaked," BleepingComputer, November 21, 2019, bleepingcomputer.com/news/security/allied-universal-breached-by-maze-ransomware-stolen-data-leaked.

104 *"first and foremost"*: Abrams, "Maze Ransomware Says Computer Type Determines Ransom Amount."

105 *Canon*: Lawrence Abrams, "Canon Confirms Ransomware Attack in Internal Memo," BleepingComputer, August 6, 2020, bleepingcomputer.com/news/security/canon-confirms-ransomware-attack-in-internal-memo/.

105 *City of Pensacola*: Lawrence Abrams, "Maze Ransomware Behind Pensacola Cyberattack, $1M Ransom Demand," BleepingComputer, December 11, 2019, bleepingcomputer.com/news/security/maze-ransomware-behind-pensacola-cyberattack-1m-ransom-demand/.

105 *"This the fault"*: Lawrence Abrams, "Maze Ransomware Releases Files Stolen from City of Pensacola," BleepingComputer, December 24, 2019, bleepingcomputer.com/news/security/maze-ransomware-releases-files-stolen-from-city-of-pensacola/.

106 *two dozen groups*: Lawrence Abrams, "List of Ransomware That Leaks Victims' Stolen Files If Not Paid," BleepingComputer, May 26, 2020, bleepingcomputer.com/news/security/list-of-ransomware-that-leaks-victims-stolen-files-if-not-paid/.

106 *Its high-profile victims*: Todd Spangler and Shirley Halperin, "Law Firm Representing Lady Gaga, Madonna, Bruce Springsteen, Others Suffers Major Data Breach," *Variety*, May 9, 2020, variety.com/2020/digital/news/entertainment-law-firm-hacked-data-breach-lady-gaga-madonna-bruce-springsteen-1234602737/.

106 *published blueprints*: Kartikay Mehrotra, "Apple Targeted in $50 Million Ransomware Hack of Supplier Quanta," Bloomberg, April 21, 2021, bloomberg.com/news/articles/2021-04-21/apple-targeted-in-50-million-ransomware-hack-of-supplier-quanta.

106 *"absolutely gorgeous"*: Dmitry Smilyanets interview with Unknown, March 16, 2021.

107 *"Yes, this is one"*: Dmitry Smilyanets interview with Unknown.

107 *"cartel"*: Lawrence Abrams, "Ransomware Gangs Team Up to Form Extortion Cartel," BleepingComputer, June 3, 2020, bleepingcomputer.com/news/security/ransomware-gangs-team-up-to-form-extortion-cartel/.

107 *"There is no way"*: Lawrence Abrams, "Scam PSA: Ransomware Gangs Don't Always Delete Stolen Data When Paid," BleepingComputer, November 4, 2020, bleepingcomputer.com/news/security/scam-psa-ransomware-gangs-dont-always-delete-stolen-data-when-paid/.

108   *One of these players*: The section describing Adrian's ransomware is drawn from an
      author interview with him over the messaging platform Telegram on February 7, 2021.

108   *Ziggy Stardust*: "Rainbow 'Ziggy Stardust' Snake Among New Mekong Delta Dis-
      coveries," BBC News, December 19, 2016, bbc.com/news/world-asia-38362315.

109   *Michael built the decryptor*: Lawrence Abrams, "Ziggy Ransomware Shuts Down and
      Releases Victims' Decryption Keys," BleepingComputer, February 7, 2021, bleep
      ingcomputer.com/news/security/ziggy-ransomware-shuts-down-and-releases
      -victims-decryption-keys/.

109   *"They plan to switch sides"*: Ionut Ilascu, "Ransomware Admin Is Refunding Victims
      Their Ransom Payments," BleepingComputer, March 28, 2021, bleepingcomputer.com
      /news/security/ransomware-admin-is-refunding-victims-their-ransom-payments/.

111   *Previously known as SynAck*: Lawrence Abrams, "SynAck Ransomware Releases
      Decryption Keys After El_Cometa Rebrand," BleepingComputer, August 13, 2021,
      bleepingcomputer.com/news/security/synack-ransomware-releases-decryption
      -keys-after-el-cometa-rebrand/.

112   *"individuals whose personal information"*: Suzanne R. Griffin, senior vice president and
      general counsel, Butterball, LLC, "Notice of Data Security Incident," October 29, 2021.

5. THE PRICE OF OBSESSION

123   *Tang*: Because Tang was a minor at the time, we are withholding her last name to
      protect her privacy.

127   *Richard Feynman wrote*: Quoted in Chris Sasaki, "Colourful Language: U of T Psy-
      chologists Discover Enhanced Language Learning in Synesthetes," *University of
      Toronto News*, May 15, 2019.

129   *$30 million in losses*: "Two Iranian Men Indicted for Deploying Ransomware to Ex-
      tort Hospitals, Municipalities, and Public Institutions, Causing over $30 Million in
      Losses," U.S. Department of Justice, press release, November 28, 2018.

129   *"You are infected"*: Lawrence Abrams, "EvilTwin's Exotic Ransomware Targets Ex-
      ecutable Files," BleepingComputer, October 14, 2016, bleepingcomputer.com/news
      /security/eviltwins-exotic-ransomware-targets-executable-files/.

131   *"a complete mess"*: Lawrence Abrams, "TeslaWare Plays Russian Roulette with Your
      Files," BleepingComputer, June 21, 2017, bleepingcomputer.com/news/security
      /teslaware-plays-russian-roulette-with-your-files/.

134   *"keeping ransomware alive"*: Renee Dudley, "The Extortion Economy: How In-
      surance Companies Are Fueling a Rise in Ransomware Attacks," ProPublica,
      August 27, 2019, propublica.org/article/the-extortion-economy-how-insurance
      -companies-are-fueling-a-rise-in-ransomware-attacks.

134   *October 2019 conference*: Beazley Cyber & Tech UK Broker Retreat.

136   *"Behind me is an empty house"*: Lawrence Abrams, "The WhiteRose Ransomware
      Is Decryptable & Tells a Strange Story," BleepingComputer, April 5, 2019, bleep
      ingcomputer.com/news/security/the-whiterose-ransomware-is-decryptable-and
      -tells-a-strange-story/.

6. STOPPING STOP

144   *master's thesis*: Article posted at Hochschule für Technik, Wirtschaft und Kultur
      [Leipzig University of Applied Sciences], October 19, 2015, htwk-leipzig.de/no
      _cache/hochschule/aktuelles/newsdetail/artikel/1209/.

145   *He analyzes ransomware*: Michael Gillespie has made a series of instructional vid-
      eos that explain his techniques, including "Analyzing Ransomware—Beginning
      Static Analysis," YouTube, November 17, 2018, youtube.com/watch?v=9nuo

-AGg4p4, and "Analyzing Ransomware—Completing a Full Analysis," YouTube, February 8, 2019, youtube.com/watch?v=rRv5vTctePE.

145 *Caesar cipher*: "Caesar Cipher," Practical Cryptography, practicalcryptography.com /ciphers/caesar-cipher/.

146 *CryptoTester*: For a more in-depth description, see Michael Gillespie's video, "Analyzing Ransomware—Using CryptoTester," YouTube, December 1, 2018, youtube .com/watch?v=vo7_ji3kd8s.

147 *prestigious Turing Prize*: Eric Mankin, "Len Adleman Wins Turing Prize," USC Viterbi School of Engineering, April 14, 2003, viterbi.usc.edu/news/news/2003/2003 _04_14_adleman.htm.

148 *"simultaneously innovative"*: Adam L. Young and Moti Yung, "Cryptovirology: The Birth, Neglect, and Explosion of Ransomware," *Communications of the ACM* 60, no. 7 (July 2017): 24–26.

149 *lava lamps*: Amanda Shendruk, "Cloudflare Uses Lava Lamps to Generate a Fundamental Resource: Randomness," *Quartz*, August 20, 2019, qz.com/1642628 /cloudflare-uses-lava-lamps-to-generate-a-crucial-resource/.

149 *Unix time*: Bobby Jack, "What Is Unix Time and When Was the Unix Epoch?," MUO, February 13, 2021, makeuseof.com/what-is-unix-time-and-when-was-the -unix-epoch/.

152 *"golden rule"*: Sarah White, "SteelCon 2019: Pouring Salt into the Crypto Wound: How Not to Be as Stupid as Ransomware Authors," YouTube, July 14, 2019, youtube .com/watch?v=XoKiBg_l4Wc.

152 *Salsa20*: "Salsa20: Stream Cipher with Symmetric Secret Key," Crypto-IT, March 9, 2020, crypto-it.net/eng/symmetric/salsa20.html.

7. RYUK REIGNS

155 *less than $6,000*: "Global Ransomware Marketplace Report—Q3 2018," Coveware, quarterly report, October 16, 2018, coveware.com/blog/global-ransomware -marketplace-report-q3-2018.

155 *more than $230,000*: "Ransomware Demands Continue to Rise as Data Exfiltration Becomes Common, and Maze Subdues," Coveware, quarterly report, November 4, 2020, coveware.com/blog/q3-2020-ransomware-marketplace-report.

155 *"Ryuk continued to set records"*: "Ransom Amounts Rise 90% in Q1 as Ryuk Increases," Coveware, quarterly report, April 16, 2019, coveware.com/blog/2019/4 /15/ransom-amounts-rise-90-in-q1-as-ryuk-ransomware-increases.

156 *Established with community funding*: DCH Regional Medical Center, dchsystem .com/locations/dch-regional-medical-center/.

156 *all nonessential events*: DCH General Counsel Chris Jones to Mia Sadler, Alabama Department of Public Health, memo, October 10, 2019.

156 *"in the best interest"*: Eddie Burkhalter, "DCH Health System Closes Three Hospitals Except 'Critical' Patients After Ransomware Attack," *Alabama Political Reporter*, October 1, 2019, alreporter.com/2019/10/01/dch-health-system-closes -three-hospitals-to-al-but-critical-patients-after-ransomware-attack/.

157 *"The 3 DCH system facilities"*: Keith Reilly, "General Notification," Alabama Department of Public Health—West Central, October 1, 2019.

157 *"network event"*: "Springhill Medical Center Says Patient Care Not Affected by Network Issue," WKRG News 5, July 9, 2019, wkrg.com/mobile-county/springhill -medical-center-says-patient-care-not-affected-by-network-issue/.

157 *"Fetal tracing information"*: Teiranni Kidd v. Springhill Hospitals Inc., First Amended Complaint, Circuit Court of Mobile County, Alabama, Civil Action No. 02-CV-2020-900171, June 4, 2020.

158   *"because the patients"*: Kevin Poulsen, Robert McMillan, and Melanie Evans, "A Hospital Hit by Hackers, a Baby in Distress: The Case of the First Alleged Ransomware Death," *Wall Street Journal*, September 30, 2021.

158   *likely Ryuk*: Poulsen, McMillan, and Evans, "A Hospital Hit by Hackers, a Baby in Distress."

158   *237 times*: Jones to Sadler memo.

158   *refined it:* Catalin Cimpanu, "Ryuk Ransomware Gang Probably Russian, Not North Korean," ZDNet, January 11, 2019, zdnet.com/article/ryuk-ransomware-gang -probably-russian-not-north-korean/.

158   *targeted more than a hundred*: "FBI Flash: Indicators of Compromise Associated with Ryuk Ransomware," Federal Bureau of Investigation, Cyber Division, Alert Number MC-000103-MW, May 2, 2019, waterisac.org/system/files/articles /FLASH-MC-000103-MW-Ryuk.pdf.

159   *National Cyber Security Centre*: "Advisory: Ryuk Ransomware Targeting Organisations Globally," National Cyber Security Centre (UK), June 22, 2019.

159   *"for government topics"*: Matt Burgess, "Inside Trickbot, Russia's Notorious Ransomware Gang," *Wired*, February 1, 2022, wired.com/story/trickbot-malware -group-internal-messages/.

159   *"À la guerre"*: John Fokker, with Bill Siegel and Alex Holdtman, "Ryuk, Exploring the Human Connection," McAfee Labs blog, February 19, 2019, mcafee.com/blogs /other-blogs/mcafee-labs/ryuk-exploring-the-human-connection/.

163   *August 2020*: John Fokker and Jambul Tologonov, "Conti Leaks: Examining the Panama Papers of Ransomware," Trellix, March 31, 2022, trellix.com/en-gb/about /newsroom/stories/threat-labs/conti-leaks-examining-the-panama-papers-of -ransomware.html.

163   *paid commissions*: Tweet by Jackie Koven (@JBurnsKoven), head of cyber threat intelligence at Chainalysis, March 1, 2022, twitter.com/JBurnsKoven.

163   *"With the public and private sector"*: Material accessed through a leak of Trickbot's messages. Downloads and translations provided by Randy Pargman of Binary Defense.

164   *"It is necessary to press"*: Material accessed through a leak of Trickbot's messages. Downloads and translations provided by Randy Pargman of Binary Defense.

165   *sixty-one Bitcoin wallets*: Vitali Kremez and Brian Carter, "Crime Laundering Primer: Inside Ryuk Crime (Crypto) Ledger & Risky Asian Crypto Traders," Adv-Intel, January 7, 2021, advintel.io/post/crime-laundering-primer-inside-ryuk -crime-crypto-ledger-risky-asian-crypto-traders.

166   *accused DCH*: Geraldine Daniels et al. vs DCH Healthcare Authority, Circuit Court of Tuscaloosa County, Alabama, 63-CV-2020-900375.00, April 17, 2020.

8. THE FBI'S DILEMMA

169   *third-highest priority*: The FBI Office of Public Affairs acknowledged but did not respond to written questions concerning material in this chapter.

169   *He invited the agents*: The meeting between FBI cyber agents and Director James Comey described in the introductory passage is reconstructed based on interviews with agents who attended. Through an intermediary, Comey declined to comment on the meeting.

172   *told counterparts*: Author interview with Jeanette Manfra, former official in the U.S. Department of Homeland Security, June 19, 2020.

172   *"best practices" document*: "How to Protect Your Networks from Ransomware," U.S. government interagency technical guidance document, 2016, justice.gov/criminal -ccips/file/872771/download.

173 *"Look, kid, did you lose"*: Cliff Stoll, *The Cuckoo's Egg: Tracking a Spy Through the Maze of Computer Espionage* (New York: Gallery Books, 1989), 77–78, 141.

173 *Clinton administration*: Details of the National Infrastructure Protection Center come from an author interview with Michael Vatis, who led it, and from a transcript of his testimony before members of the U.S. Senate Judiciary Subcommittee on Terrorism, Technology, and Government Information. Interview on April 15, 2021; testimony from June 10, 1998.

175 *the bureau's Cyber Division*: FBI Timeline, fbi.gov/history/timeline.

175 *deterring physical attacks*: Author interview with Michael Vatis, April 15, 2021.

177 *Silk Road*: Donna Leinwand Leger, "How the FBI Brought Down Cyber-Underworld Site Silk Road," *USA Today*, October 21, 2013, usatoday.com/story/news/nation /2013/10/21/fbi-cracks-silk-road/2984921/.

178 *In the seventeenth century*: "Beverwijk—The Netherlands," CityWalkSights, October 6, 2016, citywalksights.com/beverwijk%20city%20walk.htm.

178 *two thousand vendors*: "De Bazaar Beverwijk: Market in North Holland," Lonely Planet, lonelyplanet.com/the-netherlands/north-holland/shopping/de-bazaar -beverwijk/a/poi-sho/1125240/1315672.

178 *widest sand beach*: "Wijk aan Zee, the Best Kept Secret of the North Sea Coast," WijkAanZee.net, wijkaanzee.net/en/wijk-aan-zee.php#:~:text=Wijk%20aan%20 Zee%20is%20also,at%20the%20North%20Sea%20coast.

178 *fiber-optic cables*: "Submarine Cable Map: Beverwijk, Netherlands, Atlantic Crossing-1 (AC-1)," TeleGeography, submarinecablemap.com/landing-point/beverwijk -netherlands.

178 *top marks*: Author interview with Marijn Schuurbiers, team leader, Dutch National Police High Tech Crime Unit, November 5, 2021.

180 *a security competition*: The passage about the HTCU's Capture the Flag competition is drawn from author interviews with Pim Takkenberg, former HTCU team leader, September 7, 2021, and February 8, 2022.

189 *Fin7*: "Three Members of Notorious International Cybercrime Group 'Fin7' in Custody for Role in Attacking over 100 U.S. Companies," U.S. Department of Justice, press release, August 1, 2018.

190 *guarding presidents*: "Timeline of Our History," United States Secret Service, secretservice.gov/about/history/timeline.

190 *April 1865*: Erin Blakemore, "No Counterfeits. The History of the Secret Service," *Time*, April 14, 2015.

190 *The strike disabled*: Drew Hinshaw and Valentina Pop, "The Hapless Shakedown Crew That Hacked Trump's Inauguration," *Wall Street Journal*, October 25, 2019.

193 *The No More Ransom website*: "Join the Global 'No More Ransom' Initiative to Help More Victims Fight Back," Europol, press release, December 20, 2018.

194 *WildFire*: Kate Kochetkova, "WildFire Ransomware Extinguished," *Kaspersky Daily* (blog), August 24, 2016, kaspersky.com/blog/wildfire-ransomware-decryptor/12828/.

194 *take down the botnet*: Andy Greenberg, "Cops Disrupt Emotet, the Internet's 'Most Dangerous Malware,'" *Wired*, January 27, 2021, wired.com/story/emotet-botnet -takedown/.

194 *Emotet uninstaller*: Sergiu Gatlan, "Emotet Malware Nukes Itself Today from All Infected Computers Worldwide," BleepingComputer, April 25, 2021, bleepingcom puter.com/news/security/emotet-malware-nukes-itself-today-from-all-infected -computers-worldwide/.

194 *"Emotet was one"*: Lawrence Abrams, "Dutch Police Post 'Say No to Cybercrime' Warnings on Hacker Forums," BleepingComputer, February 17, 2021, bleeping computer.com/news/security/dutch-police-post-say-no-to-cybercrime-warnings -on-hacker-forums/.

9. THE G-MAN AND THE DOLPHIN

198   *Mark and Justin asked*: Through an FBI spokesperson, Mark Phelps and Justin Harris declined to respond to written questions and to comment on the material in this chapter.

198   *"Informants . . . may receive compensation"*: "About: Frequently Asked Questions," FBI, fbi.gov/about/faqs.

198   *Ron and Jane*: Record of Marriage, Vanderburgh County, Indiana.

198   *Born in 1981*: Date of birth confirmed using Illinois Online Voter Registration Lookup, ova.elections.il.gov/RegistrationLookup.aspx.

198   *two-bedroom house*: Marion County, Indiana, Assessor, maps.indy.gov/Assessor PropertyCards/.

198   *since 1911*: Britannica, s.v. "Indianapolis 500," britannica.com/sports/Indianapolis -500.

198   *Local #20*: Ron Phelps, LinkedIn, linkedin.com/in/ron-phelps-7700bb5b/.

199   *Conseco Fieldhouse*: "About Us," Horning Roofing & Sheet Metal Company, LLC, horningroofing.com/about/.

199   *As a child*: Details about Mark Phelps's and Shawn Dillard's high school years are drawn from Speedway High School's yearbooks. Copies kept on file at Speedway Public Library and provided by Ashley Bartley, adult services librarian.

199   *Shawn enrolled*: Kevin Doerr, "Veterinary Medicine—Family Style," *PVM Report* (Purdue University College of Veterinary Medicine, 2011 annual report), vet .purdue.edu/news/wp-content/uploads/2020/09/2011.pdf, 8.

199   *majored in*: Details provided by Indiana University–Purdue University Indianapolis, Office of the Registrar, Transcripts, and Enrollment Verifications.

199   *July 2004*: Ancestry.com, certificate number 26650.

199   *Mark worked briefly*: Speedway High School Alumni, AlumniClass, alumniclass .com/speedway-high-school-sparkplugs-in/.

199   *age cutoff*: "About: Frequently Asked Questions," FBI, fbi.gov/about/faqs.

199   *village of Dunlap*: Peoria County Property Tax Information, propertytax.peoria county.gov.

199   *veterinary technician's*: Illinois Department of Financial and Professional Regulation, License Lookup, online-dfpr.micropact.com/lookup/licenselookup.aspx.

199   *Nationwide*: Shawn Phelps's Facebook profile.

199   *Bald Knob Cross*: "About Us," Bald Knob Cross of Peace, baldknobcross.com/about -us/.

200   *Peoria is one of five*: "Springfield," FBI, fbi.gov/contact-us/field-offices/springfield.

200   *140 agents*: Tobias Wall, "FBI Names Lead Agent for Local Office," *State Journal-Register* (Springfield, IL), July 17, 2014.

200   *Illinois governors*: "FBI Springfield History," FBI Field Office Histories, fbi.gov /history/field-office-histories/springfield.

200   *$100 million criminal fine*: "Archer Daniels Midland Co. to Plead Guilty and Pay $100 Million for Role in Two International Price-Fixing Conspiracies," U.S. Department of Justice, press release, October 15, 1996, justice.gov/archive/opa/pr /1996/Oct96/508at.htm.

200   *embezzled $9.5 million*: Scott Kilman, "Mark Whitacre Is Sentenced to 9 Years for Swindling $9.5 Million from ADM," *Wall Street Journal*, March 5, 1998.

201   *earning a master's*: Details confirmed by University of Illinois, Springfield, Office of Records and Registration, Office of the Registrar.

206   *Created in 1990*: "About: Director's Community Leadership Award," FBI, fbi.gov /about/community-outreach/dcla.

207   *They were chosen*: "News: 2017 Director's Community Leadership Awards," FBI,

April 20, 2018, fbi.gov/news/stories/2017-directors-community-leadership -awards-042018.

207 *Wearing a dark suit*: "About: Springfield—Michael Gillespie, 2017 Director's Community Leadership Award Recipient," FBI, fbi.gov/about/community-outreach /dcla/2017/springfield-michael-gillespie.

207 *In a press release*: "Springfield: Bloomington Man Receives 2017 FBI Director's Community Leadership Award for His Efforts to Decrypt Ransomware as a Public Service," FBI, January 30, 2018, fbi.gov/contact-us/field-offices/springfield /news/press-releases/bloomington-man-receives-2017-fbi-directors-community -leadership-award-for-his-efforts-to-decrypt-ransomware-as-a-public-service.

208 *more sophisticated*: "High-Impact Ransomware Attacks Threaten U.S. Businesses and Organizations," FBI, public service announcement, October 2, 2019, ic3.gov /Media/Y2019/PSA191002.

210 *charging up to $1,000*: Lawrence Abrams, "'NamPoHyu Virus' Ransomware Targets Remote Samba Servers," BleepingComputer, April 16, 2019, bleepingcomputer.com /news/security/nampohyu-virus-ransomware-targets-remote-samba-servers/.

211 *In May 2019*: Lawrence Abrams, "Decryptor for MegaLocker and NamPoHyu Virus Ransomware Released," BleepingComputer, May 2, 2019, bleepingcomputer. com/news/security/decryptor-for-megalocker-and-nampohyu-virus-ransomware -released/.

213 *Hatch Act*: U.S. Office of Special Counsel, Federal Employee Hatch Act Information, osc.gov/Services/Pages/HatchAct-Federal.aspx#tabGroup11|tabGroup32|tabGro up51.

10. SHAKING DOWN A CITY

215 *For spending money*: Ian Duncan, "Up from the East Side: How 23 Years in Baltimore Politics Led Jack Young to Becoming Mayor—for Now," *Baltimore Sun*, April 12, 2019.

215 *sentenced to three years*: Luke Broadwater, Justin Fenton, and Kevin Rector, "Former Baltimore Mayor Catherine Pugh Sentenced to 3 Years for 'Healthy Holly' Children's Book Fraud Scheme," *Baltimore Sun*, February 27, 2020.

217 *more than a hundred*: Allan Liska, "State and Local Government Ransomware Attacks Surpass 100 for 2019," Recorded Future, December 20, 2019, recordedfuture .com/state-local-government-ransomware-attacks-2019/.

217 *about twice as many*: Allan Liska, "Early Findings: Review of State and Local Ransomware Attacks," Recorded Future, May 10, 2019, recordedfuture.com/state-local -government-ransomware-attacks/.

218 *Valdez, Alaska*: Catalin Cimpanu, "City of Valdez, Alaska, Admits to Paying Off Ransomware Infection," ZDNet, November 21, 2018, zdnet.com/article/city-of-valdez -alaska-admits-to-paying-off-ransomware-infection/.

218 *West Haven, Connecticut*: Mark Zaretsky, "West Haven Falls Victim to 'Ransomware' Cyberattack, Pays $2,000 in Bitcoin to Regain Access to Servers," *New Haven Register*, October 19, 2018.

218 *dashboard camera footage*: J. Scott Trubey, "Atlanta Police Recovering from Breach, 'Years' of Dashcam Video Lost," *Atlanta Journal-Constitution*, June 1, 2018.

218 *"It was counterintuitive to me"*: Keisha Lance Bottoms, panelist, "Preventing and Responding to Cyber Attacks," The 86th Annual Meeting of the United States Conference of Mayors, Boston, MA, June 8, 2018.

218 *348 people were murdered*: Scott Calvert, "Baltimore, New York Among Cities Fighting More Murders," *Wall Street Journal*, January 2, 2020.

218 *More than 16,500 buildings*: Ian Duncan and Christine Zhang, "Baltimore Is

Furiously Knocking Down Vacant Houses—but Barely Keeps Up as New Ones Go Empty," *Baltimore Sun*, October 18, 2019.

219 *one or two stars*: Liz Bowie, "Maryland School Star Ratings: Fewer Earn Four and Five Stars in 2019 as Schools Move Toward Middle," *Baltimore Sun*, December 3, 2019.

219 *"a natural target"*: Ian Duncan, "Baltimore's Risk Assessment Called a Pair of Aged City Computer Systems a 'Natural Target for Hackers,'" *Baltimore Sun*, May 30, 2019.

220 *A city troubleshooting team*: Kevin Rector, "Hack of Baltimore's 911 Dispatch System Was Ransomware Attack, City Officials Say," *Baltimore Sun*, March 28, 2018.

220 *"Not for one instant"*: Catherine Pugh, "Preventing and Responding to Cyber Attacks."

223 *"Unfortunately, at this time"*: Lawrence Abrams, "A Closer Look at the RobbinHood Ransomware," BleepingComputer, April 26, 2019, bleepingcomputer.com/news /security/a-closer-look-at-the-robbinhood-ransomware/.

224 *about $90 million a year*: Baltimore's tax revenue from property sales was $91.9 million in fiscal 2016, $90.4 million in fiscal 2017, $89.3 million in fiscal 2018, and $92.0 million in 2019. See the chart "Recordation and Transfer Tax Revenues," in *Executive Summary: Board of Estimates Recommendations: Fiscal 2021* (City of Baltimore, MD, 2021), bbmr.baltimorecity.gov/sites/default/files/fy21_execsumm _2020-05-06_FINAL.pdf, 37.

225 *first time in seven years*: *Comprehensive Annual Financial Report, Year Ended June 30, 2019* (City of Baltimore, MD, 2019), finance.baltimorecity.gov/sites/default /files/CAFR FY'19-Review.pdf, 16.

226 *more than doubled*: Roger Colton, *Baltimore's Conundrum: Charging for Water/ Wastewater Services That Community Residents Cannot Afford to Pay* (Baltimore, MD: Food and Water Watch, November 2018, revised), foodandwaterwatch.org/wp -content/uploads/2022/02/BaltimoreWater-RogerColton.pdf, ES-4.

226 *"I'm a working stiff"*: Paul Gessler, "Sticker Shock Hits Baltimore Residents as First Round of Water Bills Roll Out," CBS Baltimore, August 14, 2019, baltimore.cbslocal .com/2019/08/14/baltimore-city-water-bills-distributed/.

228 *"I would write the check"*: Tyler Waldman, "Councilman Says Recovery from Ransomware Attack Could Take Up to Three Months," WBAL News Radio, May 15, 2019, wbal.com/article/389236/2/councilman-says-recovery-from-ransomware -attack-could-take-up-to-three-months.

228 *"is not always a bad thing"*: Stephen L. Carter, "When It's Worth Paying a Hacker's Ransom," Bloomberg Quint, June 6, 2019, bloombergquint.com/gadfly/baltimore -computer-hack-sometimes-cities-have-to-pay-a-ransom.

228 *"If you don't like"*: Ian Duncan, "Authorities Investigating Claim That Baltimore Ransomware Group Leaked Documents to Twitter," *Baltimore Sun*, June 4, 2019.

228 *"In order to move"*: Mike Hellgren, "Mayor Jack Young Open to Paying Ransom in Computer Attack, New Fix Allows Real Estate Transactions to Resume," CBS Baltimore, May 17, 2019, baltimore.cbslocal.com/2019/05/17/ransomware-attack -continues-to-plague-baltimore-mayor-jack-young-says-city-working-to-resume -services/.

232 *"I believe the federal government"*: "Ruppersberger Provides Direction for New Funds to Help Cities Prevent Ransomware Attacks," U.S. Congressman Dutch Ruppersberger, press release, June 11, 2019, ruppersberger.house.gov/newsroom /press-releases/ruppersberger-provides-direction-for-new-funds-to-help-cities -prevent.

233 *"It's impossible to recover"*: Pieter Arntz, "Threat Spotlight: RobbinHood Ransomware Takes the Driver's Seat," Malwarebytes, February 20, 2020, malwarebytes

.com/threat-spotlight/2020/02/threat-spotlight-robbinhood-ransomware-takes
-the-drivers-seat/.

234 *$18.2 million*: Ian Duncan, "Baltimore Estimates Cost of Ransomware Attack at
$18.2 Million as Government Begins to Restore Email Accounts," *Baltimore Sun*,
May 29, 2019.

234 *annual premium of $835,000*: Kevin Rector, "Baltimore to Purchase $20M in Cyber
Insurance as It Pays Off Contractors Who Helped City Recover from Ransomware,"
Baltimore Sun, October 16, 2019.

234 *rose to $950,000*: Ethan MacLeod, "City Poised to Re-up $20M in Cyber Insurance
Adopted After Ransomware Attack," *Baltimore Business Journal*, October 27, 2020.

234 *"Paying ransomware attackers"*: Catalin Cimpanu, "US Mayors Group Adopts Resolution Not to Pay Any More Ransoms to Hackers," ZDNet, July 11, 2019, zdnet
.com/article/us-mayors-group-adopts-resolution-not-to-pay-any-more-ransoms
-to-hackers/.

234 *Florence, Alabama*: Jeremy Jackson, "City of Florence Agrees to Pay Nearly $300,000
Ransom After Cyberattack," WHNT News 19, June 10, 2020, whnt.com/news/shoals
/city-of-florence-agrees-to-pay-nearly-300000-ransom-after-cyberattack/.

11. THE EXTORTION ECONOMY

237 *30 percent return*: Sheelah Kolhatkar, *Black Edge: Inside Information, Dirty Money,
and the Quest to Bring Down the Most Wanted Man on Wall Street* (New York: Random House, 2018), xviii.

237 *"young traders longed"*: Kolhatkar, *Black Edge*, xviii.

237 *tens of millions*: Jenny Anderson, Peter Lattman, and Julie Creswell, "A Fascination
of Wall St., and Investigators," *New York Times*, December 22, 2012.

238 *news broke in 2007*: Charles Gasparino, "Details Emerge in SAC Capital Sex Ha-
rassment Case," CNBC, October 10, 2007, cnbc.com/id/21224443.

238 *$1.8 billion penalty*: "Manhattan U.S. Attorney Announces Guilty Plea Agreement
with SAC Capital Management Companies," U.S. Department of Justice, press release, November 4, 2013.

238 *two years*: Aruna Viswanatha and Juliet Chung, "Deal Ends SEC's Pursuit of Steven
Cohen," *Wall Street Journal*, January 8, 2016.

239 *make him a billionaire*: "Profile: Barry Silbert," *Forbes*, forbes.com/profile/barry
-silbert/?sh-7de813672950.

240 *Some of the businesses*: Material in this paragraph comes from an author interview
with Bill Siegel, June 24, 2020.

241 *two U.S. firms*: Material in the sections about MonsterCloud and Proven Data was
previously reported in ProPublica. See Renee Dudley and Jeff Kao, "The Trade Secret: Firms That Promised High-Tech Ransomware Solutions Almost Always Just
Pay the Hackers," ProPublica, May 15, 2019, features.propublica.org/ransomware
/ransomware-attack-data-recovery-firms-paying-hackers/.

242 *"Decryption of your files"*: "Phobos Ransomware, a Combo of CrySiS and Dharma,"
Coveware, January 18, 2019, coveware.com/blog/phobos-ransomware-distributed
-dharma-crew.

246 *Herrington's worries*: Herrington died of cancer in November 2019. See "Leif Gay-
lord Herrington, 1950–2019," obituary, *Anchorage Daily News*, December 5, 2019.

256 *"We expected to hear"*: "Introducing Coveware!," Coveware, May 7, 2018, coveware
.com/blog/2018/5/7/hello-world.

257 *inaugural quarterly report*: "Global Ransomware Marketplace Report-Q3 2018,"
Coveware, October 16, 2018, coveware.com/blog/global-ransomware-marketplace
-report-q3-2018.

257 *"The company Coveware"*: Simeon Georgiev, "Negotiating with Cybercriminals—A Risky Precedent," MonsterCloud, October 9, 2018, university.monstercloud.com /cyber-security/cybercriminals-negotiation/.

258 *"excessive fees charged"*: "Beware of Dishonest Ransomware Recovery Firms," Coveware, December 11, 2018, coveware.com/blog/2018/12/11/beware-of-dishonest -ransomware-recovery-firms.

259 *Ransomware insurance*: Material in the sections about ransomware insurance was previously reported in ProPublica. See Renee Dudley, "The Extortion Economy: How Insurance Companies Are Fueling a Rise in Ransomware Attacks," ProPublica, August 27, 2019, propublica.org/article/the-extortion-economy-how -insurance-companies-are-fueling-a-rise-in-ransomware-attacks.

262 *with 775 ransomware incidents*: Information about Beazley comes from a panel discussion on Day 2 of the FBI Cyber Division Ransomware Summit, September 2020.

263 *as many as six*: Renee Dudley, "Like Voldemort, Ransomware Is Too Scary to Be Named," ProPublica, December 23, 2019, propublica.org/article/like-voldemort -ransomware-is-too-scary-to-be-named.

263 *"far fetched"*: "Ransomware Sentiment After a Summer of Headlines," Coveware, October 8, 2019, coveware.com/blog/ransomware-debate-rages-on.

265 *on Thanksgiving Day*: Details of the construction-engineering firm's interactions with MonsterCloud come from an author interview with Kurtis Minder, Group-Sense CEO, August 27, 2021, and from Federal Trade Commission complaint, December 14, 2020.

265 *negotiating with REvil*: Rachel Monroe, "How to Negotiate with Ransomware Hackers," *New Yorker*, May 31, 2021.

265 *"After those kinds of tricks"*: Dmitry Smilyanets, "'I Scrounged Through the Trash Heaps . . . Now I'm a Millionaire:' An Interview with REvil's Unknown," The Record by Recorded Future, March 16, 2021, therecord.media/i-scrounged-through-the -trash-heaps-now-im-a-millionaire-an-interview-with-revils-unknown/.

266 *Minder filed a complaint*: After the *New Yorker* contributing writer Rachel Monroe provided a copy of the December 14, 2020, Federal Trade Commission complaint, a commission representative confirmed its authenticity.

267 *$800,000 ransom*: Jason Remillard, "Victor Congionti of Proven Data: 5 Things You Need to Know to Optimize Your Company's Approach to Data Privacy and Cybersecurity," Medium, October 6, 2020, medium.com/authority-magazine /victor-congionti-of-proven-data-5-things-you-need-to-know-to-optimize-your -companys-approach-to-9157bf9f8539.

267 *130 cases*: Presentation on Day 4 of the FBI Cyber Division Ransomware Summit, September 2020.

268 *testifying before Congress*: "Prepared Written Testimony of Bill Siegel, CEO and Co-Founder of Coveware Inc.," Federal Spending Oversight Subcommittee of the Committee on Homeland Security and Governmental Affairs," December 2, 2020, hsgac.senate.gov/imo/media/doc/Siegel Testimony1.pdf.

268 *"coerce victims into paying"*: "Ransomware Amounts Rise 3x in Q2 as Ryuk & Sodinokibi Spread," Coveware, quarterly report, July 16, 2019, coveware.com/blog/2019 /7/15/ransomware-amounts-rise-3x-in-q2-as-ryuk-amp-sodinokibi-spread.

269 *analyzed the economics*: Anja Shortland, *Kidnap: Inside the Ransom Business* (Oxford: Oxford University Press, 2019).

12. LAWRENCE'S TRUCE

272 *wrote an article*: Lawrence Abrams, "Ransomware Gangs to Stop Attacking Health Orgs During Pandemic," BleepingComputer, March 18, 2020, bleepingcomputer

.com/news/security/ransomware-gangs-to-stop-attacking-health-orgs-during
-pandemic/.

272   *"the crisis is palpable"*: Dmitry Smilyanets, "'I Scrounged Through the Trash
      Heaps...Now I'm a Millionaire:' An Interview with REvil's Unknown," The Record
      by Recorded Future, March 16, 2021, therecord.media/i-scrounged-through-the
      -trash-heaps-now-im-a-millionaire-an-interview-with-revils-unknown/.

272   *"While we will never condone"*: "Free Ransomware Help for Healthcare Providers
      During the Coronavirus Outbreak," Emsisoft blog, March 18, 2020, blog.emsisoft
      .com/en/35921/free-ransomware-help-for-healthcare-providers-during-the
      -coronavirus-outbreak/.

276   *"You hit us"*: Sam Varghese, "Big US Travel Management Firm CWT Pays Out
      U.S. $4.5m to Ransomware Gang," iTWire.com, August 2, 2020, itwire.com
      /business-it-news/security/big-us-travel-management-firm-cwt-pays-out-us$4
      -5m-to-ransomware-gang.html.

277   *"We can confirm"*: Brian Krebs, "Ransomware Group Turns to Facebook Ads," Krebs
      on Security, November 10, 2020, krebsonsecurity.com/2020/11/ransomware-group
      -turns-to-facebook-ads/.

277   *330 miles per hour*: Autumn Bows, "Here's How the Koenigsegg Jesko Absolut
      Will Reach 330MPH," HotCars, October 12, 2020, hotcars.com/heres-how-the
      -koenigsegg-jesko-absolut-will-reach-330mph/.

280   *For years now*: Daniel Gallagher, "Donations for MalwareHunterTeam," PayPal
      fundraiser, paypal.com/pools/c/8x4vKe11yu.

281   *"stop all activity"*: Davey Winder, "COVID-19 Vaccine Test Center Hit by Cyber At-
      tack, Stolen Data Posted Online," *Forbes*, March 23, 2020.

281   *"We will have to see"*: Abrams, "Ransomware Gangs to Stop Attacking Health Orgs
      During Pandemic."

282   *encrypted Boyce's files*: Felipe Erazo, "Ransomware Threatens Production of 300
      Ventilators Per Day," Cointelegraph, August 7, 2020, cointelegraph.com/news
      /ransomware-threatens-production-of-300-ventilators-per-day.

282   *"She may have died"*: William Ralston, "The Untold Story of a Cyberattack, a
      Hospital and a Dying Woman," *Wired*, November 11, 2020, wired.co.uk/article
      /ransomware-hospital-death-germany.

283   *"specifically targeted"*: "Department of Justice Launches Global Action Against
      NetWalker Ransomware," U.S. Department of Justice, press release, January 27,
      2021.

283   *Maryland nursing home chain*: Alina Bizga, "Maryland-Based Nursing Home
      Announces Ransomware Attack Affecting Nearly 50,000 Residents," Security Bou-
      levard, July 21, 2020, securityboulevard.com/2020/07/maryland-based-nursing
      -home-announces-ransomware-attack-affecting-nearly-50000-residents/.

283   *"We've poured almost all"*: Kartikay Mehrotra, "How Hackers Bled 118 Bitcoins out
      of Covid Researchers in U.S.," *Bloomberg Businessweek*, August 19, 2020, bloomberg
      .com/news/features/2020-08-19/ucsf-hack-shows-evolving-risks-of-ransomware
      -in-the-covid-era.

284   *IT technician*: Carlton C. Gammons, "Revised Record of the Case for Prosecution
      for Extradition of Sebastien Vachon-Desjardins," Canada prosecutor representing
      the United States v. Sebastien Vachon-Desjardins, Superior Court, Quebec, District
      of Gatineau, Case 550-68-000035-213, April 23, 2021, 19.

284   *"We are interested"*: Gammons, "Revised Record," 2.

284   *kept 75 percent*: Gammons, "Revised Record," 20.

284   *He also worked*: "Chainalysis in Action: U.S. Authorities Disrupt NetWalker Ran-
      somware," Chainalysis, January 27, 2021, blog.chainalysis.com/reports/netwalker
      -ransomware-disruption-arrest/.

284 *"I hit them hard bro"*: Royal Canadian Mounted Police/Gendarmerie royale du Canada report, Canada v. Vachon-Desjardins, Case 550-68-000035-213, 11.

284 *$40 million in Bitcoin*: Royal Canadian Mounted Police/Gendarmerie royale du Canada report, 8.

285 *Clark County*: Tawnell D. Hobbs, "Hacker Releases Information on Las Vegas–Area Students After Officials Don't Pay Ransom," *Wall Street Journal*, September 28, 2020.

285 *Fairfax County*: Sergiu Gatlan, "Fairfax County Schools Hit by Maze Ransomware, Student Data Leaked," BleepingComputer, September 12, 2020, bleepingcomputer .com/news/security/fairfax-county-schools-hit-by-maze-ransomware-student -data-leaked/.

285 *Chatham County*: Bill Horner III, Hannah McClellan, and D. Lars Dolder, "After Cyberattack, Stolen Chatham County Data and Sensitive Documents Posted Online," *News & Observer* (Raleigh, NC), February 11, 2021.

285 *targeted K-12 schools the most*: "Cyber Actors Target K-12 Distance Learning Education to Cause Disruptions and Steal Data," Cybersecurity & Infrastructure Security Agency, Alert (AA20-345A), December 10, 2020, cisa.gov/uscert/ncas/alerts /aa20-345a.

285 *catastrophic*: McKenna Oxenden, "Baltimore County Schools Suffered a Ransomware Attack. Here's What You Need to Know," *Baltimore Sun*, November 30, 2020.

285 *servers weren't properly isolated*: "Financial Management Practices Audit Report: Baltimore County Public Schools," Office of Legislative Audits, Department of Legislative Services, Maryland General Assembly, November 2020, 29.

287 *employee mileage reports*: Scott Travis, "Hackers Post 26,000 Broward School Files Online," *South Florida Sun Sentinel*, April 19, 2021.

287 *Microsoft investigators*: Tom Burt, "New Action to Combat Ransomware Ahead of U.S. Elections," Microsoft on the Issues (blog), October 12, 2020, blogs.microsoft .com/on-the-issues/2020/10/12/trickbot-ransomware-cyberthreat-us-elections/.

288 *Reflecting the U.S. military's*: Jason Healey, "When Should U.S. Cyber Command Take Down Criminal Botnets?," Lawfare, April 26, 2021, lawfareblog.com/when -should-us-cyber-command-take-down-criminal-botnets.

288 *it penetrated the botnet*: Ellen Nakashima, "Cyber Command Has Sought to Disrupt the World's Largest Botnet, Hoping to Reduce Its Potential Impact on the Election," *Washington Post*, October 9, 2020.

288 *false information*: Brian Krebs, "Attacks Aimed at Disrupting the Trickbot Botnet," Krebs on Security, October 2, 2020, krebsonsecurity.com/2020/10/attacks-aimed -at-disrupting-the-trickbot-botnet/.

289 *"an increased and imminent"*: "Ransomware Activity Targeting the Healthcare and Public Health Sector," Cybersecurity & Infrastructure Security Agency, Alert (AA20-302A), October 28, 2020, cisa.gov/uscert/ncas/alerts/aa20-302a.

291 *gone wrong*: Robert McMillan, Kevin Poulsen, and Dustin Volz, "Secret World of Pro-Russia Hacking Group Exposed in Leak," *Wall Street Journal*, March 28, 2022, wsj.com/articles/trickbot-pro-russia-hacking-gang-documents-ukrainian-leaker -conti-11648480564.

13. PIPELINE TO TOMORROW

293 *"I have confirmation"*: Some of the account of how Bitdefender alerted DarkSide to a flaw that the Ransomware Hunting Team had already discovered was first published in ProPublica. See Renee Dudley and Daniel Golden, "The Colonial Pipeline Ransomware Hackers Had a Secret Weapon: Self-Promoting Cybersecurity

Firms," ProPublica, May 24, 2021, propublica.org/article/the-colonial-pipeline
-ransomware-hackers-had-a-secret-weapon-self-promoting-cybersecurity-firms.

294 *"happy to announce"*: "Darkside Ransomware Decryption Tool," Bitdefender, January 11, 2021, bitdefender.com/blog/labs/darkside-ransomware-decryption-tool/.

296 *Bitdefender developed*: Bogdan Botezatu, "GandCrab Ransomware Decryption
Tool," Bitdefender, October 24, 2018, bitdefender.com/blog/labs/gandcrab-ransom
ware-decryption-tool-available-for-free/.

296 *$2 billion*: Lawrence Abrams, "GandCrab Ransomware Shutting Down After Claim-
ing to Earn $2 Billion," BleepingComputer, June 1, 2019, bleepingcomputer.com
/news/security/gandcrab-ransomware-shutting-down-after-claiming-to-earn-2
-billion/.

298 *"Companies that facilitate"*: "Advisory on Potential Sanctions Risks for Facilitating
Ransomware Payments," U.S. Department of the Treasury, October 1, 2020, home
.treasury.gov/system/files/126/ofac_ransomware_advisory_10012020_1.pdf.

299 *original thirteen colonies*: Barry Parker and Robin Hood, *Colonial Pipeline: Courage,
Passion, Commitment* (Chattanooga, TN: Parker Hill Press, 2002), 16. Much of the
account of the Colonial Pipeline's history in this section is based on this book.

299–300 *"Embracing computer technology"*: Parker and Hood, *Colonial Pipeline*, 39.

300 *pleaded guilty*: "Colonial Pipeline Pleads Guilty to Oil Spill in S.C. River," U.S. Department of Justice, press release, February 25, 1999.

300 *$13 million*: "Colonial Pipeline Will Pay to Settle Claims," *Greensboro News and
Record*, May 27, 1998.

300 *"a low point"*: Parker and Hood, *Colonial Pipeline*, 61.

300 *computer glitches*: Parker and Hood, *Colonial Pipeline*, 83.

300 *Hurricane Katrina*: "Here Are the Other Times When All or Part of the Colonial
Pipeline System Was Shut," CNBC, May 9, 2021, cnbc.com/2021/05/09/colonial
-pipeline-cyberattack-heres-when-it-was-previously-shut-down.html.

300 *begged off*: Ellen Nakashima, Lori Aratani, and Douglas MacMillan, "Colonial Hack
Exposed Government's Light-Touch Oversight of Pipeline Cybersecurity," *Washington Post*, May 30, 2021.

301 *a single password*: Stephanie Kelly and Jessica Resnick-Ault, "Hackers Only Needed
a Single Password to Disrupt Colonial Pipeline, CEO Testifies," *Insurance Journal*,
June 9, 2021, insurancejournal.com/news/national/2021/06/09/617870.htm.

301 *issued a warning*: Chris Sanders, "'Do Not Fill Plastic Bags with Gasoline' U.S.
Warns as Shortages Grow," Reuters, May 12, 2021.

301 *Almost two-thirds*: Abby Smith, "Gasoline Outages Pile Up, with Nearly Two-Thirds
of North Carolina Gas Stations out of Fuel," *Washington Examiner*, May 12, 2021.

301 *"a lot of parallels"*: Aruna Viswanatha and Dustin Volz, "FBI Director Compares
Ransomware Challenge to 9/11," *Wall Street Journal*, June 4, 2021.

301 *did not envision*: Tonya Riley, "Colonial Pipeline CEO Says Company Didn't Have
Plan for Potential Ransomware Attack," CyberScoop, June 8, 2021, cyberscoop.com
/colonial-pipeline-ransomware-senate-hack/.

301 *"It was the hardest"*: Testimony of Joseph Blount, Hearing Before the U.S. House
of Representatives Committee on Homeland Security, 117th Congress, 1st Sess.,
June 9, 2021, govinfo.gov/content/pkg/CHRG-117hhrg45085/html/CHRG-117hh
rg45085.htm.

302 *"to some degree"*: Geneva Sands and Brian Fung, "Colonial Pipeline CEO Defends
His Handling of Ransomware Attack That Crippled East Coast Fuel Supply," CNN,
June 8, 2021, cnn.com/2021/06/08/politics/colonial-pipeline-ceo-on-capitol-hill
-ransomware/index.html.

302 *cover the ransom*: Testimony of Joseph Blount.

305 *Department of Justice created*: Dustin Volz, "Ransomware Targeted by New Justice Department Task Force," *Wall Street Journal*, April 21, 2021.

305 *executive order*: Joseph R. Biden Jr., "Executive Order on Improving the Nation's Cybersecurity," The White House, May 12, 2021, whitehouse.gov/briefing-room /presidential-actions/2021/05/12/executive-order-on-improving-the-nations -cybersecurity/.

305 *same priority level*: Christopher Bing, "U.S. to Give Ransomware Hacks Similar Priority as Terrorism," Reuters, June 3, 2021.

305 *"to ensure we track"*: Bing, "U.S. to Give Ransomware Attacks Similar Priority as Terrorism."

305 *retrieve about half*: Ellen Nakashima, "Feds Recover More Than $2 Million in Ransomware Payments from Colonial Pipeline Hackers," *Washington Post*, June 7, 2021.

306 *$11 million ransom*: Jacob Bunge, "JBS Paid $11 Million to Resolve Ransomware Attack," *Wall Street Journal*, June 9, 2021.

306 *Federation Tower East*: Kartikay Mehrotra and Olga Kharif, "Ransomware HQ: Moscow's Tallest Tower Is a Cybercriminal Cash Machine," *Bloomberg Businessweek*, November 3, 2021.

306 *it didn't let Kaseya know*: Ellen Nakashima and Rachel Lerman, "FBI Held Back Ransomware Decryption Key from Businesses to Run Operation Targeting Hackers," *Washington Post*, September 21, 2021.

306 *closed again in October*: Catalin Cimpanu, "REvil Gang Shuts Down for the Second Time After Its Tor Servers Were Hacked," The Record by Recorded Future, October 18, 2021, therecord.media/revil-gang-shuts-down-for-the-second-time-after -its-tor-servers-were-hacked/.

307 *"I made it very clear"*: Ellen Nakashima and Eugene Scott, "Biden Tells Putin the U.S. Will Take 'Any Necessary Action' After Latest Ransomware Attack, White House Says," *Washington Post*, July 9, 2021.

307 *didn't invite Russia*: Zachary Basu, "Russia Left Out of White House's 30-Country Ransomware Summit," Axios, October 13, 2021, axios.com/ransomware-summit -white-house-russia-86ed85d6-e435-476b-9726-d55b3f82d1bd.html.

307 *Department of Justice announced*: "Ukrainian Arrested and Charged with Ransomware Attack on Kaseya," U.S. Department of Justice, press release, November 8, 2021.

307 *EggChange*: Catalin Cimpanu, "US Detains Crypto-Exchange Exec for Helping Ryuk Ransomware Gang Launder Profits," The Record by Recorded Future, November 12, 2021, therecord.media/us-detains-crypto-exchange-exec-for-helping -ryuk-ransomware-gang-launder-profits/.

307 *on the twenty-second floor*: Andrew E. Kramer, "Companies Linked to Russian Ransomware Hide in Plain Sight," *New York Times*, December 6, 2021.

307 *calling them "unreliable"*: "О задержании Дубникова Д.М." [About the detention of Dubnikov D.M.], Briefcase, November 5, 2021, briefcase.company/novosti /obshee/o-zaderjanii-dybnikova-dm.

308 *doubling or even tripling*: Carolyn Cohn, "Insurers Run from Ransomware Cover as Losses Mount," Reuters, November 19, 2021.

308 *stop writing*: Frank Bajak, "Insurer AXA to Stop Paying for Ransomware Crime Payments in France," *Insurance Journal*, May 9, 2021, insurancejournal.com/news /international/2021/05/09/613255.htm.

308 *Asia division*: Reuters staff, "AXA Division in Asia Hit by Ransomware Cyber Attack," Reuters, May 16, 2021.

308 *"the rising threat"*: Lyle Adriano, "AIG Reducing Cyber Limits as Costs Rise," *Insurance Business*, August 9, 2021, insurancebusinessmag.com/us/news/cyber/aig -reducing-cyber-limits-as-costs-climb-301644.aspx.

308 *Lloyd's of London*: Cohn, "Insurers Run from Ransomware Cover as Losses Mount."

308 *improve cybersecurity*: "The General Data Protection Regulation: Long Awaited EU Wide Data Protection Law Finalised," Deloitte, www2.deloitte.com/ge/en/pages /risk/articles/the-general-data-protection-regulation.html.

309 *"In case of refusal"*: Graham Cluley, "22,900 MongoDB Databases Held to Ransom by Hacker Threatening to Report Firms for GDPR Violations," Tripwire, July 2, 2020, tripwire.com/state-of-security/featured/22900-mongodb-databases -ransom-hacker-gdpr-violations/.

309 *"We're up against"*: Christopher Wray, "Working with Our Private Sector Partners to Combat the Cyber Threat," speech, Economic Club of New York, October 28, 2021, fbi.gov/news/speeches/working-with-our-private-sector-partners-to -combat-the-cyber-threat-wray-ecny-102821.

311 *released decryption keys:* Lawrence Abrams, "Ransomware Dev Releases Egregor, Maze Master Decryption Keys," BleepingComputer, February 9, 2022, bleeping computer.com/news/security/ransomware-dev-releases-egregor-maze-master -decryption-keys/.

312 *"The initial rumors"*: Fabian Wosar, "Hitting the BlackMatter Gang Where It Hurts: In the Wallet," Emsisoft blog, October 24, 2021, blog.emsisoft.com/en/39181/on -the-matter-of-blackmatter/.

314 *second major agricultural business*: Tom Polansek and Karl Plume, "Minnesota Grain Handler Targeted in Ransomware Attack," Reuters, September 23, 2021.

314 *Its affiliates shifted*: Lawrence Abrams, "BlackMatter Ransomware Moves Victims to LockBit After Shutdown," BleepingComputer, November 3, 2021, bleepingcom puter.com/news/security/blackmatter-ransomware-moves-victims-to-lockbit -after-shutdown/.

315 *"redirecting ransomware"*: "2021 Trends Show Increased Globalized Threat of Ransomware," Cybersecurity & Infrastructure Security Agency, Alert (AA22-040A), February 9, 2022, cisa.gov/uscert/ncas/alerts/aa22-040a.

315 *"thwarted admissions activities"*: "Abraham Lincoln's Namesake College to Close After 157 Years," Lincoln College, lincolncollege.edu/.

315 *new federal law*: Martin Matishak, "Biden Signs Cyber Incident Reporting Bill into Law," The Record by Recorded Future, therecord-media.cdn.ampproject.org/c/s /therecord.media/biden-signs-cyber-incident-reporting-bill-into-law/amp/.

315 *SEC proposed a rule*: Paul Kiernan, "SEC Proposes Requiring Firms to Report Cyberattacks Within Four Days," *Wall Street Journal*, March 9, 2022, wsj.com/ articles/sec-considers-rule-requiring-firms-to-report-cyber-attacks-within-four -days-11646838001.

316 *resurfaced in November 2021*: Elizabeth Montalbano, "Emotet Resurfaces on the Back of TrickBot After Nearly a Year," Threatpost, November 16, 2021, threatpost .com/emotet-resurfaces-trickbot/176362/.

316 *"the appeal of the competent"*: "ПРЕСЕЧЕНА ПРОТИВОПРАВНАЯ ДЕЯТЕЛЬНОСТЬ ЧЛЕНОВ ОРГАНИЗОВАННОГО ПРЕСТУПНОГО СООБЩЕСТВА" [Illegal activities of members of an organized criminal community stopped"], FSB, press release, January 14, 2022.

316 *The FSB*: Tom Balmforth and Maria Tsvetkova, "Russia Takes Down REvil Hacking Group at U.S. Request—FSB," Reuters, January 14, 2022.

316 *a Ukrainian researcher*: Lawrence Abrams, "Conti Ransomware's Internal Chats Leaked After Siding with Russia," BleepingComputer, February 27, 2022, bleep ingcomputer.com/news/security/conti-ransomwares-internal-chats-leaked-after -siding-with-russia/.

317 *Department of State offered*: "Reward Offers for Information to Bring Conti Ransomware Variant Co-Conspirators to Justice," U.S. Department of State, press

release, May 6, 2022, state.gov/reward-offers-for-information-to-bring-conti
-ransomware-variant-co-conspirators-to-justice/.

317   *Russian prosecutors appeared*: "Hopes of Russian Help on Ransomware Are Officially
Dead," *Washington Post*, June 1, 2022, washingtonpost.com/politics/2022/06/01
/hopes-russian-help-ransomware-are-officially-dead/.

318   *"the most effective treatment"*: "Preeclampsia: Symptoms & Causes," Mayo Clinic,
mayoclinic.org/diseases-conditions/preeclampsia/symptoms-causes/syc-20355745.

ACKNOWLEDGMENTS

When Renee started reporting on ransomware in 2018, neither she nor Dan, her editor, had ever heard of Michael Gillespie. Mentions of him in the news were scarce. Yet nearly every expert Renee interviewed praised and deferred to him, saying he knew more about ransomware strains and how to crack them than anyone else. She tried to contact Michael by phone and Twitter, but he didn't return her messages. When she reached him at Nerds on Call, he said he couldn't talk at work. He agreed to speak with Renee only following an introduction from Lawrence Abrams, his fellow ransomware hunter.

During their early phone conversations, Michael spoke authoritatively about ransomware even as he downplayed his own role in combating it. Sensing that he was being modest, Renee arranged to interview him at his home in Illinois in July 2019. There she was blown away by his dedication to helping victims despite personal hardships including cancer and financial distress. She called Dan from the BloNo airport to say that his and the Ransomware Hunting Team's story needed to be told.

And so it was, first in a ProPublica profile, and now in this book. We would like to express our deep gratitude to Michael and his ebullient wife, Morgan, who both spent dozens of hours with us on Zoom and hosted us on an unforgettable 2021 visit to Illinois. Michael patiently explained ransomware cryptography, while Morgan described their personal and family histories with unflinching candor, often answering questions directed to her more reserved husband. We're also grateful to the other members of the Ransomware Hunting Team—especially Lawrence Abrams, Fabian

Wosar, and Sarah White—for their remarkable generosity with their time, their vivid recollections, and their descriptions of hackers' culture and tactics. We are thankful to Fabian and Sarah for digging through old messages to provide us with invaluable primary source material as well as for their hospitality during a 2021 trip to London. Daniel Gallagher, Jornt van der Wiel, Marc Rivero López, and Karsten Hahn rounded out the team's story. The hunters trusted us to portray them accurately and compellingly, and we hope that they will be pleased with the result.

Other friends of the Ransomware Hunting Team, including Igor Kabina, Christian Mairoll, and Francesco Muroni, provided key insights about members' roles and evolutions. Michael's friends, colleagues, and relatives helped us understand what makes him tick. Among them, we particularly thank Rita Blanch, Dave Jacobs, Brian Ford, and Jason Hahn. We also thank the ransomware victims saved by Michael who agreed to share their stories, especially Matthew in London and Ray Orendez in the Philippines.

Other sources deepened our understanding of the world hackers occupy, providing descriptions as well as dark web screenshots, transcripts, Bitcoin tracing, and more. Thank you especially to Alex Holden, John Fokker, Brett Callow, Vincent D'Agostino, Dmitry Smilyanets, and sources at Chainalysis, especially Maddie Kennedy and Kim Grauer.

Dozens of sources shaped our understanding of the federal government's response to ransomware. Jeanette Manfra and Randy Pargman were especially generous with their time as they provided early and ongoing guidance, as were Milan Patel, Anthony Ferrante, Keith Mularski, Mark Grantz, and Chris Krebs. Thanks also to Michael Vatis, Scott Augenbaum, and Stacy Arruda, who described the government's early work against cyber crime.

A host of sources in the Netherlands informed our views on law enforcement efforts globally. We're particularly grateful to John Fokker, Pim Takkenberg, Marijn Schuurbiers, and Matthijs Jaspers for their generosity with their time—both on Zoom and during a memorable visit to Holland. Thanks also to Peter van Hofweegen, Frans de Bie, and the remarkable staff and graduates of ITvitae for sharing their world with us.

We're grateful to the dozens of sources from the 2019 ProPublica series *The Extortion Economy*, some of whom provided assistance with this book, most notably Bill Siegel. Of the hundreds of other people whom we interviewed, several were especially helpful, including Chris Ballod, Robert Sapolsky, Aaron Tantleff, Kurtis Minder, John Reed Stark, and John Bandler. Thanks also to Alec MacGillis for Baltimore contacts, Konstantin Schätz for research in Europe, and Ashley Bartley of the Speedway Public Library for going through yearbooks. We appreciate the help of many public relations professionals who facilitated illuminating conversations, including Elizabeth Clarke and Thomas Hottman. We're grateful to Sarah White, Matthew Green, and Moti Yung for their expert guidance on technical passages, and to David Glovin, Edward Wilding, Ronald Schilb, John Augustine, Sheryl Goldstein, Garen Hartunian, Jeff Kao, and James Bandler for their contributions. Our reporting also benefited from the assistance of many other sources who preferred not be named.

We'd also like to thank ProPublica editor-in-chief Stephen Engelberg and then managing editor Robin Fields for publishing Renee's 2019 series on ransomware—and, more broadly, for fostering a uniquely supportive workplace dedicated to the highest ideals of investigative journalism.

We're deeply grateful to our perceptive and indefatigable agents, Becky Sweren, of Aevitas Creative Management, and Lynn Johnston. This project wouldn't have happened without Becky, who spotted Renee's 2019 profile of Michael and insisted with enthusiasm and persistence that it had the makings of a book. Becky and Lynn brilliantly shaped and shepherded the proposal and placed it with Farrar, Straus and Giroux.

It could not have found a better home. With the utmost tact and grace, our editor, Alexander Star, encouraged our work and improved the manuscript in ways large and small. Assistant editor Ian Van Wye caught and fixed numerous ambiguities and infelicities. Thanks to Janet Renard for her copyedit, to Na Kim and Thomas Colligan for the cover image, to Hannah Goodwin, Rima Weinberg, and Laura Starrett for their smart suggestions, and to Sheila O'Shea, Sarita Varma, and Stephen Weil for generating publicity. Allison Warren and Shenel Ekici-Moling at Aevitas and Joe Veltre and Olivia Johnson at Gersh were quick to recognize the project's potential for film and television and have worked hard to find the best partners in those media.

We'd also like to thank our own families and friends for their contributions and unflagging support.

Renee's husband, Alket Mërtiri, lovingly supported her work on this book with his flexibility and healthy perspective on life's priorities. A selfless partner, he helped maintain a happy home, despite the challenges of raising young children in a pandemic—all while managing the demands of his own career as a scientist. William and Florian—a toddler and infant when the heavy lifting on this book began—were a font of boundless joy, even when they burst into the office during Zoom calls or emptied desk drawers for sport. Renee's mother-in-law, Athina Mërtiri, and father, Tom Dudley, graciously babysat the boys each week, spending extra time with them when professional deadlines loomed. Among many cherished friends, her sister, Nicole, was an especially reliable listener, celebrating Renee's successes and bemoaning her setbacks as if they were her own. Paulette Dudley, Renee's late mother, was a source of inspiration as this book came together. Her spirit radiated when FSG extended its offer of a book deal on May 28, the anniversary of her death.

Dan's son Steven, a cybersecurity professional who has studied ransomware, helped him grasp its technical underpinnings and came to the rescue whenever his computer malfunctioned or a file seemed to disappear. Dan's sister Olivia read several chapters and gave astute advice. Countless conversations with his beloved wife and best friend, Kathy, clarified his thinking and perspective through the inevitable ups and downs of an ambitious project. She resourcefully entertained children, grandchildren, friends, and their golden retriever, Sydney, as Dan disappeared into the study for hours or days on end.

This book reports history as it unfolds. Even while we write this, ransomware continues to ravage society, and Michael, Fabian, and the other hunters continue to crack it. We look forward to chronicling their future exploits.

INDEX

Abrams, Lawrence, 64–67, 71, 84, 87, 88, 107–108, 116–17, 127, 130–31, 135, 136, 164, 223, 257, 269, 280–81, 303; BleepingComputer founded by, 64, 66; early life of, 65; FBI and, 203, 208–11; Maze and, 100–105, 311; in Ransomware Hunting Team formation, 80–82; TeslaCrypt and, 64, 77–80; truce of, 271–73, 281–85, 292, 297; Zbot and, 72

ACCDFISA, 67, 71, 203

Adleman, Leonard, 147

Adrian, 108–10

AdvIntel, 164

Agutin, Leonid, 97

AIDS, AIDS Trojan, 18, 28–42, 146, 147

algorithms, 145–47, 149

Allied Universal, 101–103, 107

Amazon Web Services, 219

American International Group, 308

Anderson, Tim, 252

Apocalypse, 85–87, 98, 113

Apple, 106

Archer-Daniels-Midland, 200

Arruda, Stacy, 174–76, 185

ASN.1, 203–204

asymmetric encryption, 147–48, 152

Atlanta, Ga., 129, 218, 220

Augenbaum, Scott, 175, 176

Augustine, John, 25, 39, 41, 42

Aunt Beast, 310–11

autism, 181–83

AXA, 308

Babuk, 99

backdoors, 111

bait files, 146

Ballod, Christopher, 298, 299

Baltimore, Md., 215–35, 285, 286

Baltimore City Information & Technology (BCIT), 221–23, 226, 229

Baltimore County Public Schools (BCPS), 285–86

banking Trojans, 161

Bates, Jim, 31, 32, 35, 37–38

Baum, L. Frank, 44

Beazley, 260–63
Bendersky, Eduard, 98
Benge, Terry, 78
Beverwijk, 178
Biden, Joe, 212, 213, 305–307, 315
Binary Defense, 310
bitcoin tumblers, 95
Bitdefender, 294–96, 302, 309
BitPaymer, 97, 99
Black Lives Matter, 213
BlackMatter, 312–14
Blanch, Beth Hall, 48–50, 59
Blanch, Bobby, 48–50, 54, 58
Blanch, Rita, 48, 49, 53, 59, 124–25,
   206
BleepingComputer, 8, 10–11, 14, 31,
   60, 64–67, 71, 74, 75, 80, 81, 87, 90,
   107, 109, 115, 131, 136, 141, 142,
   210, 223, 241, 242, 257, 264, 267,
   272, 278, 281, 311; DDoS attack on,
   72, 88; founding of, 64, 66; Maze
   and, 100–104; TeslaCrypt and, 64,
   78–80, 135
block ciphers, 145–46
BloNo (Bloomington-Normal
   metropolitan area), 43–45
BloodDolly, 77–79, 81, 135, 136
Blount, Joseph, 301–302
BlueVoyant, 105
Blundell Brown, Nicky, 28, 35
Bonczoszek, Noel, 31–32, 34, 35, 37,
   38
Botezatu, Bogdan, 295–96
botnets, 92, 161
Bottoms, Keisha Lance, 218
Boyce Technologies, Inc., 282
Broward County Public Schools,
   286–87
Bryce, Cade, 245
BTCWare, 90–91
Bugat, 97
Butterball, 111–12, 312

Caesar, Julius, 12
Caesar cipher, 145
Campari Group, 277
Canon, 105

Capitol attack of January 6,
   213
Capture the Flag, 180, 192
Cargile, Lisa Marie, 156, 158
Carlin, John, 305
Carter, Stephen L., 228
Carter, Todd, 221–22, 234
Churchill, Winston, 63
ciphers, 145–47, 150, 152
CISA (Cybersecurity & Infrastructure
   Security Agency), 230–33, 306,
   312–15
Cleveland *Plain Dealer*, 19, 28, 40
Clinton administration, 173
CLOP, 272
Cobalt Strike, 92
Cohen, Steven A., 237, 268
CoinVault, 192–93
Colonial Pipeline Company, 299–302,
   305, 306, 315, 316
Comey, James, 169–73, 175, 177, 309
CompuCom, 297
Compulink Information eXchange
   (CIX), 30–31
Computer Crime Unit (CUU),
   Scotland Yard, 31–34, 36–37
Computer Fraud and Abuse Act, 210
Computer Misuse Act, 39
Congionti, Mark, 243–44, 246, 266
Congionti, Victor, 243–44, 246, 249,
   250, 266–67
Connelly, P. J., 218
Conti, 163–64, 286–87, 316–17
Cookson, Lizzie, 96
Costello, Eric, 226–27
Cotton Duck Title Co., 224, 227
Coumans, Mark, 182–84
Coveware, 155, 241, 242, 250, 255–61,
   263–65, 267–69, 272–78, 293, 299,
   303–305, 314, 318–20; Gillespie's
   joining of, 273–76
COVID-19 pandemic, 5, 154, 212, 235,
   271–74, 276, 277, 279–83, 285, 288,
   289, 291, 292, 297, 298, 300
Cowboy Ryuk, 160–61
Cox, Sean, 206
Crypsis, 268

cryptography, 12, 47, 64, 145–49, 152, 302, 315
CryptoLocker, 71–72, 80
CryptON, 88–89
cryptor providers, 95
CryptoSearch, 117
CryptoTester, 146
Crystal Valley, 314
CTB-Locker, 92
Cuckoo's Egg, The (Stoll), 173
CWT, 276
Cyber Command, 288, 315
cybercrime, 173–74, 176, 177, 186, 188, 194–95
Cybersecurity & Infrastructure Security Agency (CISA), 230–33, 306, 312–15
cybersecurity companies, 258, 265, 268–69, 295; data recovery, 239, 241–58, 264–69; insurance, 239, 259–63, 266, 268, 299, 308; ransom negotiation and payment, 239–58, 264–69, 274
cyber warfare, 98
Cyrulewski, Chris, 277–78

D'Agostino, Vincent, 105, 106
"Dane-geld" (Kipling), 217
DarkSide, 293–302, 305–306, 312, 316
dark web, 13, 75, 79, 92, 93, 96, 100, 103, 104, 106, 131, 150, 177, 178, 194, 223, 228, 297–98, 312
Darwinism, 18, 20–22, 39, 40, 42
data breaches, 104–107, 166, 228, 268
data recovery firms, 239, 241–58, 264–69
Davis, Andre, 220, 223–24, 233
Davis, David, 43, 44
DeathHiddenTear, 267
decompilers, 146
DEcovid19, 279
Defense Department, 288
demonslay335, see Gillespie, Michael
Department of Homeland Security, see DHS
Department of Public Works (DPW), 222, 225, 226

de Salis, Charles, 295
DeVore, Irven, 21, 23, 26, 28, 39, 40
Dharma, 92, 254, 255, 257
DHC Health System, 156–58, 166–67
DHS (Department of Homeland Security), 163, 165, 172, 175, 208, 217, 219, 300, 311; Cybersecurity & Infrastructure Security Agency (CISA), 230–33, 306, 312–15
Dickinson County Healthcare System (DCHS), 288
Digital Currency Group, 240
disassemblers, 146
distributed denial-of-service (DDoS) attack, 72, 88
Dixie Group, 297
Dixon, Sheila, 228
DMA Locker, 245–47
"dolphins," 185
DoppelPaymer, 96, 234, 271–72, 282, 285
double extortion, 104–108
Douglas, Stephen, 43
Doyle, Arthur Conan, 67
DPW (Department of Public Works), 222, 225, 226
Dreiband, Eric, 212
Dridex, 97–99
Dubnikov, Denis, 307
Dun, Weysan, 201
Dutch HTCU (High Tech Crime Unit), 179–85, 187–88, 191–94, 209, 210, 305, 311

Eckel, Rianna, 226
EggChange, 307
Egregor, 311
Eisenhower, Dwight D., 44
Ekeland, Tor, 22
El_Cometa, 111–12
Emotet, 161–63, 165, 194, 316
Emsisoft, 61, 67, 68, 70, 71, 73, 75, 77, 135, 137, 142, 144, 272–74, 280, 303, 304, 313, 319
Enigma, 12, 147
EpsilonRed, 320–21
Ethelred the Unready, 217

European Union (EU), 308–309
Europol, 193, 210, 211
Evans, Christopher, 40
Evil Corp, 97–100, 315
EvilTwin, 129–30
Exotic, 129

Fabiansomware, 85–86
Facet Technologies, 53–57, 60, 63, 78,
    118, 119, 124–26, 205, 274
FBI (Federal Bureau of Investigation),
    11, 98–99, 156, 159, 160, 163, 165,
    169–95, 197–214, 217, 221, 223,
    226, 245, 246, 250–52, 256, 264,
    266, 269, 283–84, 305, 307, 309–15;
    Abrams and, 203, 208–11; Gillespie
    and, 142, 197–211, 213–14, 317, 318;
    Popp and, 36–37; Ransomware
    Summits of, 208–209, 261, 263,
    273; REvil and, 306; Wosar and,
    203–204, 312–14
Federal Security Service (FSB), 98,
    99, 315, 316
Federal Trade Commission (FTC),
    266
FedEx, 71
Fell, Jesse, 43–44
Ferrante, Anthony, 175–78, 185, 186,
    188
Feynman, Richard, 127
Fin7, 189
Flashpoint, 164
Fokker, John, 95, 179–80, 185, 192,
    193, 204, 209
Fonix, 109
Ford, Brian, 53–56, 59–61, 205–207
Fossey, Dian, 24
Francis, Tim, 263
Frieson, Sheneka, 167
FTI Consulting, 177
Furlan, Timothy, 25, 28

Gaede, John, 289–91
Gage, Dorothy, 44
Gallagher, Daniel, 76–77, 79–82,
    126–33, 280
GandCrab, 95, 296–97

Garmin, 99
gasoline, 299, 301
General Data Protection Regulation
    (GDPR), 308–309
GetCrypt, 164
Getty, J. Paul, 12
Gillespie, Allison Todd, 45–47, 52, 56
Gillespie, John, 45–47, 54, 56, 58–59
Gillespie, Lukan Atlas, 318–20
Gillespie, Michael, 8–11, 13–14,
    17–19, 31, 44–48, 51–61, 63–65,
    67, 69, 73, 76, 77, 83, 84, 85, 87,
    97, 99, 100, 109, 113, 115–27, 132,
    135–38, 144, 146, 164, 180–81, 185,
    193, 195, 239, 264, 267, 277, 283,
    302–304, 317–21; BTCWare and,
    90–91; Coveware joined by, 273–76;
    DarkSide and, 293–94; early life of,
    9, 46–47; EpsilonRed and, 320–21;
    FBI and, 142, 197–211, 213–14, 317,
    318; ID Ransomware launched
    by, 115–18; Lorenz and, 278–79;
    in Ransomware Hunting Team
    formation, 80–81; Ryuk and, 159–60,
    164; STOPDjvu and, 141–43, 145,
    149–54, 275, 320; TeslaCrypt and,
    64, 78–79, 135
Gillespie, Morgan, 8, 9, 44, 48–53,
    56–59, 78–79, 118–26, 137–38, 142,
    143, 206–207, 274, 275, 317–20
Gittler, Jeremy, 261
Gmail, 14
Goldstein, Sheryl, 229–30, 232
Goodall, Jane, 28
Google, 14, 76, 81, 242, 254, 257, 265
Gould, Stephen Jay, 22, 41
Grantz, Mark, 190
Greenville, N.C., 218
GroupSense, 265–66
Guilford, Gayle, 219, 220, 222, 226,
    234

hacking back, 210
Hahn, Jason, 54–56, 119, 203,
    205–207
HakunaMatata, 87
Hall, Wade, 57

Hammersmith Medicines Research,
 281–82
Han, Karsten, 143–46, 160, 279–80
Happy Blog, 106
Harris, Justin, 197–98, 201, 211–12
Harvey, Dan, 224, 227
Hatch Act, 213
Heartbleed, 243
Heinrich Heine University, 282
Henry, Bill, 227–28
Henson, Chad, 254
Hermes, 158, 160
Herrington, Leif, 245–46
Hessler, Jason, 230
hex editors, 146
High Tech Crime Unit, see HTCU
Hogan-Burney, Amy, 288
Holden, Alex, 162–64, 223, 288–89,
 297, 315
Holdtman, Alex, 240–42, 255–56, 258,
 267, 273
Horn, Kimberly, 262–63
Horst, Yvonne, 183–84
HTCU (High Tech Crime Unit),
 179–85, 187–88, 191–94, 209, 210,
 305, 311, 316
Huffman, Bart, 249
Hutchins, Marcus, 98
hybrid encryption, 147–48, 152

ID Ransomware, 8, 13, 124–25,
 137, 143, 159, 165, 193, 197, 198,
 204, 207–209, 275–76, 293, 310;
 launching of, 115–18
Informant!, The, 200
Ingraham, Al, 227
initial access brokerages, 95
insurance companies, 239, 259–63,
 266, 268, 299, 308
Insurance Information Institute,
 262
Iran, 7, 11, 109, 189, 205, 250, 298–99,
 302
ITvitae, 182–84, 193

Jackson, Ron, 290–91
Jackson, Sherry, 290–91

Jacobs, Dave, 9, 58–59, 61, 118–20,
 125, 126, 203, 207
Jaspers, Matthijs, 194
JBS, 306
Jebsen, Johann-Nielsen "Johnny,"
 295
Jigsaw, 83–84
Johnson, Frank, 216, 220–21, 223,
 226–27, 229, 230, 234
Justice Department, 98, 178, 189, 205,
 208, 283, 307; Ransomware Task
 Force of, 305, 307, 310; see also FBI

Kabina, Igor (BloodDolly), 77–79, 81,
 135, 136
Kaseya, 306–307
Kaspersky Lab, 132, 192, 193
Kennedy, John F., Jr., 24
Kenneth Cole, 106
keys, 147–53
KGB, 173
Kidd, Teiranni, 157
Kidnap (Shortland), 269
kidnapping, 12, 261, 269
Kilroy, John, 36, 37, 39
Kipling, Rudyard, 217
Kissinger, Henry, 24, 27
Klinger, Gary, 166
Koch Industries, 299
Koenigsegg, 277, 278
Kolhatkar, Sheelah, 237
Krebs, Christopher, 231–33, 306–307,
 314
Kremez, Vitali, 164–65, 223
Kroll, 298

Lady Gaga, 106
Lake City, Fla., 259–61
lava lamps, 149
lawsuits, 166
LeChiffre, 60
Lee, Bruce, 96
Lee, Michael, 260–61
Lenin, Vladimir, 159
Lewis, Gwyneth, 34–35
LG Electronics, 105
Lincoln, Abraham, 43, 190

Lincoln College, 315
LinkedIn, 89, 211
Lloyd's of London, 308
Lorenz, 278–79, 304

Macaw Locker, 100
Mairoll, Christian, 70–71, 137
Malcolm, James, 21–22, 39
MalwareHunterTeam, 75–77, 80, 81,
    84, 103, 108–109, 115, 117, 129–31,
    146, 223, 280–81, 320
Manfra, Jeanette, 231–33
Mason Lietz & Klinger, 166
Maze, 96, 100–107, 272, 277, 281–82,
    285, 311
McAfee, 193
McCann, Eric, 56
McCarthy, Mike, 28
McCraw, Gabryella, 167
McGregor, Andre, 169
McVeigh, Timothy, 173
MegaLocker, 210, 211
Microsoft, 76, 82, 287–89, 298, 315,
    320
Minder, Kurtis, 266
Mission Health, 79, 128, 129, 133
MonsterCloud, 241–43, 250–58,
    264–66
Mr.Dec, 253
Mueller, Robert, 175, 251
Muhumuza, Joshua, 286
Muid, Robert Edward, 32–33
Mularski, Keith, 98–99
Muroni, Francesco, 90, 97
Mutual Legal Assistance Treaty
    (MLAT), 189, 191

Napier, Sam, 245
National Cyber Security Centre, 159
National Health Service, 97, 98
National Infrastructure Protection
    Center (NIPC), 173–75, 185
National Security Agency, 174
Nazi Germany, 12, 147, 295
Nefilim, 272, 285
Nerds on Call, 9, 17, 44, 54–57, 59, 115,
    118–20, 151, 197, 201, 207

Netherlands, 203–204; HTCU in,
    179–85, 187–88, 191–94, 209, 210,
    305, 311, 316
Netwalker, 109, 272, 282–84
New Cooperative, 314
Nmoreira, 87–88
No More Ransom, 193
Noriega, Manuel, 33–34, 37
North Korea, 87, 98, 158, 160, 189, 299
Northwave, 193
Nozelesn, 252
number sieve, 77

Office Depot, 297
offline keys, 149–51, 153
oil industry, 299; Colonial Pipeline
    Company, 299–302, 305, 306, 315,
    316
Oklahoma City bombing, 173
Okumu, Martin, 219
Olympus, 100
Operation Bleeding Cloud, 243
Orendez, Mara Yan, 141
Orendez, Ray, 139–42, 151, 153–54,
    156
OrthoVirginia, 165, 166
Orwell, George, 5
Ouroboros, 13
Owler, 161

Padres, Bret, 268
Pantagraph, The, 44, 119–20
Pargman, Randy, 185–89, 191–92, 201,
    310–11
Patel, Milan, 170, 175–77, 185, 186,
    188, 195, 309
PayloadBIN, 99–100
PayPal, 118
PC Business World, 30, 32, 34
PC Cyborg Corp., 29–30, 33–36
PC USA Computer Solutions
    Providers, 251
Pekin, Ill., 45, 47–52
Pekin High School, 53–56
Pensacola, Fla., 105
Pentagon, 174
PGA of America, 97

Phelps, Mark, 197–206, 209, 211–14, 318
Phelps, Ron, 198–99
Phelps, Shawn Dillard, 199–200
phishing, 12, 99, 161
Phobos, 92, 108, 242
Pierce, Chris, 31–32, 34–38
Pinhasi, Zohar, 251–55, 266
pirated software, 47–48, 140–45, 153, 192
Pistole, John, 251–53, 266
Plutarch, 12
Polyanin, Yevgeniy, 307
Popp, Joseph, 17–42, 146
Popp's Concordance to Darwin's On the Origin of Species (Popp), 42
Popular Evolution (Popp), 40–41
presidential election of 2020, 212–13, 233, 287
prime numbers, 77, 147, 152–53
private keys, 147
ProPublica, 258, 266
ProtonMail, 159
Proven Data Recovery, 241–51, 255–58, 264, 266–67
pseudorandom number generators, 149
public keys, 147, 153
Pugh, Catherine, 215, 220, 228, 229
Putin, Vladimir, 98, 159, 287, 306, 307, 316

Quanta Computer, 106

Radamant, 75
Ragnar Locker, 275–77, 284
random numbers, 148–49
RansomNoteCleaner, 117
ransomware, 4, 5, 11–13
ransomware-as-a-service, 92, 294, 298
ransomware gangs, 91–96, 107, 108, 112–13, 145–46, 155, 178, 242, 271–73, 292, 295, 302, 308–309, 315
Ransomware Hunting Team, 10–11; formation of, 80–83, 85

ransomware insurance, 239, 259–63, 266, 268, 299, 308
ransomware negotiation and payment, 239–58, 264–69, 274
Ransomware Summits, 208–209, 261, 263, 273
Rapid, 188, 208, 214
Recorded Future, 93–94, 106
Reedy River oil spill, 300, 301
REvil, 93–95, 106, 107, 265, 268, 272, 284, 297, 306–307, 316, 317
Ripley, Terri, 165
Rivero López, Marc, 80–83
Rivest, Ron, 147
Rivlin, Geoffrey, 39, 40
RobbinHood, 216, 218, 220–35
RSA, 147, 152–53, 293
Ruppersberger, C. A. "Dutch," 221, 230–32
Russia, 11, 85, 87, 89, 93, 97–99, 108, 155, 158–60, 162, 163, 167, 284, 297, 306, 307, 315–17; Ukraine invaded by, 316–17
Ryan, Christine, 17, 19, 41–42
Ryuk, 155–67, 188, 194, 240, 259–60, 271, 285–91, 303, 307, 316

SAC Capital Advisors, 237–38, 268
Safford, Ariz., 244–45
Salem4Youth, 63–64, 78
Salsa20, 152
SamSam, 128–29, 205, 218, 220, 249–50
SANS Institute, 188
Sapolsky, Robert, 25–27, 35
Schilb, Ronald, 19, 20, 25, 33, 41
Schneck, Phyllis, 219
Schroeder, Simon, 245–46
Schuurbiers, Marijn, 179, 181, 183, 188, 192–93
Scotland Yard, Computer Crime Unit of (CUU), 31–34, 36–37
Scott, Brandon, 221
script kiddies (skiddies), 84, 130, 131
SecondMarket, 239, 240, 255
Secret Intelligence Service, 295

Secret Service, 156, 174, 190, 208, 221, 289, 311
Seculore Solutions, 234
Securities and Exchange Commission (SEC), 263, 315
SecurityScorecard, 239
seeds, 149
Sentinel, 164
September 11 terrorist attacks, 50, 172, 175, 301
Shamir, Adi, 147
Shodan, 117
Shortland, Anja, 269
Siegel, Bill, 237–42, 250, 255–60, 263, 266–69, 273–74, 299, 302–305
Silar, Nicko, 157
Silbert, Barry, 239
Silk Road, 177
Sinclair Broadcast Group, 100
Sky Lakes Medical Center, 289–92
Skyline Comfort LLC, 252–53
Smilyanets, Dmitry, 94, 95
Solve, 278
Soviet Union, 173
Springhill Medical Center, 157–58
State Department, 316–17
State Farm, 43, 124, 125
Stevenson, Adlai, II, 44
Stoll, Cliff, 173, 189
STOPDjvu, 141–45, 149–54, 155–56, 275, 320
Storfer, Jonathan, 246–50
stream ciphers, 145, 152
Suncrypt, 284
symmetric encryption, 146–48, 150, 152
SynAck, 111
synesthesia, 126–27

Takkenberg, Pim, 180–81, 192, 193
Tang, 123–24, 136–37
Tantleff, Aaron, 273, 281
Telegram, 108, 109
Tequila, 70
TeslaCrypt, 64, 77–80, 135
TeslaWare, 131–32
Todd, Hugh, 45

Tor, 150
Toshiba Tec, 297
Transportation Security Administration (TSA), 300, 305
Travelers, 263
Travelex, 106
Treasury Department, 98, 99, 250, 298–99
Trellix, 95
Trench Micro, 209
TrickBot, 161–65, 287–89, 315–16
Trifiletti, Christopher, 211–12
Tripoli, 318
Trump, Donald, 190, 212–14, 233, 274
Turing, Alan, 12
Turing Prize, 147
Twitter, 73, 75–76, 80, 85, 88, 99–100, 110–12, 115, 127, 130–32, 134, 142, 164, 228, 275, 281, 314

Ukraine, 316–17
Ulbricht, Ross, 177
universal decryptor, 303–304, 307, 314
University Hospital of Düsseldorf, 282
University of California–San Francisco, 283
Unix time, 149
Unknown, 93–95, 106, 107, 272, 306
U.S. Conference of Mayors, 234

Vachon-Desjardins, Sebastien, 284
van der Wiel, Jornt, 132–33, 192–94
van Hofweegen, Peter, 182–84
VashSorena, 8, 13–14
Vasinskyi, Yaroslav, 307
Vatis, Michael, 174
Ventrone, Melissa, 229–30
Virus Bulletin, 18, 31, 38
VirusTotal, 81, 127, 143, 146, 223, 293

Wall Street Journal, The, 158
WannaCry, 98
WastedLocker, 99–100
Waters, Michael, 107

Wazix, 131–32
West, Nigel, 295
Whitacre, Mark, 200
White, Sarah, 68, 72–75, 81, 83, 90, 110, 130, 132, 133, 144, 152, 182, 243, 273, 275, 278, 280, 294, 303, 314, 319
WhiteRose, 135–36
Wildfire, 194
Wilding, Edward, 18, 35
Willems, Eddy, 29–30
Wilson, Tina, 286
Witherspoon, Joel, 253–54
Witt, Stephen, 260
WND, 212
Wonderful Wizard of Oz, The (Baum), 44
World War II, 12, 147, 295
Worters, Loretta, 262
Wosar, Fabian, 11, 60–61, 67–78, 81, 83, 85–92, 110–13, 115, 126, 127, 130, 132–35, 137, 144, 160, 239, 242–43, 261–62, 264, 273, 274, 279, 280, 295, 296, 302–304, 318–19; Apocalypse and, 85–87, 98, 113;

DarkSide and, 293–94; early life of, 68–70; EpsilonRed and, 320–21; Evil Corp and, 99–100; FBI and, 203–204, 312–14; Operation Bleeding Cloud of, 243; REvil and, 306–307
Wray, Christopher, 207, 211, 213, 301, 309

Xerox, 105

Yakubets, Maksim, 96–99, 315
YARA rules, 127
Young, Adam, 147–48
Young, Bernard "Jack," 215–18, 221, 223–24, 227–30, 234, 235
Yung, Moti, 147–48

Zbot Trojan, 72
Zeppelin, 279
ZeroAccess, 74
zero-day exploits, 298
Zeus, 96–98
Ziggy, 108–109
ZoomInfo, 161

A NOTE ABOUT THE AUTHORS

Renee Dudley is a technology reporter at ProPublica. Previously, as an investigative reporter at Reuters, she was named a 2017 Pulitzer Prize finalist for her work uncovering systematic cheating on college admissions tests. She started her career at daily newspapers in South Carolina and New England, and has won numerous journalism honors, including the Eugene S. Pulliam First Amendment Award.

Daniel Golden, a senior editor and reporter at ProPublica, has won a Pulitzer Prize and three George Polk Awards. He is the bestselling author of *The Price of Admission: How America's Ruling Class Buys Its Way into Elite Colleges—and Who Gets Left Outside the Gates* and *Spy Schools: How the CIA, FBI, and Foreign Intelligence Secretly Exploit America's Universities.*